pets
part of the family

pets
part of the family

Complete care for all your family pets

pets: part of the family
Published in 2003 by Hinkler Books Pty Ltd
17–23 Redwood Drive
Dingley VIC 3172 Australia
www.hinklerbooks.com

Published by arrangement with Rodale, Inc., Emmaus, PA, U.S.A.

ISBN 1 8651 5988 3

Printed and bound in Australia

Note: This book is intended as a reference volume only, not as a medical manual. The information given here is designed to help you make informed decisions about your pet's health. It is not intended as a substitute for any treatment that may have been prescribed by your veterinarian. If you suspect that your pet has a medical problem, we urge you to seek competent medical help.

Editorial Staff

Publishing Director: Jamie Trowbridge

Book Editor: Sharon Smith

Book Designer: Jill Shaffer

Illustrator: Anna Dewdney

Contributing Writers:

Linda Buchanan Allen, Lori Baird, Connie Hatch, Rose Kennedy, Dougald MacDonald, Kay Scheller, Christine Schultz, Michelle Seaton

Editorial Consultants:

Bill Azzolini, Diane Bachman, Jacqueline Bastien, Sharon Behan-Lanoue, Dr. Peter Borchelt, Wayne and Kimberly Brannon, Diane Cole, Diana Culp, Janet Depathy, Elizabeth Drbal, Troy Lynn Eckart, Michael Emerson, Kathy Fogg, Tricia Gagnon, Sandy Jarvis, Michele Joyce, Susan Joyce, Melissa Kaplan, Jody Kaufman, Robin Kovary, Jeanneane and Nick Kutsukos, Larry Lachman, Clare Landau, Joan Leissner, Jan Lovell, Dr. Patricia McConnell, Diane Moore, Micky Niego, Tom O'Neil, Karen Randall, Kathie Semenchuk, Elizabeth Sheley, Leslie Smythe, Tim Steelman, Kim Steffes, Fritz J. Trybus, University of Tennessee School of Veterinary Medicine, Sandy Jarvis Vesty, Sue Walsh, Bob Warren, Linda Weidemann

Fact Checkers: Tom Cavalieri, Dr. Carla Folkert, Micky Niego

Copy Editor and Proofreader: Barbara Jatkola

Indexer: Nanette Bendyna

Computer Keyboarder: Sheryl Fletcher

Editorial Assistants: Sue MacEwan, Nancy Trafford, Scott Vallee

CONTENTS

INTRODUCTION

It's not easy being a pet. Oh, sure, people *say* they love you. They feed you on a regular basis. They act as if they're glad to see you when they come home at night. They may even let you sleep at the foot of the bed. But sometimes they just don't *get* it. They get upset when Rover eats Susie's term paper, when Tabby suddenly stops using the litter box, or when the new baby ferret nips at somebody's nose. They don't always understand that maybe Rover is bored and lonely, Tabby has a urinary tract infection, or that cute little ferret was taken away from the litter too soon.

That's what this book is for: to look beyond the behavior or the symptom, consider what might be causing it, and offer practical, down-to-earth suggestions for improving the situation. Whether you're dealing with acne or allergies, a food thief or a furniture scratcher, you'll find plenty of ingenious ideas to make both you and your pet happier. And the tips don't stop with health and behavior issues. We'll also tell you how to find the right pet for you and your family (have you considered contacting a breed rescue group?). We'll explain how to make the new addition feel at home (not all pets want lots of attention right away). And we'll suggest all kinds of

ways you and your pet can really have fun together (quick, name four songs you can whistle with your parakeet or four hamster toys you can make from items already lying around your house). We'll tell you how to find a reputable pet breeder, how to grow your own catnip, what plants are poisonous to your pets, and how to calm a kitten's first-night jitters. We'll even give you our own pup-tested recipe for dog biscuits. And we'll keep it all simple, inexpensive, and safe—for you *and* your pet.

Where did we get all these terrific ideas? Simple. We used a little ingenuity and contacted everyone we could think of who might have a pet idea or two. We called veterinarians, trainers, and behaviorists; pet store managers and hobbyists; a pet-sitter and a travel agent (for hints on traveling with pets). We got in touch with dog owners' clubs and breed rescue organizations, veterinary schools and bird associations, and clubs for owners of potbellied pigs. And we asked experienced pet owners how they've dealt with their own pet peeves.

When we had more than enough tips, lists, and stories to fill this book, we showed every tip and every box to either a behaviorist or a veterinarian, who made sure that each one was safe, practical, and worth including. (They cautioned us that it's always important to suit the approach to the pet, so please be careful to consider your own animal's personality, species, and age when choosing the tips that will work best for you.) And then we took the whole thing to *another* group of experts and asked them to top everything off with their own favorite techniques and stories. It's that last group whose words and pictures you'll be seeing now and then throughout this book, as each one adds a personal stamp of approval, explains why a particular approach works, or points out some additional factors you should consider. You'll get to know them better in the chapters that follow, but in the meantime let us introduce . . .

Charles DeVinne, D.V.M. Dr. DeVinne, a graduate of Bethany College and Cornell Veterinary School, maintains a private practice in Peterborough, New Hampshire. Between college and vet school, he worked

on a dairy farm in New York and in an emergency animal clinic in Pennsylvania, and when he graduated from Cornell in 1981, he says, "I had this idea I wanted to be out in the middle of nowhere, treating a few dairy cows and the occasional pet dog." For a while, he did just that, first in Vermont and then in New Hampshire. These days, he concentrates on the dog and cat crowd—with the odd horse thrown in once in a while for variety.

Wendy Emerson, D.V.M. Dr. Emerson loves all kinds of animals (except spiders). She has a basset hound named Lucy, a cat named Frank (who has a mild heart condition but is doing fine), a Senegal parrot named Rafiki, a speckled king snake named Nugget, and an ornate box turtle named Gloria. Dr. Emerson graduated from Tufts School of Veterinary Medicine in 1985, then worked in a small-animal clinical practice until 1993. That was when she started her current practice in Topsfield, Massachusetts. These days, she spends most of her time on the road, making house calls on clients ranging from puppies to pythons throughout eastern Massachusetts.

Lisa Maue, D.V.M. Dr. Maue graduated from Tufts School of Veterinary Medicine in 1985. Since then, she has been practicing in Medford, Massachusetts—working part-time so that she can spend the rest of her day with her son, Jordan; her daughter, Hannah; and her husband, Paul. Dr. Maue loves cats, but because her son is highly allergic to them, she can see them only at work. Her black Labrador mix, Hoagie (yes, named after the sandwich), is recovering from lymphoma and a year of chemotherapy but is doing great.

Micky Niego, animal behaviorist. Micky runs her own training and consulting business, Dog's Eye View, in Airmont, New York. Her passion is puppy training, but she also trains service dogs for emotionally handicapped individuals, speaks on behavior and training issues at professional conferences and special events, and takes her own dogs to visit the elderly in nursing homes. She has taught humane animal education for the American Society for the Prevention of Cruelty to Animals (ASPCA) in New York City and has served as

training director at that organization's Dog Training Center. She created a new ASPCA department, Companion Animal Services, which still operates the free behavior help line she established in 1985. Micky, who has been training dogs since 1975, shares her home with her two bullmastiffs, Jody and Satchel, and four cats.

We hope that you and your pets will benefit from these folks' combined wisdom, along with that of all the other pet owners and pet care professionals who were so generous in sharing their time and experiences with us. To all of them, a heartfelt thanks. And to you and your pets, may the tips in these pages point the way to many years of healthy, happy times together.

—Sharon Smith
Editor

ADOPTING A PET

How Much Is That Dachshund in the Window?

To the casual observer, it might appear that finding and adopting a pet is just a matter of taking a tour of the local pet store or animal shelter, forking over the money, and bringing home a furry, cuddly puppy (or an adorable kitten or even a baby boa). If only it were that easy. Most stores and shelters are crowded with bright, fuzzy animals, all of them eager to be adopted. How do you choose the one that's right for you? You need to find the animal that's a perfect fit for your home (large house and yard vs. small apartment). You need one that's right for your budget (sky's the limit vs. just about making it). And perhaps most important, you need to find a pet that fits your lifestyle (quiet and home loving vs. adventurous and outdoorsy). If you've decided to adopt a pet, you have some major decisions ahead of you, and you could be living with the results for a long time to come.

Once you have figured out what kind of pet you want, you'll still need to do some shopping around. Instead of going to the nearest pet store, breeder, or shelter, do a little research to find out

which one has the best reputation for selling healthy animals and which ones offer exchange policies if something doesn't work out. While you are looking over that litter of kittens or that tank of exotic tropical fish, you will want to make sure that the one you plan to adopt is healthy. Do this by looking for signs of illness or malnutrition and making sure that the environment in which the animal was raised is clean. By taking the time to choose a pet carefully, even dispassionately, you will save yourself money and heartache later. After all, you want your new best friend to be your puppy—not your veterinarian.

ARE YOU READY FOR A PET?

Few things are harder to resist than that lovable mutt that followed you home or the box of new kittens looking for a family. But caring for a pet is a significant commitment—you have to be willing to keep regular hours, spend time caring for the animal and cleaning up after him, and give him plenty of love and attention. How do you know whether you're ready to be a pet owner? Here are a few things to think about.

FOR PETS IN GENERAL

Ask Your Decorator's Advice

❑ Trying to decide whether to get a pet? High on the list of determining factors should be your feelings about housekeeping. You pass the first test of prospective pet ownership if you can honestly say that you won't be squeamish about a little extra cleaning each week. Pets leave behind hair and feathers that must be vacuumed or scales that must be swept up. Their litter boxes, cages, and tanks need to be cleaned regularly. Let's face it: Virtually every animal is an Oscar

Which Type of Pet Is Right for You?

ANIMAL	GREAT FOR A SMALL APARTMENT?	OKAY FOR OLDER FOLKS?	LIKES KIDS?	WHAT IF I'M AWAY ALL DAY?	INTERACTS WITH OTHER PETS?
Chinchilla	Yes	Yes	No, he'll bite	He won't notice	Only another chinchilla
Ferret	Yes	No, a bit too active	No, he'll bite	He'll sleep and stop eating	Loves cats and dogs
Finch	Yes	Yes, perfect	No	That's okay	Other birds only
Fish	Yes	Yes	Yes	That's okay	Other communal fish only
Frog	Yes	Yes	Yes	That's okay	Some aquatic frogs live well with fish
Gerbil	Yes	Yes	Yes	That's okay	No
Hamster	Yes	Yes	Yes	That's okay	No
Lizard	Yes	Yes	Depends on the breed	That's okay	No
Mouse	Yes	Yes	Yes	That's okay	No
Parakeet	Yes	Yes	No	That's okay	Other birds only
Parrot	Yes, depending on noise level	Yes	No	He'll be lonely	Depends on the bird
Rabbit	Yes	Yes	Yes, if super-vised	That's okay	Some cats and some dogs
Snake	Yes, depending on his size	Yes	No	That's okay	No
Spider	Yes	Yes	No	That's okay	No
Turtle	Yes	Yes	Yes	That's okay	Other turtles only

Madison. If you're Felix Ungar, don't get a pet—or get a pet and a cleaning service at the same time.

❑ If you like a clean house without a lot of extra work but want the companionship of a pet, consider a gerbil, fish, or small bird—something that will live happily in a cage or tank. This will keep you from resenting your new roommate.

Can You Fence Off the Living Room?

❑ If you own valuable furniture or rugs, don't get a pet—or at least figure out a way to keep pets out of the rooms where you keep such valuables. Dogs and cats that have the run of the house will have accidents. So will birds or bunnies when they come out of their cages. They might scratch upholstery or chew shoes, wallpaper, and homework. Consider whether your house is set up in such a way that you can restrict a pet to certain areas—say, the kitchen or family room—where the furnishings aren't quite so precious.

Even Pet Rocks?

Pet owners, listen up: Thank your lucky stars that you didn't live during the 1500s in England. In those days, simply owning a cat was often grounds for someone to be accused of being a witch. Old, unmarried women who owned cats were particularly suspect, but ownership of any kind of pet was considered legitimate evidence in many witch trials.

Check with Your Landlord

❑ If you're planning to adopt from an animal shelter, be prepared to show proof that you either own your own home or have the explicit permission of your landlord to own a pet. Most shelters require such assurances before they'll release a pet to you. Their experience has been that too many animals in shelters or dog pounds have been given up by owners who didn't have their landlords' permission or who moved into apartments that don't take pets.

Make Sure That Sneeze Is Just a Sneeze

❑ If you have never had a pet before, or if your child has never been around animals, take a few minutes to pet the neighborhood dog or hold a friend's cat. The last thing you want to do is bring home a beautiful bundle of fur only to find that your child is allergic.

ADOPTING A PET

- ❑ If you or your child is allergic to fur, don't worry. You can still become exceptional owners of other friendly pets such as fish, turtles, or small snakes.
- ❑ What if you or your children suffer from asthma? Before you bring home a cuddly pet, be sure to ask your doctor whether the pet's fur will affect the illness.

A WORD FROM DR. EMERSON

The Best First Pets for Kids

DR. WENDY EMERSON
Veterinarian who makes house calls in and around Topsfield, Massachusetts, to care for cats, dogs, and a wide range of exotic pets

Many people tour the pet stores looking for good first pets for their kids, and they often settle on the wrong ones because they're cheap. People think that an inexpensive pet will be easier to care for than an expensive one. Then they look around and see the iguana, which some stores sell for under $15. I wish iguanas were the most expensive pets in the store because then people would realize how fragile they are and how much you have to know to care for them. But store owners don't always look at it that way. They know that you'll be back for another iguana when this one dies.

In my opinion, rats are the best first pets because they are so intelligent and affectionate. They'll learn their names; they'll do tricks; they'll love you. Of course, this is usually a pretty hard sell. When I tell kids they should get a rat, they say, "Cool," while right behind them Mom is saying, "No way."

ADOPTING A PET

World Travelers Need Not Apply

❑ If your job requires you to travel a lot, it would be better to hold off on adopting a pet until you're able to be home more. An animal depends on you completely for food, clean shelter, and affection. Even animals such as snakes and spiders that don't need to be fed every day need some regular attention because their cages

ONE PERSON'S SOLUTION

The Smartest Dog I Ever Owned

Times were hard in the coal camps of Wharton, West Virginia, in the 1940s, and owning a dog was out of the question, especially in a large family. One day, I found a large, half-starved dog lying in a ditch. He couldn't move, so I carried him home, made a bed for him under the house, and then sneaked him some scraps from the table. The next morning, he could stand, so I bathed him before I asked Mom if I could keep him. She said I could if he didn't bite. All of his bones showed, so I named him Boney.

Months later, a man claimed Boney and said his real name was Drum. He convinced my mom, but several weeks later he returned the dog and said he was dumb. He told Mom that he took the dog to a training school in Tennessee, but they sent him back because they couldn't teach Boney anything. On the command "Sit," he would stand; on "Run," he would roll over. When the man left, we laughed out loud because Boney was smart: I had taught him secret commands that only we knew.

—**JAMES R. McDAVID**
Biloxi, Mississippi

need to stay at a certain temperature and humidity. And all pets need someone to notice when they are ill or when their cages need cleaning.

I Promise I'll Take Care of Him!

❑ If you want a pet as a companion for a young child, it's fine to adopt the animal as soon as the child is old enough to appreciate him. But if you want the child to help care for the animal, it might be wise to wait until the youngster is older—say, 9 to 12 years old.

Settle Down

❑ If you're about to move, wait until after you've relocated to adopt that new pet. Otherwise, your new dog, ferret, or snake will suffer one trauma in learning to live away from her mother and another in getting used to your new home. (It's likely to take a week or so for the pet to adapt all over again after the move.) This is especially true if you are adopting an older pet that has had more than one owner already. Such an animal is more likely to be somewhat set in her ways and perhaps mourning the loss of her former home. To develop your pet's trust, you will need to give her time and stability.

Dogs in Space

Alan Shepard, eat your heart out. The first living creature in space, as many baby boomers remember, was not an American. It wasn't even a Russian man. It was a Russian dog named Laika (Russian for "barker"). Laika was shot into space on November 3, 1957, aboard *Sputnik 2*.

FOR DOGS ONLY

Jealous Puppy

Ideally, bring home a new baby—and give the whole family time to adjust to *that* new lifestyle—before you bring home a new puppy. Some pets actually feel jealous of new babies, just as they would of another animal.

FOR CATS ONLY

Baby First, Kitty Second

If you're expecting a baby in the near future, your safest course of action is to wait until after the baby is

A WORD FROM DR. MAUE

Keep the Baby and *the Cat*

DR. LISA MAUE
Veterinarian in private practice in Medford, Massachusetts, for more than a decade

I can't tell you the number of times pregnant women have come into my office in tears because they have been told that they have to get rid of their cats. It's true that some cats are carriers of toxoplasmosis and that this condition, if transmitted to a pregnant woman, can cause serious birth defects or even a miscarriage. So if you don't already own a cat, it's not a great idea to adopt one when you're pregnant. But if you already have a cat, you don't necessarily have to find a new home for your pet.

The key to guarding against toxoplasmosis is to watch your diet carefully and to wash your hands frequently. I've always had cats at home, and during both my pregnancies I treated sick cats every day. To keep toxoplasmosis out of your system, you have to keep it out of your mouth. To do that, you should wash your hands with antibacterial soap after cleaning your cat's litter box or after gardening out in the yard. (Flower beds often serve as litter boxes for neighborhood cats.) Keep it clean, and you can keep the cat.

born before you bring home a new cat. A pregnant woman can get toxoplasmosis—a condition that can result in serious birth defects or even a miscarriage—from cleaning a cat's litter box.

FOR REPTILES ONLY

Babies and Boas Don't Mix

S If you're expecting a new baby or have young children, wait until the kids are older before bringing home a pet reptile. Many of the reptiles available as pets have been exposed to or are carriers of salmonella bacteria, and young children and pregnant women are especially susceptible to salmonella poisoning. Besides, if you wait until all the kids in the household are 10 to 12 years old before bringing home a reptile, the youngsters will be able to follow your instructions about how to handle their pet carefully without hurting it. They also will understand why they need to wash their hands every time they come in contact with the reptile or help clean the cage.

IS THAT HOUSE BIG ENOUGH FOR ALL OF YOU?

Some animals need space to roam; others will flourish in a cozy apartment. As you try to decide what kind of animal you want, look around and figure out how much room you have for a new companion. How do you know if you have enough space to house a Saint Bernard? A goldfish? A parrot? Here are some guidelines.

FOR PETS IN GENERAL

He Used to Fit in the Palm of My Hand

❑ Before you adopt any pet, try to find out how big the animal is going to get. Just like people, all pets grow up. Make sure you have enough room not only for your new friend's bed, tank, or cage but also for the litter box, food bowls, and toys.

Can You Contain Your Pet?

❑ If you live in a tiny house or a one-room apartment, you might consider adopting a gerbil, hamster, or fish. No matter how small your living space, one of these animals can live happily in a cage or tank.

COMMON MISTAKES

Cockatoo? Ker-Choo!

Many of the same people who are allergic to cat or dog fur are sensitive to the down of certain birds. Cockatoos especially release a lot of down and feather dust into the air. If you're considering buying a bird and you live with someone who has allergies, you may want that person to visit the aviary with you, to see if he has a reaction. And it's a good idea to mention this potential problem to the breeder before you buy, to let her know that you are buying on a trial basis. Most breeders will understand.

ADOPTING A PET

FOR DOGS AND CATS

You Both Need Your Space

If you live alone and you plan to adopt an outgoing four-legged animal such as a cat or dog, make sure you have room to live with the new pet. This generally means that you'll need at least two rooms of living space. As with most roommates, sometimes you will both want to share the same room, and sometimes you won't.

> **4 *Benefits of Getting a Companion for Your "Only" Pet . . .***
>
> **1.** After the adjustment period, he'll have someone to play with.
>
> **2.** He'll have company when you're at work.
>
> **3.** Both animals will learn habits by example—such as scratching at the door to go out or using the litter box.
>
> **4.** You can double your fun without doubling your work.

FOR DOGS ONLY

Bark Twice if You're Bored

Conventional wisdom says that you shouldn't get a dog, especially a big dog, if you live in a small apartment. Generally speaking, conventional wisdom is right. If you live in a small space and want to adopt a pet, think first about getting a small, quiet animal. Big dogs love space to roam and run, and yours will pine for the outdoors if she is cooped up. She also will bark—constantly. A dog cooped up in a small apartment is likely to growl and yelp at every rustle and thump in the rooms next door and at every person who walks by on the street—it's part of the animal's protective instinct. Don't create a situation where you and your dog—to say nothing of your neighbors—will be uncomfortable.

Avoid Urban Sprawl: Take a Walk in the Park

What if you have your heart set on keeping a dog in the city and you meet the basic requirement of living in an apartment that's big enough for a dog to feel comfortable? If you're positive that you want a dog, be sure to check out the parks nearby. You'll need to find one that you like and is close enough to home that the two of you can walk there on a regular basis. Some parks

even have fenced-in areas where dog owners can let their pets run. This is an ideal space for your dog to get exercise and find playmates.

You Need a Dog with Street Smarts

If you're sure you want a canine companion in the city, consider a working dog (a small shepherd or a collie). These animals are generally intelligent, calm, and bred to follow direction. They are used to dealing with people and are less likely to shy away from all the bustle and noise of the city. They also will be smart enough to understand that they need to travel on a short leash, which means that they will be less likely to tug you out into traffic.

Home Is Where the Crate Is

When you plan for your new puppy, think about how you can set aside a spot just for him. One way is to use a dog crate (a hard plastic or wire mesh container that serves as an indoor doghouse and gives the dog his own space). A dog crate needs to be large enough that the animal can stand up in it, so make sure you have the space for such an addition.

The Laundry Room Is His Castle

If you prefer not to use a dog crate or just don't have room for one, you may want to start by confining your new pup to a small room that you can block off from the rest of the house. Ideally, you'll want to be able to cover the bottom half of the doorway with a large board or gate but leave the top half open so that your pet can hear you in the other

. . . And Drawbacks 4

1. After the adjustment period, he'll have someone to fight with.

2. He'll have someone to scheme with when you're at work.

3. Both animals will learn habits by example—such as drinking from the toilet and barking to be let out at 5:00 A.M.

4. Sometimes you really can't double your fun.

Unless you have a particularly possessive animal (one that challenges every visitor to your home or everyone you meet when out walking) or a dog so big that your house or budget can't accommodate an addition, the great things about a second pet usually outweigh the not so great. And if you're a dog owner who works away from home or spends a lot of time out and about without your pet, a second animal is a virtual necessity.

It's all in your approach. Make a new pup feel she has a room of her own, not a sentence to solitary confinement.

rooms of the house and won't feel too isolated. This will be the dog's space during the first few weeks. It will be large enough that the dog can play there either with you or on her own. But it will be small enough that she won't get lost or into trouble. Here your dog will have her toys and food bowl easily accessible, and you'll be able to spread out plenty of newspaper while she goes through the trial and error of housebreaking.

FOR CATS ONLY

Homebodies Are Healthier

Before you buy a cat for your one-room apartment, consider whether you're willing to have her inside with you all day—and whether you're willing to accept the risks of letting your pet roam around outside. Cats that live in urban or heavily developed suburban areas should not spend nights or whole days outside; they run too great a risk of being exposed to deadly diseases such as feline leukemia, feline infectious peritonitis, and the feline version of HIV (which is extremely contagious to cats, though not to people). In addition, your cat could get picked on by larger neighborhood bullies or might even be stolen.

FOR BIRDS ONLY

It's Cheaper Than an Aerobics Class

When you pick out a spot in your house for your new bird, make sure you allow for a cage that's wide

YOU'VE GOTTA LOVE 'EM

To Flee or Not to Flee? No Question!

I've heard of animals that can't be domesticated, but a rogue Angora hamster? Hamlet was born to be wild. From the first day we brought him home, he spent hours balanced on top of his sport wheel sniffing at the cage door. Open the lid to give him a treat, and Hamlet would make a bid for freedom. Put him in a box while cleaning the cage, and he'd start chewing his way out.

One night my son, David, who has trouble remembering to put lids back on, left the cage door ajar, and Hamlet made his break. Each night, we would hear him scurry between the walls to launch a commando attack on a bowl of apples (one delicate nibble out of each), a drawerful of bagged beans, and—prime tooth-sharpening material—the insulation lining the wires to the burners on our gas stove ($110 to repair). Two weeks later, David went to get a dog biscuit out of the plastic container (lid ajar, naturally), and there, at the bottom, was Hamlet, whose cookie nirvana had turned into a trap.

Hamlet served a few more months in solitary until David's carelessness struck again. Occasionally, we see Hamlet scurrying through the garage and figure he's nestled cozily in a boot, snacking on spilled birdseed and howling at the moon.

—KAY SCHELLER
Waterville, Vermont

enough for the bird to extend her wings fully once she's grown. In addition, it will have to be tall enough to allow her to climb. Birds such as finches, which may never be outside the cage, will need room to flap their wings and fly from perch to perch.

THE BATTLE OF THE BUDGET

The purchase price of an animal sometimes seems arbitrary. Why does a canary cost more than a tarantula? Actually, the price is based on the size and rarity of an animal (*and* on what people will pay). But no matter what the initial cost of the pet, that's just the beginning. You'll have expenses for food, shelter, trips to the vet, and maybe a toy or two to keep your new friend occupied. Like the original purchase price, these additional costs vary considerably from one species to another. How much does it cost to care for a goldfish, Great Dane, or boa constrictor? Here are some things to keep in mind.

FOR PETS IN GENERAL

Plumage Is Pricey

❑ Some people prefer rare animals because they are so unusual or striking. If you're thinking of buying an especially rare breed of lizard or cat, be prepared to pay top dollar—three or four times what a more common breed would cost.

❑ Expect to pay more if your new pet has to be imported (a foreign boa as opposed to a domestic garter snake) or if the animal itself is unusual or isn't carried by most pet stores.

Breeding Like . . . Rabbits

Two wild rabbits—a male and a female, that is—can produce more than four million offspring in a year. (That's not a typo.)

Don't Buy a Show-Off

❑ If cost is important to you, think twice before buying a purebred animal from a breeder. A rare breed of dog or cat can cost close to $1,000. It's true that a breeder will be able to tell you who your new pet's parents were as well as his medical history, and you'll be able to get a certification of his bloodline if you want to raise a show dog or become a breeder yourself. The question is whether you consider those advantages worth the additional expense.

The Only Thing That's Free Is the Advice

ADOPTING A PET

❑ Don't plan your pet budget on the assumption that you'll get a new pet at absolutely no cost, even if you're adopting from an animal shelter. Every shelter, breed rescue group, and other discount source requests at least a nominal fee—anything from $5 to $200—when you adopt a pet. They do this to help cover their veterinary bills and the cost of caring for animals while they try to find good homes for the pets.

FOR DOGS ONLY

How to Estimate the Cost of a Dog

Be sure to check your budget before you bring home that new puppy. You can expect to pay about $50 to $100 to adopt even the smallest mutt from the local pound. This price will include the spaying or neutering procedure and the dog's first round of shots—plus worming, testing for heartworms, and usually some temperament testing.

If you go through a breeder, expect to pay at least $200—into the thousands for rarer breeds. And that's just the price of the dog. You'll still need to have the animal spayed or neutered and pay for the dog's shots, which could cost an additional $200 for the first round and $50 to $60 annually for later booster shots.

COST CUTTERS

Puppies: The Thousand-Dollar Detail

Before you select a purebred puppy, make sure you've told the breeder that you are looking for a pet dog and not a show dog. The difference may mean several hundred dollars. Every breeder finds one or more puppies in a litter that may have the perfect look for the show ring. Those dogs will be sold to other breeders for thousands of dollars. The rest of the puppies—all of which are likely to be handsome, good quality dogs—will be sold as pets for hundreds of dollars. The breeder will have identified which are which by the time you see them.

Their Appetite Grows with Them

If you buy a big dog (or one that soon will be big), plan to spend up to $300 a year for food and treats. A dog that weighs less than 60 pounds will eat only about half that amount.

Before You Leave the Pet Store

In addition to the little critter himself, you'll need to buy a few things to make your pet feel at home. For some pets, this start-up cost far outweighs the cost of the animal.

IN ADDITION TO THE . . .	YOU'LL HAVE TO HAVE . . .	WHICH WILL COST . . .
Bird	Cage with perches, water bottle, pellets or seeds, cage cover	$40 to $100 and up
Cat	Litter box, litter and scoop, scratching post, nail clippers, flea comb and brush, plastic cat carrier, food and water bowls, food	$50 to $150
Dog	Leash and collar, flea collar, tags, food and water bowls, crate or bed, food, brush, nail clippers, pooper-scooper, chew toys	$50 to $100
Ferret	Cage, litter box, litter, several toys, food bowl and hanging water bottle, good quality cat food	$150 to $250
Gerbil, hamster, or mouse	Cage or terrarium, bedding, place to hide, things to crawl on, water bottle, food, chew toys, hay	$30 to $100
Goldfish	Bowl, food	$5 to $7
Lizard or toad	Terrarium; sand, damp moss, potting soil, or mulch; thermometer; heating pad; heat lamp; special lighting; insects and perhaps a special feeder; shallow water bowl; spray bottle; special vitamins	$60 to $120
Rabbit	Cage, litter box, litter, food (hay, pellets, fresh fruits and vegetables), salt wheel, protective tubes for electrical cords	$100 to $200
Snake	Terrarium, sand, high-range thermometer, heating pad, heat lamp, special lighting, large water dish, moss, place to hide, food (insects, mice, small fish)	$60 to $120
Tarantula	Terrarium, sand or gravel, heating pad, thermometer, water saucer, food (crickets), spray bottle, things to crawl on	$50 to $60
Tropical fish	Aquarium with cover, fluorescent tubes, air pump, filtering system, gravel, ornaments, water heater, water-conditioning chemicals, water-testing kits, food	$30 to $150

The Great American Breed

When you're choosing a breed of dog, don't forget about the mutts. A mixed breed is often every bit as happy and loving as a purebred dog, and they are usually healthier, too. When you buy a purebred, you are buying looks and breeding, not necessarily social skills or good health. In fact, many purebred dogs carry with them a hidden cost: the debilitating health problems that the animals will develop over the course of their lives.

FOR CATS ONLY

How to Estimate the Cost of a Cat

Check your pocketbook before checking out that pretty longhaired kitten. Buying from a breeder could set you back hundreds of dollars if you want, say, a purebred such as a Persian or an exotic crossbred such as a Himalayan. On top of that, plan to spend about $100 for spaying or neutering and another $100 for the first set of distemper and rabies vaccinations.

If you're looking for a companion rather than a certain breed or color of cat, you can save a lot of money by visiting your local shelter. Some shelters charge $40 to $100 for a cat, and that price includes the animal's first set of shots as well as worming and spaying or neutering.

FOR BIRDS ONLY

Talk Isn't Cheap

If you want a pet bird that has special skills, plan to pay accordingly. Male canaries cost almost twice as much as females because they are the singers. And a parrot costs hundreds more than a humble finch or lovebird because the parrot will learn to speak.

Does It Take a Pirate to Pay for a Parrot?

If you want a large bird with bright coloring, prepare yourself for a large outlay of cash. The bigger and rarer the bird, the more the bird will cost. The common

(if beautiful) finch or canary will generally cost around $25, while the regal and talkative African gray parrot can cost as much as $1,000. Owners pay more than $10,000 for very rare varieties of macaws.

Cages generally cost about $20 to $100, depending on the size. But some of the largest parrot cages run more than $400.

FOR FERRETS ONLY

If You Fancy a Ferret

Expect to pay between $80 and $150 for a pet ferret. They are still fairly unusual pets, so you might get a better deal from a ferret breeder than from a pet store. Check the ads in local newspapers to locate breeders in your area.

A pet ferret can be a fine friend.

Take On a Rescue Mission

You may be able to locate a ferret to adopt by seeking out a ferret rescue group. Several large cities have such organizations; call your local animal shelter to find out whether there is one in your area. You will pay considerably less for older rescued animals than for babies from the pet store.

FOR FISH ONLY

Fish in Local Waters

Check your wallet before promising your youngster an animal with a delicate constitution. Several species of tropical fish, for instance, have to be caught off coral reefs and carefully transported to pet stores. Many of them die on the way. The expense of collecting and transporting these fish drives the price up, so that each one may cost you more than $100, while the more common guppies generally run under $5 each.

FOR REPTILES ONLY

Snakes: The Temperature's Rising

S When you invest in a pet snake, budget the largest expense not for the animal or even the tank, but for the special light and heat the animal will need to survive. Snakes are cold-blooded animals. Their body temperature matches their environment. To keep them warm enough to survive, you will need to spend $20 to $40 on a special heating pad under the tank. You also will need to buy a thermometer to track the temperature in the

How Much Will He Cost Each Year?

You can probably keep a tropical fish happy for less than $100 a year, but maintaining a contented cat can add more than $500 to your budget annually. Here are some typical annual costs for keeping dogs, cats, and other pets.

PET	FOOD	GOING TO THE VET	OTHER	TOTAL
Bird	$60 to $150	$50 to $100	None	$110 to $250
Cat	$120 to $240	About $100	Litter: $120 to $180	$340 to $520
Dog	$150 to $200 for small dogs, $200 to $300 for large dogs	Shots and heartworm medications: $75 to $100	None	$225 to $500
Ferret	$80 to $120	$20 to $40	Litter: $120	$220 to $280
Lizard	$150 to $350	$50 to $100	Electricity: $20 to $30	$220 to $480
Rabbit	Hay, pellets, treats: $240	Less than $100	Litter: $60 to $120	$400 to $460
Snake	$175 to $350	$50 to $100	Electricity: $20 to $30	$245 to $480
Tropical fish	$60	None	Electricity: $20	$80

COST CUTTERS

Rescued from a Dinner Plate

If you're looking for the cheapest available pet, think about a species that is very common or one that is used as a feeder for other animals. In most pet stores, a little white mouse will cost only a few dollars; a cricket will cost only a few cents. That's because these animals are often fed to snakes. Pet stores need to keep the prices on "feeder" animals down so as to keep the costs of snake ownership at an affordable level.

tank and make sure it stays at an acceptable level. If a snake gets too cold, it will stop eating and may even die.

Some snakes and other reptiles require full-spectrum lighting, which gives them vitamin D and helps them to absorb calcium. If you're going to keep these animals, you'll need to buy special full-spectrum light bulbs for their terrariums. These bulbs cost about $20 to $40. Plan on replacing the bulbs every six months, even if they're still giving off light.

They'll Eat More, Too

Sure, you think that a great big snake will be a more interesting pet than a little garter snake. But before you get too wrapped up in your new purchase, consider how much that extra size is going to cost you. A two-foot corn snake may cost only $20, but a boa that will grow to be eight feet long will cost more than $500. You'll pay more to house your pet, too. Your big boa will need a tank that is at least two-thirds as long as she is, so your bill for buying a large snake will grow as she grows.

Rx for a Healthy Reptile

You are all ready to bring home that rare gecko or king snake, but first you need to make sure that you have a vet who can treat the animal. Decide on the kind of reptile you want, then find a vet who has experience treating that breed *before* you buy. You may even want

Leggo my gecko! Find a vet—and not just any vet—before you bring that appealing critter home.

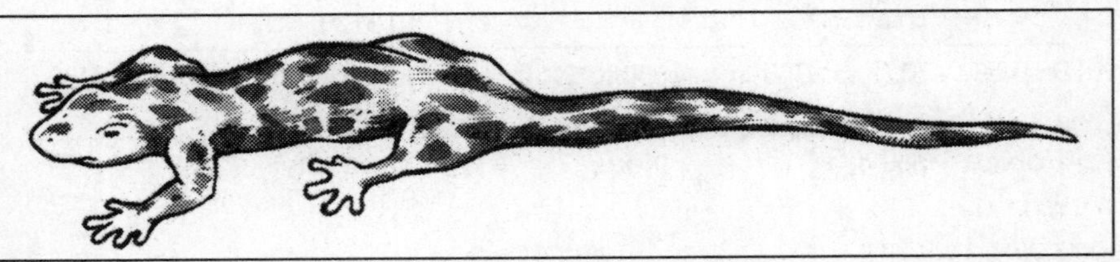

to schedule an appointment. Your new pet will need to visit a vet right away, especially if the animal was imported from another country. The vet will need to check your pet for parasites and may want to treat him for dehydration. Expect to pay between $50 and $150, depending on how healthy the animal is, for your new reptile's first visit to the vet.

FOR OTHER PETS

Will You Take to a Tarantula?

❍ The rose hair tarantula is one of the most popular breeds because of its pretty color. Most pet stores carry them, and they cost only about $20 to $25. Plan to spend at least that much more on a tank. You also will need a $20 heating pad and a small thermometer to ensure that the spider is warm enough to survive. The good news is that a tarantula is a cheap dinner date. The crickets the spider eats cost only a few cents each.

Not your usual furry creature, tarantulas make intriguing pets.

MATTERS OF TIME

You think of getting a pet because you want companionship and something to care for. Well, how *much* of each do you want? Grooming, training, exercise—they all take time. Small, fairly quiet animals such as fish and reptiles need little more than to be fed, to have their cages and tanks cleaned, and to be noticed. Dogs and cats, however, require significant amounts of time and attention every day. Here are some tips to help you make sure the pet you adopt is one your schedule can handle.

FOR PETS IN GENERAL

Are You Ready for a Long-Term Commitment?

❑ Before you adopt a pet, take a minute to think about how long that pet is likely to be around. Snakes can live for decades. Some breeds of dogs can live for 15 years. A young, healthy African gray parrot may live for 60 to

70 years—which means she may even outlive you. Before taking in a pet, think about what will happen to her if something should happen to you. Find a friend or relative who will be willing to care for the animal or who can find a good home for her. State your wishes in your will. Otherwise, your pets will be considered property of the estate and may be inherited by someone who doesn't want them.

❑ If you're not in a position to make a long-term commitment, think about adopting a fish or a mouse, which is not likely to need decades of care.

FOR DOGS ONLY

Adopt a Daily Constitutional

Before you adopt a dog, figure out a way that you can adhere to the same exercise routine every day (or face the mess when you get home). Plan on spending about an hour every day taking your dog outside. You will probably make three or four trips, depending on the rest of your schedule. A typical routine would include taking the dog out first thing in the morning, right before you leave the house, at midday or when you get home from work, and one last time before bedtime. At least one of these needs to be a 30-minute walk to keep your dog healthy and alert.

He's as Trainable as You Are

When you adopt a puppy, timing is everything. If at all possible, bring your new friend home at a time in your life when your schedule is really flexible. For the first couple of weeks, someone will need to be able to watch him during the day to coach him through the house-training process. Puppies don't have good bladder control. They need to go outside about once every two to three hours. By arranging your schedule so that you can spend extra time at home in your puppy's first couple of weeks, you are really giving him his most important lesson about living indoors. (Spending time alone with your new puppy also will keep him occupied while he gets used to your home. If

A Pet to Last a Lifetime

Knowing your pet's life expectancy at the beginning of your relationship can prepare you for a potentially early demise or a lifelong commitment. Here are typical life expectancies of some common types of pets.

ANIMAL	TYPICAL LIFE SPAN
Cats	15 to 20 years
Dogs	8 to 15 years
Birds	
Canaries	10 to 20 years
Finches	2 to 10 years
Parakeets, cockatiels, or lovebirds	15 years
Large parrots	50 to 100 years
Midsize parrots (Senegal, conure)	30 years
Fish	
Goldfish	Up to several decades
Other freshwater fish	A few years
Saltwater fish	2 months to 2 years
Reptiles	
Aquatic turtles	20 years
Box turtles	Up to 100 years
Frogs	5 to 13 years, depending on the kind
Iguanas	10 to 20 years
Lizards	5 to 20 years, depending on the kind
Salamanders	Up to 30 years
Snakes	25 to 50 years, depending on the kind
Small and Fuzzy Pets	
Chinchillas	20 years in pairs; 10 years alone
Dwarf rabbits	7 to 10 years
Ferrets	6 to 12 years
Gerbils, hamsters, or mice	2 to 4 years
Guinea pigs or hedgehogs	7 to 10 years
Rats	5 years
Tarantulas	5 years

he's left alone for several hours during the day, he'll get bored and do what puppies do best: chew.)

A Hundred Strokes

If you want a dog but would like to avoid a lot of extra vacuuming and don't want to brush anybody's hair but your own, try a shorthaired breed such as a dalmatian or Chihuahua. The longer and finer the hair on your dog, the more often you will have to brush it to keep it from matting and to keep shedding under control. A longhaired breed such as a collie or an English sheepdog will require significantly more maintenance than a shorthaired Doberman or beagle. A dog with hair as long as a Lhasa apso may have to be brushed daily.

YOU'VE GOTTA LOVE 'EM

These Pets Know How to Party

My pets' birthdays were major celebrations when I was growing up. Prince the pony celebrated his birthday in the house by marching around the dining room table to the tune of "Happy Birthday" on the player piano. When my dog Tussy had a birthday, my mother invited all the neighbor dogs. The pups sat around the table, wore party hats, and ate out of silver bowls my father had won in squash tournaments. Our horse Ginger's 36th birthday was the social event of the year on Chicago's North Shore. People came from three hours away to attend the party, which was highlighted by Ginger blowing out the candles on her birthday cake and then eating the cake—all of it.

—EDIE FARWELL
San Francisco, California

FOR CATS ONLY

Brush Up on Your Grooming Skills

The thing about longhaired cats is that they need plenty of help with their hair. Plan to spend several hours a week combing small mats out of your Persian's or Himalayan's coat. Even the Maine coon cat, which is a rugged, independent sort, will need regular brushing to keep her hair from tangling. Longhaired cats that aren't groomed on a regular basis will begin to scratch and tear at their coats and may become irritable. They also are more likely to come up with a few extra fur balls.

If you don't like the idea of grooming your cat more often than you groom yourself, think about a shorthaired breed. They also benefit from brushing, but it doesn't have to be nearly as frequent. Shorthaired cats will be perfectly satisfied if you run a comb through their hair just once or twice a month.

Cats Are Serial Killers

If you live in an old country house or have an outdoor cat, recognize up front that you will need to spend time cleaning up your cat's carnage. Cats are natural hunters that prey on smaller animals, especially rodents and birds. A cat that lives in a house with mice will kill and eat them. The good news is that you will never have to worry about buying mousetraps again. The bad news is that you will come upon little half-eaten mice every few months and will have to get rid of them.

FOR FERRETS ONLY

A Ferret Needs a Friend

If you're thinking about adopting a ferret, make sure you can set aside time to play with him every day. Ferrets are social and excitable animals. They love to play, but when they don't get enough attention, they become listless and depressed. Then they'll tend to sleep all day and may even stop eating.

You might consider getting two ferrets. They will entertain each other and still have enough energy to play with you at the end of the day.

FOR FISH ONLY

Why Fish Love Chemistry Majors

Tropical fish owners don't spend much time feeding their pets. They do spend a few hours every month checking the chemical makeup of the water in their aquariums. If you become a tropical fish owner, you will need to become an expert in water-conditioning. Your freshwater charges will need tap water that has been cleared of harsh chemicals such as ammonia and chlorine, softened to the appropriate pH level, and filtered constantly against the buildup of more ammonia and nitrates. You will need to buy the appropriate chemicals to accomplish all of this, use them on a regular basis, and routinely test the pH level of your pets' water, checking for excess ammonia and nitrates.

> **Better Change Your Will**
>
> That box turtle you just bought your kids may outlive all of you. Some turtles have been known to live 100 years or more.

Clean Water Acts

You will need to add clean water to the tank about once a month. That means siphoning off about 20 percent of the tank's water and then processing the new water before you add it to the tank. Plan on spending several hours a month just conditioning water.

FOR REPTILES ONLY

Gaze into Her Limpid Pool

A snake is a relatively independent sort (at least compared to a dog), but snakes still require a fair amount of care. Although you may need to feed your pet only once a week, you will have to change her water bowl almost daily. Many snakes need water bowls big enough for them to fit their whole bodies inside. They like to soak in the same water they drink, and it gets dirty (not to mention smelly) pretty quickly.

S Plan to spend a few minutes every day checking the temperature and lighting of your snake's tank. Even a mild change in temperature can make a snake sick or even kill the animal.

FOR OTHER PETS

Play Misty for Her

❍ Although you will have to feed your tarantula only about once a week (with live crickets, roaches, or bloodworms), you should plan to spend some time every day trying to keep the spider's environment warm and humid. In addition to checking that your pet's heating pad is keeping her tank at a constant temperature of at least 75°F, you will need to use a plant mister to keep the air humid enough for your pet.

CHOOSING THE RIGHT TYPE OF PET

Do you want a pet that will constantly seek your attention or one that will leave you alone until you have time to play? An animal that will keep up an ongoing conversation or one that won't disturb the neighbors? A friend that you can take hiking or a furry companion that will snuggle in your lap at night? Before you adopt, take stock of your personality and lifestyle, then consider these clues as to just what type of pet is likely to fit your family.

> **Kissin' Cousins**
>
> Both dogs and cats can trace their family trees to a common ancestor. That would be Miacis, a tree-climbing den animal that lived 40 million years ago, during the Eocene era.

FOR PETS IN GENERAL

Some Pets Are Early Risers

❑ If you're considering adopting a pet, consider whether you're a morning person—or willing to become one. If you don't like to get up early, you might want to think about adopting a fish, gerbil, or reptile, which will be happy to sit and wait for you to wake up on the weekends. Birds awake with the sun and are likely to start singing or chirping at first light. Dogs and cats also are early risers. Soon after you've adopted a puppy or kitten, it will figure out your sleep schedule

So Many Breeds, So Little Time

You can't complain that you don't have enough options when you decide to look for a puppy. There are more than 300 different breeds of dogs to choose from—and that's not even counting the mutts! To find out whether a particular breed is right for you, it's important to approach the breeder armed with a list of questions. Here are some of the things you might want to ask.

How bright is this breed? The more intelligent the dog, the easier she will be to train. Working and herding dogs such as collies and shepherds tend to be the most intelligent because their job is to work with people. They have been bred to take orders, make decisions, and solve problems. It's no accident that many Hollywood dogs are Border collies or Australian shepherds.

Is this the nervous type? Such breeds aren't good for older folks or children. They are more apt to bite when startled or to bark all day. They develop nervous habits —such as chewing or scratching on furniture—when they get bored. Certain terriers and some show dogs are considered high-strung because they have been bred for looks, not personality.

What's likely to ail this dog? Some breeds are very susceptible to respiratory disorders or hip dysplasia. Others have poor eyesight or are prone to certain diseases. Any of these problems will shorten the life of your pet and perhaps cost you thousands of dollars in veterinary bills.

Does he need room to move? Sometimes you can tell by the size of the dog (larger breeds tend to be more active) or by the class (sporting and working dogs are more active). But even within a particular breed, every individual is different. If your dog is active, he will need room to run and play, and he will need some obedience training if he's to become an inside dog.

Is she chatty? It's natural for dogs to bark. They do so to protect their territory and when they are feeling playful. Some dogs, such as terriers and certain hounds, bark more often than other breeds. They are exuberant and loyal, but you'll always know they're around. This makes them better dogs for homeowners than for apartment dwellers.

and wake you up faithfully every morning—Saturdays and Sundays, too. These animals get bored while you're sleeping and want some attention first thing in the morning. Dogs need to go out right away, and cats like to be fed as soon as they wake up. The best dog and cat owners have a pretty good sense of humor about the morning wake-up call and don't expect to sleep in.

His Five O'Clock Feeding

❑ If you are thinking of adopting a dog, think about adopting a regular schedule, too. If you spend long hours at work, cats or gerbils make much better companions because they can easily entertain themselves. If you suffer through long working days, so will your dog. She will be bored and depressed if you are out of the house for more than eight hours a day. Your dog may even become destructive and start overturning trash cans or chewing shoes and books.

Spiders Suffer in Silence

❑ Before you bring home a spider, fish, or lizard, think about your own personality. These animals are quiet. They don't demand attention the way dogs and cats do. They are perfect pets for watching, and they don't mind being left alone sometimes. But a quiet pet won't bark or nag you when he is hungry or needs his cage cleaned. He will just suffer quietly and die. If you are a careful, even meticulous, person, you will make a good fish or reptile owner. If you need the occasional reminder, go for the animal that can nuzzle you when necessary.

FOR DOGS ONLY

Canines Love Commotion

If yours is a bustling household with lots of kids, you should consider getting a dog rather than any other type of pet. Animals such as birds and cats shy away from loud noise, conversation, and music. Dogs, however, love stimulation. They thrive on activity,

especially if they grow up in a busy environment. And the more people there are around the house, the more likely it is that your dog will get attention and love. If one or two people are especially active or enjoy long walks, your dog will be in heaven.

Need a Jogging Companion?

If you go on long hikes or need a dog that will jog with you, you'll want an active breed such as a setter, pointer, or retriever. Some long-legged hounds also fit into this category. They love the outdoors and need space to move. When cooped up, these dogs become miserable and depressed.

Small Dogs Are Big Babies

Some people want a baby to fuss over, and there is no bigger baby than a toy dog. If you spend a lot of time at home and are prepared to lavish attention on a dog, consider one of these miniature animals. You can get miniature poodles and schnauzers, tiny terriers, even dogs so small that they will grow only to fill the palm of your hand. Small dogs don't require a lot of space, but they give and need a tremendous amount of attention and love. These dogs will follow you from room to room and pine for you when you're gone.

Promises, Promises

Before you decide to adopt a greyhound, think about where you are going to spend your next vacation. Then think about where your dog will spend it. The adoption center may ask for your guarantee that you won't put the dog in a kennel with other dogs when you go away on vacation. (Some greyhound rescue groups—organizations devoted to finding good homes for these animals after their racing days are over—have special kennel programs to house such dogs for a nominal fee while owners are away for a short time.) Once they get used to home life, greyhounds become very stressed-out if they have to go back to a kennel.

YOU'VE GOTTA LOVE 'EM

Lassie, Come Back

My brother, John, adored the TV show *Lassie*. We didn't have a dog, so his perceptions were formed entirely by the collie's brilliant and compassionate behavior. Sundays at dinner, we'd hear about her latest exploits: how she'd rescued Timmy from the well or saved the family's herd of cows.

John was convinced that all dogs were like Lassie—quick of wit and stout of heart. So nobody was surprised when, right after college, John bought a sweet-natured Border collie named Zoe. He laid in a supply of dog food and waited for Zoe to strut her stuff. When Zoe chewed an expensive book, he figured she was just adjusting to her surroundings. When she ignored repeated calls to come, she was getting acclimated to the neighborhood. But the day of the salami sandwich, John realized that all dogs aren't Lassie.

John was carrying a lunch tray on the outdoor path from the kitchen to his office when he slipped on a patch of ice and fell, the tray landing near his head. Writhing in pain and unable to get up, he was greatly relieved to see Zoe dashing toward him. He figured she'd size up the situation and run for help. Zoe stopped, cocked her head, sized up the situation, and ate the sandwich. A week later, she began obedience school.

—GREG SLACK
Hollis, New Hampshire

FOR CATS ONLY

They Want to Be Alone

If your household has many quiet hours during the day, a cat is more appropriate for you than a dog. Cats aren't as needy as dogs. In fact, they seem to pride themselves on their independence. They nap when they want to, stay up all night if they want to, and can certainly keep themselves amused while you are away at work or school. But they'll still greet you with greedy affection when you get home.

A Wait-and-See Attitude

If you know that you want a cat with a particular personality—such as a lap cat or one that is especially self-sufficient—the best thing to do is adopt a cat that is a year old. Cats don't imprint the personalities of their owners in the same way that dogs do, so a cat is likely to be the same—needy and affectionate, aloof or curious—no matter who takes care of her. The difficulty comes in identifying that personality. All kittens are pretty much alike: fuzzy, adorable, and crazy. But if you adopt an older cat instead of a kitten, you'll have a better chance of knowing everything about her habits and quirks.

Just Call Him Lucky

If you decide to adopt your cat from an animal shelter, ask the staff about the backgrounds of the cats they have. Some of the cats may have been turned over to the shelters by loving families who were moving or who could no longer care for them. The shelter will know the medical history of these animals and should know about their personalities and habits as well. They can tell you whether Fluffy is a lap cat or an independent sort.

Finally, a Friend Who Appreciates You!

Don't discount a stray cat with little or no known medical or family history. Animal rescue staffers say that the best and most loving cats are former strays.

Having been without food and shelter for a while, they are grateful for their newfound security. Unlike dogs, which turn shy and mistrustful for a while after trauma, cats seem to look on the bright side. When you give them a good home, they know they've been rescued.

ADOPTING A PET

Persians Prefer People

If you spend a lot of time in a quiet environment and are looking for a cat that will be a constant companion, consider adopting a Persian or an Abyssinian. These are generally very affectionate animals that will

Two Times a Hero

In the winter of 1925, the city of Nome, Alaska, was threatened by a diphtheria epidemic. Although a serum for the disease did exist, a road between Nome and the last stop on the mail train, Nenana, did not. Planes couldn't be used for transport because of bad weather. The only way to get the serum to Nome was via dogsled. And so on a cold January day, 20 teams took off from Nenana in what was dubbed the Great Race of Mercy to Nome.

Gunnar Kaasen's team, led by a black malamute named Balto, was the first to reach Nome. But the fact that they made it at all was due only to Balto's quick thinking. Faced with blizzard conditions, including brutal 50-below-zero temperatures, the team struggled through difficult terrain and drifting snow. This mission might easily have ended in tragedy. Just as the dogs were about to run full speed into a river—and certain death—Balto stopped them short.

Balto's bravery in this mission of mercy did not go unnoticed, and he and his teammates were hailed as national heroes, even starring in a live-action Hollywood film. Today, if you visit New York's Central Park, you'll find a statue of Balto, erected in honor of that famous dog team. The inscription reads: "Dedicated to the indomitable spirit of the sled dogs that relayed antitoxin six hundred miles over rough ice, across treacherous waters, through Arctic blizzards from Nenana to the relief of stricken Nome in the winter of 1925. Endurance. Fidelity. Intelligence."

Today that first Great Race of Mercy is commemorated in Alaska's annual Iditarod Trail Sled Dog Race, in which sled dog teams race the 1,049 miles from Nome to Anchorage.

follow an owner from room to room. They love owners who are home a lot and available to serve as furniture. They demand as much as you can give and are best for people who are willing to lavish love and attention on them. They do not do well with owners who travel a lot, and they become depressed if ignored.

YOU'VE GOTTA LOVE 'EM

Tree's Company

My neighbor is a nervous sort, always inclined to panic over situations that others might expect will resolve themselves. On one of the first nice days of spring, she let her four-month-old ginger tabby cat out for an exploration of the backyard. When an hour had gone by and kitty was nowhere to be seen, the neighbor went out to look for her—finding no cat but hearing a frightened meow overhead. She looked up, and there was her cat, 20 feet off the ground in the branches of a big maple tree. After ten minutes of clapping her hands and calling—all to no avail—the worried neighbor darted indoors and phoned the fire department. When she told the answering fireman her problem, all he said was, "Well, lady, what do you want *us* to do about it?"

"Well, don't you bring your ladders and get cats out of trees?"

"No, lady, we don't. If we ever did, it was a long time ago, or maybe it was only on TV."

"But you've just *got* to come," she begged.

"I'm telling you, lady, our job is to put out fires."

"But she'll never get down from there by herself."

"Look, lady," the exasperated fireman replied, "did you ever see a cat skeleton up in a tree?"

—ALICE MARCHITTI
Paterson, New Jersey

If you want a particularly needy cat, ask your breeder or shelter if the breed you are considering tends to bond to one person only.

Siamese Din

Some people like chatty cats that give off great big meows. If you are searching for a cat that has an opinion on everything, look no further than the Siamese. These cats often seem to be involved in an ongoing commentary on world events, and that's part of their popularity. They make great companions for people who are home a lot and are therefore able to keep up their end of the conversation.

Everybody Loves a Longhair

If you want a cat that will need a lot of attention and love, look for one of the longhaired breeds. The Persian and the Turkish Angora are two breeds that tend to be constant companions. In fact, the longhaired breeds in general tend to be vain and are often most content when they are the center of attention.

Short Hair Suits an Active Lifestyle

If you're more interested in an active playmate than a cuddly ball of fur, think about adopting a shorthaired breed. These cats tend to be more active, curious, and interested in catching mice. They love to play and interact with others, especially children and other pets.

The cat that thinks it's a dog: the Maine coon.

He Does Everything but Bark

If you are a dog owner who is trying to turn yourself into a cat owner, consider the Maine coon cat. This is North America's only natural longhaired breed, and it's just about the largest cat around. Its temperament is actually much like a dog's. It is loyal and affectionate, bonding es-

pecially to a single owner. This cat is so active that it needs lots of space and usually prefers the outdoors. In fact, a coon cat will probably spend most nights working to rid the neighborhood of mice.

She Might Not Grow Up Just Like Mom

Although it's helpful to pay attention to breed when making your selection, it's also important to recognize that breed won't tell you everything about your prospective pet's personality. When you adopt a cat, you need to be prepared to take a bit of a chance. Dogs have been bred for certain personality traits as well as for looks, so a puppy's character is often easy to spot. Cats, however, have been bred purely for their looks, with personality as an afterthought. They don't know how they are supposed to behave. No matter how many times the breeder tells you that Persians are needy, don't be so sure that the one you're holding isn't a rebel.

FOR BIRDS ONLY

Do Not Disturb

Consider getting a bird as a pet if you have a quiet, tranquil home where your new friend can get his bearings in peace. If your household is boisterous or you have small children, a bird may not be your best choice. A bird is likely to start at every sudden noise, squeal, or laugh, and if there is a lot of commotion, a bird will be forever wary and grumpy.

It Could Be a Long Conversation

If you want a bird that thinks he's a person, consider getting a parrot. This is the biggest, the smartest, one of the most expensive, and perhaps the most beautiful of all pet birds. But parrots also require the most supervision and attention. They live a long time and continue acquiring personality traits for as long as they live. You'll spend a lot of time—perhaps a lifetime—with a parrot and should be ready for a serious commitment before you buy.

Polly Wanna Chitchat

If you have a house with plenty of space and you need a little company, nothing could be better than a large talking bird. A new budgie (budgerigar) will squawk a bit, but she also will learn a few words. A new African gray parrot will learn a vocabulary of about 200 words and will become a chatty friend. Or you could get several finches or canaries or a couple of lovebirds. They will sing and chirp and provide plenty of chatty company for you.

ADOPTING A PET

A WORD FROM DR. EMERSON

Birds: It's About Time

DR. WENDY EMERSON
Veterinarian who makes house calls in and around Topsfield, Massachusetts, to care for cats, dogs, and a wide range of exotic pets

It's a good idea to schedule the arrival of your new kitten or puppy to coincide with your vacation time because these animals need extra care during the house-training period. But the exact opposite is true for your new bird.

A number of my clients have bought birds on their summer vacations and then spent 12 hours a day holding and talking to their new pets. Then their vacations end, and they go back to work for 8 hours a day, leaving the birds to sit and wonder why they have been abandoned. A bird treated that way will soon develop neurotic habits, such as picking feathers or screaming constantly. The bird might even get sick. That's why I tell people to adopt a new bird at a time when the bird can get used to the family's normal schedule, especially if that schedule includes many hours when no one is home. Then the bird will learn how to be alone.

Worse Than Singing in the Shower

If you live in a small apartment or one with paper-thin walls, think twice about investing in a raucous parrot or even a more melodious bird such as a finch or canary. Bird sounds are meant to carry over a distance, and they do. Your neighbors may not appreciate your new 5:00 A.M. wake-up calls.

Squaaawk! You Want Me Where?

Before you decide on a particular type of bird, think about how much interaction you want to have. A parrot can make a wonderfully chatty companion, but just try to get him into a cage, and you'll get quite an earful. In general, the larger and smarter the bird, the less he's going to tolerate a life behind bars.

Everybody loves a budgie. They're especially good companions for folks who don't have a lot of space.

Small Talk

Looking for a bird that doesn't take a lot of space but will keep you company by echoing your thoughts? Consider the budgerigar, or budgie. It will learn to mimic a few words if trained properly, and it is every bit as beautiful as the finch—and a bit friendlier.

They Like Short Conversations

You'll need to bring midsize birds such as parakeets out for a tour of the house and a little conversation anywhere from once a week to once a day, depending on how friendly your particular bird is. Parakeets and cockatiels will require a bit more of your attention at first than smaller birds. You'll want to spend time with them to get them used to you—and used to the idea of being outside the cage. Once they are accustomed to contact, they will be loving and friendly.

Some Birds Like Serving Time

If you aren't looking for an interactive bird, your best bet is something smaller, perhaps a canary or finch. These birds have very pleasant calls, and some have brilliant plumage as well. They are perfectly content in their cages and don't need to be brought out. In fact, they don't like much contact with people. They'd rather be admired from afar.

Raised by Hand

If you're looking for a cuddly, friendly, social bird, ask for one that has been hand-fed. As the name suggests, these birds were removed from the nest as newborns and fed by hand. They are completely tame and comfortable around people. After they warm up to you, they will not fuss or start when you try to bring them outside their cages. In fact, they love human contact. You can find a hand-fed bird in almost any variety, from an exotic parrot to a common finch. These birds cost a bit more than birds born in captivity and raised by their mothers.

If you do get a hand-fed bird, you will need to bring your pet out, hold her, and talk to her every day. Otherwise, she will be miserable. Birds raised in captivity can stay in their cages most of the time and will need only to get out for a little air about once a week.

COMMON MISTAKES

Some Prefer a Large School

Your family is setting up a fish tank for the first time, and you like the looks of the tetras, danios, Rasporas, or barbs. The fish are fairly inexpensive, so you decide to buy a couple of them—perhaps one for each child. But these are schooling fish. They like to live in groups, and they get nervous and nippy if there are only a couple of their kind around. The moral? If you buy schooling fish, purchase at least six. They'll feel more comfortable—and so will you.

FOR FISH ONLY

A Kid's Best Friend

For a very young, very inexperienced pet owner in search of a first fish, there is no better choice than the goldfish. Kids love goldfish because they are friendly and easy to maintain. They flirt and beg for food

when people are around. They're very inexpensive and need only a bowl, some fresh water, and some food every day to be happy. If goldfish are well cared for, they will live for years, even decades. By contrast, tropical saltwater fish are the most fragile of all pets. They are caught in the wild and brought into a tank environment that is extremely difficult to maintain, making the expected life span of a tropical fish between two months and one year.

FOR OTHER PETS

Give Him Nothing to Chew On

❍ If you have a small apartment, need a fuzzy animal that doesn't mind living in a cage, and are concerned about noise, consider adopting a rabbit. Rabbits are very undemanding pets that can be litter box trained and don't mind spending the entire workday in a cage. They love to be held and are smart enough to learn simple commands.

COMMON MISTAKES

Adopting from the Wild

That garter snake you just found in your yard may be adorable, its location is convenient, and it's certainly free. But it is not the ideal pet. If you don't know what you are doing, the snake could be dead in a couple of weeks. Or if your state has regulations against raising certain animals, you could find yourself in a lot of trouble.

Most people who adopt reptiles from the wild run into problems. They don't know exactly what they have, and they don't know exactly how to take care of the animal. What does this snake eat? At what temperature should you keep that frog? If you try to tame a pet from the wild, you learn about the pet *after* you have the animal. If you go to a pet store or reptile expert—even if that source is selling an animal that was initially captured in the wild—you *start* with the right information and equipment and then get the animal. That is the safest, smartest, and most humane way to bring an animal into your home.

They Can't Stand the Heat

❍ Do not adopt a rabbit, ferret, or chinchilla if you live in an especially warm climate and do not have any air-conditioning. These animals are extremely susceptible to excessive heat; it can kill them.

Gerbils Need Protective Custody

❍ If you bring small, fuzzy pets into your grown cat's territory, make sure you have room to separate and supervise them until the new pet is grown. Your cat will probably love a rabbit or ferret to play with, but a *baby* ferret or bunny is likely to awaken his killer instinct.

❍ Keep gerbils, hamsters, and other small rodents separated from cats permanently.

Lizards: Born behind Bars?

❍ If you're thinking about adopting a lizard, snake, turtle, or frog but don't have a lot of experience handling reptiles or amphibians, try to find an animal that was born in captivity (known in the business as captive-born) rather than one caught in the wild. Captive-born animals are heartier and less delicate than wild varieties. They are more likely to take their food already dead or even frozen, and they are likely to require less in the way of veterinary care.

OTHER CONSIDERATIONS

Whew! You've got the space, the money, and the time for a new pet, and you have some idea of what kind of animal may best fit your lifestyle. What else do you need to know? Here are some other things to think about before you decide to buy.

FOR DOGS ONLY

Teach That Young Dog Some Good Tricks

If you decide to bring a dog into your city apartment, plan to invest some extra time and money in her training at the very beginning. A puppy growing up in

the country can get away with less training, but a city dog will need extensive obedience training at a young age. That way, she'll learn to follow your instructions on a leash and will be polite in elevators and safe crossing streets.

FOR FERRETS ONLY

A Scentual Experience

Before you adopt a ferret, make sure that everyone in the household will be comfortable with the peculiar odor of the animal. Ferrets are closely related to minks

A WORD FROM DR. EMERSON

Your Snake Doesn't Have to Kill His Supper

DR. WENDY EMERSON

Veterinarian who makes house calls in and around Topsfield, Massachusetts, to care for cats, dogs, and a wide range of exotic pets

When I got my snake, a speckled king snake named Nugget, the pet store told me that he would eat only live mice. Like most new snake owners, I was a little upset at the idea of putting a fuzzy mouse in the cage and watching my pet chase it around until he killed the poor thing. Besides, as a vet, I've treated a lot of snakes that have sustained serious, sometimes even life-threatening, bites from the rats or mice they were expected to eat. Luckily, I discovered that almost all snakes will learn to eat the prekilled frozen mice that you can order through pet stores and other suppliers. You thaw out the mice individually in hot water, then place them in the cage. The first couple of times, you may need to put the mice and the snake in a brown paper bag for a few hours until the snake catches on. So Nugget isn't exactly a hunter. That's okay with me.

and skunks. Ferrets sold legally in this country have already been de-scented, so that they don't give off any of their natural defensive scents. Still, they have a distinctive animal odor that is stronger than that of most house pets, even gerbils and other rodents.

Ferret Out the Legal Issues

Before you try to adopt a ferret, be sure to find out (from your local pet store owner) if ferrets are legal in your state. Taking in a ferret is still against the law in several states because they have long been considered dangerous. They do have a reputation as biters, but many people consider them to be friendly pets and swear that the bites are more like nibbles. Ferrets have the rambunctious disposition of puppies and are bright and loving. Perhaps that explains why they have become so popular.

FOR REPTILES ONLY

The Better Mousetrap

Before you think of taking home that beautiful blood python, consider what you're willing to do for his diet. That python doesn't eat processed foods the way dogs and cats do. He eats mice—he may insist on live ones—and you're going to have to find those mice and serve them up once a week. (Don't worry; pet stores that sell snakes also sell mice.) In addition to serving up the mice, you'll have to supervise the feeding to make sure that the mice don't get the upper hand and injure or kill your snake.

Some captive snakes won't kill their prey, so you'll have to kill the mice for them or buy dead ones. You can get frozen mice from any pet store that sells snakes. Your vet also will know of sources for mail-order mice, which you can keep in the freezer.

SOURCES FOR PETS

Once you've decided on the kind of animal you want, you'll still have some work to do before you settle on the individual. Everyone knows that you can find the

usual assortment of baby ferrets, kittens, puppies, and goldfish at almost any large pet store, but that's certainly not your only option. What if you want an older pet? What if you want a canary with just the right coloring? What if you are searching for a rare breed of tropical fish? What if you are afraid of spending too much? Knowing all the options available will help you to choose the perfect pet from the best possible source. Here are some suggestions.

FOR PETS IN GENERAL

Find a Specialist

❑ Large area chain stores usually have a few of every kind of animal, but you are probably looking to buy only one kind. You can find a larger selection, lower prices, and a more knowledgeable sales staff if you seek out a smaller pet store that specializes in that kind of pet. Even if a small pet store carries only a few dogs, cats, and rabbits, it might have a really large selection of reptiles. So call ahead to find out which stores specialize in the type of animal you're looking for.

You'd Better Shop Around

❑ The prices of animals vary widely. To make sure you get the best price and the best quality pet, contact several breeders and the nearest animal shelter—in addition to the pet store—before you buy. Visit each one to compare prices, health guarantees, and the quality of the individual animals before you decide on the right source for your new pet.

Is This a Bargain or a Boondoggle?

❑ So maybe you shouldn't look a gift horse in the mouth, but you should look carefully at any animal offered to you for free. Owners who are hastily getting rid of a retired show dog or young iguana probably know something about the animal's health and temperament that you don't. Before you consider adopting a bargain pet, ask the owner for the name and number of the vet who cares for the animal, then call the vet.

That way, you can get a medical history and make sure you won't have any surprise health bills.

Ask for Directory Assistance

❑ Some folks say that animal breeders are everywhere, but they can be hard to find. Many of them operate on a word-of-mouth basis. One way to find a list of good breeders is to call a local veterinarian and ask for a copy of the area pet directory. This is a listing of breeders in your area, as well as breed hobbyists who occasionally have one or two animals for sale. Many veterinarians keep pet directories on hand, and so do Humane Societies and animal shelters.

Surf the Net

❑ If you're trying to find sources for pets, get on a World Wide Web search engine and type in the breed of animal you are looking for. (To narrow the choices, try to include the word "breeder" or "club" in your search request.) Every day, more and more pet enthusiasts set

YOU'VE GOTTA LOVE 'EM

The Bosom Barks

Beatrice Campbell, the famous British actress who first played the role of Eliza Doolittle in *Pygmalion,* was so fond of her pet Pekingese that she refused to be separated from him when she traveled. She loved to tell the story of the time she tried to smuggle the animal through customs by cradling him in her arms and wrapping her cape tightly around herself. "Everything was going splendidly," she would say, "until my bosom barked."

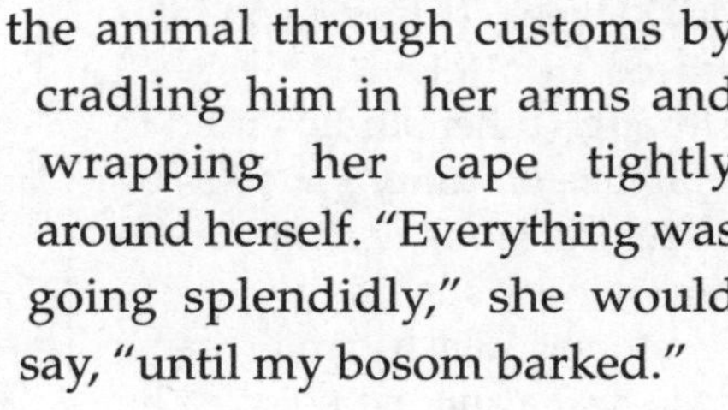

ADOPTING A PET

up Web pages full of information about different breeds and how to care for them. By now, nearly every breed has a Web page maintained by an official club or organization or by an enthusiastic breeder. Many organizations—including the Cat Fanciers' Association, the American Kennel Club, and the American Association of Aviculture—have their own Web sites. From these sites, you can easily find links to classified ads for breeders and mail-order companies nationwide.

One Good Thing That Came out of World War I

In 1918, an American airman named Lee Duncan found two German shepherd puppies in an abandoned German dugout in France. He decided to take the puppies home. It may have been the luckiest find he ever made.

One of the puppies he called Nanette. The other he named Rin Tin Tin.

Rinty, as he came to be known, starred in dozens of films for Warner Brothers and actually staved off bankruptcy for the studio. He became the toast of Hollywood, earning $1,000 week. (Rinty's son later starred in a television series.) Although other studios tried to capitalize on Rinty's success by launching films with other canine heroes such as Peter the Great and Flash, none came close to the success enjoyed by Rinty and Duncan.

I Shop Alone

❑ If your family includes children, leave them at home the first time you visit each breeder or pet store. Children can bond instantly to animals, and when they do, they will be very insistent. You need time alone with the breeder or salesperson to ask specific questions about the history of an animal you're considering and how to care for him. You also should visit several shops before you decide where to buy your pet. Once you've decided on the breeder or source, you can bring your children in to help choose from the litter.

FOR DOGS ONLY

Go Clubbing

If you aren't sure whether you want to adopt a particular breed of dog, do additional research by calling a national breed organization. Each of these clubs collects and distributes information about a particular breed of dog. They have lists of reputable breeders and can provide information about diseases and disorders common to a particular breed. To obtain a list of national breed clubs, contact the American

COST CUTTERS

Join the Rescue Squad

You want a purebred Doberman, schipperke, or malamute, but you don't want to pay hundreds or thousands of dollars for a new puppy. A great way to find a purebred dog without paying purebred prices is to contact a breed rescue group. These organizations are dedicated to recovering adult dogs from owners who can no longer care for them, then placing the dogs in good homes. Most of the dogs are older—between one and five years of age—but they are well-behaved, loving animals that have been examined by a vet and are up-to-date on their shots. All of them have been housebroken, and many have degrees from obedience school. You can find a rescue group for almost every breed of dog. Call your local animal shelter for a list of groups in your region. Or contact the American Kennel Club (get the current phone number from their Web site) for a national list.

Breed rescue groups for cats also are springing up these days. Much like the canine rescue organizations, these groups care for and place purebred adult cats whose prior owners can no longer keep them. If you are looking for a specific breed of cat and don't have your heart set on a kitten, try a breed rescue group. You can get a list of rescue groups from the Cat Fanciers' Association (check their Web site for a current phone number). Or ask a breeder who sells the kind of cat you are interested in to refer you to one of these groups.

Kennel Club. One easy way to do this is to search the Internet for the organization's name.

See a Show

To evaluate a particular breed of dog and to find a good breeder, try attending a dog show in your area. (Search the internet for the American Kennel Club to find out about upcoming shows near you.) These functions are like conventions for breeders, who gather to compete and to share information. They also bring their business cards and are available to answer questions about the breed. Touring the grooming area of a dog show is a good way to meet and interview a number of breeders without the pressure of having to buy a dog

on the spot. In fact, if someone tries to sell you a dog right there at the show, don't buy—and don't trust that breeder.

Head Off to the Races

If you are looking for a fairly big dog that is quiet and devoted, consider adopting a retired greyhound racing dog. In the past few years, dozens of groups have sprung up all over the country to rescue and place these gentle dogs after their racing days are over. The dogs that come up for adoption are available only through Greyhound Rescue Leagues. They are usually four- to five-year-olds that have had full racing careers or two- to three-year-olds that are too slow to be winners. (Finding a greyhound puppy to adopt is almost impossible, since these dogs are bred exclusively for

COMMON MISTAKES

Sure She's Cute—But Is She Healthy?

Before you buy a pet from a pet store that's located in a shopping mall, be prepared to ask some pointed questions about where the animals come from and how they are cared for. Some store owners sell dogs and cats purchased from careless breeders who are known for selling unhealthy animals. Some sell animals whose histories they know nothing about. The store owner or staff should know exactly how the animals arrived at the store, who owned them before, and who bred them.

If you want an animal such as a snake, a ferret, or an African gray parrot, you should ask how many of these animals the store has sold. Some stores buy and sell rare animals that they don't know how to care for properly. They can't recognize disease or malnutrition. Their employees sometimes handle animals from different cages without washing their hands. If so, it's a sure bet that any disease one animal has will be transmitted to the rest in short order.

Rather than deal with nonspecialists, try to go through reputable breeders (people who belong to breeders organizations or breed rescue groups) or even your local animal shelter. As a rule, these people work closely with veterinarians and genuinely care about the welfare of the pets they sell.

racing.) To find a local rescue club, look first in the Yellow Pages. If you come up empty, call the nearest animal shelter and ask for a reference.

So What if She Didn't Graduate?

If you'd like to adopt a well-behaved older dog, look for a failed service dog. All over the country, organizations train dogs to aid the blind or the hearing impaired. Trainers spend as much as five months giving extensive obedience training to these dogs, but not every dog goes on to become a working dog. A rejected animal may have a slight physical defect or some behavioral problem that is as harmless as a fear of crossing the street. They are still well-trained, lovable dogs (often purebred Labs and golden retrievers) that need homes once their training ends. To find one of these dogs, contact your local association for the blind or call your local animal shelter. They will be able to tell you which organization near you trains and places service dogs.

FOR CATS ONLY

Fancy a Cat

If you are looking for a specific breed of cat, contact the Cat Fanciers' Association (CFA). Search the Internet, using the organization's name.) Be aware, though, that the CFA doesn't screen the list. You'll have to do that yourself.

FOR BIRDS ONLY

Look for Birds of a Feather

Your best bet for finding a good pet bird may be to find a small breeder hobbyist. Such a person usually specializes in one kind of bird, so his flock is not exposed to the health problems of multiple species. You will probably be able to go into the breeder's home and find out how his birds have been raised. The breeder is more likely to have the tamer, hand-fed birds that many people prefer. And if you're not buying from

someone who expects to make a living by selling birds, you may get a better price.

The Doctor Knows Best

One of the keys to buying a bird is to find a healthy one, so calling an avian vet in your area can be a good way to find a reputable breeder. These vets are in touch with the breeders over the long term. They also visit pet stores and do health checks on the birds. And they are experts. They will know who in the area has healthy stock.

Exotic Birds Are Not for Beginners

If you go to a breeder or pet store and try to buy an expensive exotic bird, expect to answer a lot of questions about how you plan to feed and care for the bird. Even if offered thousands of dollars in cash, reputable pet stores and breeders will not sell large tropical birds to people who have never owned birds or have little experience with them. Because these birds are so smart and beautiful, the people who care for them become very attached, and they carefully screen potential buyers.

Play Telephone Tag

If you don't want to buy a bird from a local pet store because you are looking for a particularly rare breed or color, you'll need to spend some time on the phone to find an alternative source. Most bird breeders operate by word of mouth. Make contact with one you trust, and ask that person to put you in touch with someone who specializes in the breed or color you are looking for.

Try a Bird-of-the-Month Club

If you're interested in adopting a bird and have never owned one before, check out a local bird club. Such clubs can offer you a great way to get information, meet knowledgeable people, and find a pet at less than pet store or mail-order prices. Most of these clubs hold

monthly meetings. At least one member will generally bring some birds from home, and sometimes a few birds will be available for sale right at the meeting. Clubs also offer a chance for you to make friends with people who already own the type of bird you wish to adopt. They will know about hobbyists with extra birds that they will sell for a nominal price. Look in the Yellow Pages for a local avian vet and ask the vet for the names and phone numbers of area bird clubs.

A Bird in the Hand . . . Could Be Stolen

When the classified ad seems too good to be true, the first thing you should wonder about is whether the bird for sale has been stolen or smuggled. Each year, thousands of birds are stolen from aviaries or smuggled illegally from other countries. You can protect yourself by knowing what to look for and what to ask as you evaluate the bird.

Check out the seller's references. Ask for a medical history of the bird you're considering, as well as the name of the person or organization from which the bird was purchased, how long ago it was purchased, where it was raised, and how old it is. Visit the aviary or home where the bird lives and see how the owner interacts with him. (If the owner wants to meet you in a parking lot, restaurant, or other public place to sell you a bird, you're in trouble.) Finally, look for a leg band. Every legal bird has an officially authorized leg band that identifies the bird and the breeder by code. This is to help authorities identify stolen or lost birds and return them to their owners. If the leg band is missing, the bird was either smuggled or stolen, and the band has been removed.

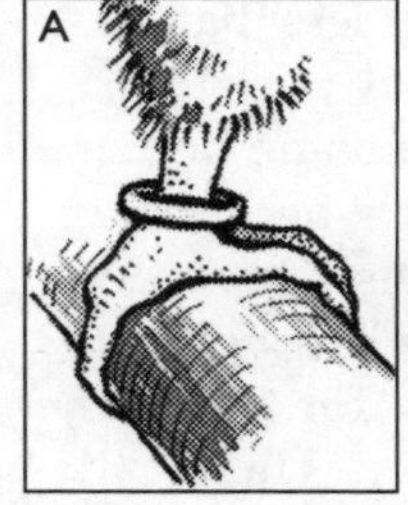

A closed band (A) means a domestically bred bird; an open one (B), a legal import.

Exotic birds are targets for theft because they are so beautiful and valuable. By being careful about whom you buy from, you will be guaranteed a healthy bird that has not been subjected to abuse or trauma. And by buying from reputable sources, you help put smugglers and thieves out of business.

COST CUTTERS

Mail-Order Macaws May Save You Money

A good way to get unusual birds at good prices is to find a company that sells birds by mail. Many people, including experienced breeders, buy parrots and other large tropical birds by mail. Many of the companies that sell avian pets this way were U.S. Department of Agriculture (USDA) import stations at one time. Now they're commercial businesses that specialize in breeding and selling pet birds. Because these are large distributors, they often sell exotic birds for less than the birds cost in local pet stores. One warning: Do some homework to find out whether the company you wish to order from is reputable. To do that, ask the company for a list of former customers. Then call those folks to make sure the birds they bought were healthy.

Ask the Pet Store Owner

If you are looking for a particular breed of bird or a particular color of finch or budgie that isn't available at your local pet store, ask the pet store owner for a list of breeders in the area who might have what you want. Many pet store owners have professional contacts with local clubs and aviaries and don't mind sharing that information. After all, they hope you'll be back to buy birdseed.

Why Is This Cheeper So Much Cheaper?

Get a price list from several sources before you buy a bird, so that you know roughly what price you should expect to pay for that macaw, canary, or parrot. Most pet stores and large distributors publish price lists on the Internet or will quote prices over the phone. Having done your homework, you'll know the going rate and can do some comparative shopping. You'll also be in a position to question an offer that seems too good to be true. If you encounter a bird that is selling for half the usual cost, ask why the bird is so cheap. The owner probably knows something that you don't. Perhaps the bird is ill. More likely the bird is surly or destructive or has been neglected.

FOR FERRETS ONLY

Look Beyond the Local Pet Store

Ferrets seem to be ubiquitous in pet stores, which are often a pretty good source for these animals. But before putting down your money, you may want to check to see if you can get a much lower price through a breeder. Breeders offer other advantages, too. They are experts in ferret care and can often provide support and advice to novice owners. The disadvantage is that ferret breeders are harder to find than dog or cat breeders. One approach is to contact the League of Independent Ferret Enthusiasts (LIFE) or the American Ferret Association (AFA) to get a list of breeders in your area. You can reach LIFE through the Internet. (Search on the organization's name.) To contact the AFA, call toll-free directory assistance (1-800-555-1212) for the current number. Another approach is to ask those organizations for lists of upcoming ferret shows, where you will find dozens of breeders.

ADOPTING A PET

FOR FISH ONLY

Check Out the Home Market

Even the most well-stocked tropical fish store will not have every available variety. If you are searching for a rare type of fish, your best bet may be to find a local hobbyist who dabbles in breeding. Hobbyists don't make a living selling fish. They do it because they enjoy it. For this reason, they often have a few extra fish available at very low prices.

To locate a hobbyist, ask a local tropical fish store (one that doesn't carry the variety you want) for the number of the aquarium society in your area. Most local breeders will be members, so if you join the organization, you'll find people who can help you. One especially popular national club is the Federation of American Aquarium Societies (FAAS). This group has chapters in most large cities.

COMMON MISTAKES

Does That Fish Come in Plaid?

First-time fish owners often try to fill their tanks with lots of different fish that look good together. They match fish the way they might match an outfit. But there's more to a fish tank than good design, and even if the colors don't fight, the fish might. Or they might all grow to be fairly large and then get aggressive as they compete for space.

The best way to build a community of fish is to look for the one kind you like best—say, the beautiful angelfish—and then round out the community with one or two other kinds, making sure these secondary fish are small. You can generally pick up these small fish for less than a couple of dollars apiece.

Read All about It

If you are having trouble locating an aquarium club, check your local pet store for a tropical fish magazine.

These magazines are great sources for regional clubs, area breeders, and suppliers of aquariums and fish.

FOR REPTILES ONLY

The Best Selection Since Noah's Ark

S If you can't decide what kind of snake to buy, or if you have your heart set on a fairly rare breed, your best chance of finding the right breeder will be at a reptile show. But how do you find a show? Most clubs for owners and breeders of reptiles, called herpetological societies, hold shows for their finest specimens. These shows are excellent opportunities to see unusual breeds not available in pet stores and often to buy snakes and lizards at prices much lower than those at pet stores. Since the herpetological community in most cities is pretty small, these shows also are a good time to ask questions about how to care for different reptiles. You may even get the chance to speak to a breeder's former customers to find out what kind of professional reputation she has. To find a herpetological society near you, check with a local vet who treats reptiles. He will be able to give you the number of the local organization.

This not so little piggy didn't go to market. To find such pets, you just have to know where to look.

FOR OTHER PETS

Pigs Are Purebred, Too

O Looking to adopt a potbellied pig? To find out about sanctuaries and rescue groups nationwide, contact the Potbellied Pig Registry Service. Search the Internet, under the registry's full name, for up-to-date contact information.

EVALUATING A SELLER

So you have this list of phone numbers for different area breeders, shelters, and pet stores and a group of ads from the paper offering puppies, kittens, or rabbits. Now you have to figure out which one has the pet for you. You want to buy from someone who is honest and who raises animals carefully. To do that, you have to ask some questions and look closely at the conditions in which your prospective pet was raised. Here are a few things to keep in mind.

ADOPTING A PET

FOR PETS IN GENERAL

Lady, This Offer Won't Last Forever

❑ The first time you meet a breeder or hobbyist, pay attention to how she treats you. Anyone who uses pressure sales tactics should be crossed off your list. If the breeder or pet store owner doesn't care about where the animals end up, she probably doesn't care about their welfare right now either. A good dealer or breeder will offer you information and a business card so that you can talk further after you've had time to think. She also will ask questions about you and will really listen to your answers.

Look for Stick-to-itiveness

❑ Ask each breeder how long he has been in business. You want a breeder you can contact over the years, someone who will answer your questions. Ask the breeder whether he has a relationship with people who purchased animals from his earlier litters.

Get References

❑ No matter what kind of animal you are buying, if you are dealing with a breeder, ask for the names and phone numbers of previous customers. Then call these people and ask about how they were treated and whether they ran into any problems. You know you are dealing with a good breeder when former cus-

COMMON MISTAKES

No Puppy Should Be Put through the Mill

You ask to see the mother and father of the puppy you want to buy, and the breeder refuses or has some excuse for why they are away at the moment. Then you notice that although you see lots of litters of puppies here, you haven't spotted a single adult. Stop. Walk away. If you don't, you may be buying from a puppy mill or from someone who supports them.

Some breeders turn out litter after litter of puppies with no regard for their health or well-being. The dogs are shipped all over the country to be sold by people claiming to be backyard breeders. Frequently, these dogs have been inbred and have serious health and temperament problems. Sometimes they have been raised in unsanitary conditions. Not only do you want to avoid puppy mill dogs, but you want to put puppy mills out of business by going to someone who is reputable.

YOU'VE GOTTA LOVE 'EM

Andy the Goose

Gene Fleming wasn't expecting to bring home a pet goose the day he stopped by his sister-in-law's farm in Harvard, Nebraska, in 1988. Then he saw Andy, a two-year-old gray goose who had been hatched without feet. Andy hobbled along awkwardly as he tried to walk. Fleming decided to help him and took the goose to his home in nearby Hastings.

Fleming started with the smallest-size baby shoes he could find and filled them with foam. For the next month, they became Andy's feet. Fleming held the 40-pound bird up while Andy figured out how to take his first steps. Pretty soon, Andy was walking everywhere. Fleming switched to baby sneakers when Andy wore out his leather shoes.

Fleming took Andy to schools, hospitals, and church groups to give talks about overcoming disabilities. Andy loved the attention. Before long, the goose was featured in *People* magazine and made an appearance on *The Tonight Show.* A sneaker company offered him a lifetime supply of shoes.

Andy might still be making the rounds at area schools, but someone broke into his pen and killed him in 1991. The people of Hastings raised a $10,000 reward for information leading to the perpetrator's arrest, but no one was ever charged with the crime. Instead, the money was used to build a monument to Andy, with an etching and an inscription that tells his story. Fleming says that people come from all over the world to visit it and to hear the story of the goose who had sneakers instead of feet.

tomers say that they've always felt comfortable calling with questions, that the pets they brought home have been free of disease or serious health problems, or that any animals with illnesses were promptly exchanged without any hassle.

Ask Around

❑ Take time to ask other breeders and hobbyists what they know about the breeder you are planning to buy from. If you suspect that the breeder you have contacted isn't honest or is selling unhealthy animals, call the local animal shelter. Every shelter generally keeps a blacklist of breeders with bad reputations and can warn you away if need be.

Does This Animal Have a Hidden Past?

❑ Before you even think about buying, ask the seller specific questions about the care she recommends for individual animals. You know you are dealing with a caring owner if she knows exactly when and what this parrot or that snake likes to eat. The seller also should be willing to give you background on an individual animal, including a specific health history of ailments and vaccinations. (Of course, if you are buying from a breed rescue group or shelter, you may not be able to get much information on the background of a particular animal, but the group should be able to give you details about what they've observed so far.)

FOR DOGS ONLY

What's the Exchange Rate?

Although most breeders will not give a written guarantee and will not even verbally guarantee the health of a dog throughout his lifetime, they should offer some reassurances. You should find out right away whether the breeder or pet store allows refunds or exchanges if the dog you take home develops a health problem within the first weeks or months of ownership. Talk about that possibility the first time you

contact a breeder, well before you get out your checkbook or choose a puppy.

Make sure you can return the animal if an unforeseen problem should develop for you or your household. For example, if someone in your household develops an allergy or in the next couple of weeks you unexpectedly need to move to an apartment that doesn't take pets, you should be able to return the pet with few questions asked. Set up the return policy before you pay for the pet and take him home.

FOR CATS ONLY

101 Himalayans?

You walk into the breeder's house, and it looks like the feline version of *101 Dalmatians*. The breeder tells you not to worry, but you should. You've heard of puppy mills. Well, there are kitty mills, too, from which disreputable breeders ship unhealthy kittens across the country to be sold as quickly as possible. To avoid buying from a kitty mill, always ask to see the parents of each litter. Most kitty mill owners won't have adult cats, but they will have plenty of flimsy excuses about why full-grown cats aren't around. If you don't believe their answers, leave. Immediately.

Another way to avoid buying from a kitty mill is to make sure that the kittens have been raised as a litter and not in tiny, overcrowded cages. If you see cages, don't buy from these folks. The best way to put these breeders out of business is to take yours elsewhere.

Don't Know Much about History . . .

If a rescue group tries to charge you market prices for a cat or tells you that they have no health history for the cat, you should move on to a more responsible shelter. Most rescue groups are in business because they want to find good, caring homes for abandoned or abused cats. But a few get into breed rescue thinking that they can make money by adopting and placing purebred cats. You can find a better (and cheaper) alternative.

YOU'VE GOTTA LOVE 'EM

Cats Will Be Cats

I was visiting an aristocratic family in Mexico City. They had gone to a bit of trouble to present a vegetarian dinner served on steaming silver platters by the maid in their formal dining room. I was the only one facing the window, through which I could see the family cat, Crystal, crouched in the well-manicured lawn. I was on my best behavior and was nodding politely to the head of the household as he continued on with a sermon against the ills of eating meat. It seems the family hadn't eaten meat for a whole year and had come to consider meat eating quite barbaric. Even their pets no longer ate meat, my host said. Their poodle enjoyed crunching on carrots rather than bones, and their cat was kept on a strict dry food diet.

Just about then, I was distracted from my host's monologue by a movement over his shoulder. Something gray was rising and falling to the ground. Looking out the window, I saw that the family cat had caught a mouse and was batting it playfully in the air. A few minutes later, she proceeded to eat it. And I, being a good guest, proceeded to keep my mouth shut.

—**CHRISTINE SCHULTZ**
Taylor, Mississippi

FOR BIRDS ONLY

Cleanliness Is Next to Healthiness

When you're evaluating a store or breeder from whom you're considering buying a bird, check to see that the birds are kept in sanitary conditions. The two

best indicators of these are clean cages and clean water. The bottom of each cage should be lined with fresh newspaper or litter. The birds' drinking water should be clear and fresh. If it's cloudy, ask why. Some breeders put vitamin supplements in the water, which will discolor it slightly, but muddy or cloudy water indicates that these birds may be carrying diseases.

One Warning Flag Will Do

If you see even one seriously ill bird in a pet store or aviary, take your business elsewhere. Birds in crowded pet store cages pass diseases around faster than schoolchildren hand off the sniffles. If a bird makes clicking noises, has labored breathing, shows mucus around the eyes and beak, or seems terribly thin with a protruding breastbone, he is really very sick. He needs a veterinarian, not a new owner. And so do his unfortunate cage-mates.

Hamsters: All from the Same Family Three

They seem so mundane, those little hamsters you see in nearly every pet store. But they're actually very exotic. In 1930, a professor from Jerusalem found a burrow of hamsters in Syria. He brought them back to the university where he taught, but only three of them—a male and two females—survived. They bred, and in 1938 some of them were shipped to the United States. Today nearly every hamster in the United States is directly descended from those three hamsters.

FOR FERRETS ONLY

He Should Be out of the Woods

When you've chosen a ferret you're ready to buy, check the bottom of her cage. A knowledgeable owner will line a ferret's cage with cloth—either cut-up T-shirts or blankets. Or the owner may use Wee-Wee Pads, sold in most pet supply stores and used primarily for training puppies. (A Wee-Wee Pad looks something like a disposable diaper that unfolds to approximately 27 by 22 inches—about the size of the unfolded newspaper it's meant to replace.) Don't buy a ferret from someone who uses cedar wood shavings to line the cage. Wood carries oils and a scent that cause upper respiratory infections in ferrets. In fact, wood shavings, especially cedar shavings, can be so toxic that

they actually kill the ferret. A pet store owner may tell you that she has to use pine or aspen shavings for cleanliness. Be forewarned: Although these woods are less toxic than cedar, they are still not as healthy as cloth.

In Search of a Third-Floor Walk-Up

Check the height of the cage before you buy a ferret. You know you are dealing with a conscientious owner if the ferret is living in a cage that has two or three levels. Many people try to keep their ferrets in tiny, wire-bottom rabbit cages—a practice that's roughly like housing your Doberman in a shoe box. Ferrets need cages with two or three levels. They need corners to wriggle into and things to climb on top of. If an owner keeps his ferret cooped up in a small cage all day, the ferret will be sleepy and depressed and prone to destructive behavior when she comes out to play.

FOR FISH ONLY

The Drinks Are on You

When you buy your first tankful of fish from a large pet store—which is usually where you'll find the best prices on the most common breeds of fish—bring along a friend who has owned fish before. These big stores often accidentally mislabel tanks and end up charging the wrong prices for their fish. By bringing along someone with more knowledge, you'll know whether you're getting a good price and whether you're really buying the breed you want.

Look, Mac! It's Dinnertime!

The best way to evaluate the quality of service in a fish store is to listen for one question: What kind of fish do you have at home? If no one asks you what you already have, how can they advise you on what to buy? The clerk should be able to tell you that the Oscar you are eyeing will gobble up your goldfish on the very first day. If you are starting to build your population from scratch, you should be able to get lots of advice on how to mix different breeds safely.

No Sign Is a Bad Sign

When you are in a store checking out fish, take a minute to check out the tanks themselves. Look for a sign on one tank that says "Not for Sale." The sign indicates that there has been a problem with one of the fish in that tank and the store has decided not to sell out of it until they have handled the problem. Far from indicating that the store itself is unsanitary, this sign actually tells you that the store managers care about the health of the fish and about potential customers. It proves that they take responsibility for the unavoidable health problems that can creep in.

Look for the Not-So-Silver Lining

If you buy a snake from a pet store, look at the lining inside the cage. A lining of cedar chips means that the snake may have a serious respiratory problem. The oil in cedar is toxic to snakes and will make them sick. Avoid snakes that live in cages lined with pine or aspen chips as well. These can get lodged in a snake's mouth.

FOR REPTILES ONLY

Does He Know Slinky's Favorite Color?

A knowledgeable and conscientious owner will volunteer a lot of information about a snake before you agree to buy the pet. He will tell you about the snake's health background, his personality, the temperature at which the tank should be kept, and how the animal likes and doesn't like to be handled. If the owner does not provide this information, you should ask questions: Does the snake take his food alive or dead? How often does he eat? Has he ever been a problem eater or refused food? Pay attention not only to the answers but also to how well the owner appears to know the pet. The more knowledgeable the owner, the more likely it is that the snake has been well cared for.

EVALUATING A SPECIFIC ANIMAL

You have decided on the right source for your new pet—someone who carefully raises healthy animals. Now you are faced with a cardboard box of wriggling puppies, an aviary of brightly colored birds, or a tankful of beautiful tropical fish that seem identical. How will you choose? Consider the health and appearance of each animal. Consider temperament. Look for signs of illness or deformity. And ask lots and lots of questions.

FOR PETS IN GENERAL

Tag Team Shopping

❑ If this is your first pet, or the first time you will be getting an animal of this kind, find a friend who already has a similar animal and invite him along. Your friend will know what questions to ask and how to look for diseases or defects in the animal. This person also can be your devil's advocate—reminding you to ask for a guarantee, for example—and can help you to resist any pressure sales tactics.

Look for Social Butterflies

❑ When you adopt an animal that you want to be able to touch or hold—such as a dog, ferret, or snake—be sure to watch how the animal reacts to the breeder or owner, as well as how it reacts to you. The moment that you first hold a new kitten or a turtle may be a little tense for both of you, but you should be able to relax. An animal that starts, bites, or cowers has probably not been socialized and will need lots of extra attention to relax.

Maybe She Was Really a Mole

Many presidents have been pet lovers. George Washington had three dogs—Sweetlips, Truelove, and Venus. Richard Nixon had Checkers, and Lyndon Johnson had Him and Her. But it was Pushinka, a Samoyed puppy that Nikita Khrushchev gave to Caroline Kennedy, that caused the biggest commotion. Rumor has it that after Khrushchev presented the dog to Caroline, the CIA checked her for bugs.

FOR DOGS ONLY

Can You Predict Your Pet's Future Health?

☞ If you are buying from a breeder, call your vet and ask what health concerns are common in the breed you're considering. Then ask the vet whether there are specific questions you should ask the breeder about the

particular animal you're looking at. Most of the purebreds have hereditary health problems. Great Danes often have stomach problems; bulldogs have respiratory problems; most large breeds suffer from hip dysplasia and heart trouble; dalmatians are known for urinary tract disorders and deafness. The breeder should know these problems well and should be able to assure you (legitimately) that these particular pups are at low risk.

Size Up Mom and Dad

If size matters to you, look at the parents of a litter before you buy any of the pups. Dogs within a breed can vary greatly in size, but the parents offer a pretty good idea of how big their pups will get. If you're not in the market for an extra-large toy poodle or a tiny Great Dane, make sure to screen the puppies.

Can He Pay the Bills?

You probably know about Seeing Eye dogs and drug-sniffing dogs. But are you familiar with service dogs? These animals can be trained to perform all sorts of functions for their masters and mistresses. For instance, dogs can assist wheelchair-bound individuals by taking deposit slips to bank tellers, picking up objects as small as a dime, or opening heavy doors. Dogs also can be trained to turn on lights and retrieve a variety of objects from high shelves.

Maybe someday they'll be able to train dogs to shovel the driveway and take out the trash.

Hey! Wake Up!

When you choose a dog out of a litter, pick one that seems particularly alert, active, and playful, not standoffish, depressed, or overly aggressive. (Think twice before adopting a pup that growls or nips as you pet her.) The puppy should have a good coat and no scaly skin or mange. She should have bright, clear eyes that aren't watery or irritated.

Look for a Doggy Diploma

If you are adopting an adult dog, ask whether the dog has been spayed or neutered. Be sure she's up-to-date on her shots and ask to see a copy of her rabies certificate. The current owner should have taken care of these things so that you don't have to once you take the dog home. (It's likely that you will always get positive answers to these questions if you are adopting from a shelter or breed rescue group. Rescue groups carefully screen their dogs for behavior and health problems before they place them.) Also ask whether she has attended obedience classes.

Miss Congeniality

Since a good breeder will have spent enough time around the litter to identify some of the dominant characteristics of each pup, ask him to help match you with the best dog for your family. Some breeders and animal shelters do personality tests on each puppy in a litter. They look for alertness, intelligence, and aggressiveness. They check to see which dogs startle easily, which are prone to barking, and which ones are easygoing. If you can tell the breeder something about your home and family, she should be able to point out the dog that will be best for you.

Greyhounds: Experience Necessary

Ask whether the greyhound you have your eye on has already been in foster care. Racing dogs have strictly regulated schedules and very little human contact. Although they are housed with dozens of other dogs and are used to kennel life, they are rarely allowed to play and may not even know how. Even a few weeks in a loving foster home give these former racers a chance to slow down and get used to the life of a pampered pet. A greyhound will be

What Happened to Fluffy?

Before you rescue that beautiful, long-legged greyhound, think about your other pets. If you have a cat, rabbit, gerbil, or any other small furry creature in the house, you might want to adopt some other breed. Although greyhounds are among the most gentle tempered dogs, they have been raised at the track. For all their lives, they have been chasing fuzzy little rabbits around a track, and they are not likely to stop just because they've retired. If you want to hang on to Fluffy, don't bring home a retired racer.

If, however, you have young children or another dog or two, that greyhound could be the perfect addition to your family. She's likely to love your other dogs and to play well with the youngsters. If she's typical of her breed, she'll rarely growl or bite and would much prefer to walk away from trouble.

A Dog's Best Friend Is His Lawyer

In 1869, George Graham Vest, who later became a U.S. senator, represented in a lawsuit a man whose dog, Old Drum, had been shot by a neighbor. The defendant all but admitted shooting the dog but protested the amount the dog's owner was asking in restitution: $150.

When Vest rose to complete his final arguments, his words brought tears to the eyes of some jurors: "If fortune drives the master forth an outcast in the world, friendless and homeless, the faithful dog asks no higher privilege than that of accompanying him to guard against danger, to fight against his enemies, and when the last scene of all comes, and death takes the master in its embrace and his body is laid away in the cold ground, no matter if all other friends pursue their way, there by his graveside will the noble dog be found, his head between his paws, his eyes sad but open in alert watchfulness, faithful and true even to death."

The jury found for the plaintiff—for $500, more than three times what he had originally sought.

less nervous and hesitant and more willing to socialize with a new family if he has spent time in foster care.

Say What?

Before you even look at a litter of dalmatians, ask the breeder whether the puppies have had their hearing tested. Many dalmatian puppies are born deaf in one or both ears. If a breeder tells you that he's had the vet check the pups and their hearing is fine, don't take his word for it. Ask to see a copy of the Brain Auditory Electronic Response (BAER) test. The results, in printout form, look kind of like an electrocardiogram (EKG). The test shows in an easy-to-interpret manner whether the dog is totally deaf or unilateral—that is, can hear out of only one ear.

Listen Carefully

Deafness in a puppy can seem like an invisible disability, but you can screen your potential puppy for hearing problems by watching his behavior and listening to him. Deaf dogs startle easily and bite often. They are frightened by sudden movements. They yowl all the time and watch all the other puppies in the litter. Deaf dogs also sleep on the top of the pile so that any stirring will warn them that it's time to get up.

FOR CATS ONLY

Size Matters

Make sure the kittens you're thinking of adopting weigh at least three to four pounds. Don't worry about getting a cat that is heavier or bigger than that. Worry instead about cats that are too small. Extreme smallness in a cat may be a sign of inbreeding. When you breed relatives to relatives, you get small bones and weak muscles. The rule of thumb is that a healthy kitten will gain one pound per month, so by the time you see a three-month-old kitten, it should weigh three pounds.

Mom Needs Time to Teach the Basics

You see a kitten that is much smaller than she should be, but the breeder insists that the parents aren't related. You should still be concerned. The other reason that a kitten may be too small is that she is too young to be separated from her mother. A cat should be 12 weeks old before being sent into a new home. If kittens are separated from their mothers before that time, they will have trouble all their lives. Experts say that they just don't know that they are cats yet and simply are not ready to leave home.

Get 'Em Bright-Eyed and Bushy-Tailed

Look for kittens that are alert and playful, especially in the morning and early evening. That's usually when kittens are on the prowl. If a kitten seems sluggish with dull, sleepy eyes even at these times, he may be unhealthy.

Not-So-Subtle Signs of Illness

Try to find a kitten with skin that's clean and shows no sign of fleas. Be sure that the animal has no

flaky skin or patches where hair is missing. These are indications of ringworm, which is very hard to get rid of. Look for an active kitten with a bright, clear expression and a full, shiny coat.

Dad Was Sick a Lot

With cats, the mother's and father's personalities are not really good indicators of how the kitten will behave. But do ask about the parents' health histories. You may even want to talk to the vet who treats them. Animals with chronic health problems—including fleas, anemia, or urinary tract infections—will produce kittens with the same problems, and similarly high veterinary bills. Ask the owner or breeder for the number of the cat's vet and make a call that could save you hundreds of dollars in medical bills.

Born to Be Held

Before you adopt from a pet store or shelter, ask whether the kitten you're considering has been held and touched. It seems crazy that any fuzzy little kitten could spend time around people without having been smothered with affection, but many young cats are raised entirely in cages. Even breeds such as Persians and Himalayans, which are known to be affectionate, can grow up timid and shy if they are raised without human contact. They will eventually come around, but you will spend months winning them over. Unless you have the time and patience to do this, you might want to move on and buy from a breeder who raises kittens with affection.

FOR BIRDS ONLY

He Should Be Proud as a Peacock

Vanity can be a good sign, especially if you are in the market for a pet bird. To confirm the health of a bird you're thinking of buying, make sure he has good posture, is perching comfortably, and has beautifully smooth, dry, shiny feathers. If the bird's feathers seem ragged, damp, or dirty, he may be suffering from mal-

YOU'VE GOTTA LOVE 'EM

Cat Goes Hunting, Saves Bear

Pam Mahoney had not owned her hamster, Bear, for very long before Bear decided to get out and see the neighborhood. Mahoney liked to take the hamster outside to get some fresh air. She was even thoughtful enough to turn his cage upside down to let him run around on the grass. One day, she turned her back on the crafty rodent, who tunneled his way out of the cage and scurried off. Mahoney was crushed. In tears, she called her friend Tammy Gibson, who worked for a local veterinarian, to commiserate. She assumed she'd never see Bear again.

About a month later, a distraught woman called the local animal shelter. When the animal control officer arrived, he found a wounded hamster and a rather self-satisfied cat. The woman told him that her cat had brought the hamster home as a trophy. Were hamsters running wild in Dover, Massachusetts? This one wasn't seriously injured but had suffered a broken leg, so the officer brought him to the local vet—who just happened to be the same vet Tammy Gibson worked for. Gibson called Pam Mahoney right away, though she wasn't convinced that this was Bear. After all, the woman and her cat lived five miles away from the Mahoney house.

Mahoney recognized Bear immediately. Today he is happy and healthy and living at home, but he probably won't be visiting any more grassy knolls.

nutrition or may be ill. Sometimes birds that are sick and uncomfortable refuse to preen themselves. (The one time this is not true is in the summer, when many birds molt.)

Get a Complete Bio

Before you adopt a bird, be sure to get a detailed medical history. Ask whether the bird has a regular veterinarian. If the bird has ever been injured, find out whether the injury may be chronic. If so, you may be visiting the vet again soon. Ask the vet what illnesses the bird has had, even if the pet is perfectly healthy now. Some birds are carriers of diseases they've had in the past. If you're bringing your new pet home to an aviary or a community of birds, you should know the risks.

Practical Parker

A troubled friend once asked writer Dorothy Parker how to get rid of an unwanted cat. She asked, "Have you tried curiosity?"

Handle with Care

Not only should you watch to see how the owner handles the bird you plan to buy, but you also should ask to hold the bird yourself. This is especially true if you are adopting a parrot or parakeet that has been advertised as hand-fed. If the owner has to struggle to gain the bird's confidence, that may indicate a skittish bird with some behavior problems. If you are unable to handle the bird at first—if she fusses and fights even though the owner is standing right there—you'll probably never be able to handle her.

FOR FERRETS ONLY

Will There Be an Inheritance Tax?

If you are adopting from a breeder, ask whether any of the litters produced from these parents have had trouble with cancer, heart problems, or adrenal disease—illnesses that ferrets are particularly prone to. Sometimes the animals will inherit from their parents a predilection for one of these ailments. If you find that there have been a lot of illnesses in the past, you may want to walk away. If the breeder has no idea whether there have been problems, you definitely should take your business elsewhere.

Ask about Dad's Mood

Ask about the parents of the ferret kit you want to adopt. What is their size and temperament? You will especially want to know the temperament of the sire. If he is overly aggressive, the kits will be, too.

Look for the Litter Box

Before you buy a ferret, make sure the mother is litter box trained. (Either ask or look for the box itself.) Having a mother that's trained gives the kits a head start on house-training because they've grown up around a litter box and know what it's for.

Did He Have a Happy Childhood?

When you look for a pet ferret, try to find one that has stayed in a happy family with Mom and lots of siblings for at least nine weeks. He also should have had some human contact every day so that he knows the difference between how much he can roughhouse with other kits and how gingerly he needs to treat human skin. Most pet stores (as opposed to breeders) sell ferrets that have been shipped out at a much younger age. They are more prone to aggressiveness and less likely to understand the concept of a litter box. They can still be wonderful pets, but they won't be as tame.

A Pack of Dogs, a Pride of Lions . . .

Would you believe that a group of ferrets is called a business?

Hey, Ferret Face! That Hurt!

If you buy a ferret from a backyard breeder who keeps the kits in a shed out back, you might be asking for trouble. These animals have probably been handled

YOU'VE GOTTA LOVE 'EM

A Trying Experience

I have a slim waist and strong calves, and finding jeans that fit is always a struggle. One time, I was in the dressing room of a women's store and had just pulled some pants up past my knees when a Scottish terrier dashed into the store and right under the curtain of my dressing room. The little dog yapped and raced around my legs. I was so startled that I tried to jump out of the way, but with the jeans around my ankles, I plunged over sideways, pulled down the curtain, and fell through the dressing room door and onto the main floor of the shop. Frightened by my tumble, the dog pooped on the carpet, where I lay half-undressed.

It turned out the terrier was lost, so after I'd recovered my dignity, I comforted the frightened animal while the store clerk cleaned up the mess and called the animal shelter, which reunited the dog and his owners.

Maybe I'll just order by mail from now on.

—LAURA ZARUBA
Boulder, Colorado

only rarely, and that means they are likely to shy away from contact. They may have no idea how to behave around people. It will take several months of very patient work to turn them into the safe and confident companions that you'll want your pets to be.

It's a Tough Job, but Somebody Has to Do It

When choosing the best pet for you from a particular group or litter of ferrets, make several trips to the breeder's house or pet store. Take some time to play with the ferrets. They won't mind; they'll play all day if someone is around to encourage them. Ask the person who spends time with them every day which ones are calm and quiet and which are more active. They may all seem alike at first, but pretty soon you'll be able to pick out the one with the personality traits you want.

Make Sure You're *Healthy*

Don't take your sniffles to the pet store if you plan to pick out a ferret. You may not be able to spend any time around the litter if you have a cold or the flu. Ferrets are extremely susceptible to both ailments, as well as to bacterial and viral infections. Wait until you feel better so that the ferret will feel better in her new home.

It's a Mite of a Problem

Ferrets wear their health on their sleeves, so you will be able to tell right away if there is a problem. A kit will look bony if he has been underfed. He will have a coarse coat and dull eyes if he is sick. Runny eyes and nose mean that the animal has a slight cold or allergy. You should also look for ear mites. Most of these problems are correctable, but you may want to ask the owner to pay for the treatment before you consider buying.

FOR FISH ONLY

The Fish That Ate Philadelphia

With fish, size matters—especially if the fish is likely to outgrow the tank. Before you buy a fish, ask how big she's likely to get. The salesperson at a pet store should level with you about this. The clerk should tell you that an Oscar or Pacu will grow to be 12 inches in length if pampered. Eventually, the fish will eat as

much for dinner as you will. If you have a small tank and don't have room to replace it with a larger one, stick to small species.

FOR REPTILES ONLY

Find a Perfect Ten

S What you want in a snake, quite simply, is perfection, especially if you are buying from a classified ad or from someone who is not an experienced breeder. Look for scales that are shiny and smooth. (If they're dry and flaky, the snake may have a vitamin deficiency.) Make sure there are no visible scars or wrinkles (which could indicate either abuse or malnutrition). And avoid a snake with sunken eyes or a protruding backbone (also signs of a poor diet).

Judge a Pet by Its Parent

S Ask to see the parents of the lizard or snake that you intend to buy. You won't be looking for any special physical characteristics—you can't tell anything about what a baby lizard will eventually look like by looking at his parents—but you do need to assure yourself that the animal was captive-bred and not captured in the wild. An animal that is captured is likely to have parasites and to shy away from human contact. A captive-bred reptile will be clean and tame.

Make Sure That Snake Isn't Bringing Any Friends

S Make sure the snake you're considering adopting is "clean"—meaning that the animal is free of parasites and worms, especially tapeworms. Reptiles need to be wormed just as dogs and cats do. If the breeder says that a snake is clean, a vet has checked the animal for parasites and has provided the appropriate treatment to get rid of any that were found.

Was There a Death in the Family?

S Snakes are born in a clutch of eggs, and most of the animals from the clutch should have survived. Before buying from a breeder, ask what percentage of the snakes born in your potential pet's clutch have died. If more than half of them have not survived, you might be dealing with weak stock, and the rest of the clutch is likely to be sickly, too. A breeder shouldn't sell animals out of a clutch that has a high mortality rate, and reputable breeders know that. You can protect yourself by asking.

ADOPTING A PET

Born to Be Wild

$ Some people try to sell snakes caught in the wild, especially ball pythons, and pass them off as being captive-bred because the latter are easier to sell. Make sure that you are buying a captive-bred snake (which will be healthy and friendly) rather than one that was captured in the wild (which will be surly and have lots of health problems). How can you tell? The best way is to look at the top of the animal's head. If the scales are discolored and dull instead of shiny, the snake has had some sun damage—and no captive-bred snake would have been exposed to the sun long enough to have developed the problem. Also look for parasites, such as ticks. If a snake has ticks, the animal was not born in a terrarium.

COMMON MISTAKES

Letting Go

If your giant day gecko, garter snake, chameleon, or scorpion doesn't work out, the last thing you should do is let it go. No captive-born reptile or insect is going to be able to survive without some special care. They're used to having the right temperature and scheduled feedings. Without someone looking out for their needs, your pets will suffer and die.

Instead of releasing the animal, contact the nearest shelter or herpetological society (the corner pet store or even the zoo will know how to get in touch with one). These groups often have a system for adopting back insects and reptiles from owners who can't care for them anymore.

Watch the Tip of the Tail

$ The key to finding a great lizard is to look at the animal's tail. A healthy lizard has a nice, fat tail. If the tail looks thin, the lizard may be malnourished. Avoid any lizard that has protruding bones on the legs, hips, or jaw. He may have a calcium deficiency that results in a condition called metabolic bone disease (MBD). Because the condition is difficult to treat, many hobbyists try to sell

lizards that have it rather than take them to the vet. It pays to look closely.

Get a Clean Belly of Health

Before you purchase a turtle, check to see that she has bright, shiny eyes, which indicates good health. Test to see that she's alert—or at least not comatose. And make sure that the tank has a fresh lining and that the underside of the turtle is clean. These are proofs that the animal has been raised in a clean environment.

THE BEST SEASONS TO ADOPT

Adopting a pet is a matter of finding the right pet in the right place at the right time. Some pets don't travel well in extreme heat or cold. Some are especially bothered by holiday stress. Here are a few guidelines to help you find the right (and avoid the wrong) time to bring home a new companion.

FOR DOGS ONLY

Avoid the Holiday Rush

Because you want to bring your new puppy into a happy home, wait until after the holidays to adopt. Experts agree that the worst time to adopt any dog is during a major holiday, which means that puppies make terrible Christmas gifts. Everyone is too rushed during the holidays. Puppies need time to adjust to a new home and enough attention from you to learn the fundamentals of house-training.

No Way I'm Going Out in This Blizzard!

Avoid bringing home a new puppy in the dead of winter. No one—puppy or owner—wants to go outside when the windchill is 30 below. By adopting a dog in harsh weather conditions, you are making

No Off-Color Jokes, Please

The Pharaoh hound is one of the oldest known breeds in the world. It's also the only breed known to blush. When one of these dogs is excited, the tan-colored areas around the animal's nose, eyes, and ears turn pink or red.

the process of house-training unpleasant for you and your pet.

FOR CATS ONLY

Love Is in the Air

If you want to have a lot of kittens to choose from, plan to adopt in the springtime. More litters are available in the spring and early fall than in the frigid months.

FOR BIRDS ONLY

There's a Reason Birds Fly South in Winter

The best time of year to bring a bird home is late spring or early fall, when the weather is balmy but not hot. The worst time is winter. It is extremely dangerous to expose birds to the cold. People who care about their birds won't bring them to bird shows in winter, and the airlines won't ship birds in harsh weather. Even if you order in October or March, you are taking a chance that the purchase will be placed on hold until the weather warms up.

The Bowser without a Bark

The basenji, a breed developed in Africa, is unusual in that it doesn't bark. Explanations for this range from physiological reasons to the idea that the breed learned not to bark because it spent so much time around people (who don't bark).

Basenjis aren't totally silent, though. They can make other doggy noises, such as growling and whining. And they make a basenji-specific sound, which is said to resemble a cross between a yodel and a chortle. According to the American Kennel Club, the dog makes the sound when it's happy.

Must be fun at parties.

FOR REPTILES ONLY

It May Be His Nap Time

You can buy a snake at any time of year, but if you plan to adopt a new ball python or other hibernating snake, your best bet is to wait until spring. If you bring home a hibernating snake after the end of October, he won't be much of a companion until he wakes up in the spring, and you won't get much practice in learning his habits or feeding schedule until then. More than one new owner has called a breeder in terror to say that a snake hasn't eaten in weeks, when the animal is really just dozing his way through the cold months.

To be doubly sure that you're adopting a new snake at the time of year when she'll be most active, read up on the native climate and behavior of any breed before you buy. Or ask the breeder to fill you in on the hibernation habits of that particular breed of snake.

FINALIZING THE ADOPTION

Once you have chosen your new pet, you will want a few assurances before you take the animal home. Even if everyone has the best intentions, some problems can creep in. Make sure the owner will take the animal back if you should change your mind. Get some guarantees that she has kept the animal as healthy as possible and ask for some last-minute advice on how to care for your pet. Here are some things to keep in mind.

FOR PETS IN GENERAL

Ask for Directions

❑ Don't buy a pet when you're in a hurry. You should ask and be asked a lot of questions before you walk out the door with your new friend. If you are buying from a pet store or experienced breeder, the owner or salesclerk should ask if this is your first pet of this type and should have a lot of information ready for you to take home. He should provide tip sheets, numbers of hot lines, and verbal advice on how to feed, train, and care for the pet. And he will have queries for you, too. A good breeder wants each animal to find a good home and will question you until satisfied that you can provide one.

FOR CATS ONLY

Shelters Practice Boosterism

When you adopt from the Humane Society, you will get a cat that has seen the vet and has been given up-to-date shots. But you should still ask whether the cat has been spayed or neutered and whether any other medical work has been done. Some shelters take extensive measures to make sure that each cat has had the same dental work and blood work that any conscientious owner would have paid for. Others simply don't have the money to do so. In that case, they can identify the cat's health problems, and the rest will be up to you.

Mom Needs to Pass This Test

Before you adopt, make sure that your new kitten's mother has tested negative for feline leukemia. The blood test for this disease can't be done on kittens, but if the mother is negative, there is a good chance that the kittens are, too.

Ask Fluffy to Say Cheese

If you are adopting an adult cat, particularly one that is more than five years old, be sure that you get the cat's medical and dental records. As cats age, they develop problems with their teeth that can be very expensive. Make sure that any necessary dental work has been done before you take the cat home. Also have the vet

When Is an Animal Old Enough to Leave Home?

One of the best tests to tell whether you are dealing with a reputable breeder or owner is to ask the age of the animals she's offering for adoption. Animals have to reach a certain maturity before they can safely be separated from their mothers. Here are some guidelines.

IF YOU ARE BUYING A . . .	IT SHOULD BE AT LEAST . . .	OR ELSE . . .
Ferret	9 to 10 weeks old	It will be aggressive
Kitten	12 weeks old	It will be antisocial and more difficult to litter box train
Potbellied pig	6 to 8 weeks old	It will be too aggressive and antisocial
Puppy	10 weeks old	It will be small, antisocial, and prone to illness
Rabbit	7 weeks old	It will be prone to illness

YOU'VE GOTTA LOVE 'EM

Stinker, the Bathing Beauty

When I was little, I got a black cat that my parents named Stinker because he was hissy and mean. In the summers, my cousin Brian, who was not a nice boy, loved to take Stinker and dunk him vigorously in my little wading pool, just to watch him struggle to run away. Sometimes he would chase the poor cat around the yard with the garden hose. After a while, Stinker grew resigned to this and gained a grudging respect for someone who was, after all, meaner than he was.

A few years later, we outgrew the wading pool, and shortly after that we had to move. We sent Stinker to live with my Aunt Linda in western Nebraska. By this time, he had grown to be a huge, middle-aged cat. That first week, Linda drew a bath for herself but left the bathroom door open. When she came back to shut off the water and get in, she found a huge feline blob almost completely submerged in the bathwater and two big yellow eyes blinking up at her through the bubbles. After that, it was Linda who had to get resigned to the fact that Stinker loved water—dishwater, bathwater, not even the dog's water bowl was safe. In the summer, she says, the cat loved to loll underneath the sprinklers in the yard. I don't know, maybe Stinker missed Brian after all.

—MICHELLE SEATON
Medford, Massachusetts

check for potential dental problems that may cost you in the future. If you are adopting from an animal shelter, the staff should already have checked the cat's teeth.

Buyer Beware

The clock is ticking on your chance to exchange a kitten after you take him home, so be sure to keep a careful eye on your new pet's health from the very beginning. Most breeders feel that it is impossible to guarantee fully the health of any cat. If you change your mind or come across a health problem, they'll usually offer to give you your money back for the first two weeks only. After that, although they probably won't refund your money, they will usually let you replace your kitten with another one from the same litter.

If you already have other cats at home, make absolutely sure any addition to the menagerie is healthy. Most breeders won't allow you to return a kitten once you have taken it home to your other cats. They believe that any health problems that arise could be the result of exposure in your home.

FOR BIRDS ONLY

She Should Have a Good Set of Lungs

If you are buying an adult bird from a breeder or small hobbyist, ask for a health check. You should insist that the bird be screened for psittacosis, a respiratory disorder similar to pneumonia. This is especially critical if you have other birds at home, since psittacosis is particularly contagious to other birds (and even to people). Even if the bird tests negative, be prepared to quarantine her for 60 days after you bring her home—in part because the trauma of moving to a new home may bring out dormant illnesses.

FOR FERRETS ONLY

Shots Should Have Been Fired

Make sure your new ferret is up-to-date on his shots before you bring him home. The animal should have received his first canine distemper shot at 6

weeks. (An older ferret should have received additional shots at 10 and 14 weeks, as well as an annual booster.)

Now That's *Brand Loyalty*

You've packed up your new ferret and are ready to walk out the door. Before you do, ask for a food sample. An owner or breeder should know exactly what brand of food your ferret likes to eat and should be willing to provide the sample to get you started. This is especially true if you are adopting an adult ferret. These animals are extremely picky eaters. They fixate on one kind of food in the first six months of life, and they won't eat anything else. A ferret would rather starve to death than try a new kind of food, so find out what the label looks like right away.

Know All That You Can Know

Before you take your new ferret home, find out how to ferret-proof your house. The seller should provide you with detailed advice on this. (*Hint:* It means sealing up every nook and cranny and throwing out the rat poison.) The seller also should give you care sheets for your animal and tell you which vaccinations have been given and which ones are due soon. If the previous owner doesn't offer you this information, be sure to ask for it.

FOR FISH ONLY

Cool, Man, Cool

No matter what time of year you buy fish, make sure the pet store is your last stop on the way home. If you are buying fish on a very hot day, bring a cooler with you to the pet store, then put the plastic bag of fish inside for the trip home. Fish can stand cooler temperatures better than warmer ones because warm water contains less oxygen than cold water.

Give Her a Thermal Jacket

If you are buying a fish in cold weather, it's a good idea to carry your fish home in an insulated cooler.

A WORD FROM DR. EMERSON

A Finicky Ferret? No Way!

DR. WENDY EMERSON
Veterinarian who makes house calls in and around Topsfield, Massachusetts, to care for cats, dogs, and a wide range of exotic pets

Although ferrets are lovable, rambunctious, and smart, like cats, they differ from cats in one major way: They eat everything they see. That's why they need constant supervision when they are out of their cages. A ferret left alone for 30 seconds will find and eat your car keys, golf tees, hair scrunchies, stray rubber bands, plastic grocery bags, bottle caps, milk carton tops, paper clips, and kids' toys. The heads of G.I. Joe dolls are a favorite snack. Ferrets will steal the lipstick from your purse and eat it—along with all the spare change at the bottom. They will crawl up into your couch and eat the foam rubber right out of the cushions. Unfortunately, what goes into the ferret must come out, and that usually requires surgery.

If you're thinking of adopting a ferret, make sure that you have a place for a large, comfortable cage and that you have time each day to supervise your pet's exercise. That doesn't mean letting the animal out while you cook dinner. Ferret owners are always saying to me, "I had my eye on him all the time." And I reply, "Well, then, you must have sat there and watched him eat these two Matchbox cars."

(Leave out the ice!) If that's not convenient and it's not *extremely* cold, at least put the bag of fish and water inside your coat or jacket before you leave the store. Even a short blast of cold air can dramatically change the temperature of the water, which will endanger the fish.

ADOPTING A PET

FOR REPTILES ONLY

Card Them

S Before you take home your new snake, lizard, or other reptile, make sure you have the phone number of the breeder or previous owner—and be absolutely certain that you have a health guarantee. The breeder's exchange policy should cover at least the first six months, and preferably a full year, during which time the breeder should encourage you to call with questions or problems. The most common health problem among reptiles is hidden parasites, and these may not become apparent for many months.

SETTLING IN
Your New Family Member

Whether you're about to adopt a dog, a cat, or a guppy, the settling-in period will go much more smoothly if you know what to expect. That adorable ball of fur isn't quite so cute when she's chewing up your new pair of shoes. But chewing is perfectly normal puppy behavior, and if your new shoes are handy . . . well, don't say we didn't warn you.

The beginning of your relationship with your pet will probably be the most difficult. She's leaving one home—possibly her mother and littermates—to join another. It's traumatic and scary, and your pet will need extra attention and care during the transition. You may have to invest a great deal of time as you help your pet adjust to new surroundings, new family, and sometimes other household pets. And you'll need to teach the new arrival what's acceptable behavior inside and outside your home.

It's wise to learn as much as you can before homecoming day. The better you prepare yourself and your home, the more you'll be

able to enjoy your new family member—and set the stage for a long and happy relationship. Here are some ideas to get you started.

FINDING A VET

For most new pets, including dogs, cats, ferrets, birds, and reptiles, the first step to good health care is a routine screening by a veterinarian. If you're about to bring an animal into your life, you'll need to establish a relationship with a vet who can examine your new pet for problems, administer any necessary shots, and advise you on diet and other requirements. Later on, it's important to have someone you can call right away if your pet becomes ill or involved in an accident.

As with any doctor, you have a right to shop around if you're not satisfied with the first vet you try. If a particular vet doesn't seem responsive to your questions or doesn't seem to interact well with your pet—or with you—keep looking.

FOR PETS IN GENERAL

First the Vet, Then the Pet

❑ It's wise to line up your vet and schedule the first appointment *before* you bring your pet home, especially if a medical guarantee is in effect. (Such a guarantee is usually good for only a limited period.) Planning the first vet appointment in advance will prevent loss of valuable time.

How to Get a Vet

❑ Word of mouth is the best way to find a good veterinarian: Ask pet-owning friends or neighbors for recommendations. You also can contact the American Animal Hospital Association (AAHA), an organization that promotes standards for pet care and pet care facilities. The AAHA maintains a membership of more than 12,000 vets in the United States and Canada who subscribe to its principles, and it provides veterinary refer-

rals as well as information and literature on pet care and health. To get in touch with the AAHA, call toll-free directory assistance (1-800-555-1212) or search the Internet using the keywords "American Animal Hospital Association."

FOR BIRDS ONLY

All Vets Aren't for the Birds

The veterinarian who takes such good care of your dog or cat may not be the right choice when it comes to caring for your new bird. Feathered pets require special handling, tests, and treatments, and if your vet is not an avian specialist, your sick bird could suffer unnecessarily. To find a good bird doctor, contact bird clubs or breeders in your area and ask for referrals.

A WORD FROM DR. EMERSON

New Snakes Want to Be Home Alone

DR. WENDY EMERSON
Veterinarian who makes house calls in and around Topsfield, Massachusetts, to care for cats, dogs, and a wide range of exotic pets

The thing your new snake will need most when you first bring him home is time alone. In fact, I tell people not to feed their snakes for the first couple of days. People think that they need to handle a snake every day for it to become tame and affectionate, but actually you need to work up to this much contact slowly. Most reptiles don't like to be handled. A lot of them get sick if they're handled too much. Many snakes will regurgitate if they are handled right after they eat. So the best thing to do is to have the cage all set up before you bring your pet home and then leave him alone for a while.

PREPARING YOUR HOME

If your new pet won't be confined to a cage or tank, you may need to do some serious pet-proofing to keep your valuables—and your pet—out of harm's way. Set up a "home base" where the animal will be comfortable and happy and where you can limit mobility for a while. At this early stage, you'll be getting to know each other, and it's safer to do it in a controlled environment. Here are some ideas on how to get ready for the new arrival.

FOR PETS IN GENERAL

Stow Your Valuables, Save Your Relationship

❑ Before bringing home a new pet, get anything that's really precious out of harm's way. Puppies chew, cats claw and scratch, and most pets are subject to "accidents" of one kind or another. If you have a valuable antique rug, piece of fine furniture, or heirloom vase, move it to a closed-off room or store it away before bringing an animal into your home. Remove the possibility of serious damage so that you can focus on giving your pet the love and affection the animal needs—and avoid anger and resentment.

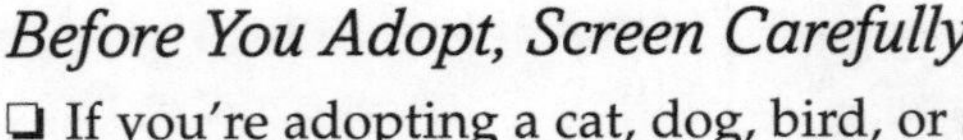

Before You Adopt, Screen Carefully

❑ If you're adopting a cat, dog, bird, or any other animal that will move freely around your house, check to see that all your windows have secure screens. Curious cats especially love to perch at windows and can fall out accidentally. A bird could easily fly out while you're not looking.

Don't let your new pet indulge in power plays. Grab a staple gun and get all electrical wires under control.

Avoid Highly Charged Situations

❑ Electrical wires pose a hazard for puppies, kittens, birds, and other animals that might chew or play with them. Get wires under control by tacking them to the floor or base-

Pet-Proofing 101

Prepare your house for a new pet as if you were acquiring a toddler with a tail. Inquisitive young animals can be amazingly clever at getting into places they don't belong. Take appropriate precautions, especially if you're bringing home a cat, dog, or any other animal that will have the run of the house. Here are some of the basics.

Use Bitter Apple (available at pet supply stores) on furniture, electrical wires, and anything else your pet shouldn't chew.

Secure all cabinets where cleaning supplies, chemicals, and other dangerous items are stored. Use a child-proof lock if necessary.

Hide garbage and trash cans behind cabinets or out of reach, or cover them securely.

Shut closet doors. This keeps your shoes and clothing safely inside and your kitten or puppy away from any plastic bags and other hazards.

Eliminate dangerous hidey-holes. Keep washer, dryer, dishwasher, oven, and refrigerator doors closed. Check the dryer vent for gaps a kitty could crawl into.

Keep toilet lids closed.

Stash small objects such as jewelry, rubber bands, twist ties, paper clips, sewing supplies, and string in drawers or covered containers. They're easy to choke on.

Securely tie shade pulls and drapery cords. A playful cat could strangle in them.

Remove all houseplants from a cat's potential reach. Kitties often like to nibble on greenery, and this can be hazardous to both the appearance of the plant and the health of the cat (many plants are poisonous to felines).

After your pet gets home, you may need to add to this list. Watch your pet's behavior carefully for clues about other potential hazards.

board. (Never insert a tack directly into a wire!) If you can't eliminate access to a particular electrical cord, cover it with Bitter Apple cream or spray (available at pet stores), which has an unpleasant taste designed to repel pets.

FOR DOGS ONLY

Make Sure Your Pet Is Safe at Home

Before you bring home that pup, decide where to set up a home base for the new arrival. Choose a spot

where the puppy can be safely confined when you can't keep an eye out: an easy-to-control environment that's not readily damaged, such as a hallway, bathroom, or enclosed porch. Set up a bed, bowls, and toys. Put down newspaper. Then close the area off with a gate that lets the puppy see out. (Don't use an accordion-style child's gate. A puppy's head can get caught in it.) Depending on what you're doing, you can move the gate to different "safety zones" around the house so that the puppy can be closer to you and feel like part of the family. Let your new pet explore the house gradually under your supervision, but return the pup to the safety zone when you can't supervise.

Whether it's a plastic carrier (A) you can transport easily or a large wire kennel (B) that lets your friend see everything that's going on, a puppy crate can be a source of comfort and security.

The Puppy Crate: A Room, Not a Prison

If there's no safe area in your house where a new pet can be restricted, or if you just want to give your new friend a space of his own, try a crate. This is where your pet will sleep and spend time when you can't supervise closely. When used correctly, it's a perfectly humane and effective way to incorporate a puppy into your home and your life. Your new dog will easily adapt and learn that it's his own special spot.

To help your pet feel secure, place some toys inside the crate along with a blanket, towel, or piece of clothing that carries your familiar scent. (Make sure any cloth you leave in the crate is unfrayed, and remove such items if your pup starts to chew on them. If an animal swallows bits of cloth, the pieces can cause an intestinal obstruction.) Confine the puppy there no more than a few hours at a time or overnight. When you're nearby and can supervise, leave the door of the crate open so that the pup can wander in and out freely. It will soon become your pet's favorite hangout.

Now This *Smells Like Home*

 If you find the cost of a crate prohibitive or simply prefer not to go that route, giving your pet a bed of her own is the next best way to help her acquire a sense of belonging and stability. For a puppy, cut down a wooden or cardboard box. (Avoid wicker beds—pups will chew on them and can hurt themselves.) Cut it low enough so that she can get in and out easily, but leave the sides high enough to form a little enclosure to keep out drafts. Line the box with an old, unfrayed towel, cushion, or blanket so that she can curl up and get cozy. (If she starts to chew on this, remove it.) The smell will become familiar, and your puppy will associate it with her special spot. Later on, if the animal outgrows the box, you can put her blanket directly on the floor.

5 *Ways to Make a Puppy Crate Feel Like Home*

In the wild, dogs live in dens that provide them with a safe and comfortable environment. If introduced correctly, a crate can become your puppy's den. It also can keep her out of trouble when you're not around and can aid in housebreaking. Here are a few ways to make sure your pup takes to her private domain.

1. Don't force her in before she's ready. Leave the door open for the first few days and feed her inside the crate. When she's done eating, praise her and call her out so that she can relieve herself. Eventually, she will go in on her own when she's tired or wants some private time.

2. Once your puppy goes in and out on her own, begin closing the door for short periods of time. This will work better if you have tired your puppy out first.

3. Lock your dog in overnight, then take her out first thing in the morning so that she can relieve herself. She won't want to mess up her own space, but if she's desperate, she will.

4. During the day, don't force your puppy to stay in the cage for more than three to four hours at a time. By then, she will need to relieve herself.

5. Always associate the crate with good things. Never use it as punishment. Some dogs will be happy to sleep in a crate all their lives.

FOR CATS ONLY

Cats That Go Bump in the Night

Before you bring home a cat, and certainly before you bring home a pair, be sure to set up your house so that they can wander around and make noise at night without bothering you. Cats are nocturnal. They often nap the day away—especially if they spend the day alone—only to get up in search of adventure just as you are going to sleep. They aren't destructive at night, just noisy. You will want to be able to shut your bedroom door so that you can sleep through the rattle toys, the bottle top hockey, and even the mouse hunting that cats enjoy at night.

Inside or Outside? The Great (Cat) Debate

If you live in a suburban or rural environment, one of the first decisions you'll need to make regarding your new cat is whether the animal will be an indoor or an outdoor pet. Here are some questions to help guide you.

Who lives next door? Your neighbors may not like your cat. For the sake of the neighbors *and* the kitty, make sure all parties get along before your new pet darts out the door and heads straight for a cat-hating neighbor's yard.

How do the neighbors keep their lawns in such good shape? Weed killers and chemical fertilizers are dangerous to cats and other animals. Find out whether any folks in your area use them before letting your pet roam their properties.

How close is the nearest highway? Don't expect your cat to understand traffic patterns. If the nearest interstate is just around the corner, forget about letting your feline run free.

How do you feel about local wildlife? Most cats will chase (and kill) small animals and birds—a habit that may be more of a problem when tabby brings home a dead chickadee than when she shows off her prowess at mouse hunting. Will your feline's natural hunting instincts make you or your neighbors unhappy?

Finally, are you comfortable with the odds? Even in rural areas, outdoor cats do not live as long as indoor cats. There are simply more hazards outside than inside your house.

Make a Nest for Catnaps

You should have a bed ready for your new kitten, but it need not be fancy or expensive. Instead, improvise a resting place from a cardboard box or old dresser drawer. Keep it in a quiet spot, away from drafts. Line it with something soft (without feathers) that can be washed periodically, along with a piece of clothing or a towel that carries your scent. Cats like a feeling of shelter, so if you offer your pet a spot that feels safe, she'll be less tempted to crawl into closets, cabinets, and other dangerous spots.

Kitty in the City

If you live in a city, letting your cat outside is not a realistic option. There are simply too many risks. According to Dr. Peter Borchelt, a behaviorist in Brooklyn, New York, a well-cared-for indoor cat can live 20 years, but the average life span of an outdoor cat in the city is only 3 years.

FOR BIRDS ONLY

Cages: The Bigger the Better

There's no such thing as a too-big birdcage. A bird should live in the largest cage you can afford and have space for. Birds are designed for flying and are happiest and most comfortable in a home that gives them room to move. (It also will help keep their weight down.) If a bird can't spread his wings, get him a larger cage. And give your bird plenty of toys—five or more—to provide added stimulation.

It's better to line the bottom of the cage with paper rather than gravel or litter. This will make it easier to monitor the bird's droppings and notice any change, which is usually the first sign of illness.

Give Your Bird a Bird's-Eye View

Place your bird's cage where she'll be healthy and happy. Birds like a well-lit location, well away from the floor. A spot near a window is excellent because your pet will be able to entertain herself by watching the birds outdoors. But make sure your bird is not subject to cold drafts or harsh, direct sunlight, either of which can be harmful. In a particularly sunny spot, be sure to

provide some shade or place the cage partly away from the window so that your pet can shelter herself if necessary.

Polly Wanna Perfect Perch

Your bird should never be out of the cage unsupervised, but there are times when your pet will enjoy coming out from behind bars and hanging out with the family under your watchful eye. Get your pet a play perch or T-stand and place it in a spot where he can be near you, preferably in a closed-off area without direct access to the outdoors. A calm bird that's accustomed to being handled may perch in such a spot for hours. But keep an eye out: A sudden noise could startle your pet and cause him to fly into a closed window or onto a hot stove. And birds love to chew, so be sure to keep yours away from all electrical wires and any other potential dangers.

The Carpenter Who Came to Call

Carpenter Larry Ames had been hired to rewire a house in Palo Alto, California, and thought he was the only one home. He pulled the electric cable through the tight crawl space, moving along on his back. While pounding the staples to the floor joist, he heard a voice from upstairs.

"Who's there?" the voice called.

"It's me," Larry answered. "I'm in the cellar. I can't come out right now."

"Who's there?" the voice called again.

"It's Larry," he said, yelling a little louder. "I'm in the crawl space."

He scooted along a little more and hammered up another staple. "Errrnnkk," he heard. "Who's there?"

At which point a chagrined Larry realized that he'd been talking to the family's pet parrot.

FOR FISH ONLY

Clean House before They Arrive

If you're planning to acquire fish for the first time, set up their new environment a day or two before bringing them home. Fill the tank and turn on the filtration system and heater, if you have one, so that the equipment will have time to clean and regulate the temperature of the water. This will create a more hospitable home for your new fish and reduce the risks to them during the transition.

Help Your Pets Avoid the Draft

SETTLING IN

When setting up a fish tank, keep in mind that fish are very sensitive to temperature. Avoid placing the tank near a window, which could expose your fish to drafts of cold air, lowering the water temperature and perhaps even killing them. (Bright sunlight also encourages the growth of algae. Although algae isn't unhealthy for fish—it even provides a food source if you miss a day of feeding—too much of the green slime is aesthetically unpleasing and can make it hard to see your fish.) Similarly, place the tank away from radiators or other heat sources that could dramatically raise the water temperature in the tank.

Put Those Fish on Solid Ground

Water is heavy—a 10-gallon fish tank weighs around 80 pounds when filled. So make sure you set up

COMMON MISTAKES

Fish Tanks: Bigger Is Better

If you are just starting out as a fish owner, the worst thing you can do is buy a tank that is too small. Overcrowding is the biggest cause of fish fatalities for the novice owner. Experts say that you should buy at minimum a 20-gallon tank and fill it slowly with fish, one small school at a time. To keep from overcrowding, allow at least 1 gallon of water for every inch of freshwater fish. For example, you could have 15 to 20 one-inch-long fish in a 20-gallon tank, or 40 fish if each one is half an inch long. For saltwater fish, the tank size depends less on the size of the fish and more on the species. But as a rule of thumb, if you allow at least 5 gallons of water for every one-inch saltwater fish, your pets should be fine. In general, no matter what kind of fish you buy, the more water you have in the tank, the more mistakes you can make without killing your fish.

A related rule is to ask the store clerk what size filter you need and then buy a filter that is at least one size bigger. You will make mistakes with filtration and the chemical balance in the tank—everyone does at first—but with the larger filter, your fish will have a fighting chance.

SETTLING IN

your fish tank on a strong, solid surface that won't collapse under the weight. You can buy a fish stand made for this purpose if you don't have an appropriate table or platform. Don't try to set up your tank on a shelf or a flimsy coffee table.

They Love Hide-and-Seek

For a well-furnished fish tank, include plenty of plants and rocks in the decor. The purpose is not just aesthetic. Fish like to have places to swim in and out of, where they can breed, hide from other fish, or just pass the time. Ceramic mermaids and treasure chests won't impress the fish one bit, but they will make swimming around more interesting.

COST CUTTERS

Offer Your Pet a Seedy Diet

Gerbils and hamsters get all their nutritional needs from the commercial seed mixtures sold in supermarkets and pet stores. It's basically the same as the birdseed you buy for your outdoor feeder, so consolidate your shopping list and stock up on the same food for the gerbil or hamster and the wild birds. (This approach is *not* appropriate for other small animals. A rabbit or guinea pig, for example, requires a specially formulated pellet-based diet.)

FOR POCKET PETS

She'll Eat Herself out of House and Home

Gerbils and hamsters are big chewers, so don't plan to put these animals in plastic cages or houses they can eat their way out of. An aquarium with a screen cover is best. Outfit it with a water bottle, a wheel for playing, and pine bedding to absorb waste. Don't use cedar shavings; they may cause respiratory problems in small animals.

Keep Pocket Pets in the Temperate Zone

Gerbils and hamsters respond well to a consistent, mild climate, so place their cages in spots where the temperature will stay between 50°F and 80°F. Hot weather doesn't agree with them, and hamsters will actually hibernate if it gets too cold. On hot summer days, put a fan in the window to draw fresh air into the room. Air-conditioning also is an option, as long as you main-

tain a moderate temperature and protect the animals from cold drafts.

Guinea Pigs Need Sound Footing

Unlike rabbits, a guinea pig should not live in a cage with a wire bottom. The rest of the cage can be wire, but the bottom should have a flat, solid surface—even if that surface is a specially designed mat that's placed over a wire cage bottom. That's because guinea pigs have only three toes on their back feet, and in a wire cage they can catch a toe and even rip it off acci-

---

A WORD FROM DR. EMERSON

Turtles: Hold the Burgers

DR. WENDY EMERSON

Veterinarian who makes house calls in and around Topsfield, Massachusetts, to care for cats, dogs, and a wide range of exotic pets

When new pet owners bring their animals to me for the pets' initial checkups, I often give the owners handouts containing pet care information, including notes on the best foods for their animals. I can't count the times I've handed an information sheet to a new box turtle owner and heard, "Earthworms? I thought they ate hamburger and lettuce." And I have to say, "No, that will pretty much kill him."

When I was little, I had a box turtle, and my family and I fed it what the pet store told us to feed it—hamburger and lettuce. But that's not right. After all, turtles don't naturally eat hamburger. Out in the wild, they eat worms and bugs as a source of protein. They do eat lots of greens, too, but be sure to give them a variety. Mine loves radicchio, parsley, spinach, and kale. Try these kinds of foods on *your* turtle—and save the hamburger for the barbecue.

dentally. Make sure there are no openings for a pet's foot to fall through.

FOR RABBITS ONLY

Wanted: A Proper Bunny House

An all-wire cage with a pan underneath to catch the rabbit's droppings is the cleanest and healthiest home for a bunny. Clean the cage every few days. For a bunny under six pounds, a 24- by 24- by 18-inch cage is fine. For an animal between six and ten pounds, the cage should be 30 by 30 inches, and for anything bigger, get a cage that's at least 36 by 30 inches.

To avoid a condition called sore hock, give your bunny a hutch or some solid surface to lie on part of the time. Place this resting surface in the cage after your bunny has chosen a soiling spot so that you can put the surface in an area that will stay relatively clean.

They Like Things Calm and Cool

When setting up your rabbit's cage, place it in a quiet spot, indoors and away from windows. Bunnies don't like a lot of excitement and should never be exposed to direct sunlight or drafts of cold air. Although they can live in environments ranging from 20°F to 85°F, they shouldn't be exposed to quick temperature changes.

Even though your new bunny will spend most of his time in a cage, it's still a good idea to rabbit-proof the rooms he will frequent. Hide or protect all electrical cords, carpets, and linoleum. And avoid leaving your pet outside the cage unsupervised, or he will chew on anything in sight.

FOR REPTILES ONLY

So Where Do You Want This 800-Gallon Tank?

Before you adopt a pet snake, figure out where in your house you can place a tank of the appropriate size. A snake needs a tank that is at least two-thirds to three-quarters as long as he is. If you are hoping to adopt a

Give Your Cold-Blooded Pet a Warm Reception

To help your reptile or amphibian adapt to your home, try to re-create the animal's natural habitat as closely as possible. Native habitats can be very different for various species, so you will need to learn about the requirements of your particular pet before you bring the animal home. Here are a few general ideas to get you started.

• For the cage, use an aquarium or a box made of screen and wood.

• Beware of falling objects! In re-creating the natural environment, be sure the materials you use are sturdy and placed securely so that they won't topple over and injure the caged animal.

• Offer your pet a choice of hiding spots, such as caves made of plastic or rock, hollow logs, or dense vegetation. He may want to hide or build tunnels in his cage—in part as a way to regulate his body temperature.

• Most reptiles and amphibians need water. The source will depend on the species, but you may need to provide a water bowl, a jug with a slow drip, or moving water, such as a waterfall.

• Simulate the heat range of your pet's natural environment by using the appropriate light bulb in his cage (the seller should be able to tell you what the animal needs), and provide a variety of shelter that leads him away from the light bulb to the cooler end of his home. Reptiles and amphibians may be cold-blooded, but that just means they have to heat their blood to warm their bodies. In the wild, they regulate their temperatures by basking in the sun, then going for cover to cool down. The light bulb and shady spots offer similar conditions.

boa that will grow to be nine feet long, you'll need a tank that is six feet long and wide enough for him to be able to coil up and turn around comfortably. Place the tank near an electrical outlet so that you can power the snake's heating pad and lights.

PET SUPPLIES

Parents-to-be have baby showers to help them prepare for the new arrival, but outfitting a nonhuman family member is relatively simple and a lot less expensive (assuming that you can ignore luxuries such as four-poster

SETTLING IN

kitty beds and cashmere doggy vests). Your new pet will be healthy, happy, and comfortable as long as you have the right food and a few basic supplies on hand. Here are some of the essentials for your shopping list.

FOR DOGS ONLY

Give That Puppy Plenty to Chew On

For teething puppies and many older dogs, chewing is an urge that's impossible to resist, so make sure you provide your new dog with plenty of alternatives to your furniture and shoes. Give her chew toys made of hard nylon, such as Nylabones, or from a cornstarch formulation, such as Booda Velvets. Start right away to draw your pet's attention to her chew toys and give her lots of praise when she uses them.

Keep Him on a Short Leash

If you'll be getting a new puppy, get a six-foot leash to start with. This length provides plenty of control for training purposes. Later on, you can buy a longer retractable leash that allows your dog a wider range of movement.

Neckwear for the Well-Dressed Dog

Get your new puppy a collar made of leather, nylon, or canvas—something strong, to which you can attach a license and ID tags. The collar should be wide enough to allow breathing and stretching room, but not so wide that the puppy can get his mouth around it or pull it off.

FOR CATS ONLY

A Scratch in the Right Place

Cats love to stretch out and exercise their claws, so it's smart to start training your new pet immediately. And that means you should

COST CUTTERS

Toys Are Everywhere

It's fun to buy rubber mice and other toys for your new cat, but it's hardly necessary. There's plenty around the house to keep cats and kittens constantly entertained. Give them a rolled-up piece of paper, a paper (not plastic) grocery bag, or a Ping-Pong ball. Try shining a flashlight and watch them chase the beam. As long as they can't swallow it or get it wrapped around their necks, it's fair game.

have a scratching post ready when kitty moves in. Cats tend to scratch when they awaken and in areas where they commonly greet others, such as doorways. A spot near your cat's bed or next to a door is a good location for a scratching post.

As soon as the cat goes for your rugs or furniture, direct the animal to the scratching post and encourage

COST CUTTERS

Low-Cost Scratching Alternatives

Your cat may turn up his nose at several scratching posts before you find one he's willing to use. To avoid expensive trial and error, start with the simplest option first: Try hanging a piece of corrugated cardboard from a doorknob. If he doesn't take to that, move on to something more elaborate, or if you're handy, make a scratching post yourself with wood and perhaps a piece of burlap.

To make your own scratching post, start with a log (complete with bark) about three feet high and a base about two feet square. Cover the bottom of the base with felt to prevent it from scratching the floor, then nail the end of the log into the base. If you're feeling adventurous, you can screw a strong spring into the top of the log and attach a bit of fluff to the end of the spring to amuse kitty.

Alternatively, instead of a log, use a pyramid-shaped block of wood and cover it with burlap, which can be applied with a staple gun or carpet glue.

Let kitty scratch a simple log (A) or a burlap-covered pyramid (B).

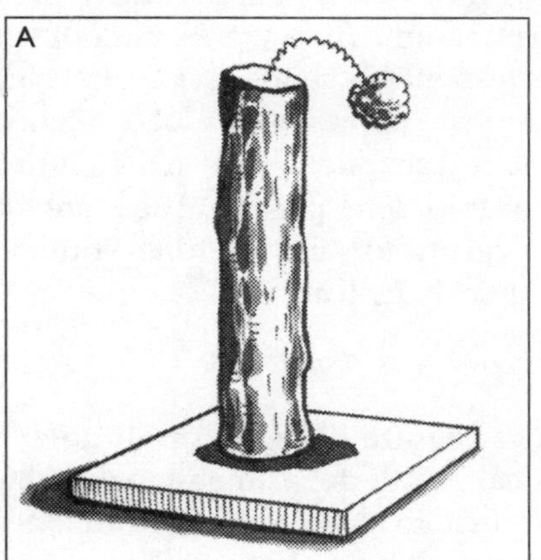

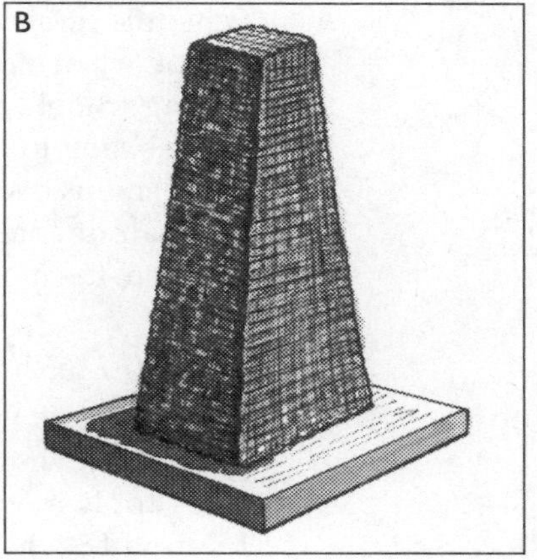

him to use it. You can even attach a few hanging toys to the post so that he'll be attracted to it. Eventually, your pet will learn that it's the approved spot for scratching.

A Bathroom on Every Floor

If your home is very spacious, or if you live on two floors, it's a good idea to set up two litter boxes for your new kitten—one at either end of the house or on each floor. Not only will this be more convenient for the cat, but it also will cut down on accidents.

OTHER CONSIDERATIONS

Every animal is an individual with a unique personality. That's part of the fun—and the challenge—of owning a pet. You can never fully anticipate how a pet will change your life, but there are many factors you can think about. How will you incorporate the new pet into the household? Where will your pet live? Will your pet go outdoors? Consider the following before you bring your new animal home.

FOR DOGS ONLY

A New Puppy? Clear Your Calendar

A new puppy shouldn't be alone for more than about three hours at a time. So if you're planning to bring one home, don't make too many other plans. Schedule some vacation time from work or adopt your puppy when older, responsible children can take charge during school vacations. Puppies need a lot of attention in the beginning and feel abandoned when their human companions disappear for long periods. The more time you can devote to caring for and training your pup early on, the more quickly he'll adjust.

Keep It Legal

Many vicinities require licenses for all dogs, so check with your local health department about which rules apply in your area. In most locations, you'll need to provide evidence of a rabies shot or other vaccination. See if your veterinarian has the necessary forms.

ONE PERSON'S SOLUTION

True Concessions

At three months old, Maggie, our Labrador retriever, was a handful. We had been fairly successful at establishing ourselves as the dominant members of the family (the "alpha dogs"), so she was respectful and was already good at sitting and staying for brief periods of time. But she had an incredible amount of energy, and since we lived in a New York City apartment, she couldn't race around outside to burn it off. (We were carefully heeding our vet's adamant advice not to take her out on the streets or to the park until she had completed her shots and had some protection against disease.)

One night when Maggie was demanding attention, we decided that, since the sofa would be replaced soon anyway, we'd relent and invite her up with us. Instantly, she became calm and happy, as if she realized she'd been given a privilege to be treasured. We didn't allow her on any of the other furniture, but as long as she could join us on the couch, she'd lie down quietly.

I'm not sure whether dog trainers would recommend this strategy, but for Maggie it turned out to be good dog psychology. She is two now and is not permitted on the new couch, but she does have an armchair she's allowed in. So far, we have never caught her on furniture that wasn't hers.

—CHERISSE BANDY
Providence, Rhode Island

SETTLING IN

Hello! My Name Is Buffie

Whether or not your dog needs a license, get the animal an ID tag with your name and phone number on it. You can be fined for having an unlicensed dog, but the consequences may be much worse if your dog is lost with no identification.

Dogs Come In and Must Go Out

All dogs need to spend time outdoors to relieve themselves and get the necessary exercise. Before you

COST CUTTERS

Doghouse vs. Poorhouse

When you first acquire a pet, you can spend a great deal of money on equipment, food, and toys. But there are a number of ways to keep your costs down.

Shop by mail. A few mail-order companies sell everything from crates to toys to health care products. The prices are generally lower than those of discount pet stores (although it pays to compare prices before you purchase), and if the items are in stock, they are shipped right away. J-B Wholesale Pet Supplies and R. C. Steele are two well-established mail-order sources. Call toll-free directory assistance (1-800-555-1212) for their phone numbers, then call and ask each company to send you its catalog. Mail-order pet supply companies usually have a minimum purchase of $25 to $50. If you need to, combine your order with a friend's to meet the minimum.

Buy in bulk. Provided you have the space to store it and the animals to use it up quickly, you can save money by purchasing pet food in 20- to 40-pound bags and storing it in airtight containers. You'll also save time by cutting down on trips to the store. Don't overdo this one, though, if you have only one or two small animals. Pet food can go rancid if stored too long.

Seek out secondhand equipment. If you need a dog crate, aquarium, gerbil cage, cat carrier, or litter box, consider buying used equipment. Many people have leftover equipment they don't plan to use and are happy to sell. Look for classified ads in the local newspaper or signs posted in your supermarket or apartment building. Or post an ad yourself. Be sure to clean such items thoroughly with disinfectant before using them.

bring home a dog, consider what kind of outdoor access she will have. To a large extent, this depends on where you live. A fenced-in backyard or dog run is ideal for exercising and keeps your dog from wandering off. City dogs will have to be walked on a leash. Plan on at least three walks a day for an older, housebroken dog and up to six or seven for a puppy. All dogs require vigorous exercise at least once a day, so factor in some playtime for the two of you.

No matter where you live, never let your dog outside unsupervised. Between traffic, other dogs, and wildlife (and even a few strange people), it's much too dangerous.

FOR CATS ONLY

Plan a Weekend with Kitty

A new cat or kitten won't require as much time as a puppy, but your new pet *will* need extra attention during his first few days at home. Plan on bringing your cat home when you'll be available to spend time with the animal, such as at the beginning of a not-too-busy weekend. This will give you both a chance to get used to each other. Observe your pet's behavior carefully so that you can address any potential problems, and keep an eye out for household hazards that might endanger his safety.

Outfit the Outdoor Cat

If your cat will be spending time outdoors, make sure she's had all her shots for rabies, distemper, and feline leukemia. And also make sure she's wearing a flea and tick collar at all times, as well as an ID tag with your name and phone number on it. This should be a breakaway model designed for cats so that your kitty won't get caught on something and strangle.

EASING THE TRANSITION

Your new pet has just left everything he knows for a strange new environment full of unfamiliar sights, sounds, and smells. Is it any wonder he's scared? All

SETTLING IN

pets need a period of adjustment—but they don't all adjust in the same way. To welcome a puppy, there's no such thing as too much love and attention, but a reptile or hamster would rather be left alone for the first few days. If you understand your pet's needs before he comes home, you'll be well prepared to make him comfortable in his new surroundings.

FOR PETS IN GENERAL

Serve Up the Usual Chow

❑ Pets have many adjustments to make when they move to a new home, so it's a good idea to continue feeding them what they've been used to for a while. Get a supply of the food your pet's been eating and keep her diet the same for a week or so. If your vet recommends a different diet, introduce it gradually so that the animal's digestive system can adapt to the new food.

FOR DOGS ONLY

Give Pup a Place to Curl Up

When you arrive home with your new puppy, have a special spot set up for him in a safe, restricted area of the house. Bring him to his area and show him his bed, bowls, and toys so that he can start to feel at home. Let your pet sniff around and explore his new surroundings at his own pace. Take it slowly at first; he'll need a little time to get familiar with his new home. But keep a close eye on the puppy if he ventures beyond his own area. After all, he's just a baby and will require supervision until he's trained and housebroken.

Meet the Family

To help your new puppy settle in, introduce her to your whole family and let everyone hold her and interact with her. This will give the puppy a chance to become familiar with everyone's scent. Dogs are social animals and love companionship, so your puppy will thrive on lots and lots of attention. Handle her gently in the beginning. Speak softly and don't overwhelm her

5 Ways to Calm Your Dog's First-Night Blues

Imagine spending your first six to eight weeks of life with your mother and brothers and sisters. You have a mother who feeds you and looks after you and a constant source of playmates and warm bodies to sleep next to. All of a sudden, a strange-smelling person picks you up and takes you away from your family. You are left on a bed or in a box without any of the warm and safe smells and other comforts you have grown up with. Sound scary? Try any of these suggestions to make your puppy's first night in her new home a little more comfortable.

1. Set a hot-water bottle on her bed next to her.

2. Place a ticking clock near her (with the alarm shut off and out of reach).

3. Give her something soft and fuzzy to sleep on, such as a fleece pullover.

4. Ask the breeder for something that smells of her mother and siblings, such as a piece of cloth or a toy.

5. Leave a radio or television on so that she hears voices all night.

with loud noises, sudden movements, or rough play. Take special care around young, overeager children. The puppy will still be getting her bearings and will need to be reassured that she's in a safe environment.

Try Diversionary Tactics

Your puppy will be happier if he can see and hear family members and know that you're nearby, even when you're busy with other things. Establish his home base in a part of the house that's well traveled and not far from the action, such as the kitchen or family room. Isolating him in a cold, damp basement or garage is a sure prescription for loneliness and antisocial behavior.

Help Him Make It Through That First Night

The first night in a new home can be lonely and frightening for a puppy. If he won't stop crying, you may want to move his bed or crate into your bedroom. Just knowing you're nearby will help him feel less isolated and may be enough to quiet him down. Keep in mind

YOU'VE GOTTA LOVE 'EM

Anybody Lose a Hot Dog?

I grew up with Charlie, an undistinguished Norwegian elkhound. (Charlie was female, but Dad called everyone Charlie, and the name somehow stuck.) The elkhound's distinctive trait is a tightly curled tail, but Charlie's tail always drooped as if it had been steamed for hours. And that wasn't the only way she embarrassed us.

One summer evening, our family was picnicking at the beach when Dad noticed Charlie slinking by. Then he noticed what she was carrying, and the next thing we knew, he was shouting and racing after her. Apparently, Charlie had grabbed a hot dog from the hamper of another group of picnickers—without realizing that the hot dog was linked to an entire string of wieners. When she realized her error, Charlie tried to sneak away, but she was unwilling to let go of her original prize. She crept through the sand, her sad tail and a six-foot wiener train dragging between her legs.

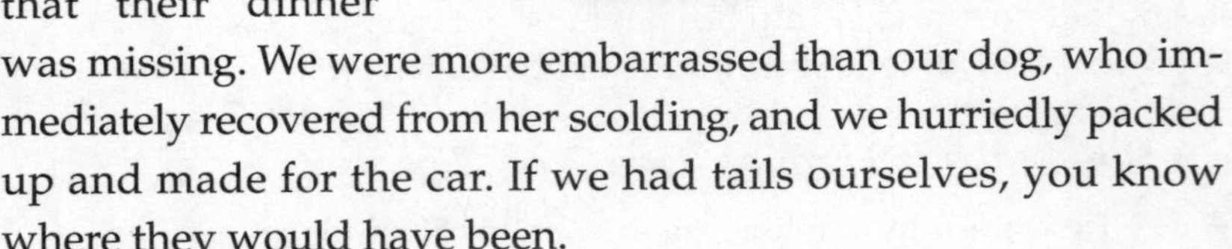

Dad grabbed Charlie and looked up and down the beach. Where had all those wieners come from? No one seemed to be aware that their dinner was missing. We were more embarrassed than our dog, who immediately recovered from her scolding, and we hurriedly packed up and made for the car. If we had tails ourselves, you know where they would have been.

—**MELISSA MacDONALD**
Portland, Maine

that your puppy will need to relieve himself during the night. While he's in his bed, keep his leash on and tie it to the leg of your bed so that he can't wander off. He'll be reluctant to soil the area so close to where he's sleeping. Be prepared for accidents, though, and plan on getting up at least once to take him outside or lead him to a separate area where you've put down newspapers.

SETTLING IN

FOR CATS ONLY

A Cat Transition Plan

A jittery cat in new surroundings will often run and hide under a bed or behind the sofa. Help make your cat's transition less scary by introducing him to your home in stages. Bring him home in a cat carrier lined with a cozy piece of clothing or a blanket. Once home, set the carrier down and open the door, but let him come out on his own and get acclimated at his own pace. In the beginning, he'll feel more secure if the environment isn't too overwhelming. Keep him in a small room or other enclosed area. As your cat becomes more comfortable, expand his world by opening doors and letting him wander about.

Have a Sleep Over

There may be nothing more distressing to a pet owner than the plaintive meows of a kitten. If you hear your new friend crying at night, you may be dealing with a case of separation anxiety (she misses her mom). Bring the kitten to bed with you, and you'll accomplish two things: First, you'll greatly comfort the kitten; second, you'll strengthen the bond between you and your new pet.

If you don't want the kitten to sleep with you, some affection may end the crying.

Too Sleepy to Be Weepy

One strategy for dealing with a weepy kitten is to play with him a lot during the day to burn up all his excess energy. By bedtime, he'll be so worn-out that he'll be too tired to cry.

SETTLING IN

FOR FERRETS ONLY

Calm Ferret Nerves

A scared young ferret will feel more secure in a cage where she can sit and look around at her new surroundings for a while. Let her settle in with a comfortable piece of bedding, preferably one with a familiar smell brought from the animal's previous home. Don't give your ferret free rein outside the cage, but do give her plenty of attention. At first, she'll need a lot of comforting, but as she gets used to the new sights, sounds, smells, and people, she'll want to play . . . and play . . . and play.

COST CUTTERS

Frugal Food for Ferrets

Many ferret owners agree that good quality cat food is fine for their pets and cheaper than commercial ferret food. If you plan to give cat food to your ferret, compare the nutritional values of various brands and choose the one with ingredients most closely matching ferret food. Also, stick to chicken-based varieties and avoid those made with fish. It will help minimize the ferret's own rather fishy smell.

Just Make Sure to Turn Off the Alarm

On those occasions when you can't be with your baby ferret to pick the animal up and offer some comfort, leave behind a soft, fuzzy toy. Also place a wound-up, ticking clock (not one with batteries or an electrical cord) near your pet's pen. The clock will approximate the sound of his mom's beating heart and may lull him to sleep.

FOR FISH ONLY

Let Them Test the Waters

When bringing home new fish, don't immediately release them from the bag into the tank. Instead, lower the entire bag into the tank and let it float there for about an hour before releasing the fish. This will allow them to adjust more gradually to the difference in water temperature.

FOR POCKET PETS

They Need Time to Themselves

The trip home from the pet store or breeder can be pretty stressful for a hamster, gerbil, or guinea pig. To

help your new pet relax, put the animal in a cage and refrain from playing with her or handling her for the first day or so. Unlike dogs, these critters prefer to be left alone for a while and won't enjoy being smothered with attention. Keep your pet's cage in a quiet place where she won't be rattled by rambunctious kids, barking dogs, and hissing cats. After she's had a chance to settle in, she'll be relaxed and ready to socialize.

FOR REPTILES ONLY

It's a Jungle in That Tank

$ Because most reptiles consume food in live form, special care is needed when feeding them. Give your pet 24 hours to adjust to his new surroundings before offering him any food. At that point, offer him a small amount to try out. If he accepts it, give him more—enough for an average-size meal. If the animal doesn't eat it within the first five minutes, remove it and try again the next day. Your pet can become stressed by the presence of potential prey if he's not ready to eat. In some cases, the prey may even attack the predator. (He's pretty stressed, too.)

PET VS. PET

In the cartoons, it's dog vs. cat and cat vs. mouse. In real life, most types of pets can learn to live together in peace and harmony—or at least to tolerate each other. The important thing is to proceed with caution when introducing a new pet to another in your household. A number of factors are at work here, including territory, sex, age, and individual personality. Even loving families get into spats, so why should we expect our pets to behave any better?

FOR PETS IN GENERAL

This Will Hurt Only for a Minute

❑ Before bringing a new pet into a household that already has resident animals, be sure the established pets are up-to-date on all their vaccinations.

SETTLING IN

Treat 'Em Like Garbo

❑ When you bring any new pet into a house that already has pets, you'll need to establish an "isolation booth" where the newcomer can acclimate to the house or be secluded if the other animals are harassing her. A spare bathroom works for a little while (even tiny kittens get bored with the small space quickly), but a laundry room is better because it's usually a little larger. In general, any spot will do as long as it has a door that shuts (or can be gated), easy-to-clean floors, and an absence of heavy foot traffic.

❑ Unless you're using a gate, outfit the door with a spring (available from a hardware or home supply store) so that it will automatically shut behind humans before troublemaking animals sneak in (or out).

Let's Get Acquainted . . . Slowly

❑ Start the "getting acquainted" process by bringing the new pet within sight—but not within fighting range—of the resident animal. Hold the new pet firmly so that she can't escape and reassure her by stroking her while the resident pet gets a peek. (This does not mean that the resident pet will take this as an endorsement and immediately love the other animal. He's much more likely to get jealous. But he has to see her sometime, and if you pet her, at least one of the two will be calm.) Then gradually work up to putting the animals near each other for a few minutes, hours, and days.

FOR DOGS AND CATS

Fluffy, Meet Rambo

Between dogs and cats, size doesn't always determine who prevails. A rambunctious new puppy may regard your cat as a toy to play with and be rewarded with a swat on the nose. The cat will hiss and scratch until the puppy backs off. Let the cat establish her own boundaries. It's best not to interfere unless one of them seems about to get hurt. Sooner or later, a pup that wants to be friends will learn to adapt his behavior to win the cat's acceptance, and eventually the two will get used to each other.

FOR DOGS ONLY

This House Isn't Big Enough for Both of Us

If you're adopting a new puppy and also have an adult dog, expect some sibling rivalry. The older dog won't like an intruder moving in on his territory and vying for your attention, and he may even try to attack

YOU'VE GOTTA LOVE 'EM

And Now for the Balcony Scene

I was living in a fifth-floor apartment a few years ago with my two cats, Barnum and Bailey. The apartment had a sliding glass door out onto a narrow balcony that was surrounded only by a narrow iron railing. I generally kept the cats off the balcony, but I had opened the sliding door just a crack to let in some air. Bailey was in one of her moods that day. Suddenly, she bolted out the door and over the railing. Cringing, I looked over the edge, expecting to see a little kitty body on the grass. She wasn't there. Then I heard a faint meow below. Somehow she had caught the railing of the balcony on the next floor down and had swung herself in to safety. I went downstairs to get her, and amazingly she didn't have a scratch. I, however, had some explaining to do. I promised my neighbors that Bailey would never just drop by again—not without calling first.

—**ANN-MARIE CUNNIFF**
Medford, Massachusetts

the pup. Keep them apart if necessary, then bring them together for short periods when you can supervise. In the meantime, feed them separately and give them both plenty of attention. Let the senior dog have something with the puppy's scent on it to help him get used to the little guy (in advance, if possible). At the very least, he'll learn to tolerate the newcomer, and as the puppy gets bigger and stronger, their relationship will stabilize.

Seniority Rules

As busy as you might be with housebreaking or puppy adoration, make extra time for your old friend and make certain that each animal gets some one-on-one attention.

The Blue Plate Special Is for Binky

When you adopt a second (or third or fourth) pup, be sure to give each dog a separate food bowl. You need

A WORD FROM DR. MAUE

Don't Let Fluffy Abuse Your New Pup

DR. LISA MAUE
Veterinarian in private practice in Medford, Massachusetts, for more than a decade

When someone brings in a new puppy with scratches on his nose and eye ulcers, I know exactly what's gone wrong. Many times people bring a new puppy into a house that already has a cat, not realizing that the cat is likely to be jealous and territorial. By contrast, the puppy is nosy, inquisitive, and ready to play. He isn't prepared for the swats and scratches that the cat will deliver. The best way to avoid injury is to make sure the cat's nails are trimmed *before* you bring home the puppy. That way, when Fluffy takes a swipe at Fido, she'll be able to teach the newcomer some manners without actually hurting the pup.

to know who's eating what. Besides, you don't want your pets to get in a lather over the second most prized possession in their lives. (The first, of course, is you.)

FOR CATS ONLY

Cat + Cat = Spat

Cats are territorial creatures and don't take kindly to newcomers. But if you'd like more feline company, it's important to know that your existing cat is more likely to accept a kitten than a rival of similar size and age. Supervise their meetings and don't leave them alone until you're sure it's safe.

Over time, most cats will learn to live together, if not love each other. Once they're past the open-warfare stage, let them work out their relationship and decide who's top cat. They may go through life avoiding each other and get into an occasional spat. Or they could become best buddies. It depends on the individual cats, but the odds of their getting along are much better if they're neutered or spayed.

FOR BIRDS ONLY

Dancing Beak to Beak?

Birds are not aggressive by nature, but birds in captivity may hurt each other if they're afraid or feel threatened. They could bite off a toe or beak, chew tail feathers, or pluck or even kill each other. If you want birds to live together, introduce them slowly and cautiously. After a new bird completes the requisite two-week isolation period to be sure she's disease-free, see how the new and old birds respond to each other when put side by side in separate cages. If they seem to interact well and sleep near each other at the sides of their cages, try a supervised visit with two people, each holding a bird. If that goes well, put them on a play gym together. If they become aggressive, clap your hands or yell to distract them, or try squirting them with a spray bottle. Whatever happens, they'll let you know whether they enjoy each other's company.

Bird-Dogging and Other Issues

A dog or cat should never be left alone with a bird unless the bird is safely out of reach in a sturdy cage. This is true even among animals that have lived together for a while and appear to be well adapted. A sudden noise or incident can easily awaken an animal's predatory instincts and upset the harmony. A dog or cat can kill a bird, and a large bird can kill a dog or cat. (In fact, a firm nip from the bird on a tail or paw can teach the four-legged pet an important lesson.) Let the dog or cat interact with your bird only when you're there to supervise.

If there's a predator in your house, invest in a strong cage for your feathered friend—not one of those flimsy cages that will keep a parakeet or canary in but may not keep a dog or cat out. Hang the cage well out of reach of the predator and make sure that the dog or cat can't climb on anything to get at the bird.

FOR FERRETS ONLY

Make the New Guy Smell Like a Friend

Planning to add to your ferret collection? In general, an older (neutered) male will be more willing to welcome a newcomer than a female that's been raised as an "only child." But most ferrets can learn to get along over time. Start the new ferret out in a separate environment and make introductions on neutral ground while you supervise. Help each ferret get to know the other's smell by swapping bedding from their cages. You also can dab vanilla extract on their necks so that they'll smell more alike. With any luck, they'll get to be pals and play together.

Take special care to protect your ferret from dogs and cats. Ferrets are generally not afraid of other animals, and sometimes their friendly, trusting nature can get them into trouble. Instead of avoiding a potential predator, they'll approach it wanting to play. And it's only natural for dogs and cats to follow their hunting instincts and go after a ferret.

COMMON MISTAKES

Birds Need Health Care Reform!

Many bird owners drop the ball when it comes to basic health care for their winged friends. But even if she's small and didn't cost much, a bird needs and deserves good veterinary care. Neglecting your new pet's health will almost certainly shorten her life and could endanger your other birds, because avian viruses are airborne and easily transmitted from bird to bird. So before you bring home that new parakeet or cockatiel, make sure she has a clean bill of health.

Schedule an appointment so that you can stop at the vet's on your way home from the pet store and your new bird can get a complete checkup and tests. The new bird should not share air space with other birds until test results indicate that she's healthy. (This usually takes about two weeks.) If you already have birds at home, isolate the new one in a separate environment—perhaps at the home of a birdless friend. If the test results indicate a serious health problem, you'll know it was there when you bought the bird. In that case, return the bird to the breeder or pet store (and beware of getting another from the same source; there may be an epidemic going on).

With a little luck, you'll have a healthy new bird that's ready to settle into her new home. And with annual return visits to the vet, she should be around for a long, long time.

FOR POCKET PETS

Quarantine the New Kid

If you're adding a new guinea pig, hamster, or gerbil to a group, keep the new arrival isolated for 60 days before introducing her to your current flock. It's possible that the new pet could be carrying a disease, and if so, the symptoms will show themselves within 60 days. In the meantime, you'll keep the original crew safe from anything the new one might be carrying.

Gerbils Prefer Longtime Friends

Gerbils love company, and if they're put together when young, they'll get along swimmingly. However, gerbils that meet as adults will fight, and one may even

What to Name the Baby

Picking a name for your new pet is fun, but it's also important. Start using your pet's name as soon as possible: It helps to establish your relationship with him and alerts him to pay attention to your voice. If you don't already have a name in mind, here are a few approaches to picking one.

• Choose a "people" name you like (Lucy, Maggie, Sam, Max). Names that end in an "ee" sound tend to carry well when you call.

• Honor a historical figure or someone you admire (Cleopatra, Beethoven, Einstein). Check an encyclopedia for ideas.

• Consider a name related to your profession. (Was the first Sparky a firehouse dog? If you're a techie, try Cyber, Chip, or Splice.)

• For a pair of pets, take a team approach (George and Gracie, Dwight and Mamie).

• Pick a character from a favorite book or play (Heathcliff, Othello, Scarlett).

• Name the pet for a place you've always wanted to go or that has special significance for you (Dakota, Quito, Kerry, Minsk).

• Select a character from mythology (Zeus, Venus, Athena, Loki, Thor).

• Sports fan? Pick a favorite athlete or team (Babe, Knute, Arnie, Sox, Dodger).

• Choose a name that reflects the animal's coloring (Blackie, Cocoa, Shadow, Snowy, Sunny).

• Base the name on a characteristic of the animal (Fluffy, Curly, Wiggles, Jaws).

• When all else fails, ask a child to suggest a name (but be prepared for the consequences).

kill the other. So if your gerbils haven't grown up together, keep them in separate cages to avoid trouble.

FOR OTHER PETS

This Bird Is Not a Toy

○ Ferrets are curious and love to play with anything that looks like a toy. Unfortunately, your bird, hamster, or other small pet might qualify as a plaything. Protect your small caged pets by not allowing a ferret anywhere near them. The fast, wiry ferrets can get at smaller animals and birds even through the bars of a cage.

HEALTH

Before You Call the Vet

One of the most important aspects of caring for a pet is caring for the animal's health. This means being able to read the signs so that you know when your pet is healthy and when he is not. It means learning ways to remedy minor problems, as well as recognizing when simple solutions aren't enough and you need to call the vet.

Do you know how (and when) to take your dog or cat's temperature? Do you know what temperature is *normal* for your pet? Suppose you do take the animal's temperature and discover that he's abnormally hot or cold—what do you do then?

And body temperature is just the beginning. Do you know how to give your pet a basic health check in less than five minutes? Can you recognize changes in the animal's everyday appearance or behavior that could be signs of trouble? And do you know what it means if a snake turns pale, a dog has bad breath, or an iguana is constipated? Read on, and you'll find the answers to all these questions and more.

HEALTH

ACNE

Acne is not a problem that's reserved for teenage humans—though it may be a greater embarrassment to your teenager than to your tomcat. Acne in pets generally appears around the chin. Your dog may scratch the area more frequently than usual, causing or exacerbating an irritation. Your cat may develop little bumps on her chin, with some swelling and maybe some hair loss. Both of these situations are signs of acne.

FOR DOGS AND CATS

Don't Feed the Problem

Acne can result when animals eat out of old, scratched plastic food bowls (which collect bacteria). Feed your pet from a metal bowl or replace plastic

A WORD FROM DR. MAUE

Pet Acne? Chin Up!

DR. LISA MAUE
Veterinarian in private practice in Medford, Massachusetts, for more than a decade

When people call to say that their dogs or cats have pimples on their chins from eating out of plastic bowls, I tell them to give their pets the same treatment they would give their teenage kids. Pet owners sometimes think that we should prescribe some special medication—and I do prescribe antibiotics when the area is really inflamed and infected—but for just a few pimples, you are better off buying an over-the-counter product such as Stridex pads from your drugstore. Any product that is designed for acne and contains a bit of benzoyl peroxide will relieve the problem. Wipe the area with a pad (or dab on a little cream) once or twice a day until the pimples are gone.

bowls regularly, and always wash the bowl after each feeding.

Wash Away the Zits

Try gently washing (patting) an acne-infected area once or twice a day with warm water and pet shampoo on a clean washcloth. If the acne does not clear up, call your vet, who may prescribe something stronger.

ALLERGIES

Your pet may be allergic to many of the same things you are: dust mites, pollen, grasses, or certain foods. Instead of coughing or sneezing, however, pets usually scratch when they are allergic to something. They also may lick the tops or bite the bottoms of their paws, and they may even chew on their tails. Other signs of allergic reactions include hair falling out in patches; dry, scaly skin; a change in coat (a dog's coat may become dry if it's normally oily or become oily if it's normally dry); body odor; and weeping eyes (look for dark tear stains under your dog's eyes). A vet can perform tests to find out whether your pet is allergic and to what. Here are some treatments that can help relieve the problem.

FOR DOGS ONLY

Can the Corn

Corn, which is a common ingredient in dog foods, can cause allergic reactions. If your dog is showing signs of allergies, read the label on her food to be certain it does not contain corn. If it does, switch to a brand without corn.

Oatmeal Isn't Just for Breakfast

If your dog scratches herself often, try bathing her with an oatmeal-based shampoo made especially for animals. Such shampoos are available at pet stores and pet supply stores. The bath won't cure an allergy, but it can relieve your pet's symptoms and discomfort.

HEALTH

Use a Shampoo with Aloe

Aloe-based shampoos, available at pet stores and pet supply stores, can help relieve allergy symptoms such as itching and skin rashes in dogs. Or you can bathe your dog with your own aloe-based shampoo. Make sure you use a product that doesn't have unnecessary ingredients (for instance, don't choose a shampoo and conditioner or a shampoo for color-treated hair), which could aggravate the situation. Use the shampoo only when your dog is exhibiting the symptoms; suspend use when the animal seems fine.

A WORD FROM DR. EMERSON

That Was One Sensitive Cat

DR. WENDY EMERSON
Veterinarian who makes house calls in and around Topsfield, Massachusetts, to care for cats, dogs, and a wide range of exotic pets

In the summer, a lot of people come in with dogs and cats that seem to have chronic ear or eye infections, and I have to tell them that their animals might be suffering from allergies. Just like people, dogs and cats can be allergic to everything from dust mites in the air to ragweed. Dogs can even be allergic to cat hair.

A cat named Leo was brought into my office one day with scabs all over his face and neck. His owner was afraid she'd have to have him put to sleep. We did a blood screen on Leo and discovered that he was allergic to almost everything, especially his food. We tried to hyposensitize him with some injections, but he was allergic to the shots. His owner began to panic. Finally, we put Leo on low doses of cortisone and tried different diets. Now he eats only boiled turkey and potatoes, which his faithful owner cooks for him.

APPETITE LOSS

HEALTH

Animals can stop eating for all kinds of reasons, and not all of them are cause for worry. Dogs can go several days without food and remain healthy. (If your dog refuses food longer than that, call the vet.) By contrast, cats that stop eating are usually sick. And when a snake refuses to eat, the animal's body temperature—and the heat level in his tank—may be too low. If your noncanine pet suddenly loses his appetite no matter what foods you offer, or if your puppy doesn't quickly regain his interest in eating, you need to pay attention.

COMMON MISTAKES

Don't Play Doctor

Some mail-order catalogs sell veterinary products such as injectible vaccines and other medications to individuals. Don't be tempted to save on vet bills by buying these and trying to use them on your own, unless you have checked with your vet to make sure she approves of your purchase and is satisfied that you know how to administer it. A mistake could be very harmful to your pet—and ultimately costly to you.

FOR CATS ONLY

This Cat's Not Fat

If your cat stops eating for more than a day, ask yourself whether there have been any sudden changes in her diet. (Did you change cat food brands? Did you suddenly shove Tuna Treat in front of her, when she's steadily and faithfully been eating Grand Grill for years? Did you take away her canned food and leave her only crunchies?) If you have changed your cat's diet, go back to her old favorites unless your vet has prescribed something else. (In that case, call the vet.)

If the animal's diet has remained the same, chances are something is wrong. Call your vet. Cats can suffer liver damage after even short periods without food.

FOR REPTILES ONLY

It's Too Cold to Eat

If your snake has stopped eating, it may be that the animal's body temperature has dropped too low and he cannot digest food properly. (Snakes are cold-blooded animals, and thus their body temperatures

ONE PERSON'S SOLUTION

Food for the Persnickety Palate

One year, our python named Monty went on a hunger strike. She refused to eat for five months. (Yes, I do mean months.) At first I thought that her body temperature had dropped too low because her tank was adjacent to an outside wall of our house. (Snakes will stop eating for long periods of time if they get cold.)

I tried heating her environment, but that didn't work. I kept offering her the mice we bred ourselves as food for Monty, but she declined.

Then one day I had an idea: Maybe Monty had lost her appetite for the same old family tree of mice. So I bought a mouse at the pet store and placed it in her cage. The mouse lasted for about eight seconds, and then it was gone. Shortly thereafter, I took Monty to the vet for a checkup, and the vet confirmed my suspicion: She was so used to "our" mice that she no longer recognized them as food.

—LESLIE SMYTHE
Medfield, Massachusetts

reflect the temperatures of their environments.) Try turning up the heat in the tank a couple of degrees.

ARTHRITIS

Arthritis is a painful disease of the joints that often develops after a pet has been injured or in older animals after years of wear and tear. It's caused when the bony ball of a joint actually rubs against the joint socket. Both cats and dogs can get arthritis. Dogs that are born with

HEALTH

the condition known as hip dysplasia are very prone to developing this ailment.

FOR DOGS AND CATS

Thinner Bodies Ache Less

An arthritic dog or cat has more trouble moving around when she gains weight. Try to help your pet maintain her optimum weight with a healthy diet and regular activity.

FOR DOGS ONLY

Walk On

Regular activity helps keep joints from getting stiff, so be sure your arthritic dog gets some exercise every day. Walk your pet at a gentle but steady pace for about 20 minutes daily.

Don't Give Fido a Hard Day's Night

If your dog has arthritis, provide her with a soft, comfortable place to sleep—either a commercial dog bed or a bed you make yourself by piling up blankets or arranging pillows. Sleeping on a hard floor will aggravate stiffness in arthritic joints.

Take Two and Call Me in the Morning

With initial permission from your vet, you can give your arthritic dog low doses of coated buffered aspirin when arthritis is causing pain. (Don't substitute unbuffered aspirin, ibuprofen, or acetaminophen, which could be harmful—even fatal—to your pet.)

5 *Quick Checks on the Health of Your Cat or Dog*

A quick check can tell you whether your cat or dog is probably healthy. Here are five key areas to check.

1. Coat. It should be shiny.

2. Eyelids. The so-called "third" eyelid, which looks like a membrane, should not be closed or swollen.

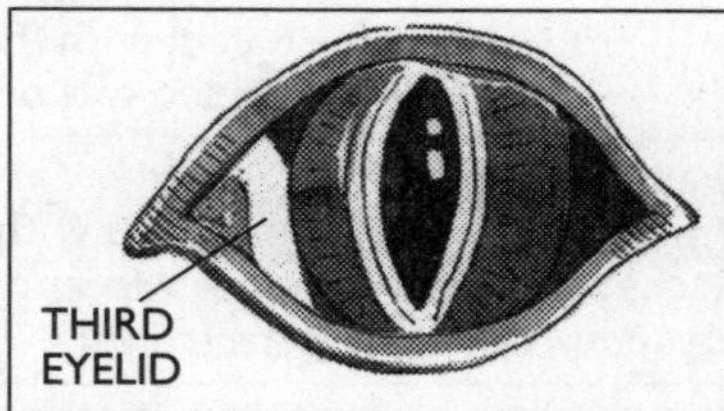

The extra eyelid: Check for swelling.

3. Eyes. They should be clear, with no discharge or discoloration.

4. Gums. They should be pink. If you press on them gently, the color should return immediately.

5. Nose. It should be cold and moist.

TIME TO CALL THE VET

Steer Clear of Contagious Cats

How can you ensure that the neighbor's cat doesn't give your kitty anything worse than fleas? In addition to making sure that your pets are properly vaccinated, you can keep them indoors, or at least avoid letting them run loose outside without supervision. You also should watch for signs of the following diseases. If you suspect that your pet may have become infected, get the animal to the vet immediately.

DISEASE	DESCRIPTION	SYMPTOMS
Calicivirus	A respiratory illness that is contracted when a cat breathes or swallows the virus.	Runny eyes and nose, sneezing, loss of appetite, mouth ulcers, drooling, and depression.
Feline leukemia	A virus that attacks a cat's immune system and is spread through contact with the saliva, blood, urine, or feces of an infected cat.	None, but associated problems may be observable. Watch for respiratory problems or mouth, eye, or skin infections.
Infectious anemia	A disease caused by a parasite that destroys the red blood cells and results in anemia. It is spread by contact with the blood of infected cats or by flea bites.	Loss of appetite and weight, depression, and difficulty breathing.
Panleukopenia (includes parvovirus and feline distemper)	A viral disease contracted by contact with the secretions or feces of an infected cat.	Severe diarrhea, fever, loss of appetite, vomiting, dehydration, and depression.
Pneumonitis	A disease caused by the organism chlamydia, which affects the tissues surrounding the eyeball and the lining of the eyelids and is contracted by contact with discharges from the eyes, nose, or mouth of an infected cat.	Squinting, teary eyes, and red eyelids, with eye discharge eventually turning yellow or green. Sometimes also sneezing or coughing.
Rhinotracheitis	A virus that involves the eyes, nasal passages, and windpipe. It is spread by contact with discharges from the eyes, nose, or mouth of an infected cat.	Sneezing, coughing, and runny eyes and nose.

FOR CATS ONLY

Play's the Thing

Arthritic cats need regular, gentle exercise to keep their joints from stiffening, so play with your pet every day for about 20 minutes. Toss him a ball made of aluminum foil. Hang a toy on a string from a doorknob and let him bat it around. Or drag a pull toy along the floor for him to pounce on.

Encourage Cozy Catnaps

Your arthritic cat may have a harder time than usual jumping up to the back of your couch or to the foot of your bed for a nap. Offer a bed or two nearer the floor, but tucked into the corner of a room or under a table, where she'll feel safe. You can buy a commercial bed at a pet store or from a catalog or make one yourself. A soft basket (such as a doll basket), with or without a towel lining, may be a favorite.

BAD BREATH

Bad breath in pets is just as offensive as it is in humans. But besides being a turnoff, halitosis can be a sign of a health problem. It may indicate an accumulation of tartar on your pet's teeth, which can result in gingivitis, or gum disease. (Bad teeth and gums also can produce bacteria that your pet will swallow, causing other health concerns.) Or it may be a sign of digestive problems. Here are some ways to get your pet's breath smelling sweeter again.

It looks like a thimble, but it acts as a toothbrush for your pet.

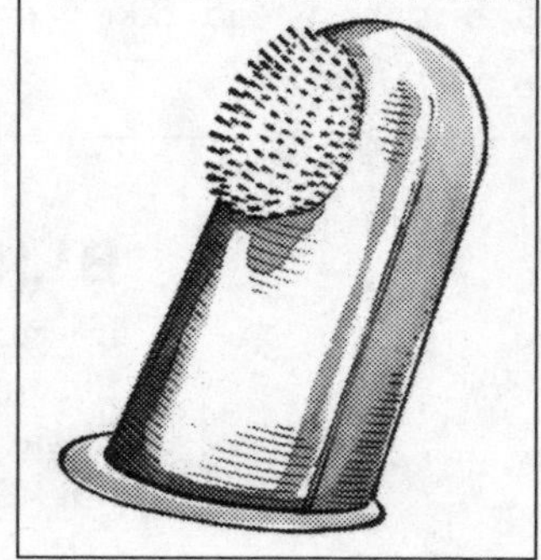

FOR DOGS AND CATS

Try a Little Tartar Control

If you check the gums of a pet with bad breath, you may see tartar—a hard, yellow-brown or grayish-white substance. If so, go to a pet store and buy a specially made rubber thimble and toothpaste, then brush the animal's teeth according to the package instructions. (You can substitute a washcloth wrapped around your finger for the rubber thimble, but

HEALTH

don't substitute human toothpaste for pet toothpaste. Toothpaste for people often contains ingredients that may be harmful to your pet, such as salicylates.)

Be the Captain of Crunch

For tartar control, feed your dog or cat some form of dry pet food, or "crunchies," every day. Or give your dog bones to chew.

BEAK PROBLEMS

If a bird's beak is allowed to grow unrestricted, it can become so long that it will curl back under his chin, not only causing discomfort but also making it difficult for him to open his mouth. But your pet is perfectly capable of handling routine beak maintenance himself if you supply the proper equipment.

TIME TO CALL THE VET

In(cyst) On Professional Treatment

Small birds such as finches and canaries are susceptible to feather cysts, which look like clumps of dried skin containing feathers. If your bird seems to have one, don't try to pick it off, which could cause bleeding (a dangerous situation for tiny birds). Instead, take your pet to the vet.

FOR BIRDS ONLY

File This under Simple Solutions

To keep your bird's beak in shape, place a cuttlebone or lava bar (available at pet stores) in your pet's cage. The bird will "sand" her own beak.

He's in a Scrape

If your young bird's beak becomes overgrown even when there's something available to scrape on, call the vet. Your pet may have a tumor or liver disease, either of which should be treated as soon as possible.

BLISTER DISEASE

If your pet snake develops little white blisters that raise the animal's scales, it's time to clean the snake's house. Blisters are caused by a cage that is too wet or that is not kept clean of feces.

FOR REPTILES ONLY

Don't Be a Slumlord

If you see blisters on your snake, clean out the animal's cage and put dry newspaper on the bottom, along with a small bowl of drinking water. Then keep the cage dry!

When you spot blisters on your snake, use a wet cloth to clean your pet's body and apply a Betadine solution with a cloth once a day. (Betadine is an antibacterial cleanser. It's typically used for people, not snakes, and is available at pharmacies.) As your snake goes through her regular shedding process, the blisters will disappear.

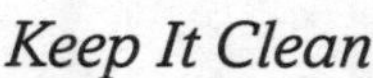

Keep It Clean

In an extreme case, the snake may go through several cycles of shedding before his skin is completely healthy again. Keep cleaning your pet on a regular basis until the blisters are replaced by healthy skin. If the snake seems sick and depressed, it's a good idea to discuss the problem with your vet. The infection may have spread.

A WORD FROM DR. MAUE

DR. LISA MAUE
Veterinarian in private practice in Medford, Massachusetts, for more than a decade

Sniff, Sniff— What's That Smell?

If your dog or cat develops an odd odor, it may not be a hygiene problem, but an infection. It's especially important to pay attention to your pet's odor if you know that the animal has a cut. The rule is that once you can smell a wound, it's not going to get better on its own. That's when you need to call the vet.

HEALTH

BODY ODOR

Bad body odor in your pet may simply mean that your little darling rolled in something unsavory. Or it may indicate a bacterial skin infection or ear infection. In either case, for your pet's sake and yours, you'll want to take steps to relieve the situation.

FOR DOGS AND CATS

Sniff Out the Problem

If your pet smells awful, try to determine where the odor is coming from. Sniff the ears and part some of the animal's fur to get a look at and a whiff of the skin. If his ears smell funky or his skin appears to have a foul-smelling rash, call your vet for treatment, which is likely to be some type of prescription antibiotic.

FOR DOGS ONLY

It's Bath Time

If your dog doesn't have an obvious infection (skin rash or foul-smelling ears), bathe and dry the animal, then check to see if she still smells bad. Still notice an odor after the bath? Call your vet. Rover may have an infection you can't locate, and your vet will need to treat it.

FOR CATS ONLY

Do You Hear What I Hear?

Cats are meticulous about grooming themselves, so barring an accidental fall into the compost bin, feline body odor is often the result of an ear infection or abscess. Sniff around your cat's ears just to be sure, then call your vet for treatment. If you can't locate the source of the odor, call your vet anyway, as there may be an infection at another site.

BODY TEMPERATURE

Every species has a certain body temperature range that is considered normal. The temperature of a warm-blooded animal such as a cat or dog should remain constant regardless of the animal's surroundings. When such a pet develops a fever, he requires a vet's attention to get things back to normal. The temperature of a cold-blooded animal such as an iguana fluctuates with the temperature of the pet's surroundings, which means that you can often solve the problem simply by turning up the heat.

A WORD FROM DR. EMERSON

Iguanas Love Warm-Ups

DR. WENDY EMERSON

Veterinarian who makes house calls in and around Topsfield, Massachusetts, to care for cats, dogs, and a wide range of exotic pets

One of the reasons I like to do house calls is that I can see exactly what in the animal's home environment might be causing problems. This is especially true for reptiles. Rather than ask a million questions at the office, I can practically diagnose the problem from the front door. That's what happened the first time I visited Jim, the four-foot iguana. Jim's owners thought that a big reptile would be more comfortable if given the run of the house. But iguanas are tropical animals; they need a temperature of 85° to 90°F to be comfortable, and most people's homes aren't that warm. That's why the usual solution is to keep an iguana in a heated cage.

In this case, instead of a cage, Jim had a shelf to sleep on and one heat lamp to keep him warm. But the lamp had no ultraviolet spectrum, and that's what an iguana needs to absorb nutrients and calcium. As a result, Jim was dehydrated, malnourished, cold, and pretty cranky. During the exam, he bit me as hard as I've ever been bitten. But I felt sorry for him. His owners' ignorance cost me only four stitches, but Jim had been cold and sick his whole life.

HEALTH

FOR DOGS AND CATS

How to Take Your Terrier's Temperature

When dogs and cats get sick, they can run fevers just like people do. The only way to tell for sure whether your pet has a fever is to take her temperature (you can't tell by feeling her nose or forehead). You can do this with a rectal thermometer made for humans, lubricated lightly. If your pet's temperature is above 101.5°F, she has a fever, and you should call the vet.

FOR FISH ONLY

Doin' the Shimmy Ain't Cool

Your tropical fish is cold-blooded, with a body temperature that mirrors the water temperature. If you find your fish hanging out near the top of the tank with his face at the water's surface and his body wiggling, he has shimmy, a condition that means he's cold. Check with your pet store to see what the optimum water (and body) temperature is for your fish, then crank up the heater on the tank.

911 for Pets

Your pet can have a health emergency just as you can. So post your veterinarian's phone number in the same prominent place you have your other emergency numbers. That way you, a baby-sitter, or anyone else in the house can call the vet quickly when necessary.

BROKEN BONES

Cats are notorious for surviving falls from high places, but that doesn't mean they always come through unscathed. Dogs have less of that wonderful ability to bounce back from falls. And every day, another family pet gets a little too close to a moving vehicle. When your favorite animal survives such a hair-raising incident, you'll need to know how to check for broken bones and what to do when you find them.

FOR DOGS AND CATS

Hit-and-Run

If your cat or dog has been hit by a car or has taken a fall and you notice that she's holding one limb at an odd angle, take the animal to the vet immediately for

YOU'VE GOTTA LOVE 'EM

Cat on an Ice-Cold Roof

Late one winter night, our cat, Pokey, who loved to climb up on the roof of our house, slipped and fell from the icy peak. She slid all the way down the shingles and over the gutter, then dropped another two stories into the cement stairwell leading to the cellar. When we got to her, she was a mess. We carried her inside, cleaned her up, checked for wounds, and determined that her back leg was broken. By now it was the middle of the night, so we settled her in a nest of towels and blankets until morning.

First thing in the morning, I made a stretcher for her from a pillowcase and took her to the vet's office, where I left her for the day. When the vet called later, he told me that he'd made a cast for her leg but she had chewed it off, so he was in the process of making another one.

When I got her home, I tried to keep Pokey quiet. For several weeks, though, I heard the *thump thump thump* of her cast bumping along the wood floors as she limped from room to room. Finally, winter turned to spring, and it was time for the cast to come off. I took Pokey back to the vet for the great release, then brought her home and watched her gingerly romp around the yard on her newly freed leg. Then I took off to do some errands.

When I returned, I couldn't find Pokey anywhere. Worried, I asked my husband whether he knew her whereabouts. Rolling his eyes, he glanced upward. There she was, stretched out and sunning herself on the peak of the roof.

—ELIZABETH B. BUCHANAN
Mendham, New Jersey

HEALTH

x-rays and treatment. (Don't attempt to splint the limb yourself. An incorrect splint can cause further damage.) If you can, carry your cat or dog to the car, supporting the possibly broken leg so that it doesn't dangle. If your dog is too large to carry or won't allow you to carry her because she's in pain, try to coax her to the car with a treat or favorite object.

Try the Touch Test

If your cat or dog has been hit by a car or taken a major fall, it's possible that his pelvis has been broken. Unlike a person, a cat or dog is able to walk with a broken pelvis, so the only way you'll know if your pet has a problem is to check the area itself. With the animal standing, gently press down on the pet's rear end. If he

7 *Essential Items for the Pet First Aid Kit*

When the cat gets cut or the dog is stung by bees, you may not have time for a quick trip to the pharmacy. Instead, take a few minutes now to visit the drugstore and stock up on the right products. Then store them together in a container designated for this purpose.

Make sure everyone in the family knows where Spot's first aid kit is kept, and make sure the container is closed and secure against curious young hands. Also, as with the products in your own medicine cabinet, be sure to replace any medicine before it reaches the expiration date on the bottle. Here's what the well-stocked first aid kit should contain.

1. Benadryl for bites and stings. The average dose is 1 milligram per pound of your pet's weight.

2. Neosporin for cuts.

3. Cotton balls for cleaning discharge, cuts, and the like.

4. Nonstick sterile gauze pads for wounds.

5. Lightweight adhesive tape that won't stick to wounds.

6. Coated buffered aspirin. You'll probably need 81-milligram tablets, but this will depend on what your vet recommends for your pet. Do not give a pet unbuffered aspirin, acetaminophen, or ibuprofen. And never give aspirin to cats without a veterinarian's supervision.

7. Your vet's phone number.

collapses or reacts as if in pain, there could be a break (and there's clearly an injury of some type). Carry him gently to the car, supporting the pelvic area, and take him to the vet immediately for x-rays and treatment.

HEALTH

BRUISES

Your pet can get a bruise just like you can. The problem is, you may not realize that your pet has been bruised because the injury is hidden beneath her fur. But if your pet seems to be favoring a spot on her body, or if you know that she's bumped against something or had a fall, look for a bruise. Be gentle. Spread the fur carefully and feel for an area that seems tender to the touch.

FOR DOGS AND CATS

This Guy's a Real Bruiser

- You can soothe the pain from a fresh bruise by applying an ice pack to the injured area. A bruise is formed by bleeding under the skin. Cooling the affected area causes the blood vessels to constrict and minimizes the extent of the bruise.
- Later, after the bruise has fully formed, try soaking a washcloth in water as hot as you can stand, then holding it against the affected area for five to ten minutes. Do this a couple of times a day for several days. Both dogs and cats seem to like this treatment, and it helps reduce the pain of a bruise while the injury heals.

BURRS IN FUR

When dogs and longhaired cats get burrs in their fur during outdoor romps, the problem is both unsightly (to you) and annoying (to your pet). Here's what you can do to get rid of these nasty nettles.

COMMON MISTAKES

Don't Cut It Too Close

If you use grooming clippers on your dog or rabbit—whether for grooming purposes, to remove matted fur, or to prepare a sore or rash for cleaning—be careful to avoid giving your pet a "clipper burn" by shaving the skin too close. If you do make this mistake, don't panic. Gently bathe the skin and apply an antibiotic cream such as Neosporin (available at pharmacies).

Your Furry Friend's Regular Checkup

Certain aspects of your dog's or cat's health should be checked by the vet once a year. Make sure you schedule time for your vet to do the following:

- Listen to heart and lungs
- Evaluate a stool sample (for worms or other parasites)
- Give a rabies vaccination (depending on the laws of your state) and any other vaccinations for which your pet may be due
- Look at teeth
- Administer flea and tick control (seasonally, depending on where you live)
- Give a heartworm test (dogs only)
- Administer a heartworm preventive
- Check carefully for bumps, lumps, or other abnormalities

In addition, many vets recommend that you have your pet's eyes checked by a veterinary ophthalmologist every few years so that the specialist can catch any cataracts or glaucoma early. Ask your regular vet for the name of a good specialist.

FOR DOGS ONLY

Brandish the Brush

If your dog comes in from a run with burrs in his fur, comb them out with a metal comb immediately. Letting them accumulate will cause the fur to mat and pull the skin (which is uncomfortable for the dog).

Don't Hesitate to Lubricate

If burrs are badly tangled in your dog's fur, rub a little vegetable oil on your fingers and work the lubrication slowly through the fur until you can pull the burrs out.

Cut Loose

When all else fails, you may have to cut stubborn burrs out of a dog's coat. To avoid accidents, wait until the dog is calm before you try this approach. Use scissors with blunt tips (such as some types of kitchen shears or even children's scissors) rather than sharp-ended sewing shears. Work slowly, being certain not to cut too close to the skin. (To avoid mistaking skin for a fur mat, try gently pinching an area with your fingers. It's better for an animal to protest a pinch than a cut.) Don't pull up on the fur. A dog's skin is loose, so if you pull up on it, you're likely to cut it at the same time you cut the fur.

FOR CATS ONLY

Brush Out Burrs

For the most part, cats like to take care of their own grooming. But if your longhaired cat has gotten herself in a tangle with a burr or two, you can help by gently working through the mess with a wire brush. (She probably won't let you cut the fur or lubricate it the way a dog will.) If you get the process going with a brush, she may be able to finish it herself with her teeth. Just watch to be sure that she doesn't swallow a burr (take it out of her mouth if need be).

CAR INJURIES

It's every pet owner's nightmare: the knock on the door or the call on the phone to tell you that a treasured cat or dog has been hit by a car. If it happens to your pet, don't panic. And don't let yourself become awash in guilt over where or why your pet was loose in the first place. There's plenty of time to analyze the accident and make some changes later. Instead, focus on your pet's immediate needs. If it's clear that Tabby or Fido has serious injuries, get him to the nearest emergency animal clinic immediately. If he doesn't *appear* to have any injuries, call the vet anyway to report the incident and ask whether you should take the animal in for treatment. Then monitor your pet's behavior and condition for at least 24 hours.

COMMON MISTAKES

Nearer My Vet to Thee

Your cat has a fishhook in her lip, or your dog has been hit by a car. You know it's an emergency, but your vet is located 30 minutes away. Don't drive the distance. Instead, take your pet to the nearest vet available. Some communities even have emergency veterinary clinics for just this purpose (look in the Yellow Pages under Veterinarians). It's also smart to be prepared: Write down the phone number and address ahead of time and keep it someplace accessible, such as in the front of your phone book or on a bulletin board near the phone.

FOR DOGS AND CATS

I Don't Like the Looks of This

Your pet has survived being hit by a car, but you're concerned about possible injuries. Quickly and gently, check the animal over—both looking and feeling for cuts, swelling in any area, and bruising or tender spots. Make note of your observations so that you can recount them later to the vet.

Is Your Pet in Shock?

Even if you see no obvious injuries, check your pet for signs of

shock: dilated pupils, shallow and rapid breathing, excessive quietness, rapid heart rate, or shivering. If she exhibits any combination of these signs, wrap your hurt pal in a blanket to keep her warm and take her to the vet immediately.

Also inspect your pet's gums. If they are gray or white or won't revert to a normal pink color when you press on them, it's a sign that the animal is in shock, probably from lack of oxygen or from internal injuries.

If She's Hiding, Maybe She's Hurting

In addition to checking over your pet's body, watch her behavior. Does she go off into a corner and curl up? Does she hide under the couch? When animals retreat to "tight" areas like these, it's another sign that they are injured. Even if you see no obvious physical injuries, call the vet if your pet's behavior changes after the accident.

Put a Sock on It

If your dog or cat has been hit by a car, he probably hurts somewhere, and no matter how much he normally trusts you, his fear may cause him to try to bite you. To prevent this, make a soft muzzle from a tube sock, panty hose leg, or cotton T-shirt ripped into strips. Tie this makeshift muzzle around the dog's snout and behind his head. Be careful to muzzle your pet in such a way that you don't hinder the animal's breathing.

An improvised muzzle, made from any soft fabric, will keep your frightened pet from biting.

Alternatively, you can buy a premade soft muzzle at a pet supply store and keep it in your animal first aid kit.

Injured Pet On Board

If your pet is injured by a car and unable to move under her own steam, or if you suspect internal or head injuries, it's best to slide the animal onto a board or

To keep your injured dog stable while you transport her to the vet, place her on a folded-up table. Keep the animal secure with pantyhose or strips of old bedsheets.

something firm to transport her to the vet. Use a plank, an old door, an ironing board, a child's sled, or a small table with folding legs. Be sure to strap your pet to the board—once near the front of her body and once near the hind end—so that she doesn't slide off. Possible emergency straps include several belts buckled together, a bedsheet torn into strips, panty hose, or, for smaller dogs, bungee cords. If nothing else is available, use a blanket.

Give Her a Lift

If your larger dog is injured but mobile, you can skip the board. Just have two people lift him and slide him into the backseat of a car so that you can get him to the vet.

CHOKING

When a cat gets into something that's supposed to be off-limits, she's likely to swallow it whole. This, of course, presents other problems, but it's unlikely to lead to choking. By contrast, a dog can get into serious trouble when trying to chew or swallow a foreign object, such as that old tennis ball she just tore apart. If this happens, you can take some steps to relieve the situation—and prevent it from recurring.

FOR DOGS ONLY

All Choked Up

If your dog starts choking, try to open the animal's jaws and look for the object that's blocking the airway.

Before You Begin Pet CPR

If your pet suddenly stops breathing, follow these steps *immediately.*

1. Lay the animal in your lap, on the floor, or on a table.

2. Wrap a thin, clean cloth (such as a thin dish towel or handkerchief) around your fingers, then extend your pet's tongue from her mouth. (The cloth will protect your fingers from a possible bite if your pet begins to breathe again.) "Sweep" her mouth and throat clear of mucus with the cloth still wrapped around your fingers.

With a cloth around your hand, extend the tongue (A), then wipe inside the mouth (B).

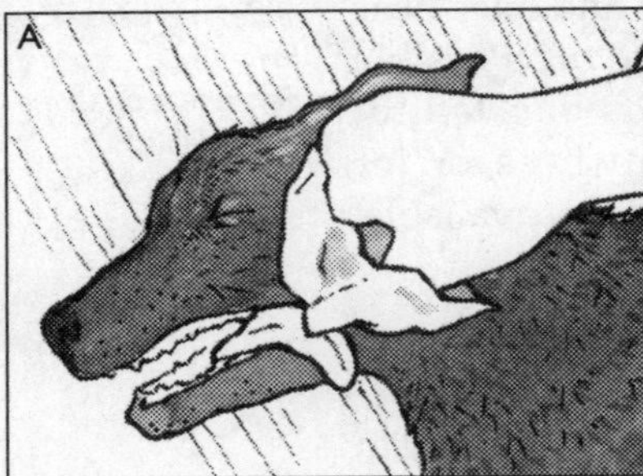

3. Look inside the mouth and throat area (and feel around with your fingers) for any foreign object or material.

4. If you find something, try to remove it gently with your fingers. If you do not find anything or cannot remove an object, you have completed the first important steps of artificial respiration.

5. Call the nearest vet or veterinary emergency clinic and tell the person who answers exactly what has happened. If the animal still is not breathing, the person on the other end of the phone may instruct you in subsequent steps of artificial respiration. If you've dislodged a foreign object and gotten your pet breathing again, you'll probably be instructed to bring the animal in immediately for treatment.

If possible, pull the object out of the dog's mouth. (Be careful to avoid being bitten.) If you can't remove the object, call the vet immediately; this is an emergency.

Sorry, Rover, Gum Balls Are Out

To prevent your dog from choking in the future, make sure he can't get hold of chicken bones, chewing gum, or tiny toys and other objects. If you give your dog a chew toy and he shreds it, take the shreds away—and avoid giving your pet more chews of that kind.

CLAW PROBLEMS

Your pet's claws—just like your nails—need regular care. In fact, lack of regular claw care can cause real health problems for your pet. In dogs and cats, too-long claws can grow around into the pads of the animals' paws, causing an infection. The overgrown claws can become ripped or torn, too, causing injury to the paw. Such problems aren't restricted to larger pets. Birds, guinea pigs, and iguanas need their claws trimmed regularly, too. Regular nail care also keeps the "quick" (the portion of the nail containing blood vessels) from growing longer and longer, ultimately preventing you from trimming the nails to the proper length. (The quick bleeds when cut—not exactly an enticement to clip away once things have gotten out of hand.)

FOR PETS IN GENERAL

If You Slip When You Clip

❑ What if you slip when you're clipping your pet's claws and cut the quick? It's a good idea to visit a pet supply store and pick up a styptic product such as Kwik Stop to stop nail bleeding, and to keep it on hand for emergencies. Be sure to check the product label and buy the right product for your type of pet. Some products are made just for dogs and cats, but others also are suitable for birds.

FOR DOGS ONLY

Deal with the Claws of the Problem

Sometimes a dog is born with an extra claw, called a dewclaw, along the side of the foot. If left alone, a dewclaw can get caught on things and tear out, bleeding profusely and causing injury to the foot.

A dewclaw can be surgically removed.

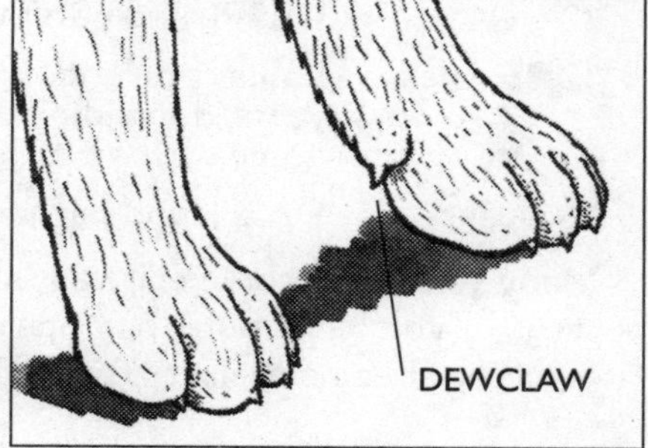

HEALTH

Some breeders remove dewclaws when their puppies are only a few days old because the procedure is simple and can be done without anesthesia. If your older dog still has a dewclaw, have it removed surgically by the vet. (You can even have it done at the same time as spaying or neutering.)

Keep Fido in Fine Trim

As a rule of thumb, it's a good idea to trim your dog's claws about every six weeks—or as soon as the claws start to snag on the rug. You may be able to go longer between trimmings if you take your pet outside for regular walks and exercise. Such activities help shed the claws' dead tissue.

Not-So-Long Shots: Recommended Vaccinations for Your Dog

One of the best ways to prevent serious illness in your dog is to have her vaccinated regularly. Your vet will give you specific recommendations for vaccinating your pet, but here are some guidelines for the first round. Most require yearly boosters, depending on the type of vaccine your vet uses.

AGE	VACCINATION
6 weeks	DA2PM (to prevent canine distemper, adnovirus, parainfluenza, measles)
8 weeks	DA2PL (to prevent canine distemper, adnovirus, parainfluenza, leptovirus)
8 weeks	Parvovirus infection prevention
8 weeks	Heartworm prevention; oral medication begins, usually continuing daily or monthly for life
12 weeks	DA2PL and parvovirus infection prevention
12–16 weeks	Rabies prevention; boosters follow every one to three years, depending on state law, or if your pet comes home with a bite wound
16 weeks	DA2PL and parvovirus infection prevention

Many vets also recommend vaccinations for kennel cough and coronavirus (if you have more than one dog or if your dog spends any time boarding elsewhere) and for Lyme disease (if you live in a high-risk area).

Soften Her Up First

The best time to clip your dog's claws is after a bath or a swim, when the nails are soft. Use clippers bought at a pet store (rather than ones intended for humans) and be careful to avoid cutting into the "quick" (the area containing blood vessels, which will bleed if cut). If your dog has clear nails, you can see the quick, so this shouldn't be a problem. If the animal has black nails, just cut a little off the end of the nail, perhaps trimming a bit more often than every six weeks.

COST CUTTERS

If You Prick Him, He Need Not Bleed

It's easy to cut too deeply when trimming your pet's claws. If you accidentally cut into the "quick" and the claw starts bleeding (or if the animal gets cut in some other way), you don't have to use a commercial styptic product to stem the flow. For a quick fix, try placing the injured paw in some flour or cornstarch, or sprinkle the cut with either of those substances.

Don't Let Him Make Snap Decisions

If your dog tries to bite or snap at you while you are clipping, drape a bath towel over his head. This technique will often quiet a dog and stop him from trying to bite.

FOR CATS ONLY

Toe the Line

Sometimes a cat is born with an extra toe and claw between the first two normal toes. The extra claw can grow too long, cutting into the foot pad and causing an abscess. You can keep the claw trimmed along with the other claws or have it surgically removed by your vet. You can combine this operation with other surgery,

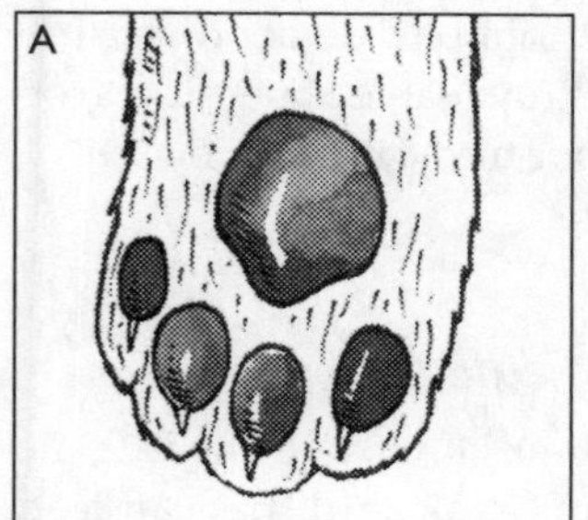

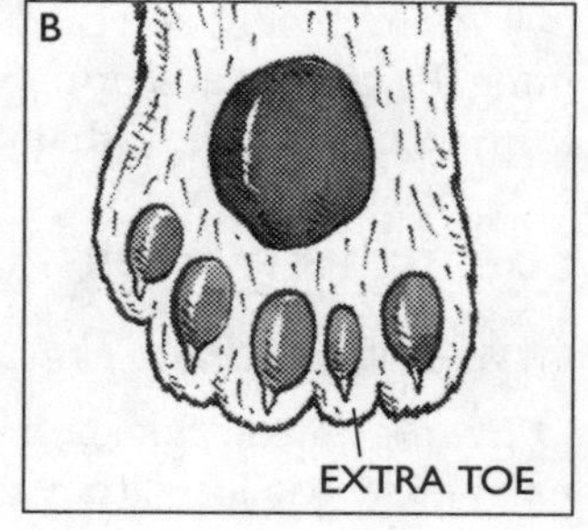

A normal cat's foot (A) and one with an extra toe and claw (B).

asking the vet to remove the extra claw while the animal is already anesthetized for spaying or neutering.

Keep the Main Claws Short

It's a good idea to check the length of your cat's claws once a month unless your pet has been surgically de-clawed by a vet. Particularly if your pet stays indoors, her claws will probably need clipping every four weeks or so.

Squeeze and Clip

For clipping, it's best to use special clippers rather than those designed for humans. (Available at pet stores, these clippers can be used for either cats or dogs.) Cats' nails are retractable, so you'll need to squeeze the paw slightly to push the claws outward. Then carefully clip well outside the "quick" (the area containing blood vessels, which will bleed if cut). Since cats' nails are clear, it's generally easy to identify the quick.

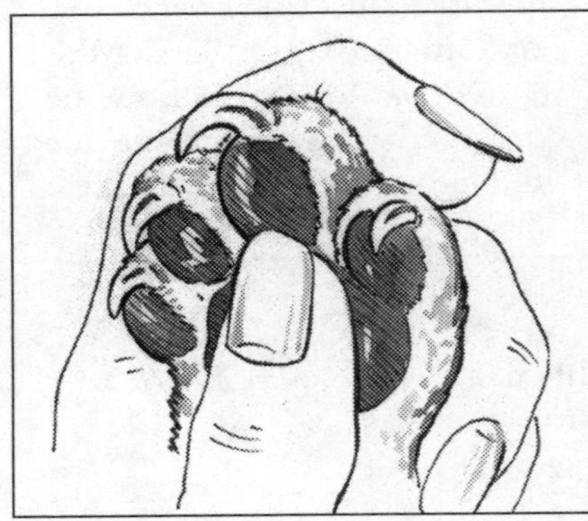

Squeeze, please. This will push your cat's claws out for clipping.

FOR BIRDS ONLY

Clip This Reminder

Clip your bird's claws two to three times a year with special bird claw clippers (available at pet or pet supply stores).

Let Polly Do It Herself

Alternatively, you can let your bird do her own trimming. Place special sandpaper (available at pet stores) on the bars of the cage so that your bird can scratch at it.

FOR OTHER PETS

Give Your Guinea Pig a Pedicure

❍ Even guinea pigs need their claws trimmed. If the nails grow too long, they can break, and that can lead to infection. A once-a-month trim with pet clippers should do the trick.

Iguanas: The Long and the Short of It

❍ Iguanas tend to have long claws, and you need to trim them every few weeks, using the same clippers you would use on a cat. (These are available at pet supply stores.) Trim each claw just at the tip, staying well outside the "quick" (the area containing blood vessels, which will bleed if cut).

CONSTIPATION

Your dog, cat, even your iguana can get constipated at some point in his life. If your pet does stop pooping, monitor the situation carefully and call the vet if home remedies don't get results within a day or two.

FOR DOGS ONLY

He's a Party Pooper

If your dog does not have a bowel movement for more than a day, the condition may be caused by stress. Have you added a new pet to the family? Have you and your dog moved recently? If you can, try to reduce the stress—separate the older dog from the new addition for a while or spend some extra time with your pet after a move, giving her special attention while she gets used to her new surroundings.

Maybe He Got into That Cheese Tray

A dog's digestive system is very sensitive to change. Try to determine whether your pet has eaten anything different from his usual diet in the last day or two. If so, put him back on familiar food. If the problem does not clear up within 48 hours, call the vet for treatment.

Tweetie, You're Grounded!

Your bird should have his wings clipped two or three times a year by a professional, such as a vet or a knowledgeable pet store owner. Since birds molt a few times a year, losing old feathers as new ones grow in, clipping is like getting a haircut. Clipping your bird's wings is a safety measure: With shortened wings, she won't be able to fly around the house and bang into windows or mirrors, and she won't be able to escape if she somehow wanders outdoors. However, be sure that when your pet is exercising outside her cage, other animals do not have access to her, because she won't be able to protect herself by flying away.

Be a Stool Pigeon: A Checklist for Your Dog's or Cat's Health

As a pet owner, you live for those wet kisses, the touch of a cold nose, the sound of purring. You don't really think too much about the other end of your furry friend. But your pet's stool can tell you a lot about his health, so it's a good idea to check on things at the rear end now and then, to be sure your pet is healthy. Here are five things to watch for and what to do if you see them.

Loose stool. Monitor the situation for up to two days. If the stool doesn't firm up by then, or if the condition turns to diarrhea, call the vet.

Blood in the stool. Try to collect a sample and call the vet.

Stool size. Stool size should always be appropriate to the size of the animal. If your big Lab is producing tiny bits of feces, or if your tiny Jack Russell is emitting huge stools, report the situation to your vet.

Worm segments in the stool. Try to collect a sample and take it to your vet.

Stool color. Know your pet's normal stool color so that if it changes, you'll be aware of the difference. If you do see a sudden change in color, try to trace it to a difference in diet, even if it was just a one-time, special treat during the past 24 hours. If you are unable to make the connection and your pet's stool remains discolored for more than 24 hours, or if your pet has other symptoms of illness or poisoning, call the vet.

FOR CATS ONLY

Hair Today, Gone Tomorrow

Constipation in cats is often caused by hair balls. You can ease your cat's condition by putting a little laxative lubricant (available at pet and pet supply stores) on your finger and letting your pet lick it off. If your pet won't lick the lubricant off your finger, wipe it on the roof of the animal's mouth. Or smear it on your pet's leg. Kitty will lick it off because cats don't like having gunk on their bodies.

Exercise Your Options

Constipation in cats can be caused or aggravated by lack of exercise. If your cat has repeated problems, make sure the animal stays active. You can help an indoor cat by playing games with him—tossing rolled-up pieces of paper or aluminum foil on the floor for your pet to bat around and chase, for example. And it's a good idea to set up a scratching post, which will help your cat flex and stretch his muscles frequently. If your pet likes to play outdoors, make sure the animal does so regularly at least for short periods of time, even in winter months.

FOR RABBITS ONLY

Give Him the Pineapple Treatment

Rabbits shed a lot, so if your bunny is constipated (and possibly not eating either), chances are he has a blockage in his intestine from ingesting fur that he has shed. You can treat your pet by putting a few tablespoons of pineapple juice in a dish for him to drink. The rabbit will like the sweet taste, and the fruit acid will break up the hair clog.

FOR REPTILES ONLY

Try Relaxation Therapy

If your iguana is constipated, it's probably because the animal has gotten cold. Here are three ways you can fix the situation: Gently immerse your pet in warm water; wrap her in a warm, wet towel; rest her against a hot-water bottle.

COMMON MISTAKES

Don't Treat Your Iguana Like a Dog

It's a myth that dog food is safe for iguanas. Your pet may actually eat it for several years before showing any ill effects, but by then it may be too late.

Too much protein, vitamin A, and vitamin E—all found in dog food—will damage your iguana's kidneys and may cause them to fail before you even have a chance to diagnose the problem.

COUGHING

Dogs and cats cough for a variety of reasons: They may be responding to a lack of humidity in the air around them, exhibiting an allergic reaction, reacting to parasites, even trying to get rid of hair balls. Whatever the cause, an astute pet owner will know several ways to help the hacker.

YOU'VE GOTTA LOVE 'EM

Tossing Cookies Can Be Fun

One day, my mom found our cocker spaniel, Meagan, sitting on the kitchen floor, eagerly devouring one of her doggy cookies. The weird thing was no one else was home, and my mom hadn't given Meagan any cookies to eat that day. When my mom glanced around the kitchen, she saw the box of cookies on the floor as well—with something rustling around inside it. There was my four-month-old Abyssinian kitten, Madison, positioned inside the box, and flipping cookies with her paw to Meagan. Madison watched Meagan swallow each one, then flipped her another. Although Meagan probably had a too-full tummy that evening, she and Madison have been best friends ever since.

—TRICIA GAGNON
Amesbury, Massachusetts

FOR DOGS AND CATS

How Dry I Am

Sometimes dogs and cats cough because the air in the house is too dry. This is particularly likely during winter months in cold climates. You can reduce the problem for your pet (and probably for yourself, too) by setting up a humidifier to moisten the air.

FOR DOGS ONLY

If Your Dog Has Coughing Companions

Dogs that board and show regularly (and thus are exposed to other dogs) may develop kennel cough—a dry cough followed by the expulsion of mucus. This is

a contagious upper respiratory disease that needs professional treatment. Call the vet.

If your dog is going to be exposed to or housed regularly with dogs outside your household, you may want to have the animal vaccinated against kennel cough.

FOR CATS ONLY

Try a New Gag

If your cat exhibits a gagging cough, with her head low to the ground, she is probably trying to expel a hair ball. You can help by buying a laxative lubricant (available at pet and pet supply stores) and letting your cat lick it off your finger. (If kitty won't eat it off your finger, smear it on her leg. She'll lick it off in an effort to keep herself clean.) The laxative will turn the hair ball into a form that can be passed with feces.

A gagging cough can indicate roundworms. It's a good idea to have the vet examine a stool sample from the cougher.

CUTS

Pets are bound to get cut from time to time, especially if they spend any time outdoors. In many cases, you can treat cuts yourself. When there's a lot of bleeding or a cut appears to be deep, you may need to call the vet. Before you do anything, carefully examine the injury.

FOR DOGS AND CATS

Help for an Unkind Cut

If your pet has a minor scratch or cut, bathe it with a clean cloth and apply an antibiotic cream such as Neosporin (available at pharmacies). Even if your pet licks the cream off—

TIME TO CALL THE VET

Put Pressure on the Situation

If your pet has a serious cut—one that's deep, bleeding profusely, or both—use a clean towel to put pressure on the wound. (Be careful when you do this. A wounded animal may try to bite even the people he loves best.) Gather up your pet and go straight to the animal hospital. This is a genuine emergency, but be reassured that most animals do not bleed to death unless the bleeding is completely uncontrollable.

which won't hurt him—enough will remain to be beneficial. For several days, watch for any swelling or discharge that could indicate an infection. If you see either of these, if the skin surrounding the cut turns black, or if your pet continually licks and chews at the cut, call the vet for treatment.

FOR DOGS ONLY

It's Just an Old Foot(ball) Injury

Your dog has a minor cut on her foot pad, which can't be sutured because the pad won't hold stitches together. Clean the cut with hydrogen peroxide (available at pharmacies), pouring the liquid on full strength. (This will sting a little.) Let the foot pad dry, then put a soft bandage, such as a gauze pad with tape, lightly around the foot. Change the bandage daily, keeping it as clean and dry as possible. After several days, check to make sure the cut is closed and shows none of the swelling or discharge that would indicate an infection. If all is clear, take the bandage off. If you notice swelling or a discharge, call the vet.

After cleaning your dog's cut foot, tape gauze in place over the injured area.

Don't let your dog outside while his foot is bandaged, except for quick toilet chores. For those, cover the bandage with a tube sock secured with tape. (Do *not* use a rubber band.)

FOR CATS ONLY

Forget the Glass Slipper

If your cat has a minor cut on her foot pad, pour a little hydrogen peroxide (available at pharmacies) on it to clean the area. Let the spot dry, then keep your kitty indoors for several days to give the cut a chance to heal.

If you notice swelling or a discharge around the wounded area, call the vet. Don't try to put a bandage on your feline's foot, as she'll tear it off right away.

FOR BIRDS ONLY

Stop the Bleeding Quickly

When your bird gets a cut, immediately apply a styptic product such as Kwik Stop (available at pet supply stores). If necessary, also apply a little pressure to the cut with a clean paper towel. Then take your pet to the vet immediately. Birds, especially small ones such as parakeets and cockatiels, don't have much blood to begin with, so any blood loss is serious. An untreated cut can be fatal to such tiny creatures.

4 *Steps to Check Your Bird's Health*

A quick check can tell you whether your bird is probably healthy. Here are four key areas to inspect.

1. Nostrils. They should be clear, without discharge.

2. Eyes. Make sure they're bright and clear.

3. Feathers. They should be in perfect condition. Make sure they're not chewed.

4. Activity level. Your bird should be active. If she is sitting at the bottom of her cage, she is probably ill. Call the vet.

FOR FISH ONLY

Isolate the Problem

When fish get cut—perhaps as a result of bites from other fish—you may not see much blood. The animals' slow metabolism means that they lose blood more slowly than some other species, and any blood that *is* lost gets rapidly diluted in the tank water. But blood or no, you can still see an actual cut. As soon as you spot it, isolate your wounded fish in a separate tank. This will protect the injured pet from further harm by other fish—an important step, since even normally placid fish have a tendency to nip at a wounded compatriot. Isolating the injured fish also will reduce the chances of infection, a potential problem when the mucus that covers the fish's scales is damaged.

How Do You Bandage a Fish?

The cut will probably heal by itself, but you also can treat the wound with an aloe-based product called

HEALTH

Stress Coat, a liquid that you add to the water in the injured pet's tank. Ask for Stress Coat at your pet store.

DENTAL PROBLEMS

Your pet isn't going to Hollywood, so why worry about whether he has perfect teeth? Healthy teeth and gums may be among the most important aspects of an animal's survival. Without them, your pet can't eat properly, groom himself, or protect himself from danger. Lack of regular dental care could lead to gum disease or abscessed teeth, either of which could result in tooth loss and other health problems.

It's easy to take care of your pet's teeth and gums. You just need to make home dental care a part of your

Not-So-Long Shots: Recommended Vaccinations for Your Cat

Even if your cat stays indoors his whole life, he should be vaccinated against certain diseases because he may come into contact with other animals or contaminated materials. Your vet will give you specific recommendations for vaccinating your pet, but here are some guidelines for the first round. Most of these require yearly boosters, depending on the type of vaccine your vet uses.

AGE	VACCINATION
8 weeks	FDRCC (to prevent feline distemper, rhinotracheitis, calicivirus, and chlamydia)
12 weeks	FDRCC
12 weeks	FeLV (for feline leukemia virus), after testing
16 weeks	FeLV
16 weeks	Rabies preventive; boosters follow every one to three years, depending on state law, or if your pet comes home with a bite wound

Many vets also recommend vaccination against feline infectious peritonitis (FIP) if a cat is considered at risk. Cats at high risk are those that spend a lot of time outdoors, live with other pets, have not been vaccinated for other diseases, or are very young. Some vets now also recommend a monthly heartworm preventive for cats, beginning at 8 weeks of age.

pet care routine and be sure that a dental examination and (if necessary) scraping of the teeth are part of your furry friend's yearly checkup with the vet. During a dental exam, the vet will look not only for tartar buildup but also for tiny cavities along the gum line, called neck lesions. Unfortunately, these can't be filled the way human dental cavities can. Instead, the decayed teeth have to be pulled.

Be sure to keep an eye out for indications of possible dental disease: bad breath, excessive drooling, difficulty chewing, loss of appetite, and loose or lost teeth. If any of these problems persists, check with your vet for treatment.

COST CUTTERS

Combine Appointments When You Can

To save on vet bills, schedule your pet's annual checkup at the same time the animal is due to begin seasonal flea or heartworm treatment (or any other seasonal treatment). For instance, in the Northeast, flea and heartworm treatments begin in the spring; try to arrange for the animal's annual physical in March or April.

FOR DOGS AND CATS

Four out of Five Dentists Recommend . . .

Brush your cat or dog's teeth regularly—daily if possible, but once a week at least. Brushing with a special pet toothbrush and pet toothpaste gets rid of foreign matter stuck between the teeth and around the gums. It also reduces plaque and tartar buildup and stimulates blood flow in the gums. And it gives you an opportunity to examine your pet's mouth for other problems, such as cuts or tumors. To help yourself remember to brush your pet's teeth, you might want to do the job at the same time every day or every week.

Let Your Finger Do the Brushing

To prepare your pet to accept tooth brushing and to get the animal used to having your hands in and around his mouth, start the dental care by just rubbing your finger back and forth along the outside of his teeth, where tartar builds up. Do this once a day for several days before graduating to toothpaste and a brushing device.

Let Her Get Her Licks In

Pet toothpastes (available at pet supply stores) come in a variety of flavors, including poultry, liver, beef, and malt. Some come packaged in a starter kit with a toothbrush shaped for your pet's mouth—cat or dog. Choose the brush and paste best suited to your pet. Put a dab of paste on the end of your finger and let your pet sniff it and lick it off your finger. Then put another dab on your finger and rub it along the outside of her teeth.

If the animal accepts the finger and toothpaste routine, next time try putting the toothpaste on the brush and actually brushing your pet's teeth, using a back-and-forth motion along the outside of the teeth. You don't need to open the mouth and brush the inside of the teeth because most of the nasty buildup occurs on the outside.

Just Water, Please

Some pets will let you brush with plain water, but they won't accept toothpaste. Don't despair. Skip the paste and use the brush anyway, with just enough water to moisten the brush and your pet's mouth. This isn't as effective as the full-scale routine, but it's much better than not brushing.

Run the Rinse Cycle

If your cat or dog simply won't stand for any kind of brushing, ask your vet to prescribe a dental rinse, which you can squirt over your pet's teeth two or three times a week to help clean them. The rinse isn't as effective as brushing, but it's better than nothing.

Ah, There's the Rub!

If either you or your pet finds the toothbrush awkward, try one of the rubber finger brushes available at pet supply stores. They look like rubber thimbles covered with nubs and are designed to fit over your finger. Just slip one on and rub it back and forth along your pet's teeth and gum line, with or without toothpaste.

YOU'VE GOTTA LOVE 'EM

Low Rider

My dad had a 1957 Thunderbird convertible. We five boys had a mutt named Bippo. Bippo liked to ride in the convertible. Dad didn't like Bippo to ride in the convertible. So when Bippo heard Dad driving his car down the driveway, Bippo would race to a corner in the road. He'd get a running start and leap right into the passenger's seat of the moving car, next to Dad. And Dad never had the heart to throw him out.

—**BOYD ALLEN III**
Exeter, New Hampshire

Control Tartar with Treats

Help control tartar buildup on your pet's teeth by giving him crunchy tartar control "treats" made especially for this purpose. You'll find them in the pet food section of the supermarket or pet supply store. Look for the words "tartar control" on the label. Don't overdo it. One or two treats a day should suffice.

Her Trouble May Be a Tumor

If your pet's mouth is swollen and smells awful, or if the animal is drooling and appears to have an appetite but can't eat, she may have a tumor inside her mouth. You may want to look inside the mouth and carefully feel around with your finger, but call the vet about the problem even if you don't find anything. The doctor will be able to determine for certain whether there is a growth and what type of treatment is best.

HEALTH

FOR DOGS ONLY

Chew on This

To promote your dog's dental health, buy him one or two different kinds of chew toys. Try any of the nylon chew toys or rubber bones with cotton centers that you can get through catalogs or at pet supply stores. While your pup plays with these toys, they will massage his gums and control the buildup of plaque and tartar. Experiment to see which types your pooch prefers, then be sure to keep him supplied.

These Rocks Don't Roll

Some dogs habitually chew rocks—not a good idea because the process grinds down their teeth and sometimes even breaks a tooth. If a tooth becomes so ground down that a nerve is exposed or near the surface, chewing will produce a sharp pain, and your pet will have trouble eating her normal dinner. To avoid this, keep an eye on your pooch while she's outside, and whenever she appears headed for a rocky repast, distract her with some other plaything or activity.

If you think your dog has actually swallowed a rock, call the vet. Sometimes a rock is vomited up or passed with feces, but if it is not, it will block the intestine and have to be removed surgically. If your pet assumes the "prayer position"—lying on the floor or ground with his paws pointing forward and his rear end raised—and appears at the same time to be in ab-

The "prayer position" is a danger signal.

dominal pain, get him to the vet immediately. It's likely that his intestine is blocked.

HEALTH

FOR POCKET PETS

Relief for Long-in-the-Tooth Rodents

Rodents have teeth that grow continuously throughout their lives. A gerbil or hamster needs to chew to keep his teeth filed down. Otherwise, the teeth will grow so long that the little guy won't be able to eat. To prevent this problem, get a pine two-by-four and cut off one-inch blocks for your pet to chew on.

FOR RABBITS ONLY

Let Them Cut Their Teeth on This

Rabbits' teeth, like those of rodents, continue to grow all their lives. This can become a problem for some animals. To keep those teeth worn down to a serviceable size, dry whole grain bread in a 350°F oven for 10 to 15 minutes, or until it is very hard, then give your pet a small piece once a day or so. (Or, to conserve energy, put the bread in the oven after you take your dinner out. Then turn off the oven and keep an eye on the bread.)

It's a Case of Tooth or Consequences

Some rabbits are unable to trim their teeth naturally, no matter what you give them to chew on. If you notice that your bunny's having trouble crunching his food, ask a vet if the animal's teeth should be trimmed. (It's not a good idea to attempt this yourself.)

COST CUTTERS

Join the Club

These days, you have access to a wide variety of nonprofit organizations devoted to gathering and disseminating information about their favorite pets. In addition to the predictable groups of cat and dog owners, you'll find societies devoted to pet birds, fish, even reptiles. By joining one of these groups, you'll get access to free (or low-cost) information about all aspects of pet care, including maintaining your animal's health, from other members, newsletters, hot lines, and the Internet.

You can locate these organizations through pet stores, veterinarians, breeders, and other pet owners. Some organizations may charge nominal dues to cover the costs of newsletters and the like.

HEALTH

DIARRHEA

When your pet gets diarrhea, the cause may be anything from simple overeating to poisoning or an intestinal blockage. The tricks are to recognize which is which and to know when to call the vet. As long as the symptoms consist only of loose stools containing no blood and the animal still has an appetite for food and water, the condition is probably mild enough to respond to home treatment. Here are some ways to firm things up.

TIME TO CALL THE VET

Oh Dear, It's Diarrhea

Your pet's severe diarrhea can be caused by things such as poisoning, parasites, an intestinal blockage, or parvovirus. It's time to call the vet if your pet shows any of these signs or if the diarrhea persists for more than one day.

- Blood in the stool
- Loss of appetite for food and/or water
- Projectile (shooting) diarrhea
- Vomiting
- Worm segments in the stool

FOR DOGS AND CATS

Try a Boiled Dinner

If your dog or cat develops mild diarrhea, feed the pet a little boiled hamburger or chicken and rice at regular mealtimes for three or four days.

You also can feed your ailing pet strained-meat baby foods from a jar. They're bland and can help return things to normal.

FOR DOGS ONLY

Go Heavy on the Starch

If your dog has mild diarrhea, feed her plain cooked pasta at mealtimes. The starch should thicken things up. If the diarrhea doesn't clear up within three or four days, or if it has gotten worse and she has lost her appetite, call the vet.

FOR RABBITS ONLY

Feed Him Pellets, Keep Him Perky

If your rabbit has a loose stool, consider whether his diet contains rabbit food pellets (available at pet stores), which promote good digestion. If it doesn't, introduce them in the amount recommended on the package. Monitor your pet for a day. If the diarrhea has not cleared up, take the animal to the vet (rabbits tend to get seriously ill much faster than other animals, so you shouldn't wait more than a day). If your pet already eats rabbit food pellets regularly and suddenly has diarrhea, call the vet. The diarrhea may be due to hair balls or internal parasites.

DROOLING

Some dogs—particularly Newfoundlands, Saint Bernards, and mastiffs—drool all the time because of the way their mouths are constructed. But if your normally fastidious dog or cat starts drooling all of a sudden, it's time to look for the cause—and the remedy.

FOR DOGS AND CATS

Stick It Out

If your pet starts drooling to an unusual degree, check inside her mouth. (Be careful not to let the animal bite you!) Your friend may have a stick, a pine needle,

TIME TO CALL THE VET

When a Pet Chews an Electrical Cord

Kittens and puppies love to chew on things, and most of the time they don't know the difference between what's safe and what isn't. So if they find an electrical cord to pounce on, to them it's fair game. The problem is if the cord is plugged in, a pet's innocent game could end with an electric shock. If your pet exhibits any combination of the symptoms listed below, *quickly* check around the house or apartment for any telltale signs that a cord has been chewed. If you find them, take the animal to the nearest emergency animal hospital. An electric shock isn't automatically fatal, but it does require treatment. Here are the symptoms that may indicate that your pet has received a shock.

1. Unconsciousness
2. Weakness or lethargy
3. Rapid, shallow breathing
4. A black "burn" line across the tongue or other similar marks on the tongue
5. Drooling
6. Gray-blue gums (indicating that the animal isn't getting enough oxygen)

a piece of bark, or some other foreign object stuck inside. If so, try to remove the object yourself. If you're not successful, take the animal to the vet.

Scrap the Treats

If your pet is not a born drooler but has been drooling a lot lately, check the animal's diet. Have you been slipping him table scraps or other treats? If so, cut them out and just feed your pet his regular diet of dog food or cat food. (And make sure the neighbors aren't giving your animal any unauthorized between-meal treats.) The drooling may stop after only a few days.

Still Waters Run Deep

Your pet may be drooling because of nerves or overexcitement about something, such as a move or the introduction of a new pet into the family. Try to calm the atmosphere if you can. Make sure your kitty has access to some of her familiar things (such as a blanket or a basket to sleep in) in her new home. Walk Fido separately from the new puppy.

DRY SKIN

Dry skin in animals can be a sign of lack of moisture in the skin, or it can signal an allergy or other illness. In rabbits, the problem may cause ear discomfort; in snakes, it may inhibit shedding. If your furry friend is doing a lot of scratching or rubbing, or if your snake doesn't seem to be shedding on schedule, dry skin may be the culprit. Don't fret; there are several things you can do to relieve the situation. But if your pet has other symptoms besides dry skin, such as severe itching or sores, or if the condition doesn't clear up within a few weeks, call your vet.

FOR DOGS AND CATS

Try Regular Brushing

Your pet's dry or flaky skin may be caused by a lack of natural oils. You can stimulate more oil and distribute it more evenly simply by brushing the animal all over every day.

Let Your Pet Feel His Oats

Relieve the itch by giving your pup or kitty a bath with an oatmeal-based shampoo made for pets (available at pet supply stores).

Or use the same kind of oatmeal bath that people use to relieve dry, itchy skin. Try Aveeno, which most doctors recommend for children with chicken pox. It's available over the counter at pharmacies.

COST CUTTERS

Friends, Romans, Rabbits: Lend Me Your Ears!

Save on vet bills by cleaning your pets' ears regularly and thus preventing infections and mites. An animal with long, floppy ears, such as a rabbit or cocker spaniel, is particularly prone to mites and infections. Try to clean such a pet's ears every day. If you have a pet with shorter ears that stand up, such as a cat or German shepherd, you can limit ear cleaning to once a week.

Clean your pet's ears as if she were a baby. Using either a cotton swab or a cotton ball, gently sweep around the outer rim of the ear, then move slightly inward. (If you are using a cotton swab, the tip should never be out of sight.) About once a month, put a drop or so of hydrogen peroxide (available at pharmacies) on the cotton before cleaning.

FOR RABBITS ONLY

Give Them an Earful

Rabbits are sometimes bothered by dry skin in their ears. It isn't serious, but you can relieve your pet's itchy symptoms by rubbing a little mineral oil (available at pharmacies) on the skin inside the ear.

FOR REPTILES ONLY

A Little Spritz Will Do

A healthy iguana's skin should be soft and silky, fleshy to the touch. If your pet's skin is dry, use a clean spray bottle to spritz his body lightly with water a few times a day. If the condition doesn't clear up within a few days, or if it is accompanied by blotches or loss of skin color, call the vet or pet store for advice and treatment.

Don't Dry for Me

If your snake's skin becomes dry, the animal won't be able to shed properly. She may not shed on schedule, the old skin may shred, or the casing on the eye may not fall off, which could blind your pet. To keep this from happening, it's a good idea to spray the animal at least three times a week with a special spray containing electrolytes and vitamins (available at pet supply stores or from vets who treat snakes). The spray works like a hand lotion, moistening the skin and making it supple for shedding.

TIME TO CALL THE VET

Ear-Reconcilable Differences

The most common ear problems among pets are ear infections and ear mites (tiny insects). Both conditions may cause your pet to show the same symptoms, and both need to be handled by the vet, but the treatments for the two ailments are very different. Call your vet if your pet exhibits any of the following:

- Scratching the head or ears constantly
- Tilting or shaking the head
- Running the head along furniture or the floor
- Redness in the ears
- Crust or crumbly material in the ears
- Shying away from having the ears touched
- Heat radiating from the ears
- Bad odor coming from the ears
- Discharge (probably green or black gunk)

EAR INFECTIONS

Keeping your dog's ears clean is the way to avoid canine ear infections. Different breeds have different needs, but the basic principle is the same: Keep those ears clear of all foreign matter and keep them dry. Here are some more ideas.

FOR DOGS ONLY

Avoid the Dunking Tank

To avoid ear infections that result from constant dampness, give your long-eared dog water in a small bowl—one that just accommodates the nose and mouth and leaves the ears high and dry. Don't offer your pet a large water bowl in which the ears get dunked with every drink.

Wipe It Off; Wipe It All *Off*

After a swim—and after your pet finishes shaking off—ward off ear infections by patting the insides of her ears with a towel. When you get back home, put a little rubbing alcohol on a cotton ball and wipe it around inside her ears. This will promote further drying.

EYE PROBLEMS

HEALTH

Pets can get eye irritations ranging from scratches to conjunctivitis (an inflammation of the membrane inside the eyelid) to allergic reactions. Common clues that your pet is suffering from some type of eye irritation are a discharge or watery eyes, rubbing or blinking the eyes, or an irritation of the eyelid or skin surrounding the eyes. Try these home treatments, and if the condition doesn't clear up promptly, consult your vet.

FOR PETS IN GENERAL

The Eyes Have It

❑ Dogs, cats, and rabbits can get conjunctivitis, also called pinkeye, which is usually caused by an infection or an allergic reaction. If your pet develops this condition, his eyes will have some gunky discharge, and the skin around the eyelids will be reddish and crusty. To relieve your pal's discomfort, soak a clean washcloth in warm water and wring it out. Then gently wipe away the discharge from both eyes.

❑ If your pet will let you, hold a clean portion of the warm, moist cloth against the closed eye for a few minutes like a compress. Do this as often as your pet seems to need it on the first day, then once or twice a day after that until the condition improves. In the meantime, it's smart to call your vet for advice, in case he recommends further treatment.

❑ If your pet will not let you touch the eye, or if she's holding the eye closed, call the vet immediately.

TIME TO CALL THE VET

Make It a Point to Check Bowser's Ears

Dogs with pointed ears, such as huskies, German shepherds, collies, and Welsh corgis, are often prone to blood blisters. Check your dog's ears regularly for troublesome areas that look like ravioli. If you see a blister, call your vet, who will drain it.

FOR DOGS AND CATS

Some Animals Just Don't Do Well with Change

🐾 If you think that your pet's eye problems may be an allergic reaction, you should try to determine what the

animal may be allergic to. Could it be a new brand of food or a new bed? If possible, change the conditions—go back to your old brand of food or try a different bed.

He's Scratched the Surface

Your dog or cat is squinting or pawing at his eye. The eye may be teary, but you don't see any obvious irritant. Your pet could have a scratched cornea. Take the animal to the vet, who will drip a dye stain into the affected eye to highlight any scratch. If she finds one, she will probably prescribe eyedrops or an ointment to treat the condition.

Don't be tempted to medicate your pet without contacting the vet. Medications for eye problems such

YOU'VE GOTTA LOVE 'EM

Jack Be Nimble, Jack Be Quick

One day, when I was at home by myself, I fainted. When I came to, I heard all kinds of strange noises in the room above the one I was in. Then my elderly mom, who lives in an apartment upstairs, burst into the room crying, "There's something wrong with Travis! What's wrong with Travis?"

Travis is my Jack Russell terrier. Apparently, when I fainted, Travis ran upstairs to my mother's apartment for help. He was jumping up and down, yelping, trying to get her attention. Sure enough, she came downstairs and found me—but had no idea that I was the one who needed help, not Travis!

—PAM HUNT
Haverhill, Massachusetts

as conjunctivitis contain steroids that will actually delay the healing of a scratch, so it's important to get the correct diagnosis from your vet.

FOR RABBITS ONLY

Your Bunny's Eyes Shouldn't Keep On Running

If your rabbit's weepy or runny eyes don't clear up quickly, call your vet. Especially if the runny eyes are accompanied by a runny nose, sneezing, and a loss of appetite, this may be a sign of a respiratory illness that can lead to pneumonia, which can be fatal in rabbits.

FOR REPTILES ONLY

Give Slinky the (Red) Carpet Treatment

If your snake's eyes appear to be irritated or uncomfortable, check her bedding. Instead of lining her cage with commercial bedding made of shredded material that can get into her eyes as she moves around, use a carpet, called terrarium lining, made especially for this purpose. This carpet is available at pet supply stores.

FEARS

Men, children, people in general, thunderstorms, cars, other animals—all are common sources of fear in animals. Often a pet's fear begins with an initial bad experience—say, being locked in a car on a hot day. Pets express their fear in different ways. They may bite or scratch, run and hide, tremble, or even urinate when afraid. Your job is to figure out what's scaring your friend and try to change those conditions.

FOR DOGS AND CATS

Tabby Gets Carried Away

It's very common for a pet to be afraid of being locked in a carrier or travel crate while in the car. This action usually leads to a trip to the vet, and pets are very good at anticipating what that may mean. You can help your pet get over that fear, but it will take some

ONE PERSON'S SOLUTION

Take the Bite out of Fear

When the Cocker Spaniel Rescue League first found Lady, she was roaming the streets of New York City. She was only a few months old, and she went from the streets to several foster homes before we adopted her.

At first Lady was quiet and gentle. But after a few weeks, she started to snarl for no apparent reason. If someone woke her up from a sound sleep, she'd bite. She had to be muzzled at the vet's. I began to worry that something was wrong. I described Lady's problems to a dog trainer, who immediately concluded that Lady was "fear biting," as the medical community describes it, meaning simply that she was biting out of fear.

Together, we put Lady on a program designed to get rid of her anxieties. We taught her how to obey commands such as "Sit" and "Stay." We also enforced other rules, such as staying off the furniture. As she learned the ground rules, her world became more consistent, giving her fewer reasons to be anxious. Ultimately, she learned that she now lived in a safe place and that people could be trusted.

Lady is now a lapdog who craves affection. She doesn't bite anymore. These days, if she's afraid of a stranger or a new situation, she just growls. And pretty soon, she warms up to her new surroundings.

—DIANE MOORE
Amesbury, Massachusetts

time. Start by leaving the carrier out on the floor with the door open and letting your pet explore it on her own. After she seems comfortable going in and around the carrier, place a treat near the entrance. If she takes the treat, put out another, a little farther into the carrier. When she takes that one, place another treat inside the carrier, even farther toward the back. You may want to put a towel or a bed in the carrier. Eventually, the pet will get into the carrier, at which point you can start picking it up. Start by simply walking into another room and then letting her out. Gradually increase the time the pet spends in the carrier and the distance until you can comfortably get her into the car.

Take Him for a Ride

If you have to drag your pet to the car or he trembles uncontrollably during the ride, ask yourself whether you take him in the car only when he has to go to the vet or kennel (or someplace else that he might find unpleasant). If the answer is yes, take him for a ride around town or go somewhere pleasant, such as a playground. Do this several times so that he gets the idea that a car ride doesn't always lead to a scary place.

Driving Miss Kitty

If your pet is afraid of the car, start to desensitize her by putting her in the car for a few minutes without turning on the engine. Then gradually expose her to more of the sensations associated with being in the vehicle—working up to starting the engine, backing the car out of the driveway, and then actually going on a short trip. If you slowly desensitize her to more and more of the elements associated with a car trip, she will eventually learn to tolerate being in the car.

FIN ROT

Fish sometimes get a condition called fin rot, which makes their fins and tails look frayed and tattered, translucent at the center, and white around the edges. There are several

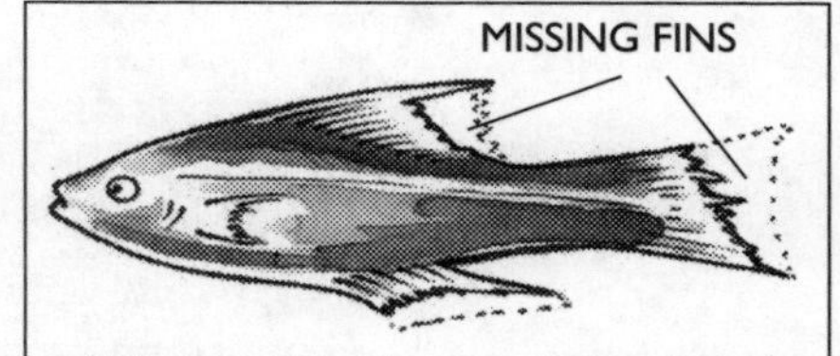

Fin rot: just what the name sounds like.

COMMON MISTAKES

Here's the Scoop!

If you need to handle any of your fish (for instance, to move a sick one to another tank), don't touch a fin. Handling a fin can disturb the protective mucus that coats your pet's body. Once this is broken, your fish is more susceptible to infection. Take a jar and scoop the fish, along with some water, right into it, then move the fish gently and quickly to the new tank.

causes, including bacterial or fungal infections or even lack of oxygen. It will be hard for you to pinpoint the cause, so it's important to cover your bases in treatment.

FOR FISH ONLY

Put Him in the Isolation Tank . . .

If one of your fish shows signs of fin rot, isolate him by putting him in a separate tank with clean, oxygenated water and a clean filter. Isolation allows you to prevent this potentially contagious condition from spreading to your other fish and lets you treat only the sick fish instead of the entire tank. Go to a pet store that handles your type of fish and ask for the proper chemical treatment to put in the water with the ailing fish.

. . . Then Clean House

In the meantime, make sure the original tank is clean and well oxygenated to prevent the other fish from getting sick and to ensure that when you return your recovered fish to his home, he'll be happy.

FLATULENCE

You're convinced that your pet has never heard of the Clean Air Act. She's passing gas at a rate that could power up a whole town. Don't worry; she's probably not sick (even though she's making *you* feel ill). Your pet might be getting gas from any of several sources—a sudden change in diet, nerves or stress, or simply aging—and you can probably do something to clear the air.

FOR DOGS AND CATS

Calm the Nerves

If your pet is suddenly gassy, she may be nervous about something. Maybe you added another new pet to the family, or you recently moved. Try to determine what's bothering her and help her calm down. Speak to her in a reassuring voice. Spend time with her separately from the time you spend with the new animal, or accompany her as she gets used to new surroundings.

Exorcise the Gas with Exercise

If flatulence is a problem for your pet, make sure the animal gets plenty of playtime. Take a dog for one or two walks each day, or toss a ball or toy for a cat to chase. Exercise is a great gas reducer.

Trash the Scraps

Table scraps, as tasty as they might seem to your pet, can have foul-smelling results if they're too rich for the animal's digestive system. Keep your pet on his regular diet of nutritious pet food, and he'll smell sweeter.

Ditch the New Diet

If you've suddenly switched your pooch or kitty to a new food, she may have problems with gas. Unless

A WORD FROM DR. DEVINNE

DR. CHARLES DEVINNE
of Peterborough, New Hampshire, who has more than 15 years of veterinary experience and whose private practice currently concentrates on dogs and cats

A Treat for Him, a Trauma for You

You may want to weigh the pros and cons before you give your dog any table scraps, even as an occasional treat. Some dogs like onions; I had a Lab who used to like them. But boy, you wouldn't want to be behind him about an hour after he ate them. Onions (and other kinds of people food) can cause serious gas. All it takes is one inappropriate snack to turn your indoor dog into an outdoor dog.

your vet has recommended the change, go back to your old standby. Or discuss the problem with your vet.

Try the Breakfast of (Four-Legged) Champions

Giving your pet food that is cereal- or grain-based rather than meat-based may help reduce gassiness. Meat-based foods could be too rich for your pet's system. That doesn't mean Fido can't have pet food with meat in it. It just means that the food should have a cereal or grain base. Check your food's label and switch if necessary, making the change gradually over several days.

Sandpaper Tongue

Anyone who's ever been "tasted" by a cat knows that a cat's tongue feels like sandpaper. That's because it's covered with hundreds of tiny, raised projections called *papillae filiformes.* The papillae curve up and back and are rough to the touch. Interestingly, they have more to do with grooming than with taste. They help the tongue act as a sort of comb, making it more efficient for picking up dirt and dust from the fur.

FLEAS

Fleas are an itchy subject for every pet owner. You're afraid of finding evidence of even one of the loathsome creatures in your home or on your pet. But the only way to keep fleas totally out of the picture is to keep all your pets indoors all the time—nearly impossible for dogs and not desirable for every cat. Keeping just one pet inside won't solve the problem either, because an outdoor pet is bound to bring a few fleas into the house, where they'll jump to an indoor pet. You need to go on flea patrol, hunting them down and knocking them dead. And you need to do it early in the season—not, say, in September, when an unchecked flea population may have reached the millions.

Wage the war against fleas on three separate fronts: (1) Shampoo your pet with flea shampoo (available at pet supply stores) and spray the animal between shampoos with flea spray; (2) collar your pet with a flea collar; and (3) treat the outdoor environment into which your pet ventures.

There are many flea products available, and they work in different ways. Those that offer immediate relief usually do so through a "quick knockdown"—in other words, they kill adult fleas on contact or when the fleas bite, but they do not harm larvae or sterilize any remaining adults. Others take longer to relieve symptoms because they work by killing larvae or sterilizing adults, but this also means that they do a more thorough job of getting rid of fleas over the long term.

To check for fleas, run your fingers through your pet's fur, spreading the fur so that you can see down to the skin. There you might see "flea dirt," a dust that is actually flea excrement. Or comb through your pet's fur with a wire brush, looking for fleas and flea dirt. Also look for the black, gritty dust in areas of your house where your pet has been lying down. If you think you have trouble, here's what you can do.

FOR DOGS AND CATS

Get in a Lather

Use a flea shampoo (available at pet supply stores) to get your pet's fur squeaky clean while simultaneously killing pests. Some shampoos are made just for dogs, others are for dogs and cats, and still others are safe even for kittens. Be sure to consult your pet supply store owner or your vet about which product is right for your pet. The answer will depend on factors such as where you live, how old your pet is, and whether the animal has sensitive skin.

It Could Be Just Her Cup of Tea

For a natural alternative to conventional flea shampoos, try one that contains tea tree oil (available at pet supply stores). The oil, which comes from the *Melaleuca alternifolia* plant, is soothing to your pet's skin and helps repel fleas. Shampoo your pet at the beginning of the flea season, then just a few times thereafter, if needed.

COMMON MISTAKES

Don't Mix Medications

It's tempting to cover your pet with every kind of flea protection you can find. But check with your vet before you combine treatments, especially if your pet has been treated with any of the prescription medications such as pills or liquid mixed with food. The chemicals in different treatments may vary, and combining them may diminish their effectiveness or even be harmful to your pet.

HEALTH

The Family That Sprays Together . . . Kills the Fleas

For immediate relief, use a flea spray on your pet. It won't solve the problem over the long term because it doesn't kill flea eggs, but it does kill adult fleas on contact and repel others. As with flea shampoos, consult with your vet or pet supply store owner about which product is best for your pet.

COMMON MISTAKES

What's Good for Fido Isn't Necessarily Good for Fluffy

It's fine to use an over-the-counter flea shampoo to keep your pet's coat and skin clean and to wash away fleas. But be sure you don't use the same shampoo on your cat that you use on your dog. They don't contain the same ingredients and could even be harmful if used on the wrong animal. Check the label carefully when you buy any flea shampoo at a pet supply store.

Collar the Critters

Another way to combat fleas is to put a flea collar on your pet. These devices are impregnated with chemicals that act in a variety of ways, depending on the individual product. They may kill fleas, repel fleas, or kill flea eggs. Consult with your vet or pet supply store owner about which product is best for your pet.

Let Your Pet Feast on Yeast

To repel fleas, feed your pet a combination of brewer's yeast and garlic once a day during flea season. You can buy this combination in tablet or powder form at most pet supply stores. Some animals like the taste of the tablets so much that they'll eat them like treats. If this doesn't work, buy the powder and mix it into your pet's meals. In either case, follow dosage instructions on the product label. The mixture will make your pet taste bad to fleas when they bite, and, as an added bonus, it will help condition the skin.

It's a Wash

To reduce the spread of fleas, keep your home clean, paying special attention to the areas inhabited by your pet. If your dog has a bed, wash it regularly. If your cat sleeps on a favorite upholstered chair, vacuum and shampoo it regularly as well. Vacuum and shampoo household carpets and rugs, too, so that fleas won't have a place to thrive.

Leave Leaves around the House

To keep fleas out of your house, buy a bunch of eucalyptus leaves, cut up the bunch, and stick both stems and leaves in open glass jars. Place a jar or two in each room of the house where your pet spends time, especially in rooms with carpets (fleas love to hide in carpeting). You can buy bunches of eucalyptus in the crafts section of a discount store.

Ban Bonzo from the Basement

Fleas love to live in old basements with dirt or cement floors. They'll dig into the dirt or make themselves at home in the cracks of the cement. If your house has a cellar with an old cement floor, vacuum the cracks regularly. If the floor is dirt, try using a flea fogger or household spray at the beginning of the flea season. And make the basement off-limits to your pet.

If You Prefer an Herbal Essence

Perhaps you prefer not to use insecticides, your pet has sensitive skin, or you have small children and you'd like to keep them away from contact with such chemicals. In any of these cases, give your pet a flea collar with active ingredients such as eucalyptus, cedar, lemongrass, rosemary, and marigold. These collars will not exterminate fleas, but they will deter the pests—without harming other living things.

COMMON MISTAKES

Are You Poisoning One Pet to Save Another?

You may be ready to try anything to get rid of your dog's fleas and ticks, but if you own a pet reptile as well as the pup, be careful not to sacrifice one pet to save another. Before you treat your home with any pesticide intended to help a dog or cat, be sure to check with a vet or pet store owner who is familiar with reptiles. Snakes, iguanas, and lizards don't metabolize pesticides the same way mammals do, and a formula that is benign to one pet may be deadly to another.

Shake Off the Visitors

If you visit someone whose pet or home has fleas, toss your clothes in the wash as soon as you return home. Otherwise, you'll bring those unwanted critters

into your house—attached to your pants leg, sneaker, or some other article of clothing.

Call In the Heavy Artillery

If all else fails, call for professional help. Your vet has some special weapons that you can launch against the insect enemy. She may prescribe pills for your dog or offer liquid medication to be mixed with your cat's food. Some vets also offer a powerful medication that is administered through just one drop of liquid on the back of a dog or cat's neck. The medicine is applied once a month or as needed.

FOR DOGS ONLY

They Can't Land—They Can't Even Live

If your dog has a flea bite allergy, often called flea allergy dermatitis, that causes him to scratch incessantly and perhaps get bumps or hives from flea bites, you may opt for a product developed specifically for animals with sensitive skin. Try applying a flea treatment such as Bio Spot. When fleas try to land on your sensitive pet, they are repelled. In addition, contact with the chemical kills them. Preventing flea bites in this manner helps prevent an allergic skin reaction in your pet. The product, available over the counter at pet supply stores, consists of one or two tubes of ointment. When dabbed on the animal's skin, it travels like an oil slick over the pet's body. It is appropriate for dogs, but it is *not* safe for cats.

HAIR BALLS

Let's face it, most cats get hair balls. Hair balls develop when your kitty sheds, then grooms herself, swallowing the fur. The fur balls up in her stomach, and she naturally tries to expel it with a gagging cough, her head held low to the ground. Every cat will probably have at least one hair ball during her life, but these little wads of irritation are particularly troublesome for longhaired breeds, simply because they shed a greater amount of fur.

FOR CATS ONLY

HEALTH

Comb It before She Swallows It

A good way to reduce the amount of hair your cat ingests is to brush her regularly with a wire grooming brush, especially when she is shedding. Clean the

ONE PERSON'S SOLUTION

Engage in Child's Play

For about a dozen years, my parents had a black, furry mixed-breed dog named Lucy. Somewhere along the line, Lucy developed arthritis, and toward the end of her life, she had great difficulty moving around. She could barely haul herself up stairs and down, and she couldn't keep up with my mom on her daily walks.

Still, it was important to keep Lucy somewhat active so that she wouldn't lose all her mobility. So each time my husband and I took our young daughter for a visit, we encouraged Marjorie to play with the dog. Marjorie was only three the last summer of Lucy's life, so she wasn't big enough to walk too fast or strong enough to do any inadvertent harm to the dog. She took Lucy under her wing, walking slowly around the yard with her, patting the dog gently on her sore back, waiting patiently when Lucy needed a rest. One day, we overheard Marjorie saying, "Don't worry, Lucy dear, you can make it," as together they walked up the long hill from the pond.

Lucy died not long after that. A year later, when Marjorie got her own pet—a little black kitten—she named her new companion Lucy.

—LINDA BUCHANAN ALLEN
Exeter, New Hampshire

brush after each grooming, removing and discarding loose hair.

Lubricate the Situation

If your cat seems to be having trouble with a hair ball, go to your local pet supply store and purchase a laxative lubricant that is specially made to break down the hair ball into a form more easily passed with feces. Just put a little on your finger, according to the package directions. Your feline friend will lick it off and swallow it. (If the animal doesn't cooperate, wipe the lubricant on her fur. She'll lick it off as she grooms herself.)

Cancel the Flea Circus

Cats try to get rid of fleas by grooming themselves more vigorously than ever—and that means they're likely to swallow more hair than ever. If your cat is infested, bear down on those nasty insects with any method of flea control you choose. Get rid of the fleas, and you'll get rid of many of the hair balls as well.

A Doggy Coat Check

Your dog's coat can tell you whether he is healthy and signal you to look further for a problem. A condition that's dangerous for one breed may be normal for another, but in general, your pet is probably fine as long as his coat is typical of his breed. Watch out for these potential problem areas.

Uncharacteristic dryness or oiliness. A German shepherd normally has a dry coat, while a Portuguese water dog or other retriever should have an oily one. If your pet's normally dry coat is suddenly oily or his normally oily coat is suddenly dry, suspect a health problem and get the animal to the vet.

Shedding. When a dog suddenly starts shedding a great deal more than usual, something may be wrong with the animal's health.

Thick or thin. Compare your dog's coat to those of other, similar animals. For example, a husky should have a big, thick coat. If your pet's coat is thin and scrawny, he may not be healthy.

HAIR LOSS

Chances are, if your pet is losing his hair, he is probably suffering from the itching or sores that often accompany such hair loss. Here are some easy ways to get hair growing again.

FOR DOGS AND CATS

Her Rings Are Rosy

If your cat or dog has developed bald patches around her ears and eyes, as well as on her front legs, she may have ringworm. Despite the name, this is not a worm infestation at all; it's a fungal infection. Your pet may scratch and enlarge the bare spots, turning them red and sore. Ringworm isn't life threatening, but it can be contagious—to other animals and to people, especially children—so call your vet to have it treated as soon as possible.

FOR RABBITS ONLY

Use a Salty Solution

If your bunny is losing fur, particularly around the hindquarters, your pet's cage is probably dirty—which means Mr. Rabbit is sitting for long periods of time on an unclean surface. Take your pet out of the cage and gently clip the fur on his feet, using grooming clippers. Be careful to clip around any wounds. Then soak the affected area for 15 minutes or so in a solution of Epsom salts (available at pharmacies and supermarkets) and water, according to the instructions on the box. Pat the area dry with a clean cloth. Clean the cage thoroughly before you return your pet to it, and clean it regularly thereafter. Repeat the soaking once or twice a day for several days, or until the skin seems to be healing. As the skin heals, fur should begin to grow back as well.

HEARING LOSS

For any of several reasons, animals sometimes lose all or some of their hearing. Rover might have had years of chronic ear infections. Snowball could be getting old. Or perhaps the problem is genetic. Some dog breeds, such as dalmatians and cocker spaniels, are especially prone to hearing problems.

To determine whether your pet might have lost some hearing, observe the animal's behavior. Does he sleep more soundly than he used to, instead of bolting awake if there's a loud noise? Does he appear unaware of the sound of familiar favorites, such as the opening of a kitchen cupboard or the cookie jar? When he's outdoors, is he oblivious to the noise of approaching cars? If your pet's behavior tells you that he's not hearing well, call your vet for an appointment. But don't panic.

Don't Bother Whispering—Your Cat Can Hear You Anyway

While dogs are justifiably renowned for their keen hearing, cats actually hear much better. People, dogs, and cats all have pretty similar abilities to hear low notes, but whereas dogs can hear notes about twice as high in pitch as humans can, cats can hear notes three times as high, perhaps so they can detect the frightened squeaks of hidden prey. The cat's hearing range covers 10 octaves, and it can distinguish notes just one-tenth of a tone apart. Moreover, cats can precisely locate sounds, using more than 20 muscles in each ear to funnel sound waves into the auditory passages. Researchers have proved the cat's ability to distinguish between two identical sounds issued at exactly the same time but 50 centimeters apart. In other words, the cat was able to hear that one sound arrived about three-millionths of a second before the other.

Regardless of the diagnosis, there are several ways you and your pet can cope with the situation.

FOR DOGS AND CATS

Tinker with a Bell

Since your deaf pet won't come running when you call, you might not know where he is at every moment. To keep track of his whereabouts and to check on him more easily, you might want to attach a little bell to his collar. Your pet may not be able to hear it, but you will, and you'll have a much better chance of knowing where he is.

I Can't See You, but I Can Smell You

It can be frustrating for a pet with a hearing problem to try locating you when you're out of sight. One way to make life easier for your pet is to wear some perfumed body lotion or scented aftershave. It makes you a little easier to track down.

Silence Can Be Deadly

If you have a pet with a hearing problem, keep her inside or walk her on a leash outside. A deaf animal can't hear any approaching danger such as cars, people, or other animals, so it's up to you to protect her by keeping her in a safe, contained environment.

FOR DOGS ONLY

Give a Show of Hands

If your dog has lost some or all of his hearing, he may not be able to hear a call to come for dinner or a

A dog that can't hear well can still learn the hand signals for "Come" (A) and "Wait" (B).

walk. But you can communicate by teaching your pet some simple hand signals. In fact, any animal that has had formal obedience training is probably already familiar with the common signals for "Come" and "Wait." When you give a command, accompany it with a hand signal that your pet can see. Be consistent. Pretty soon, even the deafest dog will understand what you want.

Flash Some Light on the Situation

Alternatively, use a few simple signals with a flashlight to tell your dog to come, sit, or stop. Soon, whenever you grab the flashlight, your pet will know you have something to say.

HEARTWORM DISEASE

In most parts of the country, mosquitoes are a fact of life. Although people in the United States rarely have to contend with any of the serious diseases that mosquitoes can carry, our pets are definitely at risk for a deadly, mosquito-borne illness: heartworm disease. Heartworms are tiny parasites transmitted by mosquitoes. When these worms mature inside a dog or cat, they clog the arteries, "choke" the heart, and ultimately kill the pet. Since the disease itself is so devastating, by far the best treatment is prevention.

FOR DOGS AND CATS

Prevention Is Good for the Heart

To prevent heartworm problems before they start, ask your vet to treat your healthy pet with heartworm

HEALTH

medication, which kills the larvae before they can grow and fill an animal's arteries. Your puppy or kitten can start treatment at an early age—as young as six to eight weeks—and can be given either a daily pill or a once-a-month chewable "treat." Heartworm medication is crucial for pets that live in areas where mosquitoes thrive—particularly in the Northwest and on the Atlantic and Gulf Coasts. But recently, cases of heartworm disease have begun to show up even in California. Most vets recommend treating your pet no matter where in the country you live.

TIME TO CALL THE VET

7 Signs of Heartworm Disease

Pet owners should be constantly on the watch for signs of heartworm disease, which include:

1. Coughing
2. Difficulty breathing
3. Increased thirst
4. Lethargy
5. Loss of appetite
6. Vomiting
7. Weight loss

If your pet shows these signs, take the animal to the vet immediately to confirm whether he has the disease. Dogs can be tested and, if infected, must be treated with doses of arsenic during a multiday stay at the animal hospital. Cats cannot tolerate the same approach, but ask your vet about appropriate treatments.

Testing, One-Two-Three

Before you start your pup on heartworm medication, you'll need to get the animal tested to determine whether she's already carrying heartworms. An animal that already has heartworm disease can't go on the preventive medication until the existing heartworms are treated, because the preventive medication doesn't cure the full-blown disease. (So far, although there is a test for heartworm in cats, it isn't considered 100 percent reliable. Unless a kitten is showing symptoms of heartworms, it's best to go ahead and put your kitty on a preventive program.)

Wait, Don't Switch

If you have both a cat and a dog, make sure you don't switch their heartworm medications. The medicines come in different doses for different types of animals.

When Mosquitoes Leave, So Do Heartworms

If you live in the Northeast or another region that gets a definite frost (effectively ending the mosquito

season), you can opt to discontinue treatment for the winter. But before you resume treatment in the spring, your pet will have to be retested. If you live in a warmer region such as the Southeast or an area that's continuously damp such as the Northwest, it's important to continue treatment year-round because mosquitoes thrive in those regions all year and thus may infect your pet with heartworm larvae at any time.

HIP DYSPLASIA

Hip dysplasia is a pain for many dogs, both large and small. Although it is more common in large dogs such as German shepherds and bullmastiffs, small dogs such as cocker spaniels can have it, too. It's a hereditary condition in which a dog's hip joints just don't fit together as neatly as they should. As the dog gets older, wear on the ill-fitting joints causes pain, and sometimes arthritis sets in.

Signs that your dog is suffering from hip dysplasia include holding a back paw off the ground, general stiffness, having trouble getting up after sitting or lying down for a while, yelping or whimpering while trying to move, and even trembling. The bad news is there's no cure. The good news is there's plenty you can do to help your dog cope.

It's a good idea to call your vet if you think your dog is showing signs of hip dysplasia. The doctor can diagnose it for certain and perhaps offer anti-inflammatory medication or recommend coated buffered aspirin for the pain. (Do not substitute acetaminophen, ibuprofen, or unbuffered aspirin.) In serious cases, surgery is a possibility. The vet can shave your dog's hip bones to reduce friction or even provide a hip replacement. But most owners opt for simple maintenance instead.

FOR DOGS ONLY

One Problem with This Joint Is Lack of Room

If you use a dog crate in your house, make sure your dog hasn't outgrown the last one you bought. Cramped spaces tend to increase joint pain, so you should see that your pet has room to stretch out and be comfortable.

TIME TO CALL THE VET

Fido's Problem Could Be Catching

Some diseases can be passed from one dog to another. If your pet shows signs of any of these—particularly if he's recently been in contact with another (possibly infected) animal—get him to the vet right away.

DISEASE	DESCRIPTION	SYMPTOMS
Brucellosis	A serious bacterial illness, often spread in kennels.	Swollen testicles in males; inability to conceive or to carry puppies to term in females; sometimes no symptoms in either sex.
Coronavirus	A virus that affects the intestinal tract and can be contracted through contact with infected feces.	Depression, vomiting, and diarrhea.
Distemper	An airborne virus that spreads like a cold.	Runny eyes and nose, severe diarrhea, vomiting, and eventually seizures.
Infectious canine hepatitis	A viral disease that attacks the liver, kidneys, lymph nodes, and other organs.	Fever, loss of appetite, increased thirst, and reddened mouth, throat, or eyelids.
Kennel cough	A contagious disease that involves both bacteria and viruses that strike the upper respiratory tract. Often spread in kennels where many dogs are housed together.	Dry, gagging cough, sometimes followed by expulsion of mucus.
Leptospirosis	A bacterial disease that attacks organs such as the kidneys, liver, and nervous system.	Vomiting and difficulty urinating.
Parvovirus	A virus contracted through contact with the infected stool of another dog.	Vomiting blood, severe bloody diarrhea, and dehydration.

Go Orthopedic

Make your dog's sleeping hours more comfortable by buying an orthopedic cushion to slip under his bed. The cushion should be made of thick "egg-crate" foam covered by a washable slipcover. You can get these cushions at a pet supply store or through a mail-order catalog.

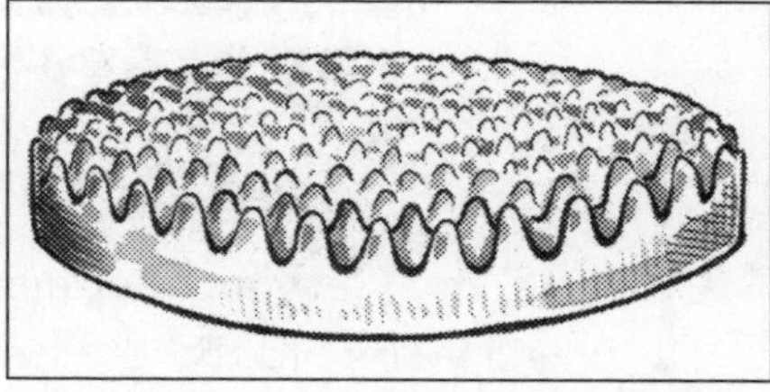

An "egg-crate" foam cushion will ease the discomfort of a dog with hip dysplasia.

Let Your Pooch Nest in Comfort

Dogs love to nest, especially when trying to escape discomfort. Put out a few beach towels or blankets—either inside her crate or in a separate spot—where your pooch can paw around, creating the perfect "nest" to sleep in.

Walk It Off

To keep your dog as limber as possible, make sure he gets mild, nonstraining exercise every day. You can even toss your pet a ball, as long as he isn't jumping up to catch it.

Don't Let Rover Jump for Joy

Pain from hip dysplasia increases when the joints are jarred or jolted. Even though you want your pet to have exercise, don't let her jump on and off furniture. Instead, make sure she takes a regular walk.

Encourage Lightweights

Dogs with hip dysplasia tend to gain weight because their exercise is less strenuous than it otherwise might be, and increased weight puts a greater strain on joints. It also makes it harder for your dog to get around without pain. Watch your pet's weight. If it increases by more than a pound or two, cut down on the animal's food. Just provide a little less than the usual amount at each meal instead of cutting out an entire meal. Your dog probably won't even notice the change.

ONE PERSON'S SOLUTION

Doggy Rest Stops

Tasha, my German shepherd, developed arthritis when she was 3 years old. By the time she was 13, it was difficult for her to get from room to room. So I put dog beds in several rooms of my house; that way, she could lie down and rest wherever she was at the moment. Commercial dog beds (available in catalogs or from pet supply stores) worked well because I could take the covers off and toss them in the washing machine. They also saved my furniture from doggy wear and tear!

—CAROLYN KIESS
Stoughton, Massachusetts

Keep Him Warm

Cold temperatures are tough on dogs with hip dysplasia. The aches and pains seem to increase when the mercury drops. So keep your ailing pooch warm. Crank up the household heat a couple of degrees if your pet seems stiff or in pain, especially if the climate outside is wintry or damp and chilly. And keep walks brief in cold weather.

Inject a Solution into the Problem

Your vet can give your hurting pup injections to temporarily ease the pain from hip dysplasia. Dosage and frequency vary with each dog.

HOT SPOTS

Fido or Fluffy seems to have a small, irritated area of skin on her haunches or belly, and she won't leave it alone. She scratches it incessantly, and pretty soon she's rubbing the spot along the carpet. She can't stop, and within a day or so, not only is the thing the size of a silver dollar, but she also has two more of the moist, smelly sores. The fur around them is matted or rubbed off entirely, and she's miserable.

Your pet has hot spots—aggravated skin sores that come from an irritating source (such as a concentration of flea eggs) on one area of the skin, dirt and dust, or even sap that is stuck to the skin. You need to pay attention to these sores because they usually won't disappear without help. And if they proliferate too much or hang around too long, they can become infected. Besides, you'll be in misery yourself just watching your pet try to cope.

FOR DOGS AND CATS

Give Him a Narrow Shave

To start your pet on the road to hot spot recovery, use grooming clippers to carefully clip the fur surrounding the area. Clip about one-half to one inch beyond the sore, increasing the clipped area if the spot gets bigger before it gets better. Clipping the fur will help the sore start to dry out and prevent hair and other dirt from aggravating it.

Take Her to the Dry Cleaner

Your immediate goal is to get that spot clean and dry. Clean the sore with a little hydrogen peroxide (available at pharmacies) on gauze or a cotton ball. After the hydrogen peroxide dries, spray the area with cortisone spray. Do this twice a day until the sore starts to dry out or a scab begins to form. If the problem area gets bigger or doesn't clear up in a couple of days, or if several spots continue to spread, call the vet for treatment.

TIME TO CALL THE VET

If Your Pet Takes a Licking

If your cat or dog continually licks one spot, she may have been bitten by another animal. (The problem may not be obvious if the pet's fur is hiding the wound.) Check carefully to see whether there is a bite wound. If you find one, call your vet. Bite wounds, particularly those inflicted by cats, are extremely likely to be infected and need to be treated with antibiotics.

TIME TO CALL THE VET

Spot Check

If your pet's hot spots don't clear up, or if she keeps on getting them over and over, call the vet. Your pet may be allergic to something that's causing a skin reaction. Your vet will ask you questions about the animal's diet, daily habits, and so forth to determine the root of the allergy. Pinpointing an allergy may take time, but it's worth the effort. Otherwise, the animal's problem could continue indefinitely.

Get Serious about Fleas

Your pet's hot spots may be the result of an irritation caused by fleas, so step up the flea treatment. Whether you choose a shampoo, collar, or spray, make sure you're doing everything you can to fluster those fleas.

FOR DOGS ONLY

Avon Calling

Just as many people feel that Avon's Skin-So-Soft is a great insect repellent, some dog owners swear by its soothing powers on hot spots. Give it a try, rubbing a little on the irritated area.

HYPERTHERMIA (OVERHEATING)

When the weather heats up, so do your pets. They can get overheated and may have a tough time releasing enough heat to cool themselves down. They have very few sweat glands, so instead they pant to release excess heat. Severe overheating, or hyperthermia, means that the body's temperature has risen above acceptable levels, which can cause brain damage and even death.

Certain animals are more prone to overheating than others. Black or furry dogs, as well as black or long-haired cats, build up plenty of body heat. And bulldogs and other breeds with "pushed-in" faces sometimes pant so hard that they can't breathe well.

Signs of severe overheating are weakness, unresponsiveness, disorientation, and rapid panting. If your pet shows any combination of these symptoms or is unconscious, you need to call the vet. But there are plenty of things you can do to help your pet cool down in less severe instances, and there are even actions you can take to lessen the effects of severe overheating before your pet gets to the animal hospital.

FOR DOGS AND CATS

A Cold Shower Will Help

If your pet is showing signs of severe overheating but is still conscious, hose the animal off with cold water, then provide water to drink. Putting an ice pack on your pet's head also will help. As soon as you finish supplying this first aid, call the vet. Taking these steps can stop your pet's temperature from rising and could help prevent brain damage or even death.

If you don't want to turn a hose on your cat, immerse her in a cold bath for several seconds (or as long as she'll stand for it). Or dunk her in a lake, pool, or brook, being careful to keep her head above water. Then give her water to drink and call the vet.

If He's Out Cold

If your pet is unconscious, use a rectal thermometer to take his temperature and determine whether the unconsciousness is probably due to hyperthermia. If your pet's temperature is 105°F or higher, immerse him in a cool bath, keeping his head above water. Remove the animal after just one minute, then take him immediately to the nearest emergency animal hospital. Do not wrap the animal in a towel; that will only keep the heat in.

If your dog is unconscious and hyperthermic but too heavy for you to lift into a tub, hose her off for several seconds before taking her to the animal hospital. If necessary, get help carrying her to the car.

Not Everyone Likes It Hot

If your dog or cat is panting rapidly, he's too hot. When animals

TIME TO CALL THE VET

Water, Water Everywhere . . . And Every Drop He Drinks

If your cat or dog is suddenly lapping up more water than usual and the weather isn't unusually hot, keep an eye on him. Thirst is a common side effect of steroids and insulin, so if he's on either of those drugs, make sure he has plenty to drink. In a pet that's not already on insulin to treat diabetes, increased thirst can indicate the *onset* of diabetes or of kidney or thyroid problems (hyperthyroidism in cats and hypothyroidism in dogs). So if your pet continues to drink more than his usual ration for a week and you aren't sure of the cause, call the vet for a diagnosis and treatment.

YOU'VE GOTTA LOVE 'EM

What Any Mother Would Do

Back in March 1996, a stray white cat was living in an abandoned garage in East New York, one of the rougher neighborhoods of New York City. She probably lived there for months, attracting little attention from anyone.

Then the garage went up in flames. After helping to put out the blaze, David Gianelli, one of the firefighters who responded to the call, caught sight of five kittens, each one more severely burned than the next, just outside the garage. In a nearby lot, he found the white cat, also badly burned. Shocked, Gianelli realized that she had returned over and over again to the burning building until she had retrieved all of her eight-week-old kittens. Gianelli gingerly placed the entire family in a box and took them to a local animal shelter.

During the next few days, Scarlett—as she was named by a shelter worker—was big news. Her picture ran on the front pages of newspapers. Because of the extensive surgery she needed, the skin on her face was drawn and taut, making her look as if she'd just had a face-lift.

During April, as Scarlett and her kittens convalesced, their story gained further attention. They were featured on the BBC and CNN, and offers to adopt the cats poured in from all over the world. Oprah Winfrey even wanted to have Scarlett and her brood on her Mother's Day show.

Of course, the story had a happy ending. Scarlett and her kittens (all but one, who didn't make it) soon found homes. But New Yorkers wouldn't quickly forget the image of the little white cat risking death to save her babies. Scarlett was hailed as a hero, and rightly so. But after all, she only did what any mom would do.

pant too hard, they create more body heat and become dehydrated from salivating. Move your distressed pet to a cool, quiet spot—under a shady tree or in a room with a fan or air conditioner turned on. Provide plenty of water for your pet to drink and try to keep the atmosphere calm.

FOR DOGS ONLY

Make Theirs on the Rocks

To help your pup cool down, give her a few ice cubes to chew on. The crunchy cubes are fun to eat and provide essential fluids your pet needs to get the cooling process going.

FOR BIRDS ONLY

He Has Hot Feet

If your bird is breathing with his mouth open and his feet feel warm to the touch, he is overheated. Cool him down carefully by moving him to a cooler room, turning on a fan (make sure it doesn't blow on him), or turning on the air conditioner at a very low level. Birds can't tolerate drafts or sudden changes in temperature, so cool your pet down slowly. Give him plenty of water to drink, too. If the bird does not seem better within an hour, call the vet.

Why Your Feathered Friend Needs a Regular Checkup

Your bird should have a checkup once a year with a vet who specializes in such care. (A good breeder, pet store owner, other vet, or even the Yellow Pages will help you identify an appropriate professional.) This is important so that the vet can:

- Check the overall condition of nose, eyes, feathers, throat, and anus
- Take a culture from the anus in order to check for bacterial problems
- Take a Gram's stain to check feces for yeast

HYPOTHERMIA

They may have fur, but those four-legged pets of ours still get cold when the temperature drops. Add snow, sleet, wind, and rain, and our friends with the natural fur coats are bound to be shivering just like the rest of us. Prolonged exposure to a chill will lead to hypothermia—a dangerous drop in core body temperature—in pets just as it will in humans. You need to

know what signs to watch for and how to "winterize" your pet.

Signs of hypothermia include prolonged and violent shivering, which speeds up an animal's metabolism and thus serves as a short-term way for the body to keep warm. But it takes energy to shiver, and if an animal is cold for too long, that energy will run out, and the body temperature will start to drop. Then signs of more advanced hypothermia—weakness, disorientation, lethargy—will start to show. Left untreated, these conditions will eventually lead to unconsciousness and even death.

It's true that some animals are built to withstand frosty temps. Huskies, malamutes, and Samoyeds, for example, have dense fur coats that make them well suited for winter weather. Even Labs and golden retrievers do pretty well. But shorthaired or small dogs such as Jack Russells just aren't up to the task. Neither are injured or sick cats or other small animals such as rabbits. Older pets have a tough time with the cold, too, especially those with arthritis, kidney ailments, or respiratory problems. Here's what you can do to help them cope.

FOR PETS IN GENERAL

These Aren't Dog Days

❑ Your pet needs to spend some time outdoors, but it's cold out there. Fine. Just keep the outside jaunt short, depending on how cold it is and your pet's individual condition. If Rover is big and strong, with a thick winter coat, let him enjoy his 20-minute walk in 25°F weather (even if *you* have to bundle up). If Fluffy is 13 years old and weighs about 5 pounds, follow her around the yard for 5 to 10 minutes, then shoo her back inside. If it's 40°F and blowing rain, put a doggy coat on your Jack Russell before you both venture out.

Shiver Me Timbers

❑ If your pet shows signs of hypothermia, bring her indoors immediately. Wrap her in blankets, then crank up

How to Take Your Pet's Pulse

Perhaps Rover's come home from a fast run, and he's panting hard even after you thought he should have slowed down. Or you discover that Tabby isn't napping; she's unconscious. In either case, you'll be better able to deal with the situation if you know how to take your pet's pulse.

Start by laying the animal on his side, then gently sliding your hand under the top back leg. Feel for the "crease" where the leg meets the body, and you'll find the little groove where the artery lies. Rest your first two fingers along the artery and count a pulse.

Take your pet's pulse under the hind leg (A) or under the chest (B).

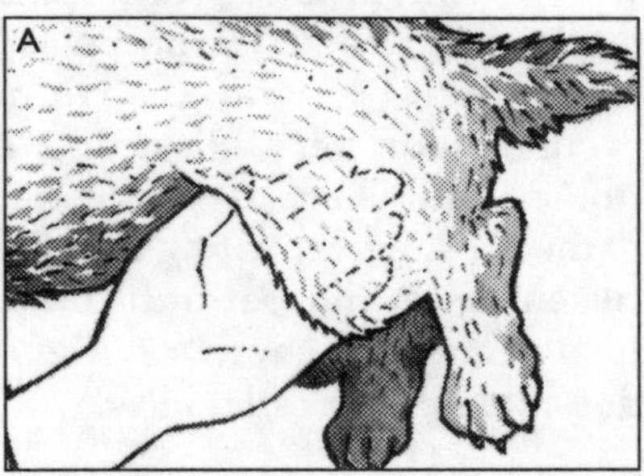

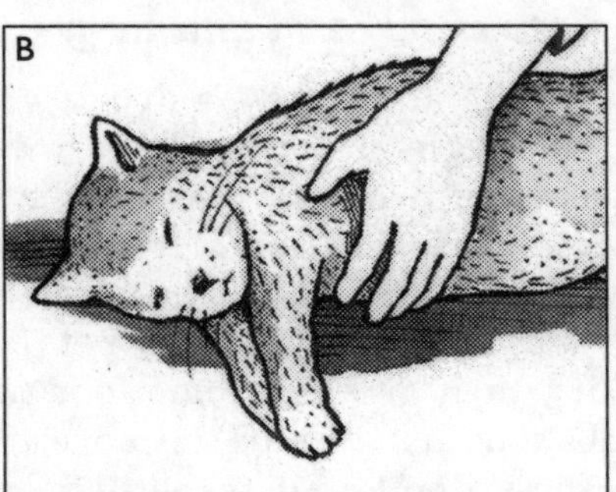

Alternatively, if you're dealing with a cat, you may prefer to lay your pet on her side and cup your hand under her chest until you can feel her pulse.

Pulse rate is generally stated in terms of a full minute, but you don't need to hold your fingers against a pet's artery quite that long. To calculate a 60-second pulse, simply take a 10-second pulse and multiply by 6, or take a 20-second pulse and multiply by 3. Then compare the result with the average healthy pulse for your type of pet, using these guidelines.

- Large dog: 60 to 80 beats per minute
- Medium dog: 120 to 140 beats per minute
- Cat or small dog: 140 to 160 beats per minute
- Rabbit: 160 to 200 beats per minute

If your pet's pulse is too rapid and he's just finished exercising, let him rest for about ten minutes before you check his pulse again. If he's healthy, his pulse should return to a normal rate. If it does not return to normal, it is too slow, he shows other signs of illness, he's unconscious, or you can't determine any cause for the unusual heart rate, call the vet immediately for a diagnosis and treatment.

HEALTH

the heat a few degrees or light a fire in the woodstove. Stay with your pet until the signs begin to disappear: She stops shivering, she seems more alert and responsive, and her temperature reaches 100°F. When the animal is comfortable, give her some food and water; fuel helps generate warmth and strength. If your pet's condition does not improve, or if she loses consciousness, call the vet immediately.

If Your Pet's All Wet

❑ Animals can easily end up with hypothermia if they get wet on a chilly day and don't have a chance to dry off. For instance, if your cat spends a night outside in a cold rain or your dog crashes through the ice on a pond or stream, hypothermia is an all-too-likely result. So if your pet gets wet and chilled, be sure to get him indoors to a warm room as quickly as possible. Throw a few beach towels or bath towels in the dryer for several minutes, then wrap them around your animal while they're still warm. Be especially careful to wrap the warmth around your pet's chest and abdomen and where the legs connect to the body. Keep rotating towels between dryer and pet until the animal's condition improves. And if it doesn't improve, call the vet.

It Hurts So Good

It's a sweltering hot day, and where's your cat? Sitting near the AC? Nope, she's lounging on your desk, right in the heat of the blazing sun. How can she do it? Whereas humans start to experience heat as pain at about 112°F, cats can tolerate temperatures of about 125°F.

Keep Her Warm and Cozy

❑ If you don't have a dryer, wrap your pet in one or two large towels anyway and drape one or two more over a radiator, near a lit woodstove or fireplace, or in front of any other available heat source. Then rotate the towels between heat source and pet. Stay with your pet until she's warm and dry, then give her some food and water. If the animal's condition does not improve, or if she loses consciousness, don't hesitate to call the vet immediately.

FOR DOGS ONLY

Maybe It's Strictly a Summer Home

Even if your dog spends hours in the backyard pen during the summer, don't assume that he'll be okay there for the same amount of time in winter. If you want to use the pen, make sure your dog can handle the cold. Is he small? Does he have short hair? Is he old, or has he been sick? If the answer is yes to any of these questions, leave the pen for summertime fun.

Make the Pen a Pal

If your pooch is young and strong, has a good coat, and seems to enjoy being outdoors in winter, go ahead and use the pen. But make sure that the enclosure has an area that is sheltered from the wind. If the pen is not attached to an outside wall of the house or garage (which provides your pet some shelter), attach a blanket or rug to one side of the fence. Also provide some type of overhead covering under which your dog can huddle. Put a bowl of warm water in the sheltered area so that she can drink. Even provide her with an old wool blanket or two or a scattered bale of straw in which she can "nest." Check on her at least several times a day and replace the drinking water if it freezes over. Above all, bring your dog inside if she shows signs of being cold.

In winter, a dog kept in a pen outside needs a space that's sheltered from the wind, some form of protection overhead, drinking water, and "nesting" material.

Button up that doggy coat when it's cold outside!

Buy a New Winter Coat

If your shorthaired or small dog starts shivering the minute he pokes his nose outside, buy him a coat. Specialty pet shops and some pet supply stores carry a variety of dog coats in many sizes, styles, and colors.

FOR CATS ONLY

Put Her on the Big Screen

If you're concerned that your outdoor cat may roam too far during the colder months, consider making use of a screened porch or balcony. Let your cat outside in this enclosed area for 15 to 20 minutes—10 minutes if the temperature is, say, less than 20°F. She'll get fresh air, survey her territory, and stretch her legs—all within a safe proximity to the warm house.

INSECT BITES AND STINGS

Mosquitoes, flies, bees, and other bugs just love to chomp on animal flesh. To them, each pet is juicier than the last. When your pal comes home whimpering or meowing after being bitten, you need to figure out what type of insect has attacked your pet. Then you can help relieve the animal's discomfort.

FOR DOGS AND CATS

Give Mosquito Bites the Cold Shoulder

The most dangerous consequence of a mosquito bite to your dog or cat is heartworm disease. But your kitty—and, less often, your pooch—also may develop a common allergic reaction to a mosquito bite. Swelling, redness, and a mild rash on or around the eyelids could very well mean that Fluffy has been bitten by a mosquito. Since it's tricky to try to apply soothing creams or lotions to the eye area, apply a cold compress instead. Dampen a clean cloth with cold water or wrap a couple of ice cubes in a clean cloth, then hold the compress against the injured eyelid for a few moments or as long as your pet will allow it. The cold should reduce both the swelling and the pain.

FOR DOGS ONLY

Make a Stinging Comment

If your dog has been stung by a bee, her face may swell and she may break out in hives. Both are allergic reactions. The first time you see such symptoms, it is wise to call the vet. He may suggest giving the animal Benadryl—the over-the-counter antihistamine commonly given to people—and tell you the correct dosage for your pet.

It's Okay to Pour Salt in the Wound

If the bee sting is in your dog's foot, you can try soaking the foot in Epsom salts and water (in the proportions given on the package) for 15 to 20 minutes to relieve pain and swelling. If you are outdoors and you have nothing else available, a handful of cool mud packed on the sting can reduce pain and swelling. Of course, when you get your pet home, wash the mud off.

Shoo Fly, Don't Bother Me

Deerflies typically attack in packs, swarming around the face and ears of your pet while he's walking in the woods. He may come home with bits of dried blood on those areas, from bites. You can do two things to prevent this. First, rub a gel-type insect repellent on the tips of the dog's ears before heading out. Second, save your jaunts in the woods for the evening, when deerflies are not as prevalent as they are during the day. Evening is generally when mosquitoes appear, however, so you may have to choose between the lesser of two evils—or avoid walking in the woods until cold weather arrives.

COMMON MISTAKES

Mosquitoes Hit Both Sides of the Screen

Even if your pet is an indoor kitty that never ventures outside, she's still susceptible to heartworm disease. In fact, studies done by veterinary clinics show that a large percentage of cats that contract the disease are indoor cats. Perhaps this is because mosquitoes don't always stay outside. Some may slip through the screen, and all it takes is one bite. It's wise to put even an indoor cat on a heartworm prevention program before it's too late.

HEALTH

ITCHING AND RASHES

A lot of itching in animals is due to allergies, ear mites, or fleas, and each of those problems has its own treatments. But itching has other sources as well, and dogs and cats aren't the only pets that suffer. Rabbits, birds, and fish get itches occasionally, too.

FOR DOGS AND CATS

Try a Cereal Approach

Some rashes and sores seem to have no obvious source. What do you do if your pet breaks out in itchy sores or a rash and you've ruled out fleas, mites, and allergies? Try bathing the animal with an oatmeal- or aloe-based shampoo (available at pet supply stores).

FOR DOGS ONLY

Is Sparky Riding a Scooter?

If you see your dog "scooting" along on her rear end or incessantly rubbing that area to scratch an itch, she may have an impacted anal gland, worms, or maggots. All three sound pretty hideous, but they can be treated. If your pet spends time in an outdoor pen, clean it thoroughly. The animal may have sat in feces, allowing maggots to develop and hatch. In any case, call your vet, who will want to see the dog to determine the exact cause of the problem and treat it.

FOR BIRDS ONLY

Polly's Got Pluck

Birds deal with itchy situations by plucking at them. If your bird keeps plucking at himself—some birds pick themselves naked quite quickly—the problem could be caused by a yeast or bacterial infection. Call the vet for treatment.

FOR FISH ONLY

Ich's No Fun

If one of your fish is scratching her body along the gravel at the bottom of the tank, or even on larger rocks or other props in the aquarium, check her body for little white spots that look like grains of salt. Your pet's fins may be twitching, too, and she may not be eating. If these signs add up, the fish is probably infested with the parasite *Ichthyophthirius multifiliis*, or "ich" for short. Isolate your contagious fish in a separate tank to protect your other aquatic pets. Then consult your pet store owner for advice on appropriate medications.

If one fish has ich, keep her isolated from tank-mates until the condition is cured.

Prepare for the Patient's Return

While your fish is receiving medication in a separate tank, change the water in his regular tank, making sure it is clean and well oxygenated when he returns. And monitor any other fish for itching and white spots, as ich can spread rapidly among fish in the same tank.

FOR RABBITS ONLY

Give Her a Fresh Start

A rabbit can get maggots around the rectal area from sitting or lying in an unclean cage, especially during hot weather. Maggots bury themselves under the skin, causing discomfort. You probably won't see them, but you can learn the signs: a strong, unusual odor in the feces and moistness on the surface of the skin around the rectal area. To kill the nasty creatures, buy a mild flea spray—one that's made for kittens. Clip or trim the fur around the affected area, then lightly spray the flea treatment on it, avoiding your pet's head and especially the eyes. The spray will kill the maggots. Let it dry, then try to keep your rabbit's tender hind end dry by making sure that her cage is immaculate. Repeat the procedure the next day if you don't see any improvement. If the problem continues, call your vet.

TIME TO CALL THE VET

Mopsy Has Mite-y Fine Dandruff

Dandruff on a rabbit usually isn't dandruff at all—it's evidence of a type of mite that is nesting in your fluffy pet's fur. If you look closely, you may even see the mites moving slightly—hence the condition's name, "walking dandruff." Call the vet for treatment.

HEALTH

She's in the Powder Room

Urine or feces that remains in contact with your rabbit's skin can "scald" the rectal area, making it burn and itch. To soothe your bunny's fanny, first stop at your local pharmacy and buy a mild drying treatment called Domeboro powder (found in the skin care section). Then trim or clip the fur around the problem area

YOU'VE GOTTA LOVE 'EM

Saba, the Mountain-Climbing Cat

My cat, Saba, is a languid, overweight five-year-old. You would not guess that, for one memorable summer, she was a mountain climber.

When Saba was little more than a kitten, I worked as manager of the Moosilauke Ravine Lodge, a Dartmouth College facility at the base of 4,810-foot Mount Moosilauke in western New Hampshire. Saba was extraordinarily interested in the outdoors. On her first time out of the house, I put her on a leash—which proved nearly disastrous for me, as she dragged me over woodpiles, up and down steep banks, and through an enormous raspberry bramble below the deck. Clearly, I had to let her chance it alone.

At Moosilauke, she found a tremendous amount to explore. One morning, I was too preoccupied with work to notice that Saba had vanished about the same time a gang of people headed up the mountain. Some hours later, I came into the dining room and overheard several hikers discussing "this mountain-climbing cat." More reports filtered in during the day, including a description of a gray cat chasing rabbits on the summit. Then, in midafternoon, Saba returned. She was rather fatigued and a bit hungry but otherwise completely unrepentant.

Thus began an extraordinary summer of feline adventures. Saba hiked the mountain nearly every time a climber came by the lodge.

and pat it dry. (Do not lift the fur to clip it because you'll risk cutting the skin as well as the fur. Instead, leave the fur flat.) Mix the Domeboro powder with water according to the package directions and apply it to your rabbit's rear end with a clean washcloth or cotton ball. Repeat once or twice a day until the condition improves. If your pet shows no improvement within two days, call the vet.

She would come back, footsore and hungry, and then head out again as soon as the next unsuspecting hiker happened along. I don't think she ever climbed the peak twice in one day, but it is possible.

It was only a matter of time before this predilection got her into trouble. There are four trails to the summit, and sometimes she headed down the wrong one. The first time, two hikers found her wandering on the other side of the mountain and brought her around to the Ravine Lodge in a fanny pack. The second time, she was picked up by a young woman who couldn't read the faded writing on Saba's collar, decided she must be a stray, and took her home to Rhode Island. The woman called two days later and explained that a coworker also had seen Saba on a hiking trip to Moosilauke and figured out the cat's connection to the Ravine Lodge. That afternoon, I drove to Rhode Island to recover my cat.

I changed jobs a few years back, and Saba has rarely been back to Mount Moosilauke. She seems to have lost her interest in mountain climbing. Although she still goes on walks occasionally, these days she seldom bestirs herself from in front of the stove.

—DAVID HOOKE
Hanover, New Hampshire

HEALTH

LAMENESS

Your pet can easily strain a muscle while running down stairs or leaping into the car. Or he might get a thorn or bit of glass caught in his paw during an outdoor romp. The most obvious sign of either injury is likely to be limping, and the first step in helping your four-legged friend is to pay attention to the *way* he's limping. If your pet is hopping along without putting weight on the injured leg but the leg isn't obviously broken, the animal may have a severe muscle strain. If your pet is limping but able to put some weight on the injured leg, he may have a mild strain, a thorn or other sharp object in his paw, or even an abscess from a wound that has been hidden by his fur. Knowing this will give you an advantage in choosing the appropriate treatment.

Those Baby Blues

Are you delighted that your cat just gave birth to four kittens that all have blue eyes? Don't get too excited; all kittens are born with blue eyes. Their true eye color doesn't develop until they are several months old.

FOR DOGS AND CATS

A Thorny Problem

If your pet comes home from a walk or a romp limping and wanting to lick a sore paw constantly, there's probably a thorn, shard of glass, or other sharp object stuck in her foot. Gently check to see what you can find, looking with special care in the pad of her paw and between the toes. If the object appears embedded near the surface of the skin, carefully pull it out. Then clean the wound with water or hydrogen peroxide (available at pharmacies) on a clean cloth. Apply a little antibacterial ointment such as Neosporin (also available at pharmacies). If your pet is a dog and the injured area is accessible, apply a bandage of gauze and tape. If your pet is a cat or the wound can't be bandaged conveniently, leave it open. In either case, monitor the situation for a few days and call the vet if the wound does not seem to be healing.

Know Your Limits

If a foreign object is really embedded in your pet's paw, or if you try to remove it and can't, don't force the issue—the object may have punctured an artery or caused other damage, and you could worsen the situation. Instead, call the vet, who can remove it safely.

HEALTH

Enforce Quiet Time

Muscle strains are not serious, but they heal best when the muscle is given a chance to rest. If you suspect that your limping pet has simply strained a muscle, try to keep the animal quiet for a few days. Minimize play, keep necessary walks short, and let her sleep a lot if she wants to. If your dog normally spends time in a crate, keep her there as long as she's comfortable staying put. This will encourage her to rest. If your pet wants to be touched, take the opportunity to do some gentle grooming, avoiding the sore area. If she does not want to be touched, leave her alone.

FOR DOGS ONLY

Buffer the Pain

With your vet's permission, you can offer your dog coated buffered aspirin to relieve the pain of a muscle strain while it is healing. The dosage is generally 1 regular strength adult tablet for every 40 to 50

YOU'VE GOTTA LOVE 'EM

They Call Him Mellow Yellow

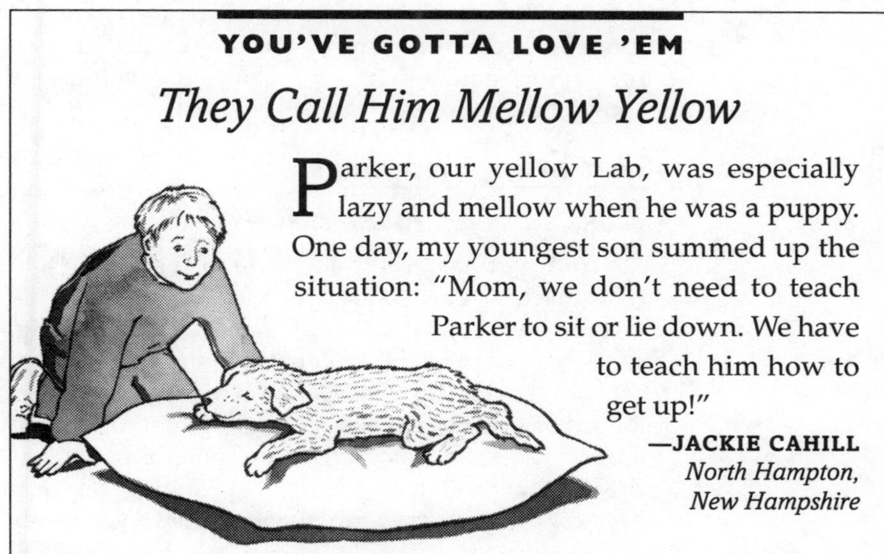

Parker, our yellow Lab, was especially lazy and mellow when he was a puppy. One day, my youngest son summed up the situation: "Mom, we don't need to teach Parker to sit or lie down. We have to teach him how to get up!"

—**JACKIE CAHILL**
North Hampton, New Hampshire

pounds of your dog's weight, administered with food once or twice a day if your dog is limping, sore, or stiff. (Do *not* substitute unbuffered aspirin, acetaminophen, or ibuprofen, as any of these medications could be harmful to your pet.)

LETHARGY

Everyone gets the blahs sometimes, and that includes pets. Tabby might be content to lounge around for a few days, or Rover might decide to take a long nap one afternoon. No big deal, you think. Maybe it's cold outside, and Tabby wants to curl up by the fire until the temperature warms up. Perhaps you and Rover took an unusually long morning walk, and he's just plain tired. Generally, your pet will snap out of this sluggishness on his own. But lethargy can be a sign of other problems, and it's important to distinguish between short-term slowdowns and something more significant.

Lethargy could be an indication that your pet is having digestive problems, including constipation, diarrhea, or even an intestinal blockage. It could be a symptom of accidental poisoning or of a serious illness such as heartworm disease. Or it could simply be your pet's reaction to prolonged exposure to excessive heat or cold. If you can't pinpoint the cause, such as a cold room, and correct it—say, by turning up the temperature in the room(s) where your pet spends time—be sure to call the vet.

FOR DOGS AND CATS

Make a List for Your Listless Pet

Your pet has been lying around for a couple of days. She doesn't want to go for a walk or play with her favorite toys. You've ruled out hot or cold weather, rigorous exercise, or some other obvious stress (such as recent surgery) as the cause. Now what? Make a list of her other symptoms. Is she drooling, vomiting, and dazed? If so, she may have eaten something toxic. Is she coughing and having difficulty breathing? She may have contracted heartworm disease. Could she possibly

be pregnant? Write down everything you observe about her behavior that's unusual.

Next, do a quick check of the condition of your pet's coat, eyes, gums, and nose. (With a cat, note whether the third eyelid is closed or swollen.) Again, write down your observations.

Now Call In Your Report

Once you've made your notations, call the vet. Because lethargy can signal a wide range of potential problems, your vet will appreciate having as much information about your pet's condition as you are able to provide.

COMMON MISTAKES

My Birdie Lies over the Counter

Don't buy over-the-counter antibiotics at the pet store in an attempt to treat a bird's infection yourself. Each over-the-counter bird medication is designed to cover a narrow spectrum of ailments, and it's unlikely the one you choose will cure whatever is ailing your bird. In fact, when you finally get your pet to the vet, an over-the-counter medication may even mask or alter the results of testing done by the doctor. In the worst case, your bird may die before you get her to the vet.

FOR BIRDS ONLY

Time's Flying— And Tweetie Isn't

If your bird seems lethargic, particularly if he is just sitting at the bottom of his cage, take him to the vet immediately. Birds are masters at masking serious symptoms, and by the time lethargy overtakes them, they are usually really ill, perhaps near death. Don't wait to see whether your pet will perk up on his own.

FOR FISH ONLY

Head Straight to the Tank

If one or more fish appear to be lethargic, hovering near the bottom of the tank, there is probably an excess of ammonia in the water, caused by too much excrement. High ammonia content is a common killer of pet fish, so it's important to correct the situation immediately. Put all of the fish in a different tank and then clean the dirty tank thoroughly before refilling it and returning the fish.

HEALTH

Maybe They Have Too Many Close Friends

If your fish seem normally active soon after you clean their tank but then become lethargic again, consider moving some of them to a different tank permanently. You could be keeping too many fish in one tank, thus allowing too much ammonia to build up in the water. If you are uncertain whether your fish tank is overpopulated, ask someone at the pet store where you bought the fish.

3 *Steps to Check Your Pet Snake's Health*

It doesn't take long to get a pretty good idea of whether your pet snake is healthy. Here are three key areas to inspect.

1. Eyes. They should be clear, unless the snake is in the process of shedding. If the latter is the case, *both* eyes should be clouded over evenly.

2. Mouth. The mouth should be clean, without mucus or "cheesy" material.

3. Body overall. The body should be free of stains or discoloration, raised or damaged scales, or bumps under the skin (signs of infection or parasites).

If you find problems, get your pet to the vet right away.

Try a Reducing Plan

Another way to deal with excess ammonia in a fish tank—after thoroughly cleaning the tank, of course—is to purchase an ammonia-reducing filter or ammonia-reducing drops for the tank. You can pick these up at a pet supply store.

FOR REPTILES ONLY

It's Alimentary, My Dear

If your reptilian friend appears listless, check to make sure that the temperature of the animal's environment falls within her optimum range. Make any necessary temperature adjustments and watch your pet for a day or so. If she doesn't perk up, she may have an alimentary canal blockage. Contact your vet, who will be able to diagnose and treat this problem.

PILL TAKING

From time to time, your pet may have to take pills, perhaps as part of a flea treatment or as a painkiller for arthritis. You can't just hand a pill to your pet with a glass of water and expect the animal to swallow it. Some pets are all too adept at identifying even those pills that you've taken great pains to conceal in a bit of food—and they have no compunction about spitting them out. Always watch carefully to be sure your pet actually swallows any pills you give him, and keep trying different approaches until the medicine really does go down. Here are some possibilities.

FOR DOGS AND CATS

Play Hide-and-Seek

Mix a pill in with your pet's moist food at mealtime. If the pill is large enough, you may be able to disguise it by breaking it up or crushing it before adding it to the food. Be sure to check with your vet first, however, as some medications are coated and should not be crushed.

A WORD FROM DR. MAUE

How to Be a Pill Pusher with Your Cat

DR. LISA MAUE
Veterinarian in private practice in Medford, Massachusetts, for more than a decade

It's one thing to get the pills from the veterinarian. It's another thing to get the cat to swallow them. You can ask your vet for what's called a syringe dispenser, which will hang on to the pill until you get the cat's jaws pried open, and then it will handily pop the pill into the cat's throat. Or you can try another method. Take a clean, brand-new pencil and dab a little petroleum jelly, butter, or peanut butter on the end of the eraser. Then stick the pill on it. Open the cat's mouth—it doesn't have to be open very wide—and push the pencil into the mouth until you reach the back of the throat. The pill will easily dislodge so that the cat can swallow it. The best part is that even if the cat resists, the pill will fall in where it's supposed to.

Alternatively, mix the pill in with a little moist pet food and hold the mixture in the palm of your hand for your pet to eat like a treat. Then follow up with something else to eat, such as a crunchy snack or, if it's mealtime, the animal's usual meal.

Give Her a Massage

One way to get a reluctant pet to take medicine is to open the animal's jaws wide and pop the pill in her mouth. Place it on top of her tongue, as far back as you can without causing her discomfort. Then hold her jaws closed and massage her throat, helping her to swallow. Don't release her jaws until she swallows. Once she does, let go of her jaws and watch to make sure she doesn't spit out the pill. If she does, try this method again.

The Painkiller That Can Kill

Never give acetaminophen to cats, no matter how much you want to relieve their minor aches and pains. It will make them sick and can even kill them. Cats don't tolerate ibuprofen well either, so don't try substituting that. Painful as it may be, it's better to let your pet endure some discomfort than to kill the animal in an attempt to be kind.

Blow in His Face, and He'll Follow You Anywhere

An alternative method of pill popping begins the same way. Open your pet's jaws wide and insert the pill as far back in his mouth, on top of his tongue, as you can without causing him discomfort. Then hold his jaws closed and blow a quick puff of air in his face. When he blinks, he'll also swallow the pill. Let go of your pet's jaws and watch to make sure he doesn't spit out the pill. If he does, try again.

If at First You Don't Succeed . . .

If you've tried all these methods and just can't convince your pal to swallow her pills, ask the vet if the medication can be given in some other form, such as a chewable treat or a liquid that can be mixed in with your pet's food. Many medications do come in more than one form.

FOR DOGS ONLY

Try This Grape Idea

Many dogs like to eat seedless grapes for snacks. Insert your dog's pill into the center of a grape and feed it to him as a treat. Then follow with several untreated grapes to complete his snack.

POISONING

From time to time, pets eat things they shouldn't. The average household is filled with toxic temptations, from houseplants to pesticides, cleaners to human medications. Then there's the outside world, where the sweet scent of antifreeze or the fun of rock chewing beckons. Sometimes pet owners even feed their pets things that seem like treats—chocolate, for instance—but turn out to be toxic.

The obvious first line of defense is to be on the alert for things that shouldn't pass through your pet's lips or beak, whether those substances are the contents of the medicine cabinet or the plants in the window box. But you can't monitor your pet's every taste, so it's important to recognize the symptoms that mean a pet may have tried something toxic. In dogs and cats, watch for drooling, glazed eyes, vomiting, apparent stomach cramps, lethargy, and seizures. Birds that have been poisoned typically have respiratory trouble and may even fall off perches.

If you suspect that your pet has been poisoned, call your vet, the nearest animal emergency clinic, or even your state poison control center. Look for the poison control center phone number on the same page as the other emergency numbers in your phone book and post it near your phone.

Antifreeze Is Fatal

Dogs and cats love the sweet taste of antifreeze that has leaked from your car onto the driveway; they'll lap it up. The trouble is that standard antifreeze is toxic, even in very small amounts. Ask your mechanic to use the new type of antifreeze that's safe for pets. And if you suspect your pet has ingested toxic antifreeze from a leak in another vehicle, *call the vet immediately,* even if there are no signs or symptoms at first. Eventually, the animal's kidneys will shut down; your pet will stop eating, urinate less frequently, vomit or have diarrhea, or even convulse.

FOR PETS IN GENERAL

Close the Door on Trash

❑ If your pet roams freely around the house, make sure he can't get into the kitchen trash, where he's bound to eat something he shouldn't. Keep your trash in a can with a secure lid or in a locked cabinet under the sink. Empty it regularly so that your pet isn't attracted by tempting odors.

Some Things Should Stay in the Closet

❑ Household cleaners, as well as medicines intended for people, can wreak havoc on an animal's system. Keep all such products out of sight and out of reach.

Find a Better Mousetrap

❑ If you have cats and dogs that roam your house freely, don't use ant or rodent poison to get rid of pests.

Don't Let Her Eat the Poisoned Apple

Iguanas love to eat fruit and plants. Although iguanas in the wild know instinctively which plants are safe and which are toxic, pet iguanas don't always know the difference. If you plan to let your iguana roam around the house periodically, she may get into plants or into bulbs and seeds that you're starting inside during cold weather. Keep an eye on your pet while she explores the house, and be sure to keep her away from these common plants and plant parts. (In cases for which no specific part is listed, the entire plant is poisonous to iguanas.)

- Amaryllis bulbs
- Apple seeds
- Avocado pits, peels, and foliage
- Azaleas
- Christmas cacti
- Cyclamens
- Daffodil bulbs and sap
- Delphiniums
- Dieffenbachia (dumbcane)
- Hyacinth bulbs
- Hydrangea flowers
- Impatiens
- Ivy (most kinds)
- Mistletoe berries and foliage
- Rhododendrons
- Tomato plant foliage and vines
- Tulips
- Wisteria

The pesticides in both are highly toxic to pets that accidentally ingest them. For example, warafin, one of the ingredients commonly found in mouse and rat poisons, prevents an animal's blood from clotting and may cause a pet to cough up blood or pass blood in the urine. Other rodent poisons cause kidney damage in pets. Find another way to get rid of those pests.

❑ If your pet does blunder into ant or rat poison, try to locate the container and save it for the vet. Information about the ingredients will be helpful in treating your pet.

If You Can't Get the Lead Out

❑ Most homes built prior to 1950, and many built before 1976, contain lead paint, which is hazardous to pets if they chew on it. Just as it does in humans, lead poisoning can cause seizures and other brain damage in animals. You can have your house professionally de-leaded, but the procedure typically costs as much as several hundred dollars per room. A cheaper alternative is to find some way to separate pet from paint. Offer the animal toys, exercise, and crunchy snacks and meals. If there is a particular area of wood that attracts him—windowsills, doorjambs, and baseboards are all likely sites—try to cover it. Or move furniture or other objects in front of that spot so that your pet can't reach it.

❑ Never assume that you can deal with lead paint in your home simply by painting over it. An animal's teeth can easily sink through several layers of paint, so woodwork may *look* better, but it will still be just as deadly.

TIME TO CALL THE VET

When Your Bird Is Poisoned

Birds are especially susceptible to poisoning from materials they eat, breathe, or merely come in contact with. If you have a bird, don't use nonstick cookware—the fumes could knock him dead, no matter where he is in the house. And don't fire up the woodstove unless it is located in a room that's far away from your pet's cage.

If your bird shows signs of respiratory distress and/or falls off his perch, it's very likely that he has been poisoned in some way, and he will die quickly without medical treatment. Call your vet immediately if you suspect that your pet has been poisoned. And keep your bird away from these other common avian toxins.

- Aerosols
- Avocados
- Ink (from leaky pens)
- Lead (in lead paint or wire)
- Secondhand smoke from cigars or cigarettes

PORCUPINE QUILLS

Fido's face is full of porcupine quills, and he's wailing like a banshee. You want to help him, but you aren't sure what to do. Pull them out yourself? Call the vet? The answer depends on just how close to the source your pooch managed to get. If he has a very few quills lodged in a paw, you may be able to remove them yourself. But if he looks like a canine pincushion, get him to the vet pronto.

The one thing you should *not* do is wait for the quills to work themselves out of your pet's skin on their own. They won't. Instead, because quills are barbed, two things may happen. First, your pet is likely to break them off as he tries to paw them out himself. This ultimately makes the quills harder to remove and also may result in abscessing. Second, since quills are designed

TIME TO CALL THE VET

Rabies Alert

Rabies is a horrifying, potentially fatal disease caused by a virus. Symptoms include restlessness, drooling, trouble swallowing, and, in more advanced stages, convulsions. Rabies is the only disease that is contagious from one warm-blooded species (raccoons, skunks, even bats) to all other warm-blooded species (including humans). Most folks know how critical it is to get dogs and cats vaccinated against rabies. It's also vital to keep these animals—as well as you and your family—away from wild creatures that could be carrying the disease. Always be suspicious of a raccoon or fox that approaches your house or seems unusually tame. Such behavior is not normal and may mean that the animal is infected and dangerous.

Rabies is transmitted through biting or contact with saliva. Dogs and cats may infect each other or may become infected when bitten by a rabid wild animal. If you suspect that your pet may have been bitten by a rabid animal, get the pet to the veterinarian immediately. If a potentially infected animal bites you, see your doctor. And notify your local game warden that a rabid animal may be on the loose. (Look under town government listings in your local phone book or call the town clerk's office and ask for the number.)

to travel one way only, they tend to bury themselves deeper with time, and eventually they can even soften and migrate far enough to puncture an internal organ. They should be removed as soon as possible.

Luckily, it's very rare for cats to get quilled. But if your pup gets a little too curious while the two of you are out hiking, here are some ways you can help.

FOR DOGS ONLY

When in Doubt, Don't Pull Them Out

If your pet has more than a few quills embedded in her (a pooch can get several hundred at a time from a single porcupine), don't fool around. Take her to the vet immediately. She's probably in a lot of pain and will be much more comfortable if anesthetized before the lengthy process of removing the quills begins.

Head straight for the vet if some of the quills are lodged inside your pet's mouth. It's very difficult to remove them from that location, and the job is best left to a professional.

Put Hand in Glove

If your pup has a half dozen or so quills in his snout, chest, or paws, and if he seems calm enough for you to approach him, it's all right for you to remove them. Begin by donning a pair of heavy work gloves or gardening gloves to protect yourself from both the quills and the bite of your frightened pet. Get a secure hold on your animal so that if he flinches, a quill won't break off while you are trying to remove it. Then, with needle-nose pliers, grasp the quill as close to your pet's skin as you can and steadily pull the quill straight out, reversing the direction in which it entered the skin. Don't wiggle the quill because the barbs could catch in the skin or the quill could break off.

If It's Tough, Don't Persist

If you try to remove the quills yourself and the first one or two come out with difficulty, stop! Don't pull half of them and then give up and call the vet. The

cost is likely to be much the same whether the vet pulls 6 quills or 60, so why put your pet through the additional trauma?

Something Soothing Is in Order

Once you're sure you've removed all the quills, cleanse the area with hydrogen peroxide (available at pharmacies) to keep dirt from entering the wounds. Your pet won't get an infection from the quills, which have on their surface a substance that is antibacterial. But if foreign substances get into the wounds later, they can cause problems.

Put Your Pet on Report

Even if you remove the quills yourself, call your vet to report the incident. Although porcupines aren't prone to rabies, the vet may want to give your pet a booster anyway, especially if there have been cases of rabies in other animals in your area.

POSTSURGICAL CARE

Whether your pet has been neutered or had a hip replaced, he is bound to feel a little punk after surgery. Your vet will give you specific instructions for the animal's care when you leave the hospital. You may be responsible for administering medication or bandaging, and you should learn the best way to carry your recuperating pet. You'll also need to be on guard for any postsurgical problems within the first few days after the operation, and you'll need to provide plenty of plain old TLC. Here are a few things you can do to keep your pal comfortable and safe during the recovery process.

FOR DOGS AND CATS

All's Quiet on the Sequestered Front

When your pet first comes home from the hospital, keep her quiet and sequestered from other animals and small children so that she doesn't feel threatened or make sudden movements.

Avoid Solitary Confinement

Keeping your pet quiet after surgery doesn't mean that you should leave the animal alone. When he's settled in a comfortable spot, such as his crate or kitty bed, check on him often to make sure he's okay. This will make your pet feel secure and will prevent him from getting up to come look for you. If the animal isn't mobile, bring food to him. Carry him to the litter box or outside for potty visits if necessary.

She's Been Down Under

After your pet has been under anesthesia, she may be groggy and disoriented. She may bump into furniture and trip over her food. She's likely to fall if she attempts to climb up or down stairs. Keep her away from these dangers for a day or two until her equilibrium returns. Show her to her food, then stay with her while she eats. Put a gate across the staircase if necessary.

A WORD FROM DR. MAUE

First on the First Aid List

DR. LISA MAUE
Veterinarian in private practice in Medford, Massachusetts, for more than a decade

People sometimes ask what first aid items they should have on hand to care for their pets. I always put hydrogen peroxide high on the list. It's available at any pharmacy and can be used to treat most minor injuries—including cuts and scratches, sores, and even hot spots. Hydrogen peroxide is a good antiseptic, as long as you make sure it's fresh. (Check the expiration date on the bottle.) Apply just enough to thoroughly clean the problem area, and be careful not to overdo it. If you have a dark-haired dog, you can easily turn her into a blonde.

HEALTH

He's Had a Close Shave

The area on which surgery is performed is generally shaved, so it's easy to see the skin afterward. Following the operation, check this area twice a day for problems—pulled sutures, bleeding, swelling, or anything else that looks unusual. Call the vet if you're concerned that the incision is not healing the way the vet told you it would.

He's in Stitches

Your pet may have sutures for a couple of weeks, so keep watching the area even after he's up and around. If he continually scratches or licks the stitches, he may be allergic to the sutures themselves, or an abscess may be developing. Call the vet.

FOR CATS ONLY

It's News to Her

For several days after surgery, line your tabby's litter box with shredded newspaper or Styrofoam packing peanuts instead of traditional kitty litter. Kitty litter may stick to the surgical wound, causing irritation and even infection. Newspaper or Styrofoam will not.

RESPIRATORY PROBLEMS

It's winter, and everyone in your household is sneezing and coughing, with a runny nose and weepy eyes. Suddenly, you notice that Fido and Fluffy have joined the club, too. What should you do? Assume they have colds and let the annoying symptoms run their course? No. Although some respiratory illnesses are not serious, others are, and they require medical attention. In addition, respiratory problems tend to differ in cats and dogs, even if the signs appear to be similar. So you should call the vet and report your pet's symptoms, especially if the animal is having difficulty breathing. She may have something caught in her throat or windpipe. Chronic labored breathing could indicate heart problems, heartworm disease, or asthma. Only your vet can tell.

FOR DOGS AND CATS

He's So Shallow

If your pet is suddenly taking very shallow breaths, he may have sustained an injury to the ribs that is interfering with his breathing, or he may be in shock. In either case, this is an emergency. Get your pet to the vet immediately.

FOR DOGS ONLY

She's Snoring Up a Storm

Dogs that have "pushed-in" faces, such as pugs and Pekingese, often have problems with snoring. If your pooch is keeping you awake nights, alert your vet to the problem. It may be the result of a mild allergic inflammation, which your vet will treat with medication. But snoring also may be related to other problems and may require surgery.

FOR CATS ONLY

Make His Discharge Honorable

If your cat has a colored discharge running from his nose, he may have a sinus infection. Call your vet, who will treat the condition with antibiotics. Then, to keep the nasal passages from becoming encrusted or plugged, clean your pet's nostrils at least twice a day with a washcloth dampened in warm water. And keep him warm and comfortable.

TIME TO CALL THE VET

Heavy Breathing Isn't Romantic

A small dog can suffer from a collapsed trachea or other respiratory problems when things get too hot. If your little dog pants so hard that she starts to cough, call the vet.

It Looks Like a Cold

If your cat is sneezing and has a runny nose and weepy eyes, she may have an upper respiratory infection, which is a viral infection that acts like a cold or the flu. The infection has to run its course, but call your vet and report the problem anyway. She may prescribe an antibiotic to prevent a secondary infection from taking hold and recommend vaccination against future illness.

HEALTH

An upper respiratory infection is much more dangerous to kittens than to full-grown cats, so it's especially important to get a young pet to the doctor for treatment as soon as possible.

Start a Steamy Affair

If your cat has a sinus infection or upper respiratory infection, put a humidifier or hot-water vaporizer on for a few hours in the room where he's resting. The warm, moist air will help clear his congestion and free up his breathing.

SHEDDING

You know it's shedding season when you find pet hair everywhere—on the couch, on the carpet, on your clothes. Most dogs and cats shed their winter coats in the spring, although some indoor pets continue light shedding all year. Even if your pet is shorthaired, expect some shedding to occur. You can't stop the fur from falling out, but you can stop it from flying around the house. A regular routine of combing and brushing will go a long way toward promoting a healthy shedding process, as well as cleaner carpets and upholstery.

Dogs and cats aren't the only animals that shed. Birds molt (lose their feathers) every six months or once a year, depending on the species, and reptiles such as snakes and iguanas shed regularly as well. Although shedding is a normal process in these animals, sometimes glitches occur that cause pain or even harm. It's a good idea to learn something about the shedding processes of these animals so that you can help them along if need be.

A reptile will shed his entire skin, from head to toe, over a period of several days. Any reptile's skin color

COST CUTTERS

Pet Grooming for Half the Price

One way to groom a longhaired cat is with one of the small-size shedding blades available at pet supply stores. But if your longhaired pet is a canine, you can substitute one of the large-size shedding blades made for horses. These tools are available at tack shops (look under Riding Apparel & Equipment in the Yellow Pages). They are exactly the same as the blades made for dogs, but they cost about half as much.

will grow dull, and a snake will develop a whitish film over his eyeballs, while an iguana's eyelids will puff out. A healthy snake will shed his skin nearly in one piece; an unhealthy one will slough off patches or shreds of skin. For an iguana, shedding skin in sections is normal.

FOR DOGS AND CATS

Give Him the Brush-Off

Brushing is probably the best way to promote a healthy shedding process in a dog or cat. Brushing not only removes loose hair, but it also stimulates the skin and enhances the natural shine of your pet's coat. If your pet has a normal coat and skin that's not sensitive, you'll probably want to use a wire brush (available at pet supply stores or from catalogs). Especially if your kitty or pup is longhaired, try to brush the animal every day, or at least twice a week. The more you brush, the less often you'll find clumps of fur clinging to your couch or clothes.

If He's the Sensitive Type

If your kitty or pooch has sensitive skin or very short hair, or if he just seems bothered by brushing during shedding season, try using a brush with soft nylon bristles instead of the wire type. A soft brush is good only for removing loose hair from the surface of the coat—it doesn't help the skin or shine the animal's coat—but it's better than not brushing at all.

Last Tangle in a Hairbrush

When you brush your cat or dog, start at the surface—the tip of the fur—and gently work deeper as you go, much as you would when de-tangling your own hair. This will prevent the brush from getting caught in tangles or clumps and tugging at the skin. If you hurt your pet with your grooming attempts, the animal won't like the brushing process. And that means it will be tougher to catch your pet—let alone get her to hold still—on future occasions.

A shedding tool has serrated edges to help catch excess fur in longhaired pets.

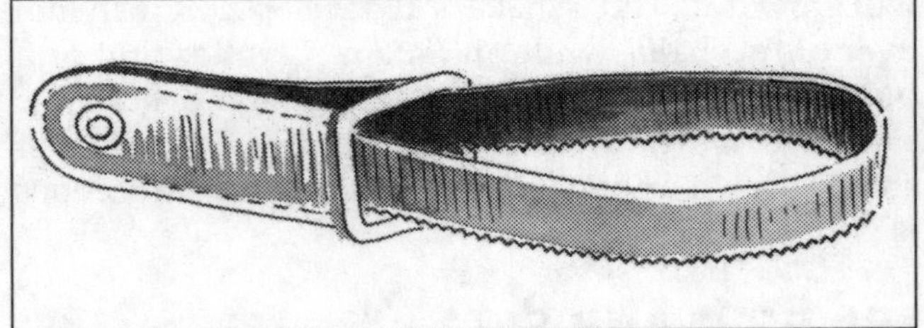

He's a Gay Blade

For longhaired cats and longhaired dogs such as golden retrievers and collies, try using a shedding tool to remove excess fur from the surface of the coat. Rake the serrated edges of the tool gently along your pet's coat in the direction the fur grows.

Groom a shorthaired dog or cat with a currycomb (A), a longhaired animal with an undercoat rake (B).

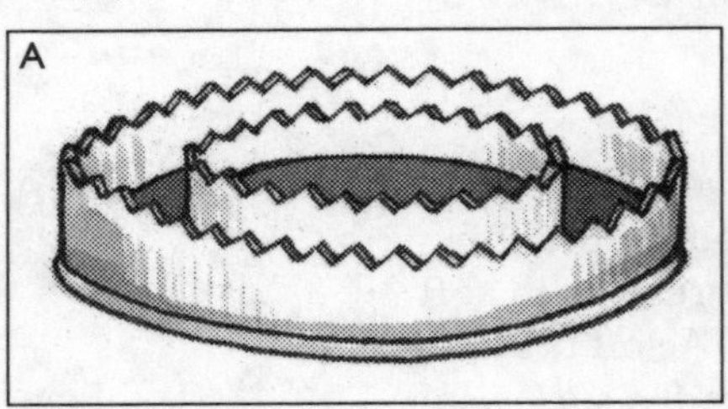

Curry Her Favor

To groom a shorthaired dog or cat, try using a rubber currycomb. This will groom your pet's coat with rounded nubs, effectively removing loose hair while massaging the skin. Currycombs are available in several sizes at horse supply shops for far less than they cost at pet supply stores. (To find a horse supply shop, look under Riding Apparel & Equipment in the Yellow Pages.) When you use a currycomb, rub in a circular motion, starting in the direction that the fur grows.

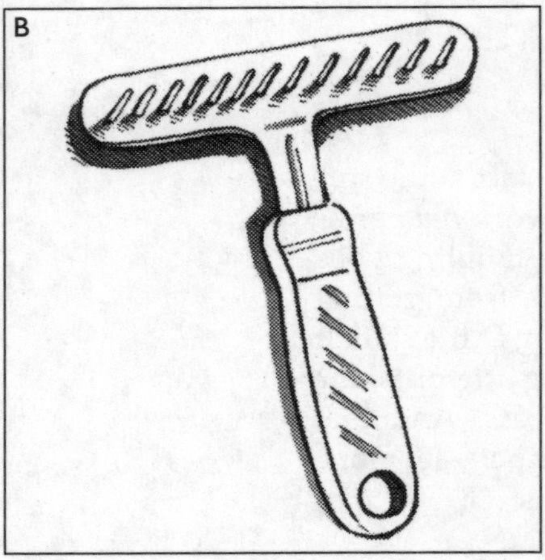

Go Undercover

For a longhaired or thick-haired breed such as a Persian or Himalayan cat or a cocker spaniel, Irish setter, malamute, poodle, or husky, try working with an undercoat rake. This gizmo, available at pet supply stores, does exactly what its name describes: It rakes out loose hair from the thick undercoat of your shedding pet.

Here Comes the Groom

Once you've brushed your way through the bulk of your pet's shedding season, take her to be groomed professionally. The groomer can finish off the job, readying your pet's coat to look and feel its summer best. This also is a nice way to pamper your pet a bit.

Try a Little Aloe

Use a pet shampoo with aloe or lanolin to restore moisture to your pet's skin and coat during shedding season.

FOR BIRDS ONLY

Vitamins May Be Vital

Ask your vet or pet store owner whether your bird might benefit from one of the over-the-counter vitamin supplements designed to promote a good molt.

Create Mist-ery

Spray your molting bird with a fine mist of warm water from a spray bottle at least once a day.

Give Him a Rubdown

While your bird is molting, rub your fingers gently through his feathers once a day. If you find a feather that seems dried out, touch the tip of it. If it falls away, it was ready to come out, and you have helped the process along. If it doesn't fall away, check it again during the next rubdown.

COST CUTTERS

The Seller Can Be a Good Teacher

When you buy a pet such as a bird, snake, or iguana from a pet store, don't be afraid to return to the pet store for health advice. A knowledgeable pet store owner will be able to assess basic health problems, recommend diet supplements or changes, and even show you how to trim claws.

Pull Out All the Stops

During the molting process, sometimes the bare shaft of a feather can pierce a bird's skin like a needle. You'll see or feel the problem during your bird's daily rubdown. If this happens, use a pair of small needle-

nose pliers to pull the feather out in a steady motion. Then apply pressure to the wound with a paper towel or your bare finger. If the bleeding doesn't stop within a few minutes, take your pet to the vet.

FOR REPTILES ONLY

Use a Little Moisturizer

S Your reptile needs moist, supple skin for a healthy shed. Spray him once a day, or at least three times a week, with warm water from a spray bottle.

S Alternatively, spray your pet with one of the vitamin oil moisturizing sprays available at pet supply stores.

A Warm Bath Can Be So Relaxing

S In addition to misting your reptile with water, you may want to soak the animal in a tub of tepid water for several minutes each day when your pet seems nearly ready to shed. This will both moisturize and loosen the skin. You can't overdo the dampening. Use any combination of spraying and soaking that works for you and your pet.

Put It on the Calendar

S Every reptile sheds regularly, and although different species have different schedules, many shed approximately once a month. A change in shedding schedule may indicate a health problem, so it's important to know your pet's normal cycle. To keep track easily, mark the beginning and end of each shed on a calendar. That way, if there is a problem, you'll be able to identify the onset of any change.

Give Your Iguana a Pat on the Head

S If you see your iguana rubbing his closed eyes against nearby objects right before he sheds, don't be alarmed. He's just trying to loosen the old skin. Help him along by gently massaging his head and eyelids with your fingers.

Inspect Those Nooks and Crannies

HEALTH

S To help your iguana get rid of dead skin between her toes, around her nostrils, at the tips of her spikes, and at the end of her tail, massage those areas and gently tug at the skin to feel whether it is ready to slough off. If it falls off when you pull, fine. If it resists your tug, leave it alone for another day.

YOU'VE GOTTA LOVE 'EM

Is That an Iguana under Your Dashboard?

One day when my iguana, Iggy, was young and a lot smaller than he is now, I had to take him somewhere in the car. Being curious (and searching for heat), he climbed up under the dashboard and slipped in behind the radio. He wouldn't come out. I called, pleaded, and poked around, but he stayed in there all day and into the night. I started to get worried about him (not to mention annoyed) because, as the outdoor temperature dropped, so would his body temperature. But how could I get him out of there? Suddenly, I thought of my friend Johnny, a race car driver who also had an auto repair shop. I drove to Johnny's and explained my predicament. He laughed. I think he thought he could get Iggy out in a flash. He couldn't. He ended up taking the whole dashboard out of my car before he got to the recalcitrant Iggy. Johnny's never let me live it down!

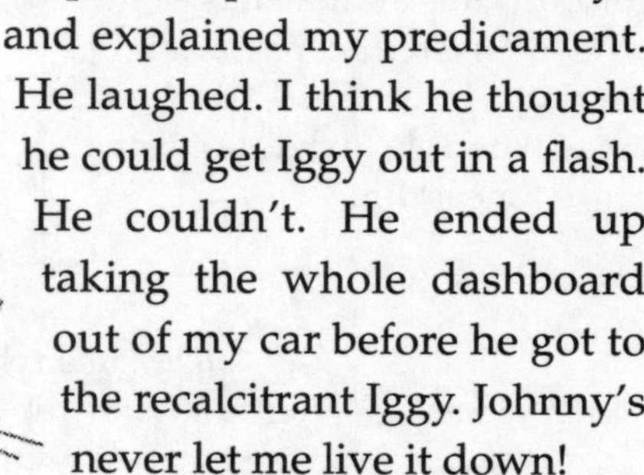

—KATHIE SEMENCHUK
Hull, Massachusetts

HEALTH

It's the Pièce de Résistance

If a spike, a tail tip, or the space between an iguana's toes seems especially stubborn about shedding after a few days, it's okay to work at it. Not doing so may leave the old skin to dry and harden, killing otherwise healthy tissue underneath and perhaps causing your pet to lose toes or spikes. Over a period of several days, keep spraying water on the area to soak the skin and keep loosening it with your fingers.

He's Whistling Dixie

If your iguana seems to be "whistling" through his nostrils as he approaches shedding time, it's likely that he has residual skin from the previous shed attached to the rim of his nostrils. Make it a point to work at this area during the upcoming shed. Gently tug at the skin after it has been loosened during bath time or after you've sprayed him.

TIME TO CALL THE VET

Snakes: Watch Out for Rough Shedding

If your snake has more than one bad shed—dead skin coming off in patches, eye caps failing to slough off, or a delay in shedding altogether—take her to the vet. An unhealthy shed usually occurs for one of two reasons: Either your pet's surroundings are too hot or too cold, or the animal has some type of systemic bacterial or parasitic infection. Only your vet will be able to determine the cause for certain.

Check Out These Snake Eyes

If your snake has a bad shed and the casing over the eye (called the eye cap) doesn't slough off, soak your pet in a warm bath for 10 to 20 minutes. Then remove the animal from the water and dab mineral oil (available at pharmacies) on each eye with a cotton swab. Return your pet to her tank and monitor the situation for 24 hours.

Never use tweezers or other sharp objects when helping your reptilian pal shed. They could cause severe harm to your pet.

Solve the Case of the Unshed Eye

If you have tried to remove unshed casings from your snake's eyes and haven't been able to get one or both off, don't force the issue. Take your pet to a reptile vet. If the eye cap goes unshed for more than two shedding cycles, infection may set in, eventually causing blindness.

SKIN DISCOLORATION

The color of your fish's or reptile's skin can tell you a lot about your pet's health. Sometimes a change in color signals the onset of a normal process—for instance, when a python's skin darkens just as his eyes turn white, or when an iguana's skin lightens right before shedding. But often discoloration indicates a problem. Perhaps your pet's surroundings are too warm or too cold, or maybe the animal has an infection. Since skin color is such a strong indicator of health in cold-blooded animals, it's important to keep an eye out for changes and to act promptly when you notice them.

FOR FISH ONLY

She's a Whiter Shade of Pale

If the colors of your fish fade quickly, she's gasping at the water's surface, and she's swimming erratically, your pet probably has suffered some type of chemical poisoning. The tank water may have some residual detergent in it, someone may have sprayed a pesticide near the tank, or some other toxic substance may be in or near the tank. Remove your fish immediately and change the tank water. Also, think back on any changes you've made recently. Did you find a cute decoration to add to the tank? If so, remove the new trinket. Once you return your fish to the clean tank, monitor her for several days. Poisoning may make her susceptible to other diseases.

Time to Call the Expert

If you just can't figure out why your pet is exhibiting symptoms of slow poisoning, or if you moved recently and introduced your fish to different tap water, consult with a local pet store owner about water conditions in the tank. He will be able to recommend ac-

HEALTH

tions—such as increasing oxygen flow to the tank or adding special corrective agents to the water—based on your specific situation.

FOR REPTILES ONLY

It Was a Dark and Stormy Night . . .

S If your iguana's skin turns dark, he may be cold or stressed in some way, or he may have an infection. Turn up the heat a few degrees and monitor his condition for 24 hours. If things don't improve, call the vet—pronto.

Fade to Black

S If your iguana's skin turns black in patches but does not form a crust, she may have a fungal infection or a thermal burn from her heat source. In either case, take her to the vet immediately for treatment.

Maybe His Skin Is as Dark as His Mood

S If the temperature of your iguana's environment is already near the top of the optimum range, try to identify any other stressors. Has your pet recently been moved? Have you changed his diet? Have you introduced other pets to the house? If you can identify a stressor, remove it if possible and monitor the iguana's condition.

S If your pet's color does not return to normal in 24 hours, or if you cannot identify a stressor, contact your vet or pet store owner, who should be able to help you identify the problem and correct it.

He's Prematurely Gray

S When an iguana's skin lightens in color or actually turns gray, she may be too warm, or she may be getting ready to shed. Consider whether this is the animal's normal shedding time. (You *do* keep track of these things, don't you?) If it is, simply wait 24 hours for the shed to begin. If this is not your pet's normal shedding time, turn down the temperature a degree or two and watch her for 24 hours. If the iguana's color does not return to normal, contact your vet or pet store owner, who should be able to help you identify the problem and correct it.

He's a Crusty Old Fellow

S If your iguana's skin develops crusty sores, your pet could have parasites or a fungal or bacterial infection (including salmonella). Take him to the vet immediately for treatment.

Color Him Troubled

S When your pet snake loses skin color but his eyes don't turn white, try increasing the temperature in the animal's cage by a few degrees. If the snake's color does not improve, call the vet.

She's Pretty in Pink

S If your snake has developed a pink belly, try to determine immediately whether she might have been burned by the heat source in her environment. If so, remove her from contact with the source and consult your vet for advice on treating the burn and selecting another heat source. Or consider providing your pet with a larger tank so that she has more room to move away from the heat source.

S If your snake clearly has not been burned and she happens to be a python or boa, she's probably getting ready to shed. Just keep an eye on her shedding process to be sure it goes smoothly.

TIME TO CALL THE VET

When Your Reptile Is under the Weather

Sometimes a reptile's behavior can alert you to potential health problems even when the animal looks healthy. Watch for prolonged soaking in water, loss of appetite or thirst, irregular defecation, a change in the shedding schedule, an increase or decrease in tameness, or constant hiding. If your pet exhibits any of these behaviors, the animal is probably not feeling well, and you should report the potential problems to your vet or pet store owner.

SKUNK SPRAY

All you need is one whiff to know that your sweet pet has been sprayed by a skunk. Poor Rover, no one wants to go near him—least of all you! But think of it this way: If he smells this bad to you from several feet away,

YOU'VE GOTTA LOVE 'EM

Anyone for Ham?

When I was about 13, we had a big bluetick coonhound named Whiskey. Our town had no leash law, so Whiskey roamed by himself. One day, Whiskey came home hauling something along the ground with his teeth. He settled down in the front yard to chew on it. As we watched him from the window, we could only guess what sad animal had become his prize.

But something about that hunk on the ground looked funny. My mom realized that Whiskey was gnawing on a huge ham shank from the supermarket—in fact, the wrapper was still on it. Mom wanted a closer look at that ham, so she sent my friend and me out to get it. My friend distracted Whiskey with a box of doggy snacks while I sneaked up and grabbed the meat, running back to the house with the heavy, greasy load cradled in my arms.

In the kitchen, my friend teased, "I'll bet you get this ham for dinner tonight."

"No way," I argued. But when my mom made several calls to the neighbors to find out whether anyone was missing a ham from their back porch, no one claimed the prize. So she cut off the bone and gave it back to Whiskey. Then she slid the rest into a pot of boiling water. Thanks to Whiskey, we had ham for dinner that night.

—**LIBBY DRBAL**
Leawood, Kansas

he must *really* smell bad to himself. You're the only one who can make him feel better. And the good news is there are some very effective remedies for the sour scent of skunk.

FOR DOGS AND CATS

Try a Tomato Juice Cocktail

To cut the stench of skunk on your pet's coat, douse him with tomato juice straight from the can or jar (don't dilute it). For a large dog, you may need several large cans of tomato juice for a single washing. (This is a job best done outside, in the garage, or in the basement, with plenty of ventilation and room to make a mess.) Be sure to keep the juice away from the animal's eyes and mouth. If he'll stand for it, leave the juice on for several minutes before rinsing it off. Once you have it out of his fur, wash him with his regular pet shampoo and dry him off, then take a sniff. You may have to repeat the procedure a couple of times, but the odor will work itself out with the washing.

Use a Feminine Touch

Premixed vinegar douche (available at any supermarket or pharmacy) is an excellent weapon against skunk odor. Just pour the liquid over your pet, keeping it out of her eyes and mouth, and let it soak in for several minutes. Then rinse it out of your pet's fur and wash her with her regular shampoo.

Alternatively, you can buy the type of vinegar douche that has to be mixed. Use about 2 ounces douche for every 1 gallon water. One gallon of treatment should be enough for a cat or small dog; you'll probably have to increase the amount to 2 gallons for a larger dog.

Keep This in Your Recipe File

Here's a home remedy that's sure to stifle the skunk stench. Mix 1 quart hydrogen peroxide (available at pharmacies; check the date on the label to be sure it's fresh) with ¼ cup baking soda. Stir in 1 tea-

spoon dishwashing liquid. Lather the brew up thoroughly in your pet's fur, keeping it out of his eyes, then rinse thoroughly.

Forewarned Is Forearmed

If you want to be ready at all times for battle against this strong foe, pick up one of the premade cleaning products, such as Skunk Kleen, from a pet supply store. Be sure to keep it where you can find it quickly!

TICKS

It happens every year: Those tricky ticks appear in early spring, hang around until midsummer, then sometimes return in early fall and linger until cold weather sets in. If you live in an area with a regular rainy season, expect to find these pests on your pet during that time as well.

These days, ticks are showing up in growing numbers and in a widening geographic area. They love to feast on the blood of pets—from cats and dogs to snakes—and in so doing can spread illnesses such as Lyme disease and, less frequently, Rocky Mountain spotted fever. In addition, they may cause temporary paralysis in an animal while they are attached.

Although Lyme disease has usually been associated with the tiny deer tick, recent evidence shows that the larger, common tick may carry the disease as well. It makes sense to treat all these pests as enemies. (Even those that don't carry disease are pretty disgusting.) Here are some ways to make those ticks take a tumble.

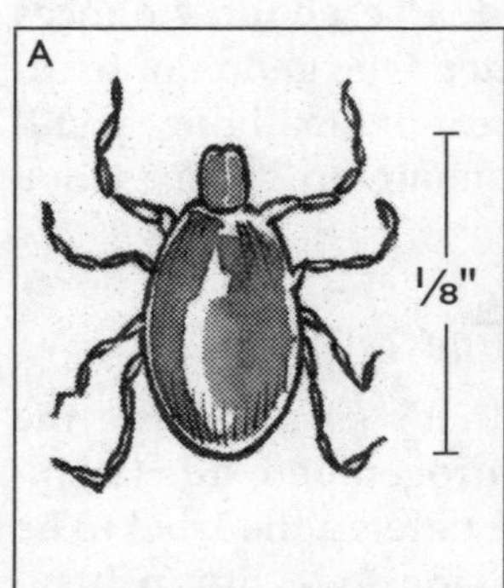

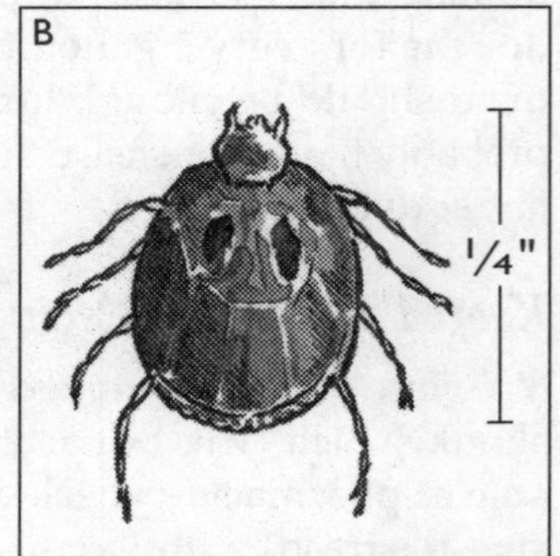

The deer tick (A) is the usual culprit in the spread of Lyme disease, but it's best to treat the common tick (B) with suspicion, too. The sizes of these adult ticks are approximate.

Check Mate

❑ During tick season, check your pet every day for ticks. If your pal is a reptile, examine his skin, especially in areas with folds. If your friend is furry, run your fingers through her coat, checking for any little bumps. If she has long hair, comb it; your comb may catch a creature or two. Examine all around her ears—inside and underneath. Check the area where her front legs join her body, as well as skin folds, under her back legs, and anywhere else a tick might be able to burrow.

Watch for Hitchhikers

❑ During the season, perform a tick inspection anytime your pet returns from being outdoors. Experts once advised people to cut their lawns so that ticks couldn't hide in tall grass, but even manicured estates aren't safe anymore. Ticks seem to be everywhere. So if your pet has been outside, assume that the animal may have given a tick a ride home.

Stay Out of Dangerous Neighborhoods

❑ Ticks especially like wet areas such as marshes, swamps, and reservoirs, so it's smart to avoid those spots—or at least to check especially carefully for the pests after returning from a jaunt to such a location.

Don't Let Them Move In

❑ Although ticks don't breed in your home the way fleas do, they enter your house clinging to pets,

Loyal to the End—And Beyond

One of the outstanding canine characteristics is loyalty, and among the most famous loyal dogs is Greyfriars Bobby. This Skye terrier lived in Edinburgh, Scotland, in the mid-nineteenth century. When the little dog's master died in 1858, the man was buried in the churchyard of Greyfriars Kirk, a historic Edinburgh church.

Bobby followed his master's funeral procession and watched as the body was interred, then refused to leave when the earth was piled over the casket. If the terrier was chased out of the churchyard, he quickly returned to stand vigil by the grave. Eventually the church officials gave in. They built a little shelter for Bobby, and neighbors donated food. Greyfriars Bobby stayed by his master's side for fourteen years, until his own death, when he too was buried in the churchyard. Today a bronze statue of the terrier stands by the church in testimony to one man's best friend.

clothes, patio furniture—anything you bring in from outdoors. You need to check your home regularly for ticks. Pay special attention to the laundry hamper, carpets, upholstered furniture, even bedding. And, of course, check the areas that your pet frequents.

Tick Them Off

❑ To remove a tick from your pet, dab a little rubbing alcohol on the tick with a cotton ball or swab. Wait two to three minutes. Then, with tweezers or a tissue, grasp the tick as close to the skin as you can without pinching your pet and gently pull the tick out. *Don't* flush the tick down the toilet. It won't necessarily drown and may even climb back out. Instead, drop the pest in a glass jar with a tablespoon or so of rubbing alcohol, then close the jar tight. That will kill the tick.

A Little Dab'll Do Ya!

❑ Another way to remove a tick from your pet—particularly if the pest has not yet locked on too securely—is to rub petroleum jelly on and around the tick, including the head. This suffocates the pest. Or use dishwashing liquid, which has the same effect. Wait a few minutes, then pull the tick out with tweezers or a tissue. Don't worry about separating the tick's head from its body, leaving the head embedded in your pet's skin. Contrary to popular belief, this rarely happens.

Get Yourself Some Extra Pull

❑ If you just can't bear to get near a tick, don't try to detach it from your pet by burning it with a lit match or lighter! You'll only succeed in burning your pet and

One version of an inexpensive tick remover.

probably yourself as well. Instead, buy a tick remover at a pet supply store and keep it on hand. Tick removers come in several versions. One type, made of metal, is about the length of a nail clipper and has a slit in the end designed to grasp the tick while you pull. It's a good, safe tool to have on hand.

URINARY TRACT INFECTIONS

Your fastidious kitty just did the unthinkable: After leaping in and out of her litter box all day, she urinated in the bathtub. Or your normally camel-like canine suddenly treats the front entrance of your house like a revolving door. And when he gets outside, he produces hardly any urine. Furthermore, you saw blood in the last trickle.

Your pet probably has a urinary tract infection. Although it's important to contact the vet immediately, this condition—unlike a urinary blockage—is not fatal. Your vet will most likely ask for a urine sample and prescribe a course of antibiotics.

A WORD FROM DR. MAUE

Is Your Cat Trying to Tell You Something?

DR. LISA MAUE
Veterinarian in private practice in Medford, Massachusetts, for more than a decade

My cat is perfectly behaved and very smart, so I couldn't believe it when she gave up on her litter box and decided to use the bathtub instead. I thought she had gone crazy—until I saw the blood. She was trying to tell me that something was wrong. Cats will do this. A cat with a bladder infection will find a light-colored spot on a carpet or comforter (or your favorite white T-shirt) to use. It's your pet's way of telling you to take her to the vet.

TIME TO CALL THE VET

This Block Isn't a Party

Your male cat is usually a tough guy, but lately he's been jumping in and out of his litter box, whimpering. When you check the box, it's nearly dry. Or he squats in the corner of a room, straining to urinate, but can't emit anything. After a couple of hours, he may be lethargic and/or vomiting. Your male cat may have a urinary obstruction—mineral deposits, blood, or mucus blocking any flow through the narrow urethra. If the obstruction remains in place for more than several hours, toxins will collect in your pet's system and may kill him within 24 to 48 hours.

If you suspect that your cat has a blockage, try to palpate his bladder. (This is a difficult undertaking with an overweight feline but perfectly manageable with one that's trim.) While he is lying on his side, cup your hand beneath his belly and pelvic area. *Gently* push your hand forward and back to locate the bladder. If your friend has an obstruction, the bladder will feel enlarged and rock solid, and your pet's reaction will show that it's sore to the touch. (A healthy bladder will feel more resilient, like a water balloon.)

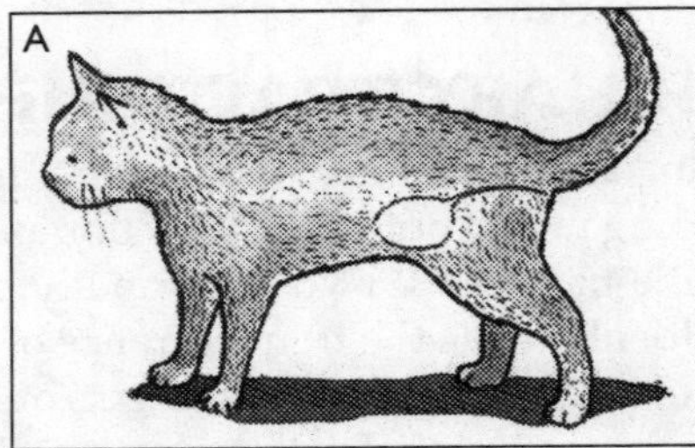

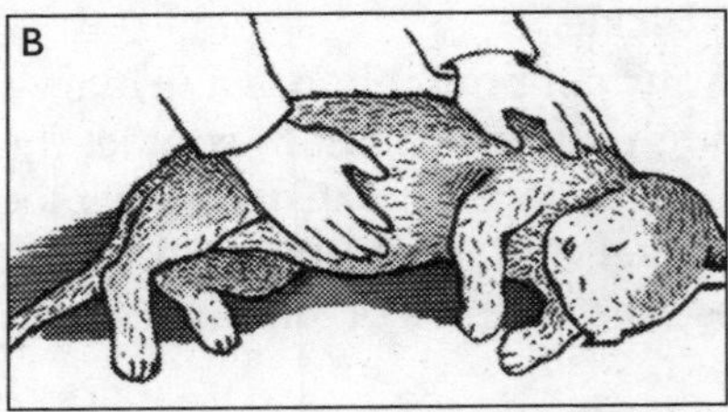

Your cat's bladder is located near the hind legs (A). Press gently (B) to check for a blockage.

If your quick check confirms your suspicions, or if you can't detect the bladder but feel that your pet is having trouble, take the animal to the nearest emergency veterinary hospital immediately. Once there, he'll be catheterized and treated with intravenous fluids if necessary.

FOR DOGS AND CATS

Feed Her with Special Care

To help clear up a urinary tract infection and prevent future ones, feed your pet a diet that's low in magnesium (read the pet food label). Or ask your pet's doctor about one of the prescription diets available only through vets.

Promote Heavy Drinking

To combat an infection and ward off future ones, be certain that your pet has plenty of water to drink. Keep the animal's water dish filled at all times.

Can the Cans

If your pet's diet includes a hefty serving of canned food, try cutting back on the canned stuff while increasing his portion of dry food. Canned food contains enough water to reduce your pet's normal thirst, causing him to drink less than he actually needs for a healthy urinary tract. By contrast, dry food will make him thirsty, so he'll drink more.

More Is Better

To prevent the buildup of infection-causing bacteria in an overfull bladder, make sure your pet has plenty of opportunities to relieve himself during the day and night. Take your pooch outside several times a day, even if he doesn't ask. Clean your tabby's box frequently so that she'll want to use it.

VISION LOSS

You always thought your pet had sharp eyes, but now she bumps into furniture. She scrambles right past the balls you toss. She tilts her head when you enter the room. She tends to settle into corners, where she feels safe. And when you look closely at her eyes, her pupils are huge.

These are all signs of vision loss, which can occur for a number of reasons. If the loss is sudden, your pet may have a detached retina, a condition in which something triggers swelling that actually causes the retina to separate from the back of the eyeball. Triggers include cancer, Lyme disease, fungal disease, autoimmune response, kidney disease, even high blood pressure. Or your pet may have lost her sight suddenly due to a blow to the head—say, from a car. More gradual vision

HEALTH

loss may be caused by cataracts or glaucoma. Signs of this include eyes that are bulging and sore to the touch. (If you touch your cat's closed eyelid, she reacts as if in pain.)

Even if there is no cure for your pet's condition, be assured that blind animals adapt relatively well to their situations. But before you start thinking about the worst-case scenario, call your vet for an accurate diagnosis and recommendations for treatment. And consider the following possibilities as well.

TIME TO CALL THE VET

When the Golden Years Aren't So Golden

Your aging dog has reached her golden years, but something is wrong. Recently, she has begun to bark at nothing; she seems disoriented; she stands in the corner of a room, staring into space; perhaps worst of all (for you), she seems to have lost all memory of her house-training.

Your friend may be growing senile. The good news is treatment is available. Take her to the vet, who will examine her to rule out other causes of her behavior, such as a brain tumor. If the diagnosis is senility, your doctor may prescribe L-Deprenyl, a medication used to treat canine cognitive disorder. The drug isn't a cure, but it does reduce the severity of symptoms. It costs about $60 per month for a 20-pound dog (dosage depends on the dog's weight).

FOR DOGS AND CATS

This Is No Time to Remodel

A pet with deteriorating eyesight needs to memorize the lay of the land. Try to leave the furniture in its familiar layout, at least in the rooms where your pet spends most of his time. If you must move things, be sure to show your pet around, walking through each room with him until he's comfortable with the new floor plan.

Follow the Scent

To help your pet find her way around the house, put a dab of perfume on the corner of the couch or any other large or sharp piece of furniture. Use good perfume—the cheap stuff will damage your furniture—and test it first in an inconspicuous spot to be sure it won't do any harm. Don't overdo it; if the whole room smells like perfume, you'll defeat your purpose.

Just Say the Word

To help your pet navigate through the house safely, teach him a few words associated with location or danger. When he's near the stairs, say "Stairs." When he's near the fireplace, say "Fire." Reinforce each word by removing him from a dangerous spot or helping him negotiate a difficult obstacle.

Give Her Aid and Comfort

The loss of sight is frightening, so remember to comfort and reassure your pet whenever possible. Talk to her when you enter or leave a room so that she knows where you are. Reassure her as you carry her to the car. Pet her and comfort her if something startles her during a walk outside. She'll adapt much more easily to vision loss—whether it's short- or long-term—with your coaching.

FOR CATS ONLY

Let Him Enjoy the Wide Screen

If your indoor/outdoor cat is having vision problems, let him out on a screened porch. Make sure that the outside door is shut and the screens are in good repair. Check on him regularly while he's out there.

VOMITING

Rover stuck his nose in the garbage and sucked down all the nasty treats he could find. Tabby dropped a dead mouse on your doorstep. Now both are sick from—if not sorry for—their escapades. Vomiting is a natural reaction to something that shouldn't be in your pet's system. The animal may vomit after swallowing garbage, table scraps, or prey—or a hair ball, rock, sock, or string. Or the problem could be a symptom of poisoning, parasites, food allergies, kidney or thyroid malfunction, or a disease such as distemper, parvovirus, diabetes, or cancer.

If your pet has vomited more than two or three times in 24 hours, appears to have lost weight, or is lethargic or dehydrated, call the vet. Report any details that may be helpful. Has the animal's diet or appetite changed? Could he have swallowed a foreign object or been poisoned? Does he have a fever? Does his breath have a urinelike smell, which could indicate kidney failure or diabetes? Any information you can give the vet will help in your pet's diagnosis and treatment.

If your pet vomits no more than three times in a 24-hour period, shows no other signs of illness, or has a condition that the vet has already identified and given you the green light to treat, it's safe to use appropriate home remedies to help your pet feel in the pink again.

FOR DOGS AND CATS

Fast after Food

If your pet has vomited a couple of times but still appears alert, without other symptoms of illness, remove food and water for 24 hours. Withholding nourishment may seem cruel, but it's not. It gives your pet's tummy a chance to rest and return to normal. Giving

ONE PERSON'S SOLUTION

A Whole New Take on Toilet Training

Our dog has always had a delicate stomach, particularly when he was a puppy. It got so that I could tell ahead of time that he was getting ready to vomit or spit up a bit, so I'd carry him into the bathroom and aim his head so that he'd vomit in the toilet. We've done this so many times that now if he's going to be sick, he heads into the bathroom and throws up in the toilet. Interestingly, he recognizes only the upstairs toilet as a place to do this—never the downstairs one.

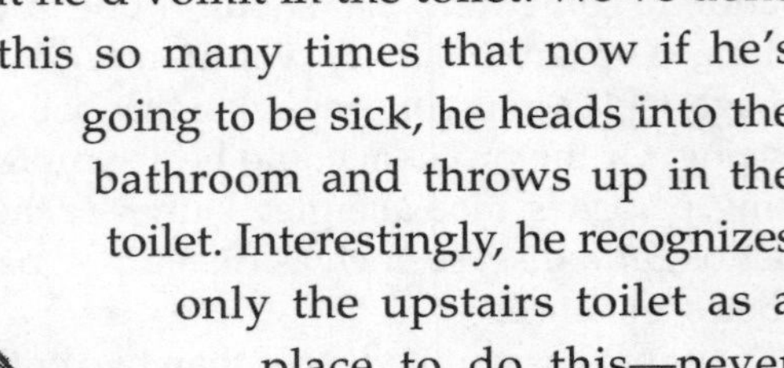

—PAT ANDREWS
Knoxville, Tennessee

your pet water at this time could make him queasy again, and he might vomit even more fluid, which could lead to dehydration.

Ice Is Nice

After 12 hours of fasting, if your pet seems quiet and comfortable and is not vomiting, offer her an ice cube to lick or crunch on. This will help reintroduce fluids to her body without putting too much in her stomach.

Take a Sip

If your pet is still not vomiting after 24 hours without food, offer him a small amount of water. If he drinks it without vomiting, offer him another small drink an hour or so later. Although he does need fluids, too much water may make him queasy, starting the vomiting process all over again.

Strike Up the Bland

If your kitty or pup stops vomiting during the 24-hour fast, it's okay to start feeding her again. But don't return immediately to her normal diet. Instead, introduce bland foods. Mix together equal parts cooked white rice and cottage cheese, feeding her about one-quarter to one-half cup at regular mealtimes for two or three days. Then start working her normal food back into the routine, continuing the rice-cheese mixture for most meals but replacing one rice-cheese meal with a small helping of the animal's usual food. Continue this pattern for three days. If she's still holding down her food after that, return to her regular diet.

TIME TO CALL THE VET

Bloating Is Bad News

If your dog has a distended abdomen or foam around his mouth; appears lethargic; licks the floor, wall, you, and everything else in sight; or tries to vomit with no result, he is probably experiencing gastric torsion, also known as bloat—a true medical emergency from which he could die within an hour. Take your pet to the nearest veterinary emergency hospital immediately.

Gastric torsion is most common in breeds with large chest cavities, such as Irish wolfhounds, German shepherds, boxers, and Great Danes. It occurs when the stomach literally twists around inside the chest cavity. Although vets and researchers have been unable to pinpoint a single cause of gastric torsion, theories include stress (from a move, time spent in a kennel, or any other trauma in a dog's life), vigorous exercise right before or after eating, and gulping food.

HEALTH

If the Fast Fails

If your pet begins vomiting again once you resume feedings or didn't stop after the 24-hour fast, call the vet.

Give Him a Pinch

Vomiting can leave an animal dehydrated, especially if he is very old, very young, or very small. Check by pinching your pet's skin; if it doesn't snap back into place, your pal is probably dehydrated. Offering him water to drink isn't enough to solve the problem. Call

A WORD FROM DR. MAUE

The Worst Part of Cat Ownership

DR. LISA MAUE
Veterinarian in private practice in Medford, Massachusetts, for more than a decade

If your cat takes to the litter box really well at first and then seems to go haywire and forget all her manners, the trouble may not be with the cat. It may be with you. Sometimes new pet owners accept the idea of cat box odor—until there really *is* odor. Then they switch to scented litter or, worse, put a cover on the litter box to contain the odor. Cats can be very sensitive to the amount, the kind, and the depth of litter. A change in any of these things can derail all your good training. Putting a lid on the box can be especially bad if you do it strictly to contain the smell. It does keep the odor in, but your cat doesn't want to walk into an intensely smelly bathroom any more than you do. If the box bothers you, put it in an area that doesn't get as much use, or keep it in a room—such as the bathroom—where you don't spend a lot of time. And clean and empty it more often!

the vet, who will want to rehydrate your animal with intravenous fluids.

Please Keep Off the Grass

Some pets develop a habit of eating grass, then vomiting it. This isn't an indication of medical problems, but it isn't pleasant for either you or your pet. So if your pet has a taste for the green stuff, try to discourage the habit. When you walk your dog, keep moving. Toss your kitty a little ball, a wadded-up piece of aluminum foil, or a toy mouse to play with. Throw your pup a Frisbee. In other words, distract your pal any way you can while he's outdoors.

Serve Him the Early Bird Special

If your pet vomits routinely overnight, she may have acid reflux—a condition in which digestive juices back up out of the stomach and into the esophagus. Nothing is medically wrong with her, but the results are messy, inconvenient, and upsetting to both of you. Try feeding her dinner an hour or so earlier in the evening than you usually do—say, at 5:00 P.M. instead of at 6:00. That way, she'll be able to rid her system of waste before she goes to sleep. And if your pet still throws up, at least you'll be prepared to clean up before you both retire for the night.

Three Meals Are Better Than Two

If the vet diagnoses your pet with acid reflux, try feeding her three small meals a day instead of two larger ones. If she has less food in her stomach at any given time, she may be less apt to vomit it. Don't change the overall amount of food you give her; just split it into three portions instead of two.

FOR DOGS ONLY

Will He Swallow This?

Dogs with acid reflux sometimes benefit from a preventive such as Tagamet caplets, an over-the-counter medication available at pharmacies. Ask your

vet whether this type of medication might help your pet and, if so, how much to give the animal.

FOR CATS ONLY

Another Helping?

If your cat wolfs down his food, vomits, and continues munching, he's eating too fast. Try offering your pet smaller portions of food at mealtimes. Divide his breakfast or dinner in half. Wait until he's through with the first helping before giving him the second. This will force your pet to slow down.

WEIGHT GAIN

The media constantly tell us that we're a nation of overweight people. But what about our pets? Do they have the same tendency to gain weight, with the same consequences? The answer is yes—pets often consume more calories than their bodies need. Obesity can aggravate respiratory problems, diabetes, arthritis, and heart disease. Just a pound or two may make a difference in an animal's health, so it's important to watch your pet's diet, exercise routine, and weight.

An average-size cat should weigh between 8 and 10 pounds; so should an average-size rabbit. Dogs' weights vary more because of the great variation in breed sizes. A small dog, such as a Jack Russell terrier, may weigh the same as a cat; a larger breed, such as a golden or Labrador retriever, may weigh 60 pounds. Irish wolfhounds and Newfoundlands weigh even more. Ask your vet or breeder what your pet's optimum weight is.

FOR DOGS AND CATS

Try This Rib Joint

The easiest way to tell whether your pet is overweight is by feeling for his ribs. Place the palm of your hand on the side of his rib cage and press gently. If you feel his ribs with this gentle pressure, he probably weighs the right amount. If you have to push harder to feel the ribs, he's overweight.

Help Lassie to Lighten Up

HEALTH

If you're concerned about your pet's weight, ask the animal's doctor if she recommends one of the prescription weight-reduction diets that are available only through vets. Be forewarned, however, that these are not intended to be used for more than a year.

YOU'VE GOTTA LOVE 'EM

A Punishing Thirst

A few years ago, I had just moved to New York. Since I didn't have an apartment yet, I was staying with my friend's mother. One weekend, she went away and asked me to take care of her Australian kelpie, Charly. That same weekend, I invited my new boyfriend over for dinner.

For appetizers, I got some marinated anchovies and a big block of feta—a very salty Greek cheese. After we'd finished, I started clearing the table, walking back and forth between the dining room and kitchen. I wasn't paying much attention to Charly, who seemed to be just hanging out. After I finished with the table, I went into the kitchen to wrap the cheese, but I couldn't find it. The plate was on the counter, undisturbed and totally clean. I asked Tom whether he'd put it away, but he hadn't. Just then, we heard a terrific gulping sound. We went back into the kitchen and there was Charly, draining his two-quart water dish, which only seconds earlier had been full. I bet Charly's glad he didn't get hold of the anchovies, too.

—**LORI BAIRD**
Astoria, New York

HEALTH

Give Her a Senior Discount

Senior diets help dogs and cats over six years of age maintain their optimum weights. Supermarkets and pet supply stores carry these foods, which are easily identified by their labels. Check with your vet before switching your pet to a senior diet.

The Four-Step Diet Plan

Anytime you introduce your pet to a new diet, do so gradually. On the first day, mix one part new food with three parts old food at each meal. Keep this up for a few days, then start mixing equal amounts of new and old food at each meal. Next, move to three parts new food and one part old. Finally, after a few days or a week, start serving just the new food.

Save the "People Food" for the People

Table scraps—those juicy morsels of meat, butter, and bacon grease—are notorious pound packers for pets. Seal food scraps tight or stash them where your animal can't reach them—for instance, in a covered trash can in the garage.

Nix the Snacks

If you're in the habit of giving your pet snacks during the day, cut back. Either give her a smaller portion each time or cut down on the number of times you offer a snack each day. Your pet's regular meals should be designed to give her all the calories she needs, making snacks superfluous.

Check with the Neighbors

If you've increased your pet's exercise and cut down on snacks but your pal still isn't losing weight (and the vet has given him an otherwise clean bill of health), check with your neighbors. Is anyone slipping your pet treats? Is your kitty trotting next door for a bowl of milk? Are the neighborhood kids tossing table scraps to your pup while he's in his outdoor pen? If so, explain that although you appreciate the intended kindness, your pet is on a diet.

FOR DOGS ONLY

This Carrot Is a Gem

Many dogs actually like the taste and crunch of raw vegetables such as carrots, broccoli, and green beans. Toss your pet a few of these each day instead of higher-calorie snacks. If these treats seem to cause indigestion, with excessive gas or diarrhea, back off and try an alternative.

An Apple a Day Keeps the Pounds Away

Apples and oranges are low-fat snacks that your pup can eat, but they may loosen the stool. If your pet develops a chronic loose stool or even diarrhea from these fruits, switch to something else.

Zero Temperature, Zero Calories

If your pooch has trouble digesting raw vegetables or fruits, or if the weather is hot, give her a couple of ice cubes to crunch on. She'll have the fun of eating a treat without gaining an ounce.

Try the Grape Escape

Many dogs love the taste of seedless grapes, so give your pup two or three of these instead of a higher-calorie snack.

Play a Game of Squash

Diets are rough on everyone, including pets. If your pup doesn't get enough to eat, he'll whine and follow you everywhere. Satisfy his hunger by replacing

Don't Lose Too Fast

If your pet is overweight, he needs to shed the excess pounds through diet and exercise—but not so fast as to endanger his health. As a general rule of thumb, figure that an average cat, rabbit, or small dog should lose one-quarter to one-half pound per week. For a medium to large dog, a loss of one pound per week is appropriate.

Be patient. If your pet takes longer to lose weight, don't fret—and don't put her on a crash diet! For some large dogs, losing three pounds over the course of six months is good progress.

HEALTH

half of his canned food ration at each meal with an equal amount of canned pumpkin or squash. His tummy will feel full, but he'll be consuming far fewer calories.

Pick up the Pace

Both you and your dog need exercise to maintain your optimum weights and health. Take a brisk walk together twice a day, keeping up the pace for 15 to 20 minutes each time. If you and your pet haven't been walking regularly, or if your dog has arthritis or other

ONE PERSON'S SOLUTION

She's No Heavyweight, but She's a Champ

When I adopted my dog, Blackie, she was 13 years old and weighed 127 pounds. Her extra weight, combined with arthritis, caused her so much pain that she couldn't get up without crying. But there was another problem as well. She had developed a hypothyroid condition, meaning that she had a low thyroid hormone level. This reduced her level of energy further and made her gain weight even more easily. Once I figured out the thyroid problem (I'm a vet) and put her on an inexpensive thyroid replacement therapy, Blackie began to shed the pounds.

Two years after she came to live with me, Blackie was down to a svelte 58 pounds. With the hypothyroidism under control, her weight dropped. And when her weight dropped, her arthritis pain eased. Now she can go for short walks and even play a tame game of fetch.

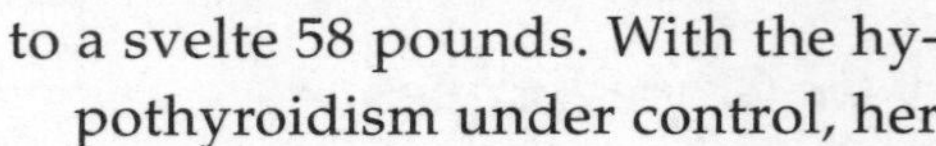

—**DR. JODY KAUFMAN**
Exeter, New Hampshire

health problems, start with, say, 10 minutes of slow walking at a time. When your pet seems more fit and energetic, increase the workout.

FOR CATS ONLY

He Likes to Play, Right?

Your cat needs exercise if he's going to lose weight. Even if you don't let him loose outside, set aside a little playtime each day. Toss a ball of aluminum foil for him to chase, or dangle one of those faux mice from the pet supply store in front of him. Leave a few toys around the house for him to play with by himself. Try to see that he gets at least 15 minutes of exercise twice a day.

Don't Let Her Go on Strike

If your kitty refuses to eat her new diet food, don't force the issue. An obese cat that goes on a hunger strike may develop fatty liver disease, which must be treated by a vet with intravenous fluids and force-feeding. If you've introduced her new food gradually over a period of three days and she's turned up her nose at it, discuss alternatives with your vet.

FOR RABBITS ONLY

Hay There!

Since rabbits don't get two squares a day—they should be allowed to graze or nibble whenever they want—putting them on a diet may be tricky. But there is a way to help your bunny lose weight without starving him. Simply offer plenty of hay and carrots and cut back on the pellets. The substitutions contain fewer calories, but they'll fill him up and nourish him just the same.

WORMS AND INTERNAL PARASITES

The worms crawl in, the worms crawl out, the worms wreak havoc on your pet's health. They can cause weight loss, weakness, dehydration, even anemia in pets, and some types can be transmitted to humans.

HEALTH

You can bet that your pet's intestine or stomach will contain at least one or two of these wiggly little creatures at some time in his life, so it's a good idea to brush up on your worm wisdom.

Most kittens and puppies have some form of worm infestation—either because they contracted the problem while in the womb or because they ingested worm larvae from their mother's milk while nursing. For that reason, it's important to have your new kitten or pup tested for worms at his first checkup with the vet. If you are adopting an animal from a professional breeder, ask whether your new pet has already been wormed.

Worms are fairly easy to treat, usually with a prescription for several days' worth of oral medication and a follow-up visit to the vet three to four weeks later. Note, however, that although cats and dogs often receive the same type of medication for worm treatment, the dosages differ. If you own both types of animals, don't give Fido's medication to Fluffy or vice versa. Doing so could be harmful to your pets.

COMMON MISTAKES

Don't Try to Worm Your Way out of This One

Although it's tempting to pick up an over-the-counter worming preparation at the pet supply store, your pet—and probably your pocketbook—will benefit much more from a prescription from your vet. That's because over-the-counter worming products are too broad-based and not strong enough to be completely effective. Furthermore, if you've made an incorrect diagnosis, you might buy the wrong type of wormer. Do it right the first time: Get an accurate diagnosis and the correct medication from your vet. It's smarter and safer than continuing to buy treatments that don't work.

FOR DOGS AND CATS

Tape This Segment

If you see your kitty or pup scooting along the ground on her fanny, or if she suddenly seems obsessed with licking her anal area, check her for tapeworms. Tapeworm segments, found on the skin and in the hair around the anal area, look like bits of rice. You also may find segments in her stool. Take her to the vet, who will prescribe medication.

Encourage Playing, Not Preying

If your cat or dog is an avid hunter, check the animal regularly for tapeworms. Rodents, in particular, tend to carry tapeworms that are transmitted easily to your pet when he goes hunting. Although you can't completely prevent your pet from doing what comes naturally, you can discourage the behavior. Keep your dog on a leash when he's outside or minimize the amount of time your cat spends roaming free. Make sure your pet has plenty of food he likes at home and plenty of toys to play with.

Beat the Fleas

If your pet has a tapeworm problem, be sure you are doing all you can to battle fleas as well. The tapeworm segments released by your pet are filled with eggs, which in turn are eaten by flea larvae. When the infected flea larvae become adults, they will reinfect your pet with tapeworms.

Hop Off the Merry-Go-Round

If you see spaghetti-like strands in your pet's droppings or vomit, she probably has roundworms. If she's had them for a while, she also may lose weight and appear weak. Have your pet treated by the vet as soon as possible—for the animal's benefit and your own. Roundworms can be transmitted to humans, causing a disease called visceral larva migrans, in which the worms infect different parts of the body, such as the inside of the eye. Prompt attention from the vet can stop the problem before it progresses.

Roundworms look like miniature strands of spaghetti—but they're considerably more dangerous.

Be the Dean of Clean

To prevent any future infestation of roundworms in your pet, clean up carefully after your animal. Keep the dog's outdoor play area or the cat's litter box pristine at all times.

He's Captain Hook

If your kitty or pup has diarrhea—possibly with blood in it or very dark in color—have the vet check a sample for hookworms. You won't see the actual worms in your pet's stool because they literally hook themselves to your pet's intestinal walls. But the vet will be able to spot the eggs through a microscope. He'll prescribe medication and most likely recommend a follow-up check in two to four weeks.

As with roundworms, prevent future infestations by keeping your pet's litter box or outdoor play area as clean as possible.

Be Heartless

If your dog or cat seems to have ongoing worm problems, ask your vet about heartworm medication that also combats other types of worms. For instance, Heartgard for Cats contains ivermectin to control heartworms as well as other medication to remove and control hookworms. No preventive will eradicate all types of worms, but since you need to be protecting your pet from heartworms on an ongoing basis, you may be able to solve a couple of problems at once.

Crack the Whip

Dogs are much more likely than cats to contract whipworms, but it is possible for your kitty to have them as well. The main symptom is a bloody stool. Try to collect a sample and take it to the vet for testing. (You won't actually see the worms, but your vet will be able to detect the eggs with a microscope.) The doctor will prescribe medication for about a week and recommend a follow-up check in three to four weeks.

FOR RABBITS ONLY

Get an Early Sample

When you first adopt a rabbit, have a stool sample checked by the vet for coccidia, tiny organisms that irritate the intestinal lining. If these organisms are present, the vet will prescribe medication. Once you've had your rabbit for a while without exposing her to other rabbits, she's unlikely to suffer a recurrence of coccidia. But if she develops diarrhea, have another stool sample tested immediately.

BEHAVIOR

Getting a Jump on Training

Just like people, pets can develop some pretty unhealthy, nasty, annoying, and sometimes dangerous habits. But pets are like children: They need guidance and discipline to live happily and healthily with the "adults" in their lives. Setting limits doesn't mean unkindness. It means being clear about what behaviors you will and won't accept from the animal. One trainer describes it as a "well-organized expression of love." And the only way to communicate that is by being consistent. If you allow your dog to pounce on the sofa cushions one day and reprimand the animal for the same behavior the next, you'll end up with a very confused pup.

Along with consistency, the other cardinal rule is immediacy. It's important to correct your pet for an undesirable behavior as he is commiting the offense, not two hours or even two minutes later. Animals don't reason the way we do. For instance, let's say your cat chews your houseplant and you squirt her with a spray bottle an hour later, after you've realized what's happened. Only when you get around to squirting her, she's lying on her bed playing with a toy. She'll associate

being squirted with lying on her bed playing with a toy, not with chewing a houseplant.

Remember, too, that anytime your pet exhibits an unacceptable behavior, you must try to find the motive behind the behavior. Let's say your dog is chewing his tail; you obviously want to change that behavior, but you need to know *why* he's chewing his tail. If the dog had a bad rash, you'd treat the self-mutilation very differently than you would if you found that he was simply bored.

We hope it goes without saying that there is never, ever any reason to hit, strike, shake, scream at, or otherwise harm an animal. You always have options for dealing with any behavior in a positive manner. Here are some of them.

BARKING

A dog barks for all sorts of reasons, but the most common are (1) he's trying to get your attention or else (2) he sees something that frightens or intimidates him. As with any undesired behavior, you need to treat the underlying problem, not just the symptom. And depending on the cause for the barking, your approach to solving the problem will differ. Here's some advice for dealing with your chatty canine.

FOR DOGS ONLY

Shake, Rattle, and Roll

Dogs hate to be startled by sudden, loud noises (who doesn't?), and you can use that to your advantage when you're trying to break a dog of barking. Drop a few pennies, screws, or pebbles into a clean, empty soda can. Seal the opening well with some duct tape, which you can find at any hardware store. When the dog barks, say "Quiet" or "Hush" in a firm tone as you either toss the can on the ground or give it a few good shakes. (If you toss it, just drop it on the ground so that it rolls and makes noise. Don't throw it at the dog.) The sound will startle the dog, and he'll stop barking. He'll also learn the "Quiet" command.

It Keeps Mosquitoes Away, Too

One high-tech way to check inappropriate barking is to invest in a citronella collar. The dog wears the collar like any other, but when the animal barks, the movement of her neck causes citronella to squirt out of the collar. The citronella is the same stuff that's in the

A WORD FROM MICKY NIEGO

Know Your Dog: Breed

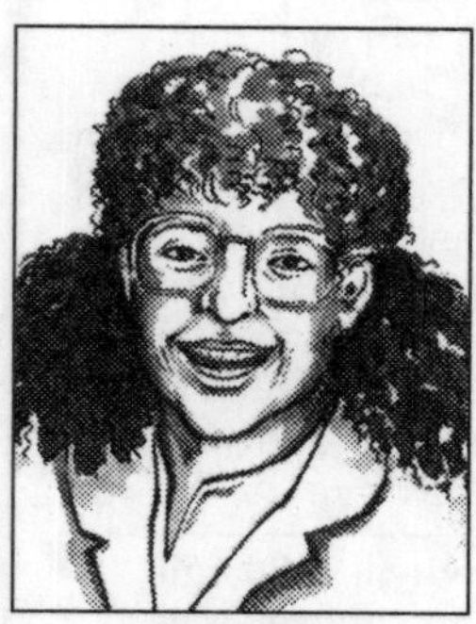

MICKY NIEGO
Animal behaviorist in Airmont, New York, who trains puppies and service dogs in addition to speaking and consulting on animal behavior and training issues

You need to get a dog whose activity level roughly matches yours, but there's more to it than that. When a behavior you find unacceptable is related to your dog's particular breed, standard corrections may not be the answer. You may need to manage, rather than try to change, the behavior. For instance, some terriers love to dig—it's characteristic of the breed. Rather than trying to stop your terrier from digging up your yard, you're probably better off giving him his own spot to dig in.

Before you decide how to deal with your pet's behavior, take a look at the box on the following page and see whether that particular behavior may be related to your dog's breed. Then plan your own actions accordingly.

Bred in the Bone

Is your dog's behavior something that's characteristic of his breed? Take a look below to find out.

TYPE	SOME SPECIFIC BREEDS	WERE BRED . . .	QUALITIES, LIMITATIONS, AND LIABILITIES
Herding dogs	Collies, Shetland sheepdogs, corgis	To move and herd livestock without displaying predatory behavior toward them. Work as part of human-dog teams.	Moderate to high activity/energy level. Basically cooperative. Prone to excessive barking in excitement and to chasing, snapping, or nipping (misplaced herding behavior). If underexercised, tend to roam and be restless.
Sporting hounds	Setters, spaniels, pointers	As tracking and hunting animals. They have keen senses of smell and sight.	High energy/activity levels. Prone to whining, excessive barking, or baying in excitement. If underexercised, they'll roam and chew destructively.
Terriers	Border, fox, Irish, Scottish	To chase rats and other pests in barns.	Very high activity/energy level. Can be persistent, impatient, uncooperative. Prone to alarm or excessive barking, chasing, and fighting. Like to dig holes (in yard and flooring). When bored, will chew destructively. Can be willfully disobedient. Can be mouthy and snappy. May bite.
Toy/non-sporting dogs	Chihuahuas, toy spaniels, shih tzus	As companions; they are strictly ornamental. These dogs are artificial. They need human care to survive.	High activity level. High-strung. Sensitive to extremes in temperature. Dependent and demanding. Can be yappy. Prone to snapping and biting.
Working dogs	Malamutes, huskies, Akitas	To be companion and guard dogs. Many can pull sleds or carts. These are large (75 pounds) or giant (more than 125 pounds) dogs.	Sedentary. Prone to growling around food, toys, and strangers to protect territory. May howl or dig. Tendency toward excessive barking, snapping, or biting as a result of overprotection or aggression.

antimosquito candles you keep on your porch. It's harmless, but the sound of the spray, coupled with the smell, startles and quiets the dog. At nearly $200 (and $15 or more for the citronella refills), the collars aren't cheap, but they work. One mail-order supplier that sells them is R. C. Steele; call toll-free directory assistance (1-800-555-1212) for the company's phone number. If you don't have time to wait for mail delivery, check your local pet supply store or with your vet.

A little squirt will do it! When it comes to stopping a dog's incessant barking, try a citronella collar.

Music Soothes the Savage Beast

If your dog has the habit of barking when you leave your house or apartment, you may be dealing with a mild case of separation anxiety. One way to put a lid on the barking is to make your dog feel as though he's not alone. Some folks accomplish this by turning a radio or television on when they leave the house—providing white noise to block out street sounds that can suddenly become intimidating when the pack leader (that's you) is gone. Music stations are especially good because the rhythm is soothing to pets.

Give Her Something Else to Think About

Do your neighbors complain that your dog barks while you're away? You may be able to keep your pet occupied in your absence by leaving her a good chew toy. Before you leave the house, rub your hands all over the toy. Your scent will make it more appealing, which will increase the likelihood of her chewing it. And if she's chewing, she won't be incessantly barking.

Cheese It!

If there's anything that can make a chew toy more inviting than leaving your scent on it, it's leaving food in it. Visit a local pet supply store and purchase a hollow bone. Stuff the bone with cheese or peanut

butter. Your dog will be so busy trying to get the food out that he may not have the time or the inclination to bark.

Pavlov's Pooch

Some dogs seem to think that the doorbell or a knock on the door is their signal to start barking. But with a little patience—and a little help from an assistant—you can condition your dog to look forward to the ringing of the bell or knocking without the vocal hysterics. Position a family member or friend outside the front door. Attach your dog's leash and, keeping her inside, take her near the door. Give the "Sit" or "Down" command. Next, have the helper knock on the door or ring the bell. If the dog barks, say in a firm voice, "No. Quiet." At the same time, snap the leash. When the barking stops, offer praise and a treat. Keep repeating this drill until your pooch gets the idea that barking results in disapproval, but sitting or lying down and being quiet earns praise and a treat.

YOU'VE GOTTA LOVE 'EM

Kitty in a Bottle

My kitten, Smudge, loves to drink water out of cups. One day, after we'd just gotten him, I was sitting in our living room when I heard *bop bop* coming from the other room. I went into the kitchen to see what was going on. Smudge had his head stuck in a tall glass that he was trying to drink from, and he was whacking his head against the wall trying to get it off!

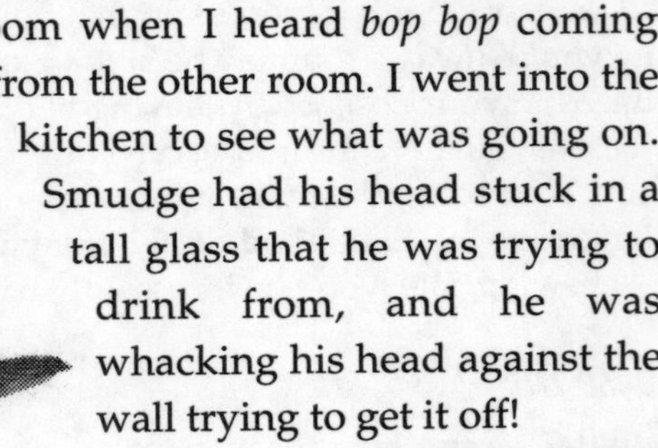

—MATT PINAUD
Boston, Massachusetts

BEGGING

The greatest problem in a pet's begging for food is probably the annoyance it causes the owner. But if you're the type who continually gives in and doles out treats on demand, you may be doing more harm than good. After all, being overweight is just as unhealthy for animals as it is for humans.

FOR PETS IN GENERAL

Consistency Is the Key

❑ Be consistent about both the amount of pet food you give your pet and when you give it, and you'll greatly lessen the chances that he'll beg or scavenge at other times. Although it is fine to feed your pets at a time of day that's convenient for you (as long as it's every day), you need to decide on a particular time of day when you're going to feed them—in the morning, afternoon, or evening—and stick to that schedule.

Just Say No to Begging

❑ Feeding your pet table scraps while you're eating is a surefire way to encourage begging. Your pet will come to expect his share when you sit down to eat. Feed your animal pet food, not people food, and you won't find a wet nose next to your plate on the dinner table.

FOR DOGS ONLY

Dinnertime Is Nap Time

One way to keep your dog from begging is to teach her to associate your dinnertime with something completely unrelated to food. For

Tailor the Punishment to the Pup

Reading through some of the tips offered in this chapter, you may be thinking, "If I used a 'shake can' (for instance) with *my* dog, I'd scare the living daylights out of him." Or "My dog would laugh in my face if I used a 'shake can' to correct her." Trust your own judgment because you're probably right.

Anytime you're dealing with an unwanted behavior, you need to tailor the correction to your dog's individual personality. If he's bold, a stern "No" may have no effect at all. But that response may be just right for a shy dog.

How can you tell whether your correction has had the appropriate impact? You want the dog to signal submission. If his ears and tail drop, you've gotten the right response. Stop there. If, however, your dog cowers and leaves a small puddle of urine on the floor, that particular correction was too harsh. File the experience away in your brain, and next time choose a milder correction.

instance, you could train your dog to go to a quiet spot and lie down anytime people are sitting at the dinner table or anytime you ring the dinner chime. (You can purchase a small bell for this purpose at almost any discount store.)

BITING

Animals bite for all sorts of reasons, including teething, fear, a desire to play, and illness. There are lots of steps you can take to curb this behavior, but if you ever feel frightened or intimidated by a pet that bites, it's time to call your vet or an animal behaviorist.

Time to Give It a Rest

Jeanneane and Nick Kutsukos of Pro Dog Training in Springfield, Virginia, recommend that puppy owners take a break from obedience training after about 20 to 30 minutes. That gives your dog (and you) a chance to take a breather and play around for a while. It also makes training time more fun for both of you—and more effective for the pup.

FOR PETS IN GENERAL

Slow and Steady Wins His Trust

❑ Any animal is liable to bite if he feels threatened or cornered. So if you've just brought a new animal into your home from a pet store, a breeder, or a shelter, you need to gain the animal's trust. Always approach the animal in a calm, measured way. Talk quietly and reassuringly to your pet, and never grab or lunge for him. Place a treat in your hand and let the animal come to you for it. Then slowly reach toward him. The calm approach is especially important with a shy or timid pet or one (say, from a shelter) with a history of abuse or neglect.

FOR DOGS ONLY

Worse Than Her Bark

If you have a large, powerful dog that bites, contact a professional trainer (look in the Yellow Pages under Pet & Dog Training) before someone gets hurt. Don't ever try to hit, shake, or physically confront a biting dog. That serves only to escalate the confrontation, and you or someone else is liable to be injured.

We Have Contact!

You can lessen the chances that your dog will grow up to be a biter by making sure the animal gets lots of human contact early. When you bring the puppy home, start a handling regimen right away. Pet the dog often. Handle his paws and gently rub his ears. That will teach the dog that being touched by a human is a social interaction to look forward to, not fear.

When the puppy is comfortable with the immediate family, invite friends or neighbors over to handle and play with her. This will reinforce the lesson.

Ask before You Touch

One way to keep your dog from biting a stranger who might intimidate her—even if your dog's not a biter—is to set boundaries around your dog with other people. Just as you wouldn't let a stranger walk up to you and pick up your child, step in when someone you don't know approaches your dog to pet her. Ask the stranger to approach the dog quietly and calmly and to hold out her hand with the palm down and the fingers under the thumb in a fist (to protect the fingers). That way the dog can get a good whiff of the person right away.

You've Gotta Be Thick-Skinned

When your puppy digs those sharp little baby teeth into your hand, try your best to leave your hand where it is and not pull it away—even though your reflex is to recoil. A dog's instinct is to give chase, and if you pull your hand away quickly, that's exactly what your pet will do. Instead, yelp loudly, and the puppy will let go.

A Gift? For Me?

Both dogs and cats occasionally bring their owners "presents," usually a dead animal of some sort. Although the actions smack of gift giving, the reasons behind the gifts vary considerably depending on whether the bearer is a dog or a cat.

If your dog brings you a dead animal, he's acknowledging you as the leader of the pack. He's telling you, "I know you're in charge."

By contrast, cats feed only their own young. So when your cat deposits a dead bird on your doorstep, it's her way of saying, "Good Lord, I know these idiots can't fend for themselves. I'll have to feed them." Or words to that effect.

BEHAVIOR

FOR CATS ONLY

Enough Already!

Fluffy's on your lap, purring. You're petting him, running your hand over his head and down along his back to his tail. Suddenly—and seemingly without provocation—he bites you. What the heck? A cat is a highly sensitive animal. Sometimes a cat will become overstimulated if you continually stroke the animal along his entire body, from head to tail. And that can provoke an attack. The answer? Keep your petting sessions short and sweet and stop at the first signs—

A WORD FROM MICKY NIEGO

Know Your Animal: Species

MICKY NIEGO
Animal behaviorist in Airmont, New York, who trains puppies and service dogs in addition to speaking and consulting on animal behavior and training issues

Before you use any particular training or correction technique with your pet, you need to understand some things about the animal. First, whether you have an iguana, a fish, or a cat, you need to know the personality traits characteristic of the animal's species. For instance:

Dogs are pack animals. Each pack has a definite leader: the alpha dog, the lead dog, the head dog. Once you know what it takes to be a leader and start acting like one, you'll be better able to train and direct your dog.

So what's a dog leader like? The leader sets the pace. When you go for a walk, you don't allow yourself to be dragged along by the dog. Leaders don't move out of the way. If Fido is lying in the doorway, you don't step over him; you make sure he moves. Leaders don't repeat commands more than once. And most impor-

twitching tail, flickering ears, or dancing eyes—that kitty is revving up and about to pounce.

Cat Got Your Thumb?

You can effectively discourage a cat from biting by squirting the animal with a spray bottle filled with water at room temperature. The key here is to keep the bottle with you at all times so that you can use it immediately when your pet starts in. Pick up a spray bottle at any plant shop or discount store. Or substitute a toy water pistol—it works just as well, and it's more fun to use!

tant, leaders are in control. Once you've established yourself as the leader, the struggle almost disappears. When you say "No!" as your dog tries to get on the sofa, he's going to obey you because he knows you're the boss.

Cat social hierarchies, on the other hand, are based on territory. You can't teach a cat to do something just because you say so. You're not the leader to your cat because cats don't think in terms of leaders. If a visitor comes over and sits on the cat's favorite rocking chair (a territory issue), the cat pees on the visitor's jacket. The cat is peeing because her territory has been invaded by someone whom she perceives as an intruder. If you yell "No!" as she starts to pee, you'll certainly have addressed the symptom (the peeing) but not the problem (she feels her territory has been usurped). When you yell at her, sure, she'll run away from the chair, but she's just as likely to pee in your friend's shoes. The way to deal with the real problem is to give her more time to get used to your friend—and, in the meantime, give her a safe place to call her own.

No matter what kind of animal you have, you need to know something about the species to understand how to train, teach, and guide the animal effectively. Ask your vet, or ask an animal trainer, but find out.

BEHAVIOR

See Puff; See Puff Bite

Biting is a fairly common behavior in kittens, and it often becomes more pronounced at about 12 weeks and again at 8 months. Although you can't entirely eliminate the behavior, you can go a long way toward curbing it. Play gently with your new kitten, and don't tease her with your hands and feet. Teasing only encourages the biting that's characteristic of predatory play.

Another way to discourage biting is always to put a toy between you and your kitten. This lets your kitten know *you're* not the toy!

What You Knead to Know

Cat owners have long been puzzled by the behavior known as kneading—when a cat hunches over a blanket or your lap, grabbing at it rhythmically with her front paws. What is it? Your cat looks as though she's having a good time, but what does it mean? Next time your cat starts to knead when she's on your lap, feel lucky. According to Diana Culp of the Pet Behavior Clinic in Rockville, Maryland, kneading is a kind of "infantile, affectionate behavior." Like the way we talk baby talk to our loved ones. Your cat's saying, "I like you." So kneading isn't a problem—unless you're wearing shorts. Your best defense may be to put a blanket on your lap before you invite her up. And keep your cat's claws clipped!

FOR BIRDS ONLY

Show Him Who's Boss

Birds often bite out of a desire to dominate you—in other words, to stay at the top of the pecking order. If your bird is so determined, the most important step to take is to keep the bird, when he's outside his cage, at or below your chest level. Don't allow the bird to perch on your shoulder or near your face, where even a small bird can do serious damage.

Tweetie Has a Toy

If your bird has nothing to do 24 hours a day but sit on the perch in her cage, you can bet she'll be ready to bite anything that comes near her. The answer? Toys, toys, and more toys. You don't have to spend much. A bird will enjoy a toy as simple as a small block of soft, untreated wood. (Pine works well, and you can probably get a piece free from your local lumberyard.) Leave the wood on the floor of the cage. Or drill a hole

in the block and hang it with a chain or a piece of soft cotton cloth from the bird's T-bar or from the top of the cage.

If you don't mind spending a little money, visit your local department store's baby department and pick up some infant toys for your pet. They're inexpensive and sturdy, and many birds love them. (Examine the toys carefully, because not everything that's safe for babies also is safe for birds. Rattles and teething rings are especially good, but steer clear of toys that have small, removable parts.)

I Feel the Earth Move . . .

One way to train a bird not to bite while she's on your finger is to jiggle or drop your finger gently, just

Birds: Break Those Plucky Habits

Just like some people who bite their nails or tap their toes to release nervous energy, birds sometimes pull out their feathers. One behaviorist explains that birds caught in the wild are used to spending about 60 percent of their time finding and opening their food. When the birds are brought into captivity, their owners provide them with plenty of food at all times. So a bird that is used to getting and opening his own food now has an enormous amount of energy to burn off.

Birds raised in captivity sometimes start to pull out their feathers when they reach sexual maturity. Just like a human teenager, a bird that has hit puberty is experiencing a surge of hormones. Unless you have the bird sexed and bred (birds don't get spayed or neutered), you're going to have one very frustrated, feather-picking pet on your hands.

The way to help your bird channel all that extra energy is to enrich his environment by letting him tear open his own food. Rather than giving your pet a bowlful of seeds, give him a banana with the peel still on. Or offer him an entire apple to tackle. You could also crack a piece of coconut and put the shell with the flesh inside the cage. Your bird will have a ball digging into some fresh, challenging food—and burn up some of that excess energy in the process.

to throw the bird a little off balance. Do this when she starts to bite you, and she'll eventually learn to associate biting with the unpleasant sensation of falling.

Grin and Bear It

You can usually put an end to biting once and for all by simply ignoring it when your bird bites you. It may hurt like crazy, but if you act as if it's no big deal, the bird will eventually give up.

The Squeaky Wheel Gets the . . . Graphite

Squeak, squeak, squeak, squeak, squeak, squeak. Ah, the hamster wheel, one of the world's most sophisticated forms of aural torture. What hamster owner hasn't been kept awake at night by the sound of her hamster running in the wheel? It's true, you can oil the wheel with vegetable or lubricating oil, but those substances tend to gum up with dust. A better solution is powdered graphite, a dry lubricant that you can find at most hardware stores. Take the wheel out of the cage and apply a small amount of graphite where the axle meets the stand. Spray it on, give the wheel a spin, and then blow off any excess powder. Put the wheel back into the cage and get ready for a good night's sleep.

FOR FERRETS ONLY

Don't Let Him Take a Little Nip

Ferrets sometimes gently nip at their owners' hands when they play, but if your ferret occasionally plays too rough and gives you a real bite, pick the animal up by the scruff of the neck and say "No" or "No bite" firmly (don't yell). Then put your pet down and ignore him. Make sure you correct the ferret the moment the animal bites you, and be consistent. Don't allow the ferret to bite with impunity sometimes and then lose your temper at other times. If you're consistent, sooner or later your pet will begin to associate biting with a strong negative reaction from you.

FOR POCKET PETS

Let Sleeping Hamsters Lie

Hamsters are nocturnal. That means they sleep through the day and are more active at night. And they can be more than a tad cranky if roused from a sound slumber (aren't you?). If you want to be sure that you don't get bitten, save your playtime for the nighttime.

CHEWING

Puppies use their mouths to explore their new worlds. (Gee, this is interesting. Wonder what it tastes like?) Other animals chew to keep their teeth short, and some do it when they're bored. But if your pet is chewing on your shoes or furniture or munching on the kids' homework, both you and the pet (not to mention the young student) are in trouble. Here are some ways to tackle problem chewing.

FOR PETS IN GENERAL

Put 'Em in the Lockup

❑ If your pet chews, confine her to one room or area where there are few chewable objects. A puppy gate, which you can find in department and discount stores, is terrific for confining animals to rooms where they're least likely to do damage—the kitchen or laundry room, for instance.

A puppy gate will let your pet see what's going on and feel like a part of the family—and it will also keep the animal away from your favorite loafers.

❑ Even a kitchen or laundry room is likely to have walls, floors, and molding that can be damaged by a curious puppy. To prevent such problems, use a dog crate when you can't be present to supervise. This is a dog-size wire or plastic kennel that serves as the dog's private space—and keeps the animal from damaging yours.

A Bitter Pill

❑ A commercial spray deterrent such as Bitter Apple, Bitter Orange, or Bitter Lime (available at pet stores) can be effective against chewing. Following the label instructions, just spray the deterrent on items you want to protect. The smell and taste will keep your pets away from areas you've sprayed.

FOR DOGS ONLY

Wood Chew?

You can keep your dog from chewing woodwork by sprinkling it with oil of cloves (available at pharmacies).

BEHAVIOR

Cool and Tasty

When puppies are teething, they chew anything they can find to relieve their discomfort. The best way to keep your teething puppy from destroying your precious belongings is to redirect her attention to items that she *is* allowed to chew on. Pick up a few good chew toys at the pet store. To make one of these toys even more appealing to your puppy, place it in the freezer for a few hours. The cold will be very soothing to her sore mouth.

He Needs a Little Excitement

Chewing is often interpreted by vets and trainers as a sign of boredom. If your dog chews inappropriately—on shoes, woodwork, or his own tail—you need to examine his activity level based on his breed. Some

BASIC TRAINING

Teach Your Dog to Sit

It's the first command many puppies learn and one of the easiest to teach. Here's how it's done.

Start by giving the dog a few "free" treats. Then show the animal a treat by holding it in front of his nose. Let him get very interested. Next, with the treat grasped firmly between your fingers, slowly raise your hand up and over the dog's head—not too high, or he'll jump up to get it. As he angles himself to get the treat, he'll raise his head and lower his back end. Say "Sit" as his rear end makes contact with the floor and immediately release the treat into his mouth.

Keep repeating this exercise until the puppy sits right away when presented with the hand signal and treat. (This will take several short, frequent practice sessions.) Then—and only then—should you verbally direct the puppy to sit *before* you give the hand signal with no treat in your hand. When the pup sits, give him a treat as a reward. Phase out using the treat as a lure as the puppy becomes more proficient in increasingly distracting surroundings.

Keep it fun—for you *and* the puppy. If you feel yourself getting tired or exasperated, give it a rest, because your puppy can hear the aggravation in your voice.

dogs, such as rottweilers and other guard dogs, were bred to be sedentary; they don't need much exercise. Other breeds, such as dalmatians, need several hours of vigorous play each day. Talk to your vet or a dog trainer to get an idea about how much exercise your dog needs. If your pet isn't getting enough exercise, play with him more, take him on more frequent walks, or set up play dates with other dogs in your neighborhood. With just a little more of a workout in the dog's daily schedule, he may give up inappropriate chewing.

BEHAVIOR

Get Stuffed

One method for coping with a dog who's chewing up your house is to redirect her behavior by giving her toys that you allow and encourage her to chew. Unfortunately, sometimes your Italian loafers are just a little tastier than that boring old chew toy you've offered your pet. The solution? Visit your local pet store, purchase a hollow bone, and stuff it full of low-fat or nonfat cheese or peanut butter. Once your pup gets a taste of the treat, she'll most likely ignore your shoes.

Just Like the Real Thing

You may have better luck curbing your dog's inappropriate chewing by replacing the object you don't want him to damage with a chew toy of a similar texture. For instance, if he's munching on chair legs, give him something hard, such as a chew toy from a pet supply store. If your mutt is tearing your pillows to pieces, he may prefer a fabric toy—a doll, for instance. (Make sure the toy is sturdy enough to stand up

COMMON MISTAKES

Solitary Confinement

You're getting ready to leave the house, and you don't want your dog to tear the place apart. So being a smart dog owner who knows about diversionary tactics, you toss your dog a toy—the Frisbee. When you come home, the house is a mess. What went wrong? Although it is true that you can prevent many kinds of destructive behavior by channeling your pet's energy into another activity, you need to make sure that if you leave the animal a toy, it's a toy she can play with by herself. Otherwise, you might as well leave no toys at all. A Frisbee or a tug-of-war toy is of no use to a dog left alone. Choose toys that wobble or roll—or anything else that the dog can handle without a playmate.

to serious chewing!) If the replacement is similar to the item the pup went for originally, chances are he'll see it as a palatable substitute. To keep your pet from going back to the original chew object, praise him for chewing the new toy and guide him back to the toy if his mouth wanders.

FOR CATS ONLY

Hey, Mom! Fluffy Just Ate the Ferns!

Some cats just love to chew stuff. If your houseplants have fallen prey to the jaws of your feline, try spraying a dose of Bitter Apple (available at pet supply stores) on the plants.

Keep These Houseplants off the Kitty Menu

It's bad enough that your ivy plant has tiny teeth marks all over it. What's worse is that the plant can make your cat ill or even kill her. All of these common houseplants are harmful to cats that eat them.

- Caladiums
- Carnations
- Cyclamens
- Dieffenbachia (dumbcane)
- Forced indoor bulbs, such as narcissus (paper whites)
- Holly
- Hydrangeas
- Ivy
- Mistletoe
- Philodendrons
- Rubber plants

If you have a cat, it's safest to avoid these plants altogether. If you just can't bear to part with your greenery, invest in some hanging pots and baskets and place your plants where the cat can't get at them. That means away from counters, tables, bookshelves, or any other furniture that your cat could climb on and jump from. Also watch out for falling leaves and flowers and pick them up before kitty can grab them.

Warning signs that your cat may have been poisoned by a plant include diarrhea, vomiting, disorientation, and lack of appetite. If you suspect that your pet has been nibbling the wrong leaves, get her to the vet immediately. And if you know which plant she's been eating, take it along, too.

Tiger-Proof Plants

If you've tried everything and your cat just won't leave your houseplants alone, you may want to consider limiting your plant purchases to varieties that do well in hanging pots. Hang the plants well away from shelves, counters, or anything else that the cat could launch herself from.

Alternatively, invest in plants that your cat won't want to chew, such as cacti.

Fake It

If all else fails, replace your live plants with low-cost, ultra-low-maintenance silk or plastic plants. If your cats have been chewing your real plants, they'll probably leave the fake ones alone.

FOR BIRDS ONLY

A Nutty Idea

If your bird is chewing the wallpaper near his cage, he's probably bored stiff. Move the cage farther away from the wall and make sure your pet has plenty of toys. Here's one that will keep him busy: Let your bird watch you place a peanut in a small paper cup. Then crumple the cup and place it inside the cage. He'll have a great time getting the nut out, and you'll have a great time watching him.

FOR POCKET PETS

Chews Your Weapon

If you find that your gerbil or hamster is chewing her water bottle or the water bottle mouthpiece, the problem may be that you haven't given the animal enough variety in her chew toys. These little creatures have to chew to keep their teeth, which grow continuously, at a manageable length. Provide your pet with a small dog bone, a little rat or monkey chow, or some dried kernels of corn, all of which are available at any good pet supply store.

ONE PERSON'S SOLUTION

When She Takes the Toilet Paper and Runs

Kim Steffes of Kim's Canine Training Center in Grand Rapids, Michigan, has a lot of experience with puppies and all the mischief they can get into. You know how puppies sometimes pull the toilet paper off the roll and run with it? "I think it's kind of cute," says Kim. "The first time."

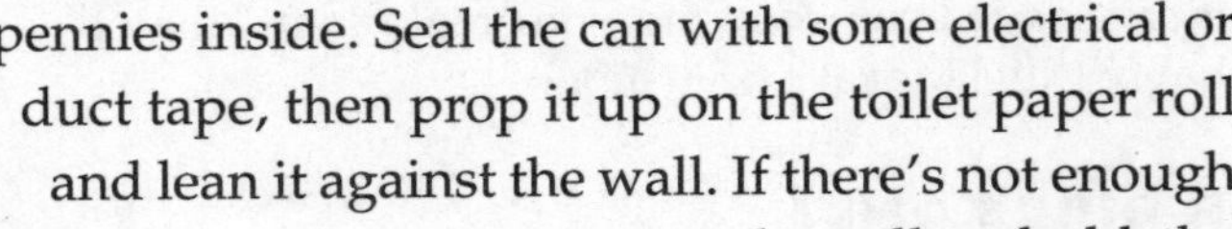

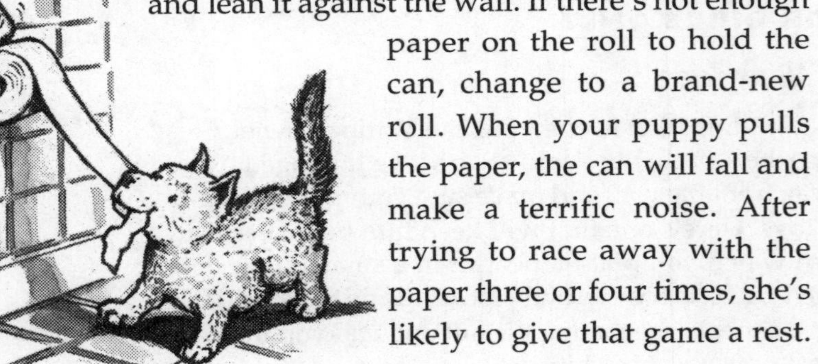

Kim's solution is a slight variation on the ever-popular "shake can." Rinse and drip-dry an empty soda can, then drop about ten pennies inside. Seal the can with some electrical or duct tape, then prop it up on the toilet paper roll and lean it against the wall. If there's not enough paper on the roll to hold the can, change to a brand-new roll. When your puppy pulls the paper, the can will fall and make a terrific noise. After trying to race away with the paper three or four times, she's likely to give that game a rest.

Alternatively, visit your local lumberyard and ask for a small (two- by two-inch) piece of untreated pine. (If they try to charge you for it, go somewhere else.)

DIGGING

Animals dig for all sorts of reasons. Dogs do it to burn off energy or because they're bored. In the summer, they may dig to lie in the cool soil. Cats tend to dig simply because they like the consistency of whatever it is they're digging in. Of course, if your backyard looks like a minefield and your potting soil is scattered all over the living room floor, figuring out *why* they're digging is only the first step. Here are some ways to cope with the behavior.

FOR PETS IN GENERAL

Camphor Care

❑ Mothballs are terrific repellents for keeping pets out of your garden, but they're toxic, so you need to make sure animals get a whiff of them without getting a taste. Here's one way to do that if you're dealing with a relatively small animal. Place several mothballs in a one-pound coffee can. Put the lid on and secure it well with duct or electrical tape. Then, with a knife or awl, punch lots of holes in the lid. The holes will let the odor out but keep the mothballs in. Place the cans wherever you don't want pets to dig. (This approach is not appropriate for large dogs, which may be able to get into the cans and eat the toxic mothballs.)

FOR DOGS ONLY

Bored No More

Constant digging, like many other destructive behaviors, can be a sign that your dog isn't getting enough exercise. If it's possible, take your dog on more frequent or longer walks or set up play dates with other dogs in your neighborhood. The amount of exercise a dog needs depends on the breed. Sporting dogs such as retrievers may need as much as a couple of hours of brisk exercise a day, while dogs bred as sedentary guard dogs or lapdogs (think rottweilers or shih tzus) can get by on much less. Talk to your vet or a dog trainer to get an idea of how much exercise is right for your dog, and remember to be careful not to overdo it with young dogs.

Surprise!

Here's a good way to keep your dog from destroying the backyard. First, purchase some small, inexpensive balloons from a discount store. Next, dig a

hole where the dog normally digs. Blow up the balloons, tie them, place them in the hole, and gently cover them with soil. When your pooch starts to dig in the dirt, his toenails will pop the balloons, sending him scurrying. If he's a sensitive dog, breaking two or three balloons will make an impression. Repeat until the dog shows no interest, being careful to pick up the remnants of the burst balloons before your pooch or some other animal swallows them.

FOR CATS ONLY

Keep Her Clean

Cats are very clean creatures and will let you know, one way or another, if their litter boxes aren't kept scrupulously clean. If your cat is spending a lot of time digging in her litter box, she's probably sending you a message that you're not cleaning it out frequently enough. Scoop out the box at least once a day and change the litter frequently, especially if you have several cats.

BASIC TRAINING

Teach Your Dog "Down"

It's a good idea to teach this one on a smooth surface such as a wood or vinyl floor—or, if you're working with a toy dog, a tabletop. Start the same way you started teaching the pup to sit: Hold a treat in your hand and get the puppy interested in it. When the animal is really going for the treat, bring your hand down to the floor and hold it there. The puppy will try all kinds of things to get the treat, but eventually and quite randomly she will lie down. Release the treat into the pup's mouth.

Repeat this process again and again until the puppy lies down quickly when presented with the hand signal and treat. Then—and only then—add the word "Down" as the puppy predictably lowers her body to the floor. Repeat this new version of the exercise frequently, saying "Down" only after the puppy has committed to the posture. As with the sit command, you can gently guide the puppy down, but don't push on the dog's back or pull on her legs. You want the animal to respond to your voice and the treat alone.

Dig This

Do the neighborhood cats consider your garden the local digging spot? Cats commonly dig in soil because they like the consistency. But you can put a stop to the habit. Gather some pine cones (it's worth a visit to the nearest pine forest) and spread them over the soil in your garden, covering as much of the dirt as possible. Cats don't like the texture of pinecones, and when they find them in your garden, they'll head somewhere else.

BEHAVIOR

COMMON MISTAKES

No Extra Cargo

Cats love to be warm, especially in cold weather. And that means if your cat goes outdoors in the winter, she's going to head anywhere that looks and feels like a good spot to get warm. Unfortunately, after your car's been running, it's very warm and inviting to a feline—who's all too likely to climb up through the wheel well and under the hood of the car, then lounge on the warm engine block. The problem is the animal can be seriously hurt or even killed if someone starts the engine.

The solution? Always give your hood a thump with your fist before you start your car. The kitty you save may be your own.

Make It a Rock Garden

Cats like to dig in plants because the texture of the potting soil feels like kitty litter to them. One easy and attractive way to keep your feline from digging around the greenery is to cover the soil with some decorative stones or large decorative wood chips, which you can purchase at any garden center. Or use marbles from a toy or discount store. Your cat won't like the feel of the new surface material, but you'll still be able to water the plants easily.

FOR FERRETS ONLY

Oh, What a Mesh!

One way to stop your ferret from digging in your houseplants is to purchase some lightweight wire mesh from a lawn and garden center and place the mesh over the dirt in the pot. If the ferret can't get to the dirt, he can't dig in it.

Use Pieces of Feces

Ferrets like to dig in clean dirt and sand, but they won't dig where they go to the toilet. If your pet ferrets are digging in your houseplants, bury a few bits of their

BEHAVIOR

feces in the dirt around the plants. The animals will stop digging immediately.

FOR REPTILES ONLY

She Needs Room to Unwind

If your snake is using her nose to dig in the soil of her tank, she's trying to tell you that the tank is too small. Try moving the snake to a larger home. If you handle her a lot (and thus give her other opportunities for stretching), choose a tank that is big enough for her to stretch out to two-thirds of her full length. If you don't handle her much, the tank should be big enough so that your pet can stretch to three-quarters of her length.

COMMON MISTAKES

Don't Try to Force-Feed Him

For the most part, pet snakes eat live prey such as rats. But they eat only when they're hungry, and that can lead to a fatal mistake.

Melissa Kaplan, a West Coast reptile expert, describes an upsetting experience. She received a phone call from a couple who had been away for a week and had come home to find their pet snake dead. Because they knew that they'd be away, the couple had decided to leave two rats in the snake's tank. That was their mistake. Snakes will not eat if they're not hungry, and, in fact, some snakes are afraid of rats. In the end, one of the rats they left in the tank actually started eating the snake.

If you need to be away from home, never leave live prey in the tank with your snake—it'll only lead to problems. It's far better to ask a snake-friendly pal to stop by and feed your snake rather than risk losing your valued pet.

DOMINANCE

A dominant dog isn't necessarily an aggressive dog. Dominance is related to the fact that dogs are pack animals. A dominant dog strives to be the leader of the pack—and you and your family are the pack. How can you tell if your dog has dominant tendencies? If he displays the following four behaviors, he wants to be in charge. First, a dominant dog will often stare at you in a direct or hostile way in response to a command. Second, with his body stiff and tense, he'll lean on you or push you. Third, the animal will try to stay out in front of you at all times. Finally, a dominant dog tends to be possessive. If you approach or try to take a bone or toy away from him, he will react by growing stiff or still and growling or snarling. Keep in mind that your dog might not dis-

play these behaviors with strangers. After all, they're not his pack. But if your pet consistently tries to dominate you and your family, it's important for you to deal with the problem. Your dog needs to know that you are in charge.

FOR DOGS ONLY

Oh Baby, No Baby

If you know your dog has a tendency toward dominance, don't talk baby talk to her or speak in a cooing voice. To the dog, such an approach sounds as though you're being submissive.

Command His Attention

If your dog consistently leaps ahead of you and pulls on the leash when you take him for a walk, and if he displays other signs of dominance, here's a way you can send him a signal about who is in charge. Before you take your dog out for a walk, give him a command such as "Sit" or "Down." After he obeys—and *only* after he obeys—put a leash on him and take him out. The message is that to get what he wants, he must comply with a directive from the pack leader (you). Then make him sit at curbs, doorways, and gate entries. As the leader, you must always control the direction and the pace.

Show Her Who's Boss

Here's another way to send a nonconfrontational message to your dominant dog about who is in charge. Before giving her any treat or toy, or before releasing her to play, give her a directive, such as "Sit" or "Down. Stay." Reward her only after she has responded appropriately.

Demanding Doggy

One way dominant dogs exert control over their owners is to demand attention from them. You've finished playing a game of fetch, but the dog wants to continue, so he brings the ball back, leans on you, and

BEHAVIOR

continually nudges your hand and whines or paws you. You can put an end to that pushiness by ending the game. Or you can give the dog a command—"Sit" or "Down. Stay"—before you continue the game, so that he knows you are in charge.

Beddy-bye

One way dogs exhibit dominance is by being possessive of objects such as furniture. An animal may

Boot Camp for Bowser

Your puppy is about six months old. Or you're just not having much luck training your grown dog at home. You decide to give obedience school a try, so you open up the Yellow Pages to Pet & Dog Training. To your utter bewilderment, you find pages upon pages of trainers listed. How do you decide on one of them? Robin Kovary of the American Dog Trainers Network offers some tips on what to consider.

Reputation. Get recommendations from some reliable sources—your vet, a nearby Humane Society or SPCA (look in the Yellow Pages under Animal Shelters), a local breeder or breeding club. If any or all of those sources recommend the same one, two, or three trainers, you're on the right track.

Experience and expertise. Once you have some names, you need to call each of the prospective trainers and ask some questions. How long has the trainer been in the business? What are her areas of expertise? Some trainers specialize in basic skill training—heel, sit, stay, and so on. Others may concentrate solely on resolving problem behaviors (biting, digging, barking). You need to find a trainer suited to your (and your dog's) needs.

A humane approach. Any good trainer will know that abuse—hitting, forcing, and yelling—is unnecessary and unproductive.

Up-to-date knowledge. Just as you expect your physician to keep up with the latest advances in medicine, you should expect a trainer to attend periodic workshops and seminars. Don't be reluctant to ask.

Sense of humor. This may not sound important, but stress inhibits learning for people and dogs. An uptight trainer won't accomplish much.

growl, for example, if you try to get her off a bed or chair. To eliminate such a problem before it starts, don't allow your pup on the furniture without permission.

FECES EATING

Dogs will sometimes eat their own or the cat's feces, for reasons ranging from a vitamin deficiency to boredom. (The scientific name for the behavior is coprophagy.) If your dog indulges, be sure to report this to your vet. Even though it's very common, it's one of the behaviors associated with rabies, and any dog that eats another dog's feces can get worms. If your feline has taken up the behavior, see a vet right away. It is highly unusual for a cat to eat feces and is very likely a sign of health problems.

COMMON MISTAKES

Change the Water

Plant misters are one correction method recommended over and over again for both dogs and cats. Just give a quick squirt when your pet misbehaves, many experts say, and the animal will soon learn more appropriate behavior. But as your pet learns and you find yourself using this disciplinary treatment less often, you could actually end up punishing your pet more severely than you intend. Dust and bacteria can develop in any bottle that gets little use.

If you do use a spray bottle to train your pet, be sure to change the water every day. That way, if the water gets into your pet's eyes, nose, or mouth, the animal won't be getting dosed with anything unexpected.

FOR DOGS ONLY

Be a Pooper-Scooper

Whichever other solutions you choose to keep your dog from eating his own feces, one of the best is to pick up all fecal matter before your pet can get to it, rather than gaping in revulsion.

Hey, I'm Hungry Already!

There's a saying that the simplest explanation for a phenomenon is usually correct. In this case, that means if your dog is eating her or the cat's feces, she may simply be hungry. Try increasing the frequency of feedings. If you usually give her a meal once a day, try giving her food twice each day for about a week and see whether that stops the behavior.

BEHAVIOR

Give Him Lots of Room

Generally speaking, dogs don't like to sleep or live too close to where they go to the bathroom, and if they're being kept on a dog run or in a laundry room that's too small, they may eat their feces just to keep their space clean. If your pup is exhibiting this behavior and you keep the animal in a rather confined area, you may be able to put a stop to the practice by giving the pooch a little more living space.

Now Doesn't That Taste Better?

If your dog actually has the gall to eat his poop while he's on a leash (doesn't he know it's gross?), you need to use some diversionary tactics to break him of the habit. Take some doggy treats along on the walk, and after your dog does his business—but before he can turn around and eat it—distract him with a treat and have him take a couple of steps forward. While he's eating his treat, clean up the feces.

A WORD FROM DR. DeVINNE

DR. CHARLES DeVINNE
of Peterborough, New Hampshire, who has more than 15 years of veterinary experience and whose private practice currently concentrates on dogs and cats

Brick by Brick

Dogs sometimes like to get into cat boxes and eat the stuff inside. That can be pretty disgusting in and of itself, but if the litter in the box happens to be the clumping kind, it can be really bad for the dog. That stuff turns into a brick inside a dog's stomach, and it's difficult to remove.

If you have both a dog and a cat, either don't use clumping litter at all or put the cat box where you're positive your dog can't get at it.

Like It Doesn't Already?

One way to stop a dog from eating her own feces is to visit your vet and ask for a product called ForBid. Adding this to the dog's regular food will make the feces taste bad.

Litter Box Lunch

There probably isn't a dog around that wouldn't grab a quick snack from the cat's litter box if given half a chance. That's because cat food (and therefore cat dung) is very rich. Your first course of action when faced with this situation is to clean out the litter box right after your cats use it. But you can't spend your day standing sentry over the box. Try placing the box where your cats can get to it—in a small nook or behind a piece of furniture—but your dog can't.

Ugh!

Ah, the wonders of the animal kingdom. We often blame dogs for exhibiting the most disgusting behavior (such as leg humping and crotch sniffing), but they haven't totally cornered the market.

Hamsters eat their feces just as dogs do. In fact, in hamsters (unlike dogs) it's a perfectly natural behavior. Hamsters excrete two types of feces—one that is made up of pure waste and another that is made up of partially digested, but still usable, material. The little dears will often eat the latter kind. So the next time you see your hamster munching away on something you're sure isn't his regular food, don't panic. Just close your eyes.

FIGHTING

There are no two ways about it: Animal fights are scary, especially if your own animal is involved. You don't want your pet to injure another, and you certainly don't want him to get hurt. Here are some suggestions—both preventives and cures—that will make an animal altercation a little easier to handle.

FOR DOGS ONLY

At Leash He Won't Fight

One of the easiest ways to protect your dog from a fight when you leave the house is to keep the animal on a leash with a properly fitting collar, head halter, or harness.

BEHAVIOR

Make a Proper Introduction

To greatly reduce the chances of a fight when you want your dog to meet another, conduct the introductions on neutral ground. Bring the pets together at a local park, for example, rather than at the home where one of the dogs lives. When two dogs meet on what one of them considers home turf, the "host" may feel a need to defend his territory.

Now Shake on It

Some folks find that a "shake can" works well in aborting potential dogfights. To make one, you'll need a clean, dry soda can and about ten pennies. Place the

A WORD FROM MICKY NIEGO

The Correct Correction

MICKY NIEGO
Animal behaviorist in Airmont, New York, who trains puppies and service dogs in addition to speaking and consulting on animal behavior and training issues

There are as many ways to correct dogs as there are to correct children, but my philosophy is that your animal is part of your family, and you're forming a relationship with him.

Let's say you have a dog who's chewing the sofa leg. Some people recommend putting a little Tabasco on that sofa leg, but let's go through what that means.

The "heat" of Tabasco and hot peppers comes from an oil that stays on your tongue. We've all eaten a dip that was too hot and then drunk 46 glasses of water, which didn't do a bit of good because water won't wash off oil. So the dog bites the sofa with the pepper on it, he drinks and drinks and drinks, and it

pennies in the can, then seal the top with electrical or duct tape. Take the can with you on your dog walks. If you encounter an aggressive dog, throw the shake can on the ground in front of the dog. In many cases, that will be enough to discourage him.

Walk, Don't Run

If, despite your best efforts, an aggressive dog lunges at your pooch when you're out for a walk, back away slowly and calmly, pulling your leashed dog gently along with you. Don't pick up your dog and beat a hasty retreat. If you turn your back and run, the aggressive dog will simply give in to its instincts, and that means she'll chase you.

doesn't do any more for the dog than it does for you and me. The correction is effective, but it's overkill, because no matter what the dog does—he stops chewing, he regrets his action, he drinks water—he can't make the consequence stop. Imagine being sent to jail even after you paid your $25 parking ticket. That's how the Tabasco treatment makes the dog feel.

So what's an appropriate correction? One that's instant and temporary. Think of what happens when you go to the museum and you get just a little too close to a painting. The alarm goes off: bzzzzzz! You get startled and back away, and the instant you do, the buzzing stops. "Safe" booby traps such as Scat Mats are good for pets because they make an animal uncomfortable as soon as, say, he approaches the trash. But the minute he moves away, the discomfort stops.

Or use a motion detector. Whenever your cat gets near the sofa, it emits an unpleasant sound, and your cat thinks, "I'd better get out of here!" The cat leaves, and the sound stops. That's the kind of correction you want: a fair correction that stops as soon as the unwanted behavior stops.

Give 'Em a Shower

One of the most frightening situations a dog owner can encounter is to find her dog in a knock-down-drag-out fight. If possible, dump some cold water or other liquid on the dogs. The shock may cause them to stop fighting. Whatever you do, don't step in and try to break up the fight. You're liable to get bitten, and you may end up making the animals more aggressive toward each other.

Should You Resort to Chemical Warfare?

One tactic you can use to stop a dogfight is to throw an ammonia-soaked rag over the dogs' noses. It is guaranteed to stop them in their tracks.

FOR CATS ONLY

Don't Reach In

What should you do if you see two cats fighting? One course of action is to pour some cold water over the felines. A good dousing will usually break up the fight. Never reach into a cat fight, and don't hit the cats with a broom, even if your cat is getting pummeled. It may make one or both of the cats more aggressive, and you risk getting ripped to shreds.

Sound Advice

If you're confronted with a cat fight and you don't have any water handy, start making noise—yelling, clapping, banging a trash can lid against the pavement. Cats hate loud sounds, and a sharp, sudden noise may end the confrontation.

You Smell Funny

You've just taken Fluffy in for her annual checkup. When you bring her home, her sisters, Puff and Tiger, hiss and growl whenever Fluffy comes near them. Before the trip to the vet, harmony reigned. What happened? The cats that stayed home can smell the vet on poor Fluffy, and it may take days before they'll accept her again. There is a way to speed up her reacclimation, and all you need is a towel. To begin, rub the towel all over one or both of the cats that stayed behind (they smell like home), then rub the towel all over the cat that went to the vet. Now all the cats will smell (sort of) the same, and peace will be restored.

Create Separate Apartments

Some folks with more than one cat never have a problem with fights, but others find that their cats are always going at it. One reason cats in the same home fight is that there isn't enough "territory" for each one. This is not a question of square feet. Rather, each cat has

Cat Fight! Is It Real or Just a Game?

If you have more than one cat, you may have watched as the two wrestled—and you probably wondered whether they were just playing or really fighting. If you stepped in, would you be breaking up a friendly wrestling match? Or would you be saving the life of one of your cats? Next time, watch for these verbal and nonverbal behaviors, and you'll be better able to see the difference.

It's Real Aggression If . . .

- You hear a deep, low growl
- The cats' ears flatten against their heads
- The mouths open as if to hiss, even though there's no sound
- The cats hiss at each other
- The cats' fur stands up all over their bodies
- The teeth are bared
- Either kitty rolls over to scratch and punch with all four feet

It's Only Play If . . .

- The ears stay forward
- There's no growling or hissing (You may see or hear some huffing, puffing, and yowling.)
- Any biting is not accompanied by punching with the feet
- Bites don't draw blood
- Slaps are gentle and usually with only one or two paws
- Tails are wiggling

If there's a yelp and the yelper runs back or chases the other cat, he's ready for more play. If, however, he hides behind the sofa or retreats to your lap, he's had enough.

his own internal sense of space. To satisfy each animal's need for a separate territory, try repositioning a large piece of furniture—a large chair, a sofa, or an armoire—so that it breaks up a large space, creating two or three smaller areas. If each cat has a space of his own, it may put an end to the fighting.

Try a Screen Saver

You can create more separate kitty spaces in your home by setting up decorative paneled screens, which you can find at furniture stores. Set one up in a corner to create space in front of and behind the screen.

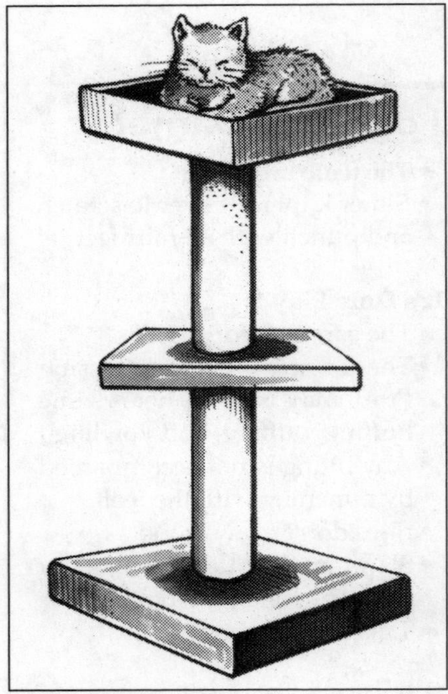

It's a tree for two (or more) cats.

Build Up, Not Out

Don't overlook vertical space in your home when you're trying to create more space for warring cats. Find out if your local pet supply store sells cat trees—tall towers with several carpeted shelves. When you bring one of these trees home, each cat gets her own shelf—and since she has a space of her own, she's less likely to initiate a fight over territory.

The Hardest Solution of All

You've tried scolding, separating, and spraying them with water, but your felines won't stop fighting. You may be surprised to learn that by continually breaking up their fights, you may be prolonging the agony. That's because what they're fighting over—who's top cat, for instance—never gets settled. If your nerves are up to it, let your cats duke it out as long as they aren't getting torn to pieces. Chances are one of them will cry uncle and submit well before either one gets seriously hurt. And after they decide on the boundaries, the fighting may end completely.

FOR FISH ONLY

Stay on Your Side!

One way to deal with a group of fish that seem to have problems coexisting peacefully is to increase the size of the tank. If the fish are fighting over territory, providing additional space for everyone may eliminate the bickering.

Spread the Wealth

Fish sometimes fight if there are too few females relative to the number of males in a tank. If your males are fighting, try purchasing some additional female fish so that there will be enough to go around.

Create a Safe Haven

If you find that one or two particularly aggressive fish are bullying some of the less aggressive fish in your tank, one solution is to provide the less aggressive fish with a place to hide. You can do that by placing some large, leafy plants or sculptures in your aquarium. These items are available at any pet store that sells fish.

COST CUTTERS

Equal—But Separate

To stop different species of fish from fighting each other, you don't necessarily have to purchase a separate tank (and all the associated paraphernalia) for each species. Instead, look for a cheaper solution at your local pet supply store. Many stores sell tank separators—plastic screens that you place in the tank, effectively creating two separate tanks with one filter system. The screen lets the water circulate, but it keeps the fish from getting to each other.

They Just Can't Get Along

Sometimes you just have to face the fact that no amount of hoping on your part will keep aggressive fish from bullying nonaggressive ones. The best solution may be to keep the varieties in separate tanks.

FOOD STEALING

Has food been disappearing from your counters, your dinner table, even—heaven forbid—your plate? If you've already ruled out all bipedal family members, there's probably a furry four-legged thief afoot. Don't

YOU'VE GOTTA LOVE 'EM

The Seeing Eye Kleptomaniac

Helene Kirschbaum of Concord, New Hampshire, tells the story of a Seeing Eye dog she helped train when she lived in Queens, New York. Soon after working with Maggie, a very smart chocolate Lab, Helene was surprised to hear that the dog's new owner, a blind woman, was getting ready to retire her. After Helene heard the reason, the plan made a little more sense.

Maggie was a bright dog, but, as it turned out, she may have been a little too bright for her own good. It seems that Maggie had picked up the unseemly habit of shoplifting. Whenever the dog's owner took her out shopping and Maggie became annoyed at the owner for any reason, the dog would walk out of the shop with a "heavily discounted" item in her mouth. Small, easily concealed items such as candy bars were her favorites, but once she made off with a pair of shoes. Of course, her poor owner had no idea that any of this was going on until a frantic shopkeeper came tearing after her.

Things finally came to a head when Maggie decided to teach her owner a lesson by walking right by the owner's house when it was time to go home. Frustrated, Maggie's owner decided she'd had enough. There's no telling what Maggie's next assignment will be, but you can be sure it won't be with the police department.

call the pet police. Instead, try these ideas for getting your pet back on the straight and narrow.

FOR PETS IN GENERAL

This May Come as a Shock . . .

❑ You can teach your pets to stay away from table and counter perimeters by both supervising and safely booby-trapping those areas. Visit a pet supply store and check out products designed specifically for that purpose. One possibility is a vinyl mat, such as a Scat Mat, that you position wherever you want to make a spot off-limits to your pet. When the mat is plugged in, it emits a weak electrical impulse, similar to a static charge. When your pet steps on the mat, she'll get an unpleasant but harmless shock. The mat is safe for kittens, puppies, and larger cats and dogs because it has variable correction levels. These devices are not cheap—depending on size, some cost more than $100—but as needs change, you can move them from place to place with no problem.

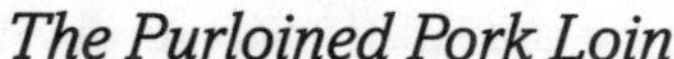

The Purloined Pork Loin

❑ When you catch your pet in the act of sneaking some food when he shouldn't, stop him in his tracks with a loud "No!" and a simultaneous squirt from a spray bottle, plant mister, or water pistol.

For Her Own Good

❑ If your pet has a habit of stealing food, it's best to keep her inside during the family barbecue. The animal may get severely burned if she tries to snatch a burger from the grill.

FOR DOGS ONLY

How Can Humans Eat That Stuff?

One way to teach a dog not to steal food is to sprinkle some lime juice on a sandwich and set it near the edge of the table. Once a pup gets a taste of that sour meal, he'll learn to leave people food alone.

One for You, One for Me

If your dog plays the thief only during your mealtimes, find a treat that she really likes—say, cheese or cut-up hot dogs. Stuff that food inside a hollow bone from a pet supply store and give her the treat, on her blanket, only when you're eating. You need to be consistent, but your dog will learn that if she goes to her place, she'll get a terrific treat.

FURNITURE SCRATCHING

The cat's claw is a marvel of natural engineering, as anyone who owns a feline knows. The claws retract when your cat isn't using them, but when he needs them—say, to scratch your sofa to shreds—they spring right out. How handy. Here are some ideas for redirecting your cat's clawing inclination before you have to buy a new sofa.

FOR CATS ONLY

A Cat Owner's Best Friend

A good, strong blast from a squirt gun or plant mister is sure to stop your kitty when she's about to scratch a piece of furniture. Be consistent about it, and she'll eventually learn to give it up—at least when you're around.

Take the High-Minded Approach

Your cat needs to sharpen his claws somewhere, and the easiest way for you to make sure it's not on your sofa is to provide him with an alternative—a scratching post that he'll like and use. (These posts are available from pet supply stores.) A key element is height. Next time kitty wakes up from a nap, watch him as he stretches and pay attention to how long he really is. That's how high the scratching post needs to be. Cats like to stretch to their full length when they scratch, and if the post you're providing is too short, your cat is going to opt for the back of your sofa instead. One behaviorist recommends that a scratching post be at least

three feet high, but use your judgment. If you have a very small cat, you can get a smaller model, but it needs to be long enough for her to stretch out fully.

Lean on Me

Another variable that determines whether your cat will use her scratching post is its sturdiness. Make sure that when you purchase or build a scratching post, the base is either heavy or wide enough so that the post won't wobble when your cat tries to use it. If the post isn't stable enough for your pet to really lean into it, she'll head straight for a piece of furniture that stays put when she scratches.

If You Build It, He Will Come

Here's a way to make a scratching board that will never budge when your cat uses it. Visit a lumberyard

ONE PERSON'S SOLUTION

A Rug of His Own

One of our cats, Thunder, took right to the scratching post we bought for him. The other, E. B., didn't. We tried everything to keep him from scratching our upholstered armchair and sofa, with little success. One day, we realized that he had a particular affinity for an old throw rug lying in the hallway. Since it was pretty inexpensive but sturdy, we decided to allow E. B. that scratching spot. Over time, he began to leave the furniture alone as long as we let him scratch that rug.

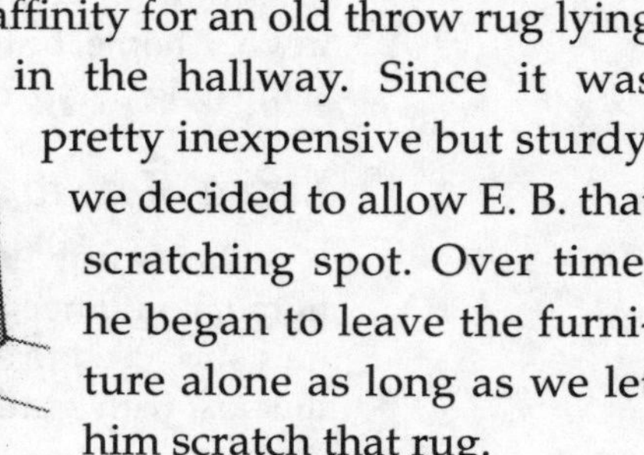

—**SUSAN JOYCE**
Cranston, Rhode Island

Ah, that feels good. Nail burlap over plywood to give kitty a sturdy scratching board.

and purchase a piece of plywood at least three feet long and about a foot or so wide (the thickness doesn't matter). Wrap the board well with several layers of heavy burlap, then nail the burlap into place all along the sides of the board. Lean the board against a wall in an out-of-the-way spot. That gives your cat privacy (and hides the board, which isn't exactly aesthetically pleasing). Anchor the board to the wall with some screws, and you have a perfect scratching board. And this homemade piece of pet equipment will last for a while, too. When your kitty has shredded one side, just remove the anchors, flip the board over, and reattach it to the wall.

Cats Don't Like Wall-to-Wall Carpeting

When you're out shopping for a good scratching post, skip the carpet-covered ones. Most cats don't like them because carpeting doesn't snag their claws well. Purchase a post covered with sisal or burlap, materials most cats prefer.

If you've already bought a piece of carpeting to make your own scratching post, you're not out of luck. Just turn the piece inside out so that the carpet backing faces out. It may not be the prettiest piece of furniture in your home, but it will certainly get more use than a scratching post with the carpet side out.

Like a Moth to a Flame

Once you've installed a scratching post in your home, you'll need to show your cat that that's where he's supposed to scratch. One way to do that is to rub the post with a little catnip. It's a sure way to attract his attention.

String Her Along

Make going to the scratching post a game for your new kitten. Dangle some string or yarn around the post or put some of her toys near it. She'll get the idea that it's a fun place to be.

Hot Legs

You can keep your cat from scratching the wooden legs of your furniture by rubbing them with a little eucalyptus oil (available at many health food stores). The odor will repel the cat, and if you give the wood a good buff afterward, you won't harm the finish.

Don't Use Catnip

One of the reasons your cat returns to the sofa or upholstered chair to scratch is that it smells like you. If you can get it to smell more like something she *doesn't* like, you can keep her away from it. Try purchasing

BASIC TRAINING

Introduce Your Cat to the Great Outdoors

How can you tell whether your cat wants to go outside? Well, you could send her out and wait for her to return. But here's a better strategy.

At a pet supply store, get a figure eight harness for your kitten. Attach to it about 20 feet of light nylon rope, which you can get at any hardware store. The harness and rope will keep your cat from escaping up a tree or from chasing birds. Head outside with your kitten. If she immediately freezes in fear or bolts wildly when she hears an approaching car or the neighbor's lawn mower, perhaps you'd better keep her inside. If, however, she happily darts around chasing leaves, she's a natural.

Cats that startle and recover may be good candidates for leash training. Start these cats out by taking short, frequent jaunts in familiar places during a quiet, well-lit time of day. Then slowly increase their exposure to outdoor chaos in areas that are less familiar, less well lit, and less quiet.

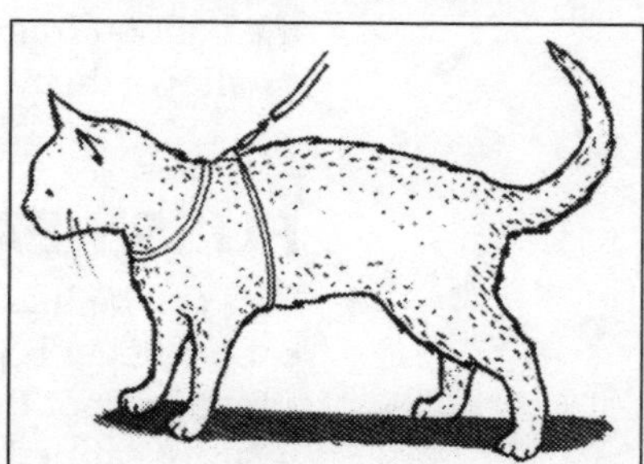

Use a figure eight harness to test a kitten's outdoor skills.

some strong-smelling dried herbs or tea from a local health food store. (Lemon tea works well because cats tend not to like citrus odors.) Stuff some of the herbs or tea into small cloth sacks. (The cheesecloth kind designed for bouquet garni is perfect. You can find them at any kitchen specialty shop. Or you can make your own from a square of scrap fabric and some string.) Stuff the bags between the cushions of your furniture. Once your cat gets a good whiff of the herbs, she'll stay away from the upholstery.

He'll Think It's a Party

Another way to keep your cat from scratching your furniture is to blow up some balloons and tape them in clusters to the spots on your furniture where your cat usually scratches. One behaviorist says she likes this method because it's so festive. When your cat tries to scratch, he'll burst the balloons with his claws. The noise and flying balloon remnants will discourage him from repeating that mistake. If you keep the balloons in place for several days, he'll learn to stop scratching. Be sure to pick up the balloon fragments before an animal or young child swallows them.

No Wonder—They Work So Hard

Cats spend about two-thirds of their lives asleep. That's about twice as much time as other mammals.

FUSSY EATING

Pets can be like people when it comes to eating. Some eat whatever is put in front of them; others want everything just so. But just as parents can help encourage healthy eating habits in their children, pet owners can discourage finicky eating in their pets. Here's how.

FOR PETS IN GENERAL

Seal the Meals

❑ Dry pet food usually comes in a box or bag, neither of which reseals very well. To keep the food fresh longer, treat it as you would your own. Transfer it to a jar with a lid, an airtight plastic container, or a tightly sealed plastic bag.

BEHAVIOR

FOR DOGS ONLY

Don't Spoil His Dinner

Some dogs won't eat when they're given their food because they've been snacking on and off all day on people food and treats. Sound familiar? If so, putting your pup on a consistent feeding schedule is a surefire way to cure him of his fussy eating. Whenever you feed your dog (usually twice a day), set the bowl out and leave it there for 15 to 20 minutes. When the

---

ONE PERSON'S SOLUTION

Give Her a Midnight Snack

Every morning at around 6:00 A.M., my cats Honey and Scout would jump on my bed, walk on my face, and start meowing right in my ear. They were hungry, of course, and wanted me to get out of bed and feed them. (Even though there was always some dry food out for them, they wanted their daily dose of wet cat chow.) Finally, it dawned on me that if I gave them their wet food at night rather than first thing in the morning, they just might let me sleep a little longer. So I switched their feeding time to just before I went to bed. It was misery for a few weeks, but they finally got used to the new routine, and soon I was sleeping in until well after 8:00.

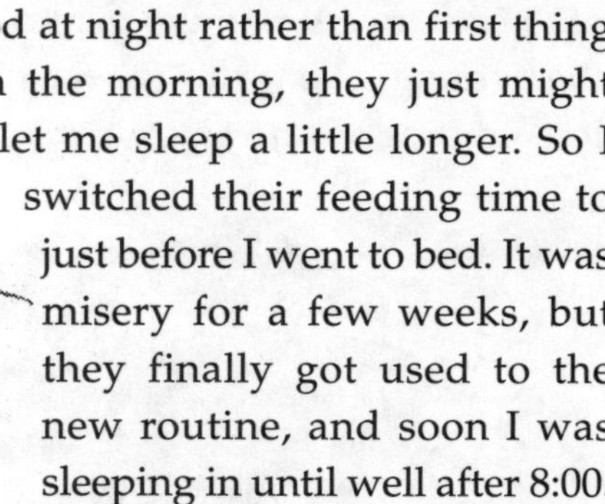

—LORI BAIRD
Astoria, New York

BEHAVIOR

time is up, pick up the food and put it away. Repeat this every time you feed your pup, and very soon he'll learn to eat what is available when it's available. Be forewarned, however: This strategy will be harder for you to carry out than it will be for your dog to get used to. Stick to your guns.

FOR CATS ONLY

She'd Rather Fight Than Switch

One sure way to encourage fussy eating in a cat is to switch brands and flavors of cat food frequently. Some cats will latch onto a particular flavor or texture. Then they'll avoid all the other flavors and eat only what they like. If your cat exhibits this tendency, your safest bet is to buy one kind of food and stick with it.

YOU'VE GOTTA LOVE 'EM

Uneasy Rider

Cats often are afraid to ride in cars. When it came to my old cat, Tilly, I could understand why. I was late heading back to work one day after lunch at home, and I jumped in my truck and drove the eight miles to work as fast as I could, covering much of the distance at 60 miles per hour. When I got out of the truck in the parking lot, I heard the whine of a seriously scared animal. I looked around the truck, expecting to see dripping blood. Finally, I found Tilly under the truck, on top of the spare tire. No physical harm done, but I'm not so sure about the psychological effects.

—**JEFF ELLISON**
Fort Collins, Colorado

Avoid a Stalemate

If your cat normally has a healthy appetite for her dry food dinner but has suddenly become finicky, you may need to replace the food with some that's fresh. Especially in humid summer weather, dry food left down too long tends to absorb moisture and become stale, which could turn even the least discerning cat into a fussy eater.

Warm Her Up to the Idea

If your cat's turning up his nose at the canned cat food you just gave him, it may be because you just pulled it out of the refrigerator. Cold food doesn't have much of an aroma, and cats won't eat what they can't smell. You can make cat food more appealing by heating it over very low heat or in the microwave just until it's warm to the touch. The heat will release the food's aroma and stimulate your cat's appetite.

Bowl Her Over

Some cats are finicky enough that they won't eat out of a bowl that has bits of old food in it. So before you dash out to the store to purchase a new brand of cat food, give your kitty a clean bowl and see whether that solves the problem. And get into the habit of washing out food and water bowls after each use, just as you do for yourself. Rancid fat and bacteria are no better for cats than they are for humans.

HOUSE-TRAINING

It may be the biggest obstacle for any new pet owner: getting the animal to go to the bathroom where he's supposed to, instead of heading for your chaise longue or your 5,000-year-old oriental rug. No one savors the prospect of housebreaking a new pet. Especially with dogs, it takes a lot of work. Still, it really is worth the effort. So if you're tired of running around behind your pet holding a piece of newspaper, read on. We have some ways to help you cope.

FOR DOGS ONLY

All the News That's Fit To . . .

In most urban areas, puppies aren't allowed to go outside until they've had all their shots. If you live in a city, you'll need to paper-train your new puppy—that is, teach him to go on newspaper in your house for the first four months or so of his life. Later, you'll need to retrain him to go outside. That intermediate step can make things a little tricky, but it doesn't have to be an insurmountable obstacle. One way to help things go more smoothly is to make the newspaper an incidental variable in the process. Do that by putting your puppy on a leash and collar every time you take him to the paper to urinate or defecate (or at least as many times as possible). That way, your puppy will learn that he goes to the toilet when (1) he's with you and (2) he's wearing his leash and collar.

Listen to the Rhythm . . .

The second step in the process of short-term paper-training is the little chant. Every puppy owner needs one. When your puppy squats and as soon as the stream of urine (or the feces) starts, begin to say "pee pee," "potty potty," or whatever you like best. This becomes, along with you and the leash and collar, yet another constant that your puppy will associate with going to the toilet. When it's finally time to take your puppy outside, the transition will be much easier. Rather than becoming confused and thinking, "Where's the paper?" she'll think, "I'm on my leash and collar, I'm near my person,

And *Never* Move the Litter Box

Let's say you leave home for a long time—a year or more. Then you come home to your pets—a dog, Poochy, and a cat, Whiskers. Will they remember you?

Poochy most definitely will. In fact, she may have spent the year you were away just sitting at the front door, pining, waiting for you to return.

But Whiskers . . . well, at the risk of breaking your heart, let's just say that whereas dogs become attached to people, cats get more attached to places. You could move a dog to three different houses, and as long as her people were around, she wouldn't suffer much. A cat, however, could go through three different owners without much heartache, as long as they all lived in the same house. (Though if you move the furniture in that house, you'll throw his whole system off kilter.)

But hey, you didn't get a cat for loyalty anyway. Right?

and she's chanting 'pee pee.' The only thing that's different is that I'm outside. Guess I'll go to the bathroom."

Where's the Bathroom Today?

Another way to make the newspaper incidental in the paper-training process is to keep moving the paper to different spots in your house or apartment. For instance, one day you might place it in the bathroom and the next near the refrigerator in the kitchen. The point is for your puppy to get used to going to the toilet when with you, when on the leash and collar, and when he hears his "potty" cue—no matter where that may be. If your pet knows only to aim for the newspaper, training him to go outside will be all the more difficult.

Don't Give Her Any Privacy

Paper-trainers take note: Given their druthers, dogs would rather go to the toilet alone. They're pack animals, it's true, but they don't go to the bathroom in groups. To make sure your dog doesn't get used to going to the toilet alone—and therefore becomes too distracted to go when people are present or she's surrounded by activity—it's important that your puppy has company when she goes. Talk to her a lot. If you make sure she can go with an audience and a brass band, she'll have no trouble going outside with the hustle and bustle of the city.

COST CUTTERS

Make It Neutral Territory

When your pet makes a mistake and goes to the bathroom on your rug, or if he sprays a spot on the wall to mark his territory, it's vital that you thoroughly eliminate the odor of the urine. If your pet can smell the urine, he'll continue to pee in that spot. There are urinary neutralizers on the market, but a homemade solution of baking soda and vinegar works just as well.

Combine equal amounts of white vinegar and baking soda in a bowl. (It will foam up for a second or two, but the bubbles will subside quickly.) Sponge the mixture on the urine spot, then rinse well with water. Let the spot dry, then give it a sniff. The odor should be gone, but if it's not, repeat the process.

Treats Are for Training

When you're house-training your puppy—or doing any kind of skill training—it's a good idea to put

BEHAVIOR

a moratorium on all treats. Save treats for when your puppy goes to the bathroom in the right spot—or otherwise correctly responds to directives—and the rewards will have a greater impact.

Familiarity Breeds Content

If you live in an area where you can take your puppy outside right away, your job is a bit simpler than if you have to paper-train, but it still takes time. One way

A WORD FROM MICKY NIEGO

Know Your Pet: Age

MICKY NIEGO
Animal behaviorist in Airmont, New York, who trains puppies and service dogs in addition to speaking and consulting on animal behavior and training issues

Animals go through developmental stages just as people do. And just as you have different expectations about people in those different stages, you need to find out about and be aware of what happens to your pets during each period.

I used to work for the American Society for the Prevention of Cruelty to Animals (ASPCA), and I can't tell you how many people brought their birds in to us when the birds hit adolescence. People would cry, "We've had him for ten years, and all of a sudden he started biting, and he won't let anyone near him." They were dealing with sexually mature adolescent birds, and we had to explain to them that they didn't need to change training techniques; they needed to stand firm and maintain limits. If they'd known what was coming, they wouldn't have been taken aback.

Let me give you some guidelines. You'll probably get your pet as a juvenile—that's about 6 weeks to 6 months old for dogs and

to make it easier on both of you is to designate a toilet area and take the animal to it every time. This might be near a fence, for instance, or under a tree. Going to the same spot every time makes the training less confusing for your puppy and cleanup easier for you.

Know Where to Go

If you choose to designate one spot in your yard as your puppy's toilet area, you can make the spot more

cats. (All age categories for birds depend on the type of bird, so check with your vet to find out about the species you have.) The animal is likely to be impressionable and to learn quickly and easily. This is the best time to train and to set lifelong habits.

As an adolescent (6 to 18 months for both dogs and cats), your pet becomes sexually mature and acts like a typical headstrong teenager. She becomes rebellious and belligerent. At this point, training for dogs and birds should emphasize control and leadership. (Cats won't usually accept such training at any age!)

An adult (18 months to 7 years for dogs and cats) is usually emotionally mature, so the animal's behavior is predictable. Just maintain training for dogs and birds.

In a geriatric pet (over 7 years for dogs and cats), the senses become less keen. This sometimes leads to confusion or irritability. Motor skills also decline. For dogs and birds, maintain training according to the animal's ability.

If you know what to expect, you won't freak out the first time you see a new behavior associated with a particular developmental stage in your pet. You'll say, "Well, Tweetie is around 12 years old now. They told us he was going to get horrible and start snapping. Now we know it's time to lower the cage so that he can recognize that we're literally standing above him and are still the ones in charge here."

BEHAVIOR

appealing and memorable by leaving a few small bits of his feces there all the time during training. That's not to say you have to let your yard become filthy. If the designated area is too funky, your pet will avoid it rather than be attracted to it. But just as a puppy will urinate in the same spot on your rug over and over again, he'll be attracted to the same place in your yard if he recognizes the scent.

It's as if She Laid the Golden Egg

Praise is very important in paper-training and in getting your new puppy to go to the bathroom outside. So when she does hit the paper or release outside rather

COMMON MISTAKES

Like a Broken Record

One of the most common mistakes dog owners make when they're teaching a dog or simply giving him a command is repeating it over and over again. For example, let's say it's feeding time, and as a matter of course, you give your dog the command "Sit" before he gets his bowl. You give the command, but he stares at you rather blankly, wagging his tail, ready to eat. You know you've taught him the meaning of the word, so ignorance is no excuse. You give the command again. Same reaction. By now you're pleading, and he still won't sit. You get annoyed, give him his food, and walk away.

When you repeat a command, you're telling the dog that he has a choice in the matter. If he doesn't sit the first time you tell him, he will always get another opportunity to sit and get a meal.

There's a better way to let your dog know that a command isn't an option. It works best if it's tied to something the dog wants, such as his dinner. Pour the food into the animal's bowl and give the command "Sit," but only once. If he doesn't move, simply put the bowl away out of his reach and leave the room, resuming whatever activity you were involved in earlier. You don't need to leave for long—about five minutes should do the trick—but it's important for your dog to see that he's not getting fed. After the time is up, go back into the kitchen and try it again, remembering to give the command only once.

than on the way out, be sure to give her genuine praise and a yummy treat.

BEHAVIOR

He Needs On-the-Spot Correction

Accidents will happen, so don't rub your dog's nose in it. If you happen to catch your puppy making a mistake, all you need to do is say "No" in a stern voice and either put him on the paper or take him outside right away. It does no good to correct the puppy if you come home and find that he soiled the floor an hour earlier. Even if you show him the spot, the puppy will not understand why he's being corrected.

Again?

How often does a puppy need to go to the bathroom? It depends on how old she is. Up to around 12 weeks, most pups have to go constantly—every 20 minutes or so when active. Count on having to take a slightly older puppy out or to the paper about 30 minutes after she eats or drinks, anytime she wakes up (usually once during the night), and always during and after playtime.

Talk About Age Spots

Dalmatian puppies are born completely white and develop their black spots as they get older.

Put Him on a Schedule

After about 16 weeks, puppies start to gain better muscle control, and most are able to hold on through the night. You can speed up that process a bit if you carefully time your puppy's evening routine. Give him his last meal for the day at around 6:30 or 7:00 P.M. Play with him vigorously to wear him out, then take him to the toilet. Don't give him any food, water, or treats after about 8:30. Schedule lights-out by 11:00 or 11:30 (after another trip outside). Of course, you'll need to take the puppy out first thing in the morning.

Gotta Go

Here's a hint. If you're holding your puppy and she suddenly starts to squirm and seems panicked to get off

BEHAVIOR

your lap, you can be pretty sure she has to go to the bathroom. Your puppy doesn't want to urinate on your lap and will try to get down if at all possible. Squirming is your cue to get your pet to the paper or outside.

He Doesn't Have to Hold It

Many pet owners complain that even when they take their animals outside frequently for potty and play trips, the puppies urinate in the house soon after coming back inside. It makes sense if you think about it from the dog's perspective. It's not unusual for an owner to send a dog out to the yard to play and go to the bathroom, then call or bring the dog in as soon as the animal "does his business." After going through this drill 10 or 12 times, the puppy starts to think, "Gee, I'll have to go inside right after I pee. I'm going to hold it as long as I can so I can stay outside longer." The owner thinks, "Well, I guess he doesn't have to go." So the dog comes inside and urinates on the carpet.

You can prevent that kind of behavior right from the start if you set up a routine. When you let your pet outside, take the animal directly to the toilet area without allowing any exploring or playing. When he's done, give him a treat, then release him to play and explore. You're teaching him that (1) nothing fun happens until he goes to the bathroom and (2) the faster he does it, the sooner he's free to play and explore.

How Cats Get into (and out of) Tight Situations

Watching cats slink through a partly open door, you have to wonder whether they're related to snakes. They're not, but cats *have* evolved in numerous ways to make them slithery creatures. Their backbones have as many as 26 more vertebrae than human spines—despite their smaller size—and these bones are held together by muscles rather than ligaments, making them far more mobile. Feline shoulder joints allow the forelegs to turn nearly 360 degrees. And cats have no collarbones, so they're able to squeeze their shoulders easily through narrow openings.

FOR CATS ONLY

Excuse Me, Where's the Ladies' Room?

When you bring home a new kitten, don't make things harder on yourself than they have to be. All it may take for your kitten to go in her litter box is for you to show her where it is. Walk her to it and let her at it.

Follow Me, Sir

Kittens eat frequently, and that means they go to the bathroom frequently. (One way to look at it is that this provides you and your kitten plenty of opportunity to practice litter box training.) After you feed your kitten, wait about 10 to 15 minutes, then lead him to the litter

YOU'VE GOTTA LOVE 'EM

Toilet-Trained Cat

My cat, Milo, is absolutely crazy. He's crabby a lot and avoids people all the time. He's like a hermit. When he's not being cranky, he's being wild—streaking around the house, stopping suddenly, then running back the way he came, hunched up all the time. It's because of his occasional crazed episodes that we always leave the toilet lid down.

Once I was brushing my teeth with the bathroom door open. Milo was streaking around in one of his usual wild fits. Suddenly, he ran into the bathroom and started to jump up on the toilet—only whoever had been in the bathroom before me had left the toilet lid up. Realizing there was nothing under him, he grabbed the fuzzy lid cover, but he fell anyway, pulling the lid right down on top of himself. I was laughing so hard he had to meow before I realized he wanted out!

—MEGAN SULLIVANT
St. Louis, Missouri

BEHAVIOR

box. Don't pick him up and take him; he has to learn to find it himself. Make it a game. Trail a piece of string along to the box, but don't take any detours over shaggy rugs or other "diggable" surfaces. Continue the drill for a couple of weeks. Then, to test your cat, leave one of your fuzzy sweaters (not your best one!) or a shaggy rug in the middle of the floor. If your kitten skips over it and proceeds to the box, you can claim success.

(Not So) Heaven Scent

You can reinforce the idea that the litter box is *the* place to go by leaving a little urine in the box. Go ahead

---

A WORD FROM MICKY NIEGO

Short of a Neon Sign

MICKY NIEGO
Animal behaviorist in Airmont, New York, who trains puppies and service dogs in addition to speaking and consulting on animal behavior and training issues

Teaching a kitten to use the litter box is usually fairly easy. But some well-meaning new owners make it difficult for kitty to know where to go. For instance, they place the litter box in the bathroom, but then they also leave a shaggy bath mat there, too. How is the kitten supposed to know the difference between digging in a fuzzy rug and digging in a gravelly box? She doesn't, and so she digs around and defecates on the mat. Other owners leave the litter box in the same room with a big potted floor plant. Guess what they find when they get home?

The litter box must be a beacon. Don't give your pet a choice about where to go. That means no rugs or towels on the floor in the bathroom (if that's where you leave the litter box). And no matter where you place that box, don't leave anything else nearby with a texture that may confuse your pet.

and scoop out the feces, but resist the urge to change the whole box. If your kitten can smell it, she'll know where to go. Of course, after a few days, when your kitten knows where to go and you know that she knows (you'll know because she'll be using the box), you'll need to clean the box.

Tiny Kittens Can't Handle High-Rises

It's a good idea to watch your new kitten get into the litter box at least two or three times to be sure he can make it. Some boxes have awfully high sides, and your kitten may be too small to climb over them. If he has trouble, put a small piece of scrap wood—or any other appropriate-size object—beside the box to act as a sort of step.

COST CUTTERS

Toward an Odorless Litter Box

Sure, you could spend money on a container of expensive kitty litter deodorizer, but here's a cheaper solution. After you've emptied and cleaned your cat's litter box but before you've poured in the fresh litter, sprinkle in a thin layer—about one-sixteenth inch thick—of baking soda. The soda will keep the odor down, and it's far less expensive.

It's a Litter Mistake

Cats are notoriously fussy, and if you find that your kitten won't use the litter box despite your best efforts, the problem may be that she doesn't like a particular brand of litter. Try a different brand and give her a few days to check it out. Her litter preferences may not be as obvious as you expect. A particular brand is acceptable only if she goes to the bathroom in it and covers up her waste. If she goes but doesn't cover it, you still have a problem. Keep trying new brands until you find one she likes.

Some Prefer Mahogany

If you're having trouble finding a litter that your kitty likes, use your imagination. You're certainly not limited to commercial types. Some cats prefer wood shavings or animal bedding wood chips—the kind that hamsters, guinea pigs, and gerbils sleep in—to the traditional gravel litters. You can find wood chips at any pet supply store.

BEHAVIOR

FOR FERRETS ONLY

Anyplace Will Do

When you're trying to house-train a ferret, you'll save yourself a lot of aggravation and heartache if, early on, you resign yourself to the fact that although most ferrets will use a litter box most of the time, sometimes your little friend will go where he wants to. When you get a new ferret, keep him confined to one room or a small space for the first several weeks or until he shows that he knows what the boxes are for. Put a litter box in each corner (ferrets like to go in, among other places, corners). When he goes in one of the boxes, praise him well. Gradually expand the space you give him.

Back Him Up . . .

If you want to try to house-train your ferret, you'll have an easier time if you watch for the visual cues that tell you he's about to let loose. After your ferret eats, take him into the bathroom and put newspaper or a litter box down where you want him to go. Then watch him. When the ferret suddenly stops in the middle of scampering about and starts to back up, that means he's about to go. That's your cue to pick him up and put him in the litter box. To reinforce the idea, leave a few bits of feces in the box with him.

. . . Or Leave the Doors Open

For some unexplainable reason, ferrets like to go to the bathroom right outside closed doors. So take the hint. If you give your ferret the run of the house, place a litter box near each closed door, then place a few bits of your pet's feces in each one to attract her.

BASIC TRAINING

Teach Your Bird to Perch on Your Finger

Birds don't naturally want to stand on your finger—it's an acquired skill. Although it is generally not a difficult trick to teach your pet, it does require repetition and patience.

Start by gently pushing your extended finger against the bird's chest, just above the legs. The bird will eventually step up as she loses her balance. Say the word "Up" as the bird steps onto your finger.

When you're teaching the command, don't flinch if the bird reaches out with her beak to touch your finger or hand. She's simply testing the sturdiness of the perch (your finger), so keep your hand steady and still as the bird climbs up.

HOWLING

BEHAVIOR

Dogs howl for a variety of reasons, one of which is to communicate with the pack. Most dogs howl at one time or another, and when they do it only occasionally, it's usually not a problem. But if your dog is howling morning, noon, and night, try some of these ideas to quiet him down.

FOR DOGS ONLY

Howl Long Will This Go On?

If your puppy howls a lot when he's separated from you or can't see you, relax. This is common with very young dogs. Your pet is calling you or trying to locate you. This behavior generally diminishes greatly when the pup is between eight and ten weeks old. In the meantime, don't inadvertently reward the behavior by returning and petting the puppy. Act as though nothing's the matter (of course, make sure nothing really *is* the matter) or offer a quick reassurance—"I'll be right back"—and nothing more. Your puppy will learn that howling is not a way to get your attention.

Play with Me

Chronic howling, like nuisance barking, can be a sign that your dog is stressed-out from being separated from his pack (that is, your family). If you keep your dog isolated a great deal of the time, you may be able to put an end to his howling simply by spending more time with him. Take your pet on more frequent walks and schedule in some playtime each day.

BASIC TRAINING

Teach Your Bird to Talk

One of the first sounds most talking birds mimic is the telephone or the doorbell. That's because those sounds elicit a reaction from you. Think about it: You're sitting quietly reading the newspaper. The phone or doorbell rings, and you jump up immediately. Your bird thinks he can get a similar response if he makes the same sound.

How do you teach him words? One good way is to begin labeling things that are meaningful to the bird. For instance, when you give your pet water, say "Water." When you offer food, say "Cracker," "Food," or "Treat." Or, if you want to train your pet to be funny or cute, say "Thank you" when you give the bird water or food. Sooner or later, your feathered friend will say "Thank you" whenever you give him either.

If you want to expand your pet's vocabulary, you could record a word or short phrase on a cassette and play it for about 15 minutes several times a day.

BEHAVIOR

Bowser Wants to Be Part of the Family

If you are using a dog crate for your puppy, you may be able to put an end to the howling by placing the crate in an area frequented by the family. Isolation is the enemy here. Dogs are social creatures.

JUMPING ON FURNITURE

Off. Get off the chair. Off. Get off the *other* chair. Do you sound like a broken record? Is your divan covered with dog hair? Is your footstool coated with feline fur? Don't give up the ship. Here are some ways to keep your furry friends off the furniture, both when you are home and—better yet—when you're not.

FOR PETS IN GENERAL

Shake-Down

❑ Loud noises will stop your pet before she jumps on the furniture. When Fluffy starts to make her way onto the easy chair, clap your hands, slap your hand on a table, or use a "shake can." To make a shake can, rinse and drip-dry an empty soda can. Drop about ten pennies or screws into the can and seal it well with duct or electrical tape. Whenever your pet goes near the furniture, give the can a good shake. The noise should send the offender scurrying.

Wet the Heck?

❑ Let's say that you want to keep your large dog off the bed when you turn in for the night (it gets a little cramped) but don't object to her lying there at other times. Or you want your cat to stay off the sofa when you're on it but don't mind him curling up there when you're not around. A plant mister or spray bottle filled with water should do the trick. Just say the word "Away" as you give your pet a squirt. You must be consistent, and that means having the spray bottle at the ready for at least six to eight weeks. Soon your pet will get the idea that "Away" means you don't want to

share your territory—and that's a very proper attitude for the leader of the pack.

Shocking Solution

❑ One way to keep your pets off the furniture when you're not home is to (safely) booby-trap the furniture. If you don't want to put a lot of effort into your plan, the best thing to do is to visit a pet supply store and check out products designed for this purpose. One is a vinyl mat, such as a Scat Mat, that you position anyplace you want to make off-limits to your pet—perhaps beneath the drapes (for cats that climb) or on the sofa. When the mat is plugged in and the pet makes contact, the mat emits a weak electrical impulse. The pet gets an unpleasant but harmless shock. The mat is safe for kittens, puppies, and larger cats and dogs because it has variable correction levels. These devices are not

ONE PERSON'S SOLUTION

Foiled Again!

We solved the problem of keeping our three-year-old dalmatian off the furniture when we are home by giving him a squirt with a spray bottle whenever he headed for forbidden territory. But we were stumped about how to keep him off when we were out. Our solution: aluminum foil on the couch cushions! I bought a 75-foot roll and lay foil over the cushions every time we go out. I'm not quite sure why it works—I think he's afraid of the sound it makes—but it does work.

—**ANNE HOGG**
Carmel, New York

BEHAVIOR

cheap—depending on size, some cost more than $100—but as needs change, you can move them from place to place with no problem.

Like Fingernails on a Blackboard

❑ Another product designed to keep pets off furniture works by emitting a loud noise that lasts as long as your pet stays on the furniture. These devices are sold in many pet supply stores and catalogs—usually for about a third of the price of an electrified mat. They can work well for a bold pet, but they're not appropriate for a timid animal. If Tiger or Bandit runs under the bed and quivers the first time you try this approach, switch to a different method.

A WORD FROM MICKY NIEGO

Attractions and Distractions

MICKY NIEGO
Animal behaviorist in Airmont, New York, who trains puppies and service dogs in addition to speaking and consulting on animal behavior and training issues

You taught your bird to say hello when you make a finger signal, and you want to show off. So now there are 16 people watching, eating, and making noise, and you say, "Fred, say hello!" And Fred just goes to the bottom of his cage and ignores you.

What happened? He said hello when it was just you and him. What happened was that you added all the people and activity. When the activity level goes up, the animal's focus goes down.

It happens to us, too. You're at a party talking to two people, and then there are six people, and then you hear a side conversation, and then two other people start talking to you. You haven't finished that conversation

FOR DOGS ONLY

BEHAVIOR

Flag Him Down

If you've been using an invisible fence to keep your dog in your yard, you may have a ready-made tool for keeping him off the furniture (or away from other verboten areas of your home). Once your dog has learned to recognize and steer clear of the flags marking your invisible fence, move the "danger sign" indoors. Before you leave the house, put several of the flags in empty soda bottles—one flag to a bottle. Then create a border of flags in bottles around the area of the home you want your dog to avoid. He'll see the flags, and making the association with the fence should keep him well clear of your furniture.

---

with Susie, but now some guy is asking you another question, and, oh dear, you've lost your train of thought. That's distraction. Or maybe the problem is an attraction. You're talking to somebody at that party, and over his shoulder you see the best-looking strawberry shortcake go by. Now you don't have any idea what this man is saying about tax shelters—you want a piece of that shortcake. You've lost his words. You're right there, he's right there, but you've completely lost the thread of the conversation. Now all you care about is shortcake.

You can see the same thing with pets. You teach Fido to sit, and he can sit like nobody's business. But then one day the kids are screaming on the swing set outside, and your spouse walks in with a bunch of groceries. When you tell Fido to sit, he just looks confused.

Here's the answer. Initially, teach your pet away from those distractions and attractions. Then, as he learns a specific command, incrementally increase the amount of activity around him when you give the command. It will take time, but eventually you'll have a pet who's less likely to be distracted by strawberry shortcake, er, screaming kids.

BEHAVIOR

FOR CATS ONLY

Take Her to a Higher Plane

Your kitty may be lounging on the back of the sofa or on top of the television cabinet because she likes to be up high, where she can survey her domain. If you provide her with her own higher place, she may stay

ONE PERSON'S SOLUTION

Insert Your Pet's Name Here

My wife and I are foster parents for two German shepherds that are retired from Guide Dogs for the Blind in San Rafael, California. We are always looking for new ways to keep them off the furniture and were lucky enough to happen upon this method. At Halloween, we saw a novelty doormat for sale at our local Walgreen's. It had a recording device inside that allowed you to record a message, and when someone stepped on the mat, the message would play. I brought it home and recorded a special message for my dogs. When they got up on the living room couch by stepping on the mat, it called them by name and told them to get off. It turned out to be a great tool, and it cost only about $6.

—**JIMMIE MONSOOR**
Danville, California

off your furniture. Visit your local pet supply store and ask whether they sell cat trees—vertical carpeted shelves designed just for cats. Install one of these in your house, and your cat will be able to get high, so to speak, without damaging your divan.

JUMPING ON PEOPLE

Tired of being literally bowled over when you walk through the door at night? Here are some ways to train your dog to keep all four feet firmly on the ground.

FOR DOGS ONLY

Don't Even Think about It

Here's a common scenario: Working at the kitchen counter, you fill your dog's bowl with food. Your dog jumps up on you. You say "Off." Your dog jumps off. You praise your dog. What's wrong with this picture? Your dog has not learned not to jump up on you. He's only learned to get off when you tell him to. After all, you praised him when he did, right? The way to show him that jumping isn't okay is to catch him before he does it. Watch his body language, and you'll be able to anticipate when he's about to jump. When he makes even the suggestion of the motion, very sternly tell him "No. Off." Then walk away and ignore him. He'll learn that jumping not only gets him a rebuff, but it also gets him ignored—exactly the opposite reaction from what he's hoping for.

Stoop to Her Level

If your dog is a habitual jumper, try this strategy: Next time you walk in the door, crouch down to your dog's level right away, before she has a chance to jump up on you. Praise her warmly and pet her. Combine this method with a firm correction—a stern "No" at the first sign of impending jumping—and your dog should learn that keeping her feet on the ground earns her praise and much-coveted social interaction, but jumping gets her nothing but a correction.

Knock, Knock

It generally takes at least three to ten well-timed repetitions of an action-consequence sequence for most dogs to catch on. But what if you get company only once a month? How can you teach your dog not to jump up on people? Set up a practice situation. Enlist the help of one or two friends or neighbors, asking them to stop by briefly at specified times each day for about a week. Then put your dog on his leash when the agreed-upon hour approaches.

As your "bait" comes through the door, give the command "Off," but don't pull the leash. If the dog obeys—meaning that he keeps his feet on the ground—praise him and have your visitor praise him softly, too. If the dog tries to jump, give a quick snap on the leash and tell him "No. Off." At the same time, close the door quickly so that the dog gets no praise, no attention, nothing but a correction. (You'll need to explain the whole routine to your assistant in advance, of course, so you don't offend the friend while training the dog.) Do this several times every day for a week or so, depending on your dog, and it should cure him of jumping.

Shall We Dance?

Next time your dog greets you at the door by jumping up on you, try this. Hold her two front paws, so that your dog is actually standing on her two back feet. Maintain that position until you can tell she doesn't like it. She may start to struggle or whine a bit. As you release her, tell her "No," "No jump," or "Off." Dogs don't like to stay in the standing position, so if you repeat this exercise each time she jumps, your pet will eventually get the hint that jumping up is only going to cause her discomfort.

LEASH PULLING

You know the old joke about your dog taking *you* for a walk? Well, it's not funny if you're the one on the other end of the leash. Then it's just plain annoying. Here are

A WORD FROM MICKY NIEGO

They Know What's Coming

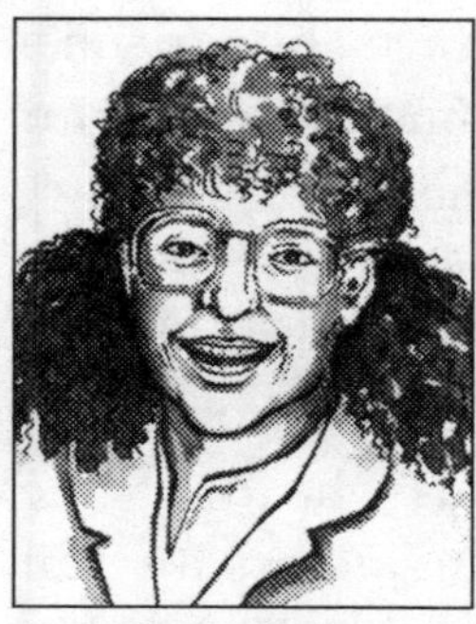

MICKY NIEGO
Animal behaviorist in Airmont, New York, who trains puppies and service dogs in addition to speaking and consulting on animal behavior and training issues

You grab your handbag, you pick up your car keys, and your dog's ready to go. He's been watching you all his life, and he knows: You never pick up that handbag to go to the bathroom. You never pick up that handbag to go to the kitchen. You pick up that handbag when you go out. And he says, "Oh boy, when she grabs that handbag, I know she's headed for the door." He's learned from past experience—and he's right.

Frequency, timing, and consistency of outcome all come into play when your dog is learning. Frequency means that you leave the house often enough (and therefore pick up your handbag often enough) for the dog to see a pattern. Timing means that you grab your handbag *just before* you leave the house (if you picked it up 15 minutes before you left, the dog probably wouldn't associate it with your leaving). And consistency of outcome means that nine times out of ten, if you pick up your handbag, you do leave the house. So how can you apply each of these when you *want* a dog to learn something?

Let's say you want to teach your dog not to beg at the table. Timing, frequency, and consistency of outcome dictate that every single time she comes to the table for a scrap, you tell her, in no uncertain terms, "No!" You tell her at every meal (frequency), you tell her at the exact moment she puts her head on the table (timing), and you tell her every single time she tries to beg (consistency of outcome).

Then all you have to do is train Grandma to do the same when she pet-sits.

YOU'VE GOTTA LOVE 'EM

Playing for Keeps

Buried by an avalanche in Colorado, I was saved by a friend's mongrel dog, Bungie. But the dog didn't find me simply for the sake of rescuing me. She had an ulterior motive.

We were skiing in 18 inches of fresh snow in the San Juan Mountains near Telluride. Returning to our cabin after ski touring up to see a frozen waterfall, I was ahead of the group, cutting across a small slope, when the avalanche hit. I grabbed onto a tree to stop myself as the snow buried me completely, except for an 8-inch hole leading to the surface. I could breathe, but I couldn't move. After four or five minutes, Bungie poked her head through the hole—with a stick in her mouth. She wanted to play fetch. I was glad to see her, but I said, "Not now, Bungie!" Shortly, the others arrived, saw Bungie's tail wagging, and dug me out of the snow. As soon as I was free, I happily threw the stick for Bungie.

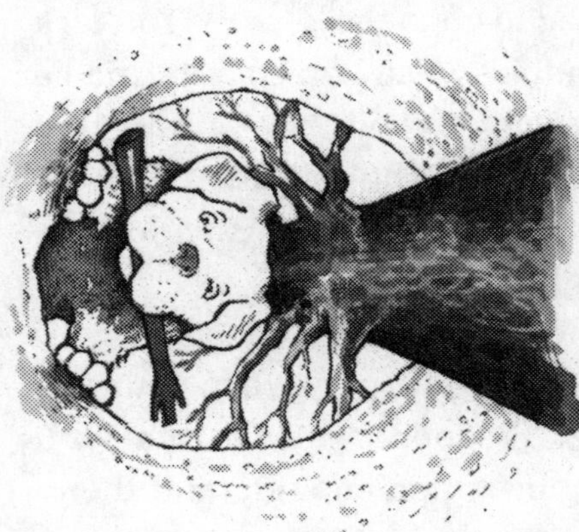

—**EUGENE BUCHANAN**
Steamboat Springs, Colorado

some strategies the experts recommend for pulling your dog back into line.

FOR DOGS ONLY

Make Your Intentions Clear

Leash pulling is one of those undesirable behaviors that dogs get a lot of mixed messages about. One

day, your dog pulls and you get angry. Another day, you feel like jogging along behind, so you let him do it. The moral of the story? Be consistent. If you correct your dog once for leash pulling, correct him every time. Otherwise, you'll end up with a confused leash puller.

Get Off to a Good Start

Leash pulling is very easy to prevent if you start the training while your puppy is still brand-new. When you begin walking the pup with a leash and collar (*not* a choke collar) and he starts to pull ahead of you, just give the leash a sharp tug back. Keep in mind your strength and the size of your dog. A sharp tug back on a Saint Bernard puppy is different from a sharp tug back on a Chihuahua. After two or three times, the puppy will realize that when she fights the resistance in the leash, she suddenly gets jarred backward.

An ordinary halter (A) is safer than a collar for training small dogs. A no-pull halter (B) is good for training persistent leash pullers.

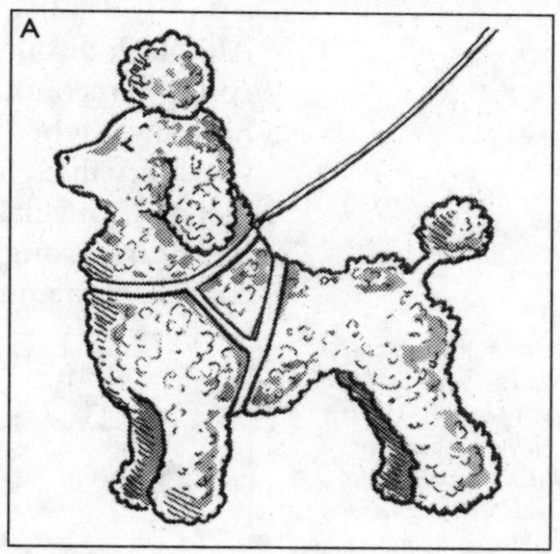

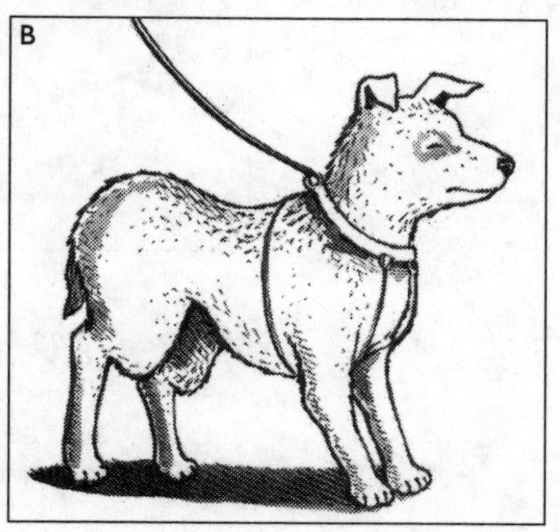

Harness His Energy

If your dog is very small or delicate, you may want to opt for a harness rather than a collar when you're teaching him not to pull ahead. A harness fits over the dog's body, rather than just around his neck, which could get injured if you snapped back on a collar sharply. If you do use a harness, the correction is the same. When the pooch pulls ahead, give the leash a sharp jerk back to teach the animal that pulling the leader about is not acceptable.

Halt!

To help teach your leash puller new tricks, you may want to invest in a no-pull halter, a favorite tool of trainers who want to discourage dogs from pulling. A no-pull halter

has two straps that extend off the halter and wrap around the back of the dog's front legs. When the dog tries to run ahead of you, the straps tighten, pulling the animal's head down toward her front legs and making it uncomfortable to pull ahead. The tension on the halter relaxes immediately when the dog slows down. These halters, which cost about $16, are available at some pet supply stores. You also may be able to get one from your vet.

A Multipronged Defense

For some dogs with thick coats or very muscular necks, the usual pulling prevention techniques have little effect. If this applies to your dog, consider trying a pronged collar, also known as a spike or pinch collar. Although it sounds like a medieval torture device, the collar is recommended by trainers as effective—and humane—when used correctly on persistent pullers with very thick fur or strong necks. The pronged collar (generally available at any store that sells dog supplies) has blunt prongs that prod the dog's neck when the collar is tightened by a sharp, quick snap of the leash.

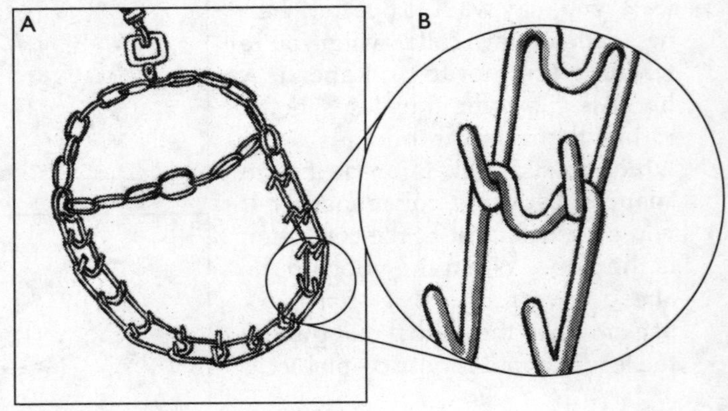

A pronged collar (A) may be your best bet for restraining a dog with an especially thick coat or strong neck. The blunt prongs (B) prod the neck when you snap the leash.

Where'd She Go?

When your dog pulls at her leash, she isn't openly defying you. She's probably just excited and not paying attention to where you're going. Here's how to remind her to pay more attention. Next time you're walking with your dog and she starts to pull, simply turn around and walk in another direction. Don't yank, just abruptly change your path and walk away. Do this consistently, and she'll begin to realize that she has to pay attention to you, the leader.

LEG HUMPING

Between this behavior and eating their own feces, it seems that dogs have cornered the market on disgusting behavior. You may be surprised to learn that this behavior isn't necessarily sexual. Puppies of both sexes do it to each other as a way of testing their relationships. But it's still disturbing. Take heart: Unless your dog's leg humping is a sign of dominant behavior—a more serious overall behavioral problem than leg humping in and of itself—you can probably break your pet of the habit. (If the real issue is dominance, you'll need to watch your own behavior, making sure you give your pet the firm message that you're the one in charge.)

COMMON MISTAKES

Well, Which Is It?

Professional trainers stress that it's important for owners who are trying to train their dogs to remember the difference between the directives "Off" and "Down." It's easy to confuse the two in the heat of the moment. To a dog that is learning standard obedience training, "Down" means to lie down. "Off" is the command you give when the dog places her feet on either a person or an object and you want her to remove them. To give one when you mean the other only confuses the dog.

FOR DOGS ONLY

That'll Teach Him

One quick way to get the message across to your dog that leg humping isn't going to win him any friends is to give him a blast of clean water from a spray bottle when you see that he's about to start in. Repeat the correction each time he repeats the action, and he'll give it up.

Not My Leg, Pal

A loud noise is one way to distract your dog from what he's doing. Clap your hands, slap your hand on a

table, or use an air horn. At the same time, tell the dog "No" in a stern voice.

He Needs Adult Supervision

For adults, leg humping is a slightly embarrassing experience. But for a small child confronted with a large dog, it can be truly frightening. If your dog is a habitual humper, you need always to supervise his interactions with people, especially children, and correct him firmly each time he attempts it.

"Fix" the Problem

One easy way to lessen the likelihood that your male dog will become a chronic leg humper—and to avoid all sorts of other problems—is to have him neutered by the time he's six months old. If you wait much longer than that, the operation may not have much effect on this behavior.

LITTER BOX WOES

What happened? Your feline has never had a problem hitting the litter box, but now she's going on the kitchen floor, in the bathtub, in the middle of the down comforter on your bed. (If your cat is urinating on the walls, she's spraying, and that's a different problem altogether.) No, your cat isn't angry with you, but something has gone awry. Once you've consulted your vet and ruled out a possible health problem, try these ways to get her to go in the box again.

FOR CATS ONLY

But It Smells *Like the Toilet*

Once your cat (intentionally) misses the litter box, you need to remove the odor of feces and urine completely, or she'll continue to use the same spot outside the box over and over again. One way to kill the odor is to clean the spot with a urine neutralizer called Nature's Miracle, available from vets and pet supply stores.

This Is the Dining Area, Not the Bathroom

BEHAVIOR

Another way to discourage your cat from using the same (wrong) bathroom spot over and over is to put a plate of her food in the spot every day for at least 21 days. She'll get the idea that that particular location is a feeding area, and she'll avoid soiling it.

Try a Double Scoop

If you're not cleaning the litter box often enough, your cat will let you know by using another spot—like

BASIC TRAINING

Come Here!

Two factors make it tough for new puppy owners to teach their dogs to come when called.

First, for the initial 3½ to 4½ months of their lives, most puppies will come when you call them. That's because developmentally they are juveniles and therefore are utterly attached to and dependent on you (for the moment). Unfortunately, that behavior often lulls an owner into thinking her puppy already knows the command. Then, when the puppy gets a little older—and less dependent—he stops coming.

The second factor is actually a mistake that some owners make: failing to put a dog on a leash when trying to teach the animal to come. If your puppy's not on a leash, you're giving him a choice about whether he wants to comply—and that's a training no-no.

To train your puppy to come when you call him, put on his collar and attach a long, retractable leash. Have some treats ready. Call the puppy enthusiastically—clap your hands, stoop down, or run backward while laughing and clapping. Give him a small treat when he comes to you. Once he's finished the treat, let him go explore again. (That teaches him that there's no reason to avoid you when you call him, because "Come" doesn't always mean that it's time to go inside or playtime is over.)

Repeat the exercise over and over again on the leash—gradually increasing the number and the closeness of distractions that are luring him—until he comes automatically every time. Then, and only then, take off the leash and start the process over again until he comes each time you call him.

your fifth-century Turkish rug. Try scooping the soiled litter every time she uses the box, rather than once a day or so. If that doesn't do the trick, try cleaning the entire litter box more often.

Time for a New Box

Nearly every litter box on the market today is made of plastic. That makes the boxes durable and inexpensive, but over time they all tend to absorb odors. So if your cat has an old box and is going to the toilet everywhere except in the box, it may not make any difference how often you scoop, change the litter, or clean the box. You may simply need a new litter box, which you can buy at any pet supply store.

If you do purchase a new litter box, choose one that resembles the old one as closely as possible. Cats are notoriously sensitive to changes in their environments, and a totally different litter box may actually exacerbate the problem.

PLAYING IN THE WATER DISH

Has the great flood come to your home? Some dogs love to play in their water bowls, dropping their toys in them or just splashing the water around. It looks like fun—unless you're the one cleaning up afterward. So if you're tired of stepping in poodles, er, puddles, in your kitchen, take some expert advice on how to tell your pooch to dry up.

Let your dog be a bottle-fed baby if you want to eliminate playing in the water dish.

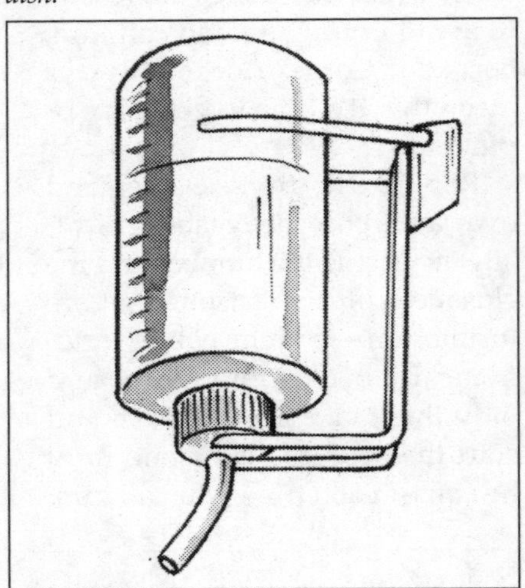

FOR DOGS ONLY

Try a Bottled Remedy

Your dog won't be able to play in her water dish if she doesn't have a water dish to play in. Many folks have had success conquering the water dish problem by replacing a dog's dish with a water bottle—basically a one-quart version of the type of bottle you would typically use with a hamster, gerbil, or guinea pig. You can find these bottles at most pet supply stores.

Remote Control

One way to deal with a dog that likes to play in his water dish is with a remote correction. You'll need a "shake can," which you can make with a clean, empty soda can. Place about ten pennies or screws in the can, then seal it with some duct or electrical tape. Fill your dog's water dish and leave the room, but stay within sight (and throwing distance) of the dish. When your dog enters the room and starts to play in the water, toss the can onto the floor near him. The noise will startle him and distract him from what he's doing. Repeat this drill frequently, and you'll put an end to the behavior—at least when you're around.

To avoid water dish play, bring the dish up (A) or cut the opening down (B).

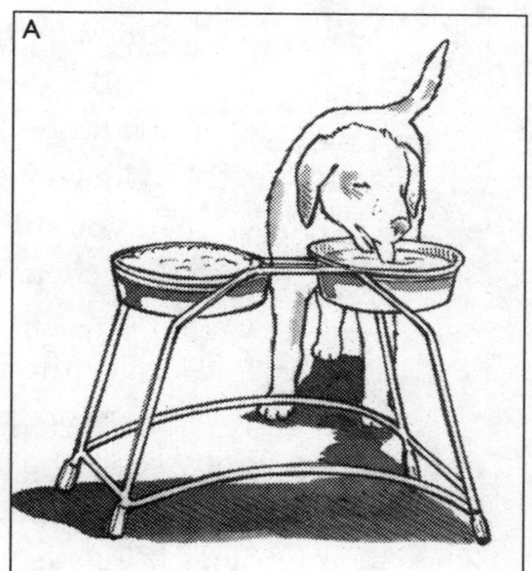

Get Him off the Ground

Some dogs like to put their two front feet in their water dishes. (There are some strange dogs out there.) If that's your dilemma, visit your local pet supply store and check out the elevated water and food dishes. Originally designed for dogs with physical problems, for which reaching down is painful, the contraptions are simply high racks that hold the food and water dishes. Especially if your dog is small, putting his bowl up at shoulder level will make him stop putting his feet in his dish.

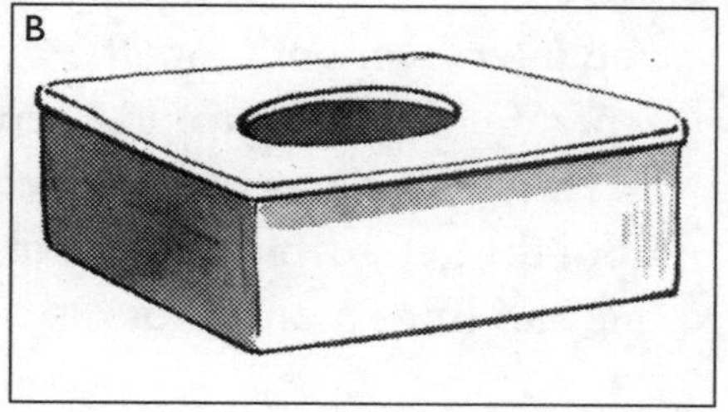

Cut the Dish Down to Size

Some dogs treat their water dishes like mini pools. You can put an end to those antics by making a water dish that only your pet's snout will fit into. First, buy a large plastic storage container with a lid (avail-

BEHAVIOR

able at any discount or grocery store). Next, cut into the lid with a utility knife or scissors, making a hole that's large enough only for your dog's snout. Fill the container with water, replace the lid, and you have the perfect water dish for dogs that like water sports.

A WORD FROM DR. DEVINNE

Getting to Know You

DR. CHARLES DEVINNE
of Peterborough, New Hampshire, who has more than 15 years of veterinary experience and whose private practice currently concentrates on dogs and cats

Let's say you're going to introduce a new cat into a household. In my experience, there are three main things that may cause problems with the new addition to the family: competition for food and water, competition for the litter area, and competition for human affection.

Besides setting up separate feeding and bathroom areas for the new pet, you can go a long way toward minimizing the fighting if you minimize the competition for your affection. What usually happens is that the new cat comes in, and the owner fawns over the newcomer, spending time with her and making a big fuss—all in front of the "old" cat. Pretty soon, the resentment starts to build—especially with females. They seem to get a lot more upset than males when their territory is invaded.

So be a little careful how you divide your attention. Make sure you fawn over both (or all) your cats, and be sure to give each a separate feeding area and a separate litter area.

Hey, sometimes a new cat comes in, and they're best buddies from the get-go, but in my experience, it usually takes between one and three months for the cats to work out their hierarchy.

SPRAYING AND MARKING TERRITORY

When your cat urinates all over the walls of your house, it's called spraying. If it's your dog, the experts call it marking territory. To make things more confusing, animals of both sexes do this, although the behavior is more common in males. It is a problem best caught early, as putting a stop to spraying once it really gets established can be a challenge. Here are some proven remedies.

FOR DOGS AND CATS

Eliminate the Urge

To prevent your pet from spraying the same spot over and over again, you need to eliminate the urine odor completely. That means it's not a good idea to use ammonia to clean the spot. To an animal, ammonia smells like urine. Visit a local pet supply store and ask for a pet urine neutralizer such as Nature's Miracle, which is designed to kill urine odors. If your pet can't smell the urine, he won't refresh the fading odor on that spot.

Shed New Light on the Problem

To make sure you catch all the problem spots when cleaning up after your pet, pick up a special black light from a pet or home supply store. It will show urine-soiled areas of the carpet in white or eerie blue, in places you can't see in daylight.

That'll Fix Him

Although the problem is not always related to sex, you can sometimes prevent a male dog or cat from marking or spraying inside the house by having the animal neutered as soon as is appropriate. If you're not sure just when that is for your particular pet, check with your vet or local Society for the Prevention of Cruelty to Animals (SPCA). You'll find the number for the SPCA in the Yellow Pages of your local phone book, listed under Animal Shelters.

BEHAVIOR

Keep an Eye on Him

You can prevent later unpleasant surprises if, when you get a new pet, you supervise the animal at all times—or as much as possible. A very small dog can mark a spot in your house for months, and you may not even know it (unless you catch her in the act). That's because a tiny dog has an even tinier bladder, so she releases an almost unnoticeable amount of urine. Similarly, the urine of fixed cats is not very pungent, so you may not smell it right away. Three months later, when you notice an unpleasant smell in the sofa, it may be too late to correct the behavior.

FOR DOGS ONLY

Make Up Your Mind!

One way to keep your dog from urinating or marking in the house is to teach him the "Inside" and

A WORD FROM MICKY NIEGO

Lures and Rewards

MICKY NIEGO
Animal behaviorist in Airmont, New York, who trains puppies and service dogs in addition to speaking and consulting on animal behavior and training issues

How do you initially teach a dog a behavior? You lure him. To teach "Sit," you hold the treat above the dog's head, and his little bottom falls to the ground. Then you put the treat in his mouth. That's luring. When we teach animals, it's wonderful to lure them because they want to do the behavior; you're not forcing them. Any animal can be lured. The most timid animal can be lured. The most aggressive animal can be lured. All you have to do is supply the thing that is just irresistible: a treat, a tennis ball, a Frisbee.

After an animal knows a behavior, you switch from lures to rewards. You want that

"Outside" commands. Here's how it works. Get yourself a handful of treats. Take Bowser to the open front door, then toss one treat outside. As he runs to get the treat, give the command "Outside" or just "Out." Next, toss a treat inside the house and give the command "Inside" or "In." Repeat this exercise over and over again, until you're confident that your dog knows the meaning of these directives. The next step is supervision. When you see your dog starting to sniff an area, or when you think he's about to lift his leg, give the "Outside" command in a firm voice, then get him outside. He'll learn that this behavior is okay when he's outside but unacceptable inside.

Gotcha!

To stop your dog from marking territory, you must catch him in the act. One good correction to use is a "shake can." To make a shake can, rinse and drip-dry a

behavior to keep happening, so the next step is to say "Spotty, sit," and Spotty sits. Only now, instead of showing him the treat ahead of time, you just give it to him after he sits.

How do you make the transition from luring to rewarding? You keep using the hand gesture but without the treat. You hold your hand above Spotty's head and give the command "Sit." Or you hold your hand as if you have a treat, and you say "Come."

You want to aim for giving random treats (rewards). In the beginning (once the behavior is learned), you give Spotty a treat four out of five times. Then you make it two out of five times, and then you totally randomize the treat. During the day, you keep five treats in your pocket, and you give them for superlative performance. The dog never knows where he's going to get them or when he's going to get them, but he knows that when you issue a directive and he complies, there may be a treat at the end of the rainbow.

And if you don't have a treat on you, there's always praise. Petting, eye contact, and a kind smile on your face are all rewards to a dog.

soda can and place about ten pennies or screws inside. Tape the can opening closed with some electrical or duct tape. When you see your dog starting to sniff or raise his leg, shout "No!" Simultaneously, toss the shake can onto the floor near him or just give it a good shake. The sound, coupled with your verbal correction, will stop him from doing what he was about to do—which was to mark *your* territory.

FOR CATS ONLY

Lemon Tea for Kitty Pee

If your cat is spraying the walls of your house, here's a way to break the habit. Dip a cotton ball in some lemon extract (available in the spice section of your supermarket). Squeeze out the excess and place the cotton in a metal tea ball (designed to hold loose tea). Hang the ball by its hook near where your cat is spraying. The smell will repel some cats. Refresh the ball once a week until the cat is retrained.

> **You're All Mine**
>
> Does it give you a warm and fuzzy feeling when your cat rubs her face or tail against you? "Such an expression of love," you think. Actually, it's an expression of ownership. Cats have scent glands on each side of their foreheads, on their lips and chins, and on their tails. They mark their territory by rubbing those scent glands on the objects they wish to delineate as their own.

Dining Room This Way, Toilet That Way

Once you've cleaned up a spot where your cat has been spraying, you can reinforce the idea that she shouldn't mark that area by placing a small plate or bowl of food in the spot. That lets her know that the area is a feeding station. Leave food there every day for at least 21 days, and the spraying in that spot should end.

STALKING AT BIRD FEEDERS

Cats are hunters. Period. You may hear stories about felines that learn to coexist peacefully with backyard birdies, but those instances are the exception, not the rule. You may as well try to train your fish not to swim, your birds not to fly, and your rabbits not to . . . well, you get the idea. Even though we can't advise you how to genetically reprogram your cat, we *can* offer some advice about protecting the local avian population.

FOR CATS ONLY

Fish Gotta Swim; Cats Gotta . . . Hunt

Your cat is going to hunt birds no matter how much you explain to her that it's not nice. And since you're not going to be able to teach your cat to leave the birds alone, the most humane option you can exercise is to resist the urge to put up a bird feeder in your backyard.

Early Warning System

Although you can't train the hunting instinct out of your cat, you *can* give the birds a fighting chance. Many folks recommend placing a small bell on your cat's collar when he goes outside. When your kitty moves or tries to pounce, the bell will ring. That will scare the birds away before your cat can get to them.

One popular style of bird feeder is designed to baffle all four-legged critters.

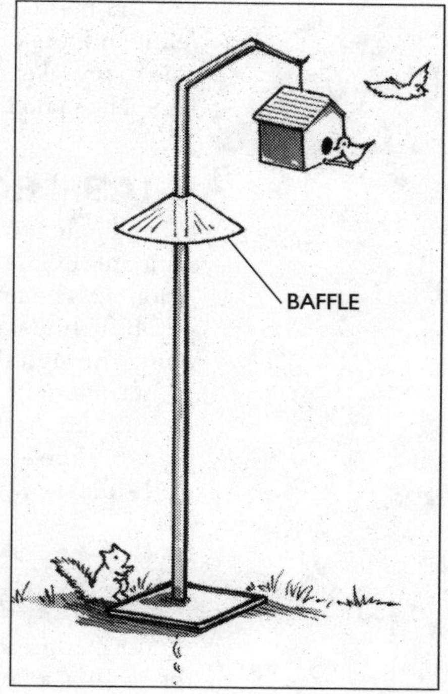

Good for the Lawn, Too

If you just can't bring yourself to give up your bird feeders, or if the neighbor's cat considers your feeder an invitation to dinner, try this strategy. Whenever a cat is outside and posing a potential threat to the feeder, turn on a sprinkler close by. Birds are more than happy to get wet while they're eating, but cats will definitely stay away.

No Heavyweights Allowed

Bird lovers have been combating squirrels and raccoons since the dawn of time, so there's a big market out there for varmint-proof bird feeders. If you're a cat owner who wants to protect the local avian population, it's a good idea to visit a

garden center and investigate different models of feeders. Some of them work by shutting down when something heavier than a bird tries to climb the supporting pole. Others have baffles to block any animal that tries to clamber up. Although your cat may not speak to you for weeks after you install one of these feeders, the birds will sing your praises.

Keep the Peace

Maybe you don't have a bird feeder, but what if your neighbor does? That can be a source of problems if you plan to let your cat outdoors. One strategy you can use to protect the local birds and your relationship with your neighbor is to purchase a cat-proof bird feeder as a gift for the folks next door. The family will most likely appreciate both the gift and the fact that you're taking responsibility for your cat. Best of all, it will prevent any Hatfield and McCoy–style feuding.

They're as Different as Night and Day

Another way to protect local birds is to keep your feline indoors during the daytime and to let him outside to prowl at night. Since birds do not feed at night, they'll be in no danger from your cat.

TRASH ROOTING

What a pain it is to walk into the kitchen and find the remnants of last night's dinner strewn across the floor. And it can be unhealthy—even dangerous—for your pet. If he finds and chews a chicken carcass (he's not going through the trash to eat your leftover tofu and groats, after all), he can easily get a bone lodged in his throat. And that will, at the very least, require a visit to the vet. Here are some ways to put a lid on your pet's trash-rooting ways.

FOR DOGS AND CATS

She'll Get a Charge out of It

One approach to keeping your pets from rooting in the trash is to keep them completely away from your trash bins. A good way to do that is to place a deterrent in front of the cans. Consider visiting a pet supply store and picking up a special vinyl mat, such as a Scat Mat, that you can position in front of the trash can. When the mat is plugged in, it emits a weak electrical impulse, similar to a static charge. When your pet jumps on the mat, she'll get an unpleasant but harmless shock. The charge can be set to varying correction levels, making the mat safe for kittens, puppies, and larger cats and dogs. And the mat can be moved from place to place. The one negative aspect is that one of these mats can cost upward of $100, but you may find that it's worth the price.

BEHAVIOR

Spray the Problem Away

A simple way to keep your pet away from the trash is to spray the can with a commercial deterrent called Bitter Apple. You can buy Bitter Apple at most pet supply stores.

FOR DOGS ONLY

Set a Trap

Many dog trainers and other experts recommend booby-trapping the trash. Booby traps are effective be-

ONE PERSON'S SOLUTION

Rock Solid

When I was a kid, we had a dog, Shadow, who liked to knock over our kitchen trash can to get at the food inside. We finally solved the problem by placing a big rock in the bottom of the bin. The rock weighted the can so that Shadow couldn't knock it over.

—**TOM CAVALIERI**
Astoria, New York

cause they correct the animal at the exact moment of the unwanted behavior, so the dog learns precisely what not to do. Here's one booby trap that's effective with submissive dogs (ones that are easily corrected), but it's best used with dogs larger than cocker spaniels. Purchase several Snappy Trainers from a pet supply store or mail-order catalog. A Snappy Trainer has a mechanism much like that of a mousetrap, but it won't catch your pet's paw or injure the animal in any way. Set the Snappy Trainers and lay them, upside down, on top of the trash in the can or on the floor in front of it. When your dog tries to dig through the trash, the Snappy Trainers will go off, snapping and popping in the air. The sound and motion will send your pet the message that trash rooting gets him nothing but a good scare.

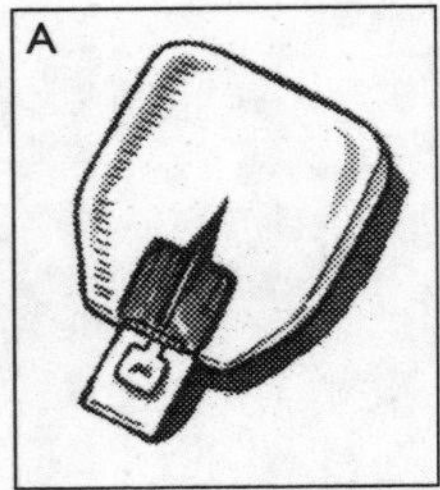

A Snappy Trainer (A) is designed to scare a dog away from trouble —especially trouble in the form of a tempting trash can (B).

Teach Her the Cancan

Here's an expert-recommended booby trap you can make for bold, confident dogs without spending a lot of cash. For it to work, you'll need to make eight to ten "shake cans." (For each one, rinse and drip-dry a soda can and place about ten pennies or screws inside. Tape the can closed with some electrical or duct tape.) You'll also need a piece of cardboard large enough to hold all the cans. Finally, you'll need some strong thread or fishing line. Punch a hole in one end of the cardboard, then place the cardboard somewhere above the trash can—on the back of the toilet if you're rigging the bathroom trash or on the counter near the kitchen trash.

Stack the cans, pyramid style, on the cardboard. Tie the thread or fishing line to the cardboard, threading it through the hole, then bait the line. If your dog always goes for the empty toilet paper roll, use that. If he usually goes after food, tie the line to a paper towel that you've used to pat dry a piece of meat. Place the baited line on top of the trash, then wait a bit. Sooner or later, your pooch will take the bait, setting off an enormous cacophony of noise. After three or four times, he'll get tired of scaring himself and leave the trash alone.

The best booby traps are painless, but oh, the commotion they cause! To discourage a trash rooter, set a pyramid of shake cans in a precarious spot next to the trash, then link them to the garbage with fishing line.

Don't Make It Worth His Trouble

If every time your dog roots through the trash he finds a tasty ham bone or juicy piece of leftover steak, it won't matter much how you booby-trap the can. Most dogs will tolerate whatever slings and arrows their owners throw their way as long as there's a delectable treat waiting for them. Your only chance in that case may be to move the really tasty trash into a closet trash can or out to the porch or garage. Or if your dog sleeps outside at night, store the trash indoors.

Lock Him Out

Putting the trash on the porch isn't always an option for apartment dwellers. An alternative is to purchase a sturdy can that comes with a locking lid. You'll find such cans at most home supply stores.

WANDERING

Few things are worse than looking in the kitchen, den, or backyard and realizing that your pet's not there. Unfortunately, pets run off, escape, and sometimes are taken from us. Here are some steps you can take to prevent your pet from flying the coop—as well as some ideas to follow if your friend has already disappeared.

BEHAVIOR

FOR PETS IN GENERAL

It Should Go without Saying . . .

❑ Some pets, especially cats, don't like collars and tags, but you need to get your pet used to them as early as possible. Keep an ID tag, which includes your name, address, and phone number, on your pet at all times because you never know when she'll dart away. You can order tags through your vet or local animal shelter.

COMMON MISTAKES

Fence Me In

Many dog owners use a product known as an invisible fence to keep a dog in the yard. Here's how the system works. Antenna wires are buried along the perimeter of the yard and then marked with small flags. The dog wears a computerized collar that beeps when he gets too close to the boundary marked by the flags. If the dog tries to cross the boundary, he receives a shock—a mild one, but unpleasant nonetheless.

The invisible fence is a popular tool, but even if you have one, you should not leave your dog unattended. Although the fence does keep your pet in the yard, it doesn't keep other dogs or people out. Pets need protection and attention from their owners. It's fine to use an invisible fence to monitor your dog's activity, but don't use it as a pet-sitter.

If Found, Return to Grand Canyon

❑ If a pet wanders away from your home, you have a pretty good chance of finding him. But if he escapes during a family vacation, you'll have a problem, especially if his tags list your home address and phone number. Make sure the tag your pet wears while traveling with you includes the address and phone number of your vacation accommodations, as well as your home address and phone number. (If you don't feel comfortable broadcasting your address to the world, include your work phone number or E-mail address.) That way, if your pet wanders off, whoever finds him will be able to contact you wherever you are. If you know you'll be incommunicado on the road, list the name, address, and phone number of a willing friend or neighbor, and make sure to alert that person to any medical conditions your pet may have.

And He'll Fit Right In at the Biker Bar

❑ It's a sad fact that stray animals are often picked up by dishonest folks who sell them to laboratories that use them for research. Tags and collars offer little protection, since they can be easily removed. Tattooing has become a more popular way of permanently identifying animals, since reputable labs won't buy dogs that are tattooed. Your vet tattoos a code, unique to your pet, on the inside of his hind leg. That code is entered into a database. If your pet is found, the shelter staff calls the database and can identify your pet and return him to you. To find out more about tattooing, ask your vet or contact your local animal shelter.

Take a Mug Shot

❑ Smart homeowners know it's a good idea to have photos of their valuables on hand for insurance pur-

How Long Is Long Enough?

How long do you continue a correction or training method before you know it's either working or not working? There's no one answer to that question. It depends on the dog. But here are some things to keep in mind.

1. Evaluate whether you're being consistent, correcting the dog each and every time she exhibits the behavior you don't want. If you're not, you're sending the dog mixed messages.

2. Consider the breed of the dog. Sporting and hunting dogs—retrievers, for instance—were bred to work as part of a cooperative team. They are likely to respond fairly quickly to well-timed and consistent guidance. Other dogs were bred to work alone or only with other dogs. Terriers, for example, were bred for their determination and persistence (they were used for vermin control). You may have to repeat a correction or rechannel an activity dozens of times before such a dog changes or redirects her behavior.

3. Think about the individual personality of your dog. Is she bold? Shy? Compliant? Remember that no matter what the "standard" personality traits of your dog's breed, every dog is an individual.

So how do you know when to say when? If you've tried a correction method consistently every day for five to seven days and have seen no improvement in your dog's behavior, it's time to reassess your training strategy.

poses. But it's also a good idea to have good, clear photos of your pet in case she runs away. If Fluffy disappears, you can photocopy the photos for posters and leave copies with your local animal shelter.

Rover, Come Home

❑ If your pet runs away, your first course of action should be to search the immediate neighborhood. Take a walk or a drive around the block, calling your pet's name.

Put Out an APB

❑ After you're sure your pet is missing (and not just hiding on top of the refrigerator), contact the local animal control officer, the nearby Humane Society and animal shelters, your vet, and other vets in your area (you'll find them listed under Veterinarians in the Yellow Pages). If you live in a large city, you'll find the phone number for your animal control officer listed in the blue government pages of your local phone directory under Animals. If you live in a small town or just don't have blue pages in your phone book, contact your local city or town hall.

Tell all the officials you contact that you've lost your dog or cat (or other pet) and give them a good description of the animal, including what name the animal answers to. If the pet has any special medical conditions, be sure to mention that to the animal control officer and the shelters as well. Don't forget to leave your name, address, and day and evening phone numbers so people can reach you if they do find your pet.

Ferrets: He Hides, You Seek

Ferrets are funny little creatures. They'll scamper all around your house and get into every kind of mischief, crawling behind the sofa, into the dryer, and up into the recliner. The problem is once their batteries run down, they fall asleep—no matter where they are. So if your ferret suddenly gets tired just as he's burrowed under your sofa cushion, he'll zonk out right under the cushion. That means he's in danger of being squished if someone decides to have a seat.

So ferret owners, be careful. It's best never to let your pal roam around the house unattended. And if he should get out of your sight, make sure to check carefully before you switch on the dryer. Or pull out the sofa bed. Or throw out the trash. Or . . .

Wanted: Sparky

❑ Many folks find their missing pets by putting up posters around the areas where they lost their animals. To do this, make photocopies of your pet's picture and mount one on each poster. Then add a complete description of the animal—height, weight, identifying characteristics, and what name she answers to. Include the date the pet disappeared, and don't forget to list your phone number. Post the flyers all over your town or neighborhood, including bulletin boards in Laundromats, grocery stores, and other public places. If you always take your dog to the same park or dog walk, make sure to put up plenty of posters there, too.

It Pays to Advertise

❑ Consider placing a classified ad in your local newspaper to report your pet's disappearance. People who find animals often check the lost and found section of the paper when they're trying to locate a pet's owner.

Pet Net

❑ If you have access to a computer and an Internet connection, check out the U.S. Department of Agriculture's Web site devoted to lost and found pets. (Search using the keywords "USDA," "lost," and "pet.") On that site, you can enter information about your missing pet and check out descriptions of found pets. If you don't have a computer, visit your local library. Many now offer free Internet connection time and instruction.

COST CUTTERS

How to Create Missing-Pet Posters That Don't Fall Apart

Your pet is missing, and you've gone to a lot of effort to put together posters seeking the animal's safe return. The trouble is once it rains or snows, your posters will probably get ruined. If you don't want to pay to have the posters laminated (which is quite expensive), try this solution.

Visit a local home center or discount store and purchase rolls of clear contact paper. Roll out a sheet, backing side up, on the bare floor or another large, flat surface. Anchor the corners so that the paper won't roll up, then peel off the backing. Lay the posters, printed side down, on the contact paper, placing them as close together as possible. Then roll out another piece of contact paper, peel off the backing, and lay it on top of the posters. (This will be a lot easier if you have someone helping you.) Finally, cut the posters out, using a box cutter and a yardstick to guide you. Your posters will last until Lassie comes home.

FOR CATS ONLY

In a Thimble?

Cats can squeeze into some mighty small spaces, so if yours has disappeared and you're sure she could not have gotten outside, check even the tiniest spaces in your house. That means looking between sofa cushions, behind furniture, under the sink, in the attic, in drawers, and in filing cabinets.

She's Just Homesick

Since cats become attached to places rather than people, it's not unusual for them to try to return to their old homes when their families move. If you've recently moved and your former residence is not far from your new one, that's the first place to look.

Let Him Settle In

If you have moved and you own a cat, you can prevent your pet from making a beeline to the old house by keeping him inside, even if he's an outdoor cat, for the first several weeks after you relocate. That way, he'll have some time to get used to your new place and begin to think of it as home. Of course, you'll have to provide a litter box or two in the interim. (Use soil instead of litter to minimize the adjustment required.) As long as your cat knows where the boxes are, there shouldn't be any problem. The easiest way to show your pet the way to each box is to lead him there. Try making a game of the process by playing "chase the string."

She Won't Go Far

If your indoor cat darts out the door when you're not looking, start your search right in your own yard, close to the house. Once they actually escape, many indoor cats become so nervous that they don't go very far. Check around the front porch, under the house, in the shrubs, and in any other small, secure spaces.

LIVING WITH PETS

Whose House Is It, Anyway?

You've made it past the hectic, irritating, glorious first weeks with your pet. And now you discover that, even though (most) of the puddle cleaning and "getting to know you" conflicts are behind you, living with a pet on a daily basis presents plenty of demands. The challenges really fall into two categories: the self-discipline you must develop to keep your pet clean, fit, and well-tended over the long haul; and the creativity you must call on to keep enjoying your pet and to keep your pet loving life in your household. In other words, you need routine, but not so much that it becomes monotonous.

To walk that fine line, you'll need to learn the practical stuff: how to be heart-healthy exercise buddies, how and when to be travel pals, how to find the right pet-sitter, how best to pick up shedding hair or salvage cat-scratched furniture, how to coerce your child into feeding the dog.

But you'll also need to concentrate on ways to enjoy your pet, day after day, at every phase of the animal's adult life. Not only does

that ensure that your pet won't be neglected, but it also ensures that you'll have some fun, too, whether you're creating an instant hideaway for a hamster, playing cat and mouse with kitty, or swimming laps with your dog by your side.

Sometimes you'll need the right words to go with your actions. Your new role as proud pet owner calls for a repertoire of diplomatic approaches to dealing with those trying people who don't appreciate your beloved friend, who let their children tease your pet, or who simply don't realize that they are mistreating their own animals. In this chapter, we offer lots of options for all these sticky situations.

Last, although nobody likes to think about it, you must prepare yourself to deal with your pet's waning days and death—always offering due respect, love, and compassion. After all, that's what pet ownership is all about: being there from the beginning and seeing your pet through to the end.

FIRST THINGS FIRST: SPAYING AND NEUTERING

Unless your dog or cat is a champion breed, has a rock-solid pedigree, or has eight to ten good homes lined up for her offspring because she's so good-tempered or talented, you should opt not to add to the world's dog population. Although this seems to bring up some emotional issues, particularly for male owners, rest assured: The operation in no way degrades the animal (animals really don't have the same feelings about their sexuality as humans do). It is safe, and the pain is carefully countered with anesthesia. Here's how to go about getting your pet "fixed."

FOR DOGS AND CATS

Coming of Age

When should your pet be spayed or neutered? The surgery can be performed as early as age 10 to 12

A WORD FROM DR. DEVINNE

What on Earth . . . ?

DR. CHARLES DEVINNE
of Peterborough, New Hampshire, who has more than 15 years of veterinary experience and whose private practice currently concentrates on dogs and cats

Seeing dogs mating can be a disturbing experience if you don't know what's going on. And we've had instances where people have been really confused by it—especially if they happen to catch the dogs during a particular stage, when the two animals are facing in opposite directions.

Take my word for it: He's really locked in there. A male dog gets a very large bulb on the penis at that point, making it nearly impossible to disengage. Unfortunately, we've seen people try all sorts of things to separate them, either not knowing what's going on or trying to prevent an unplanned mating. They dump water on the animals, spray them with a hose, even try to manually pull them apart. In the process, they can do a lot of damage to the female as well as to the male.

Take my advice: Leave them alone. They know what they're doing. And if you're trying to prevent a pregnancy from an unplanned mating, forget about it; the damage has been done. By the time you spot them, it's just too late.

5 *Good Reasons to Have Your Pet Snipped*

No one wants to add to the world's population of unwanted animals. But if you need more motivation than that before you decide to get your cat or dog spayed or neutered, consider these additional benefits of the operation.

1. Marmaduke will be less likely to take issue with every male dog in the vicinity, as well as the letter carrier and the two-year-old next door. Neutering reduces aggression in dogs.

2. Fluffy or Tom will no longer spray his territory—probably. There's no guarantee here, but *most* animals will stop.

3. Neighborhood dogs will no longer scrap and howl at the back door when Millie's in heat.

4. Marmaduke won't break chains or bolt to strange neighborhoods and through traffic to satisfy biological urges.

5. Tom won't yowl at all hours or come home missing half an ear after trying to win his lady love.

weeks. It's generally recommended that you have the procedure done before the animal reaches puberty—that's about age 6 months. Check with your vet to find out more precisely when your pet is ready.

If cats start spraying, they're past the age of readiness. But fear not, neutering or spaying usually eliminates the spraying habit, or at least cuts down on the supersmelly hormones in the spray.

Do You Have an Appointment?

Neutering and spaying are often day surgeries. Unless your vet prefers to keep the animal overnight to be sure the recovery from anesthesia is complete, it's a good idea to make the appointment early in the day so that you can drop your pet off first thing and pick her up in the late afternoon or early evening.

Unless you're at home during the workweek, try to get a Friday appointment. That gives you the weekend to keep an eye on your recuperating pet.

Please Don't Eat the Stitches

Cats and dogs want to lick their wounds, and they don't make an exception for surgical cuts. To keep animals from disturbing the sutures, veterinarians have devised an E, or Elizabethan, collar, which looks really weird but does the job. The collar fits around an animal's head, blocking any attempts at licking. If your vet doesn't provide your pet with such a device, ask him about it.

A low-cost alternative to the Elizabethan collar is simply a bucket (for dogs) or margarine tub (for cats) with the bottom removed, inverted and fitted to your pet's neck. Your veterinarian or clinic may use the low-cost alternative, but find out. If the vet is planning to use the Elizabethan collar, ask her about using the bucket or tub approach instead. You might even start a trend in your area!

After surgery, an old plastic bucket fitted around a dog's neck will keep the animal from licking the stitches. And it's less expensive than a more traditional Elizabethan collar.

DIET FOR A SMALL MENAGERIE

There are three categories of food for pets: food they need, food they'll eat, and food they want. Your job is to sort out your pets' nutritional needs, make sure what they need gets in their mouths, and find ways to let them enjoy their food without just "living to eat." Here are ways to balance your roles as dietitian, chef, server, and food psychologist.

FOR DOGS AND CATS

That Package Was Too Big to Lift Anyway

Always transfer leftover dry food to an airtight container as soon as you open the package—or at least close the bag tightly. And avoid buying large, economy-size bags of food if you have only one small dog or cat. Pet foods can become rancid if stored improperly or for too long.

FOR DOGS ONLY

Crunch and Munch

Feed your pooch dry food. In addition to providing the nutrition density a dog needs, it provides crunch and munch, which is critical for healthy teeth and gums.

Kick the Canned

Avoid canned foods. They average 65 to 75 percent water, and virtually all are messy and smelly to deal with. Dogs will quickly pick up the soft, mushy habit, too, because canned food is tastier than dry and easy to gulp down.

If you can't resist giving your pet canned food, go for the "science formula" foods made by such upscale producers as Iams and Science Diet. These are the canned foods that come closest to meeting a dog's nutritional needs, but even they should be mixed with dry kibble for healthy teeth and gums.

The Gradual Mix and Switch

If your adult dog has always eaten strictly canned food, switch to kibble in increments, starting with one part kibble and three parts canned the first week and moving to an additional part kibble during successive weeks. If you introduce the switch too quickly, your dog's digestive system could react violently.

Get Your Dog to Eat—But Not Too Much

Generally speaking, you should feed your dog morning and evening. (If your dog will eat only one of those times, you'll have to go with that choice.) But clear the dishes after 15 minutes. This practice sets up a good habit for any dog and corrects bad habits for already overweight dogs because it discourages eating too much—a real temptation if there's a full dish at all times. Plus it will keep your hound from eating food to comfort himself when you're not around. You can start the timed feedings anytime, even if a dog has followed a different routine for ten years or more.

FOR CATS ONLY

Kitties Can Do

If your cat's not already addicted, don't choose canned food. Although it will meet your pet's nutritional requirements, it costs more than dry food, it's fussy to open, and it makes cats have loose stools that smell worse than normal. Plus, the canned foods that cats really like tend to give them fish breath.

When They'd Rather Pine Than Switch

 Show cats aside, most "canned food only" cats can adjust to a hard chow diet or a new brand of food if you introduce it over a period of weeks. Start by replacing one-fourth of your cat's food with the new stuff. After three or four days, increase the proportion so that the new brand makes up half the meal. Keep this up until you're feeding your cat only the new food. As long as you keep the process gradual, most cats will accept it.

5 *Reasons Not to Give Kitty an All-Day Buffet*

The best way to feed cats is to set out food twice a day, for about 20 minutes each time, and then toss whatever's left. The advantages:

1. Fluffy will know *you're* in control of the vittles, not her. This discourages cats from making food yet another control issue, which can make them eat too much or ignore food just to show they're the ones in charge. Your being in charge of the food also makes it simpler to change diets or administer a regulated diet.

2. You won't have trouble with rotting food or vermin. Old canned food gets stinky, old dry food gets stale, and either is a lure for mice or roaches.

3. Tom's teeth won't suffer. The saliva and acid associated with constant crunching and nibbling make cats more susceptible to resorptive lesions—the kitty equivalent of cavities.

4. Fluffy's less likely to gain weight. Cats that just don't know when to quit—particularly adopted strays, which are used to feast-or-famine bingeing—will have to quit when the food is gone.

5. There's less eating to win. In a multicat family, some cats will eat more than they want just to keep another cat from getting more than his fair share. The 20-minute time limit cuts down on competition.

LIVING WITH PETS

FOR FISH ONLY

Some Like Live Bait

Oscars, firemouths, and other cichlids prefer live fish in their diets. You'll have to sacrifice some small goldfish or guppies from the pet store or the pet department of a discount store to feed the larger fish. Or you can raise them to accept large flakes, floating pellets, or food sticks.

COMMON MISTAKES

Fish Don't Eat Like Whales

Many people dump enough food in their fish tanks to feed the fish for a month. But when it comes to eating, less is better than more for fish. They continually look for food, and if they consume too much of it too fast, they can get sick and die. Feed them once a day at a regular time so that they'll get used to a schedule. Give them only as much as they can eat in about five minutes, but if they eat it very quickly, give them a pinch more.

If you're going away for a couple of days, put a weekend feeder in the tank. This is actually compressed food that dissolves slowly to provide a food source for your fish over a period of time.

FOR POCKET PETS

Descended from Desert Stock

Feed your gerbils a seed mix, also known as lab chow, that comes in a block and contains the vitamins and minerals these animals need. As desert-type animals, gerbils don't need much water, but they are sure to welcome a few extra seeds or the crumbs from a piece of shelled walnut.

Oh, Say, Where's the C?

Be sure to feed your guinea pigs a mix designated specifically for that type of animal. Don't give them rabbit pellets, which may look much the same but don't contain the vitamin C that guinea pigs need. Without food formulated especially for them, guinea pigs will develop scurvy.

Eating as an Art Form

Guinea pigs genuinely adore chowing down, so you can give them produce extras without the risk that they won't eat their pellet mix. They share food likes with rabbits (which also can partake freely of produce and still want pellets): a little hay; some homegrown green beans, peas, or

A WORD FROM DR. EMERSON

Your Bird Needs Food for Thought

DR. WENDY EMERSON
Veterinarian who makes house calls in and around Topsfield, Massachusetts, to care for cats, dogs, and a wide range of exotic pets

It used to be that people fed their birds one thing: seed. But new information on exotic birds says that the less seed they get, the better. In fact, I call seed the death diet because the birds I see that have eaten nothing but seed all their lives have many more health problems, age faster, and die much younger than birds whose primary diet is formula pellets.

When I tell this to new bird owners, they resist. It doesn't seem natural, they say, for a bird to eat these phony pellets. My response: Hey, there aren't any parrots in South America sitting around eating sunflower seeds. That's not natural either. Pellets have the exact nutritional formula that your bird requires. Augment them if you want with some fresh fruits and vegetables, a little rice or pasta, or dried fruits. My pet bird loves sweet potatoes and watermelon. And when you're choosing foods for your bird, think in terms of things that are interesting to eat. Birds are smart. Unlike other pets, they need foods that make them think. My dog has been eating the same food every day for eight years, and he still gets excited to see it. But I know my Senegal parrot, Rafiki, will get bored with the same old thing. Once in a while, he needs to peel a few grapes.

turnips; a bit of watermelon rind. Don't overdo the lettuce, which has little food value and will cause diarrhea. Other than that, just keep it fresh and make sure to remove the decayed food at the end of every day. Neither animal will eat anything wilted.

LIVING WITH PETS

FOR RABBITS ONLY

Food Fight!

Feed your rabbit from a heavy ceramic bowl. These animals are unrepentant food dish flingers, using their buckteeth to toss their dinner plates. This wastes a lot of food and makes a mess. So if you feed your pet from a lightweight container, you may regret it.

FOOD TREATS

Most pets—even tropical fish—appreciate a little tickle of the taste buds. Those with less sophisticated palates (golden retrievers come to mind) may not know what they're eating but will relish a little extra anything from their much-adored owners. Still, a food treat should be a rare indulgence, sold or prepared especially for animals. For the most part, it should *not* be a helping of whatever the owners are indulging in. And before you go spend your mad money on beluga caviar, be fore-

Taste Treats for Your Pup

The foods that dogs consider treats vary widely, so it's worth your while to experiment, keeping in mind that some dogs like spicy foods and some will retch on your carpet at a hint of garlic. Some pups also have grain allergies and downright weird preferences (just like humans). No pet should be given human food on a regular basis, but on special occasions, treats could include any of the following:

1. Two dice-size cubes of hard cheese
2. Two or three slices of raw carrot
3. A piece of sourdough bread
4. One-half cup of cooked chicken (be sure to remove all the bones)
5. A meatball or bit of cooked hamburger
6. A few sections of an orange
7. A few slices of apple

Commercial biscuits and jerky also are fine if offered no more than once a day. (You may need to increase the treat giving while you're training the pup.) Make certain that the treats are not so small that they'll lodge in your dog's throat if she decides to down one in a single gulp.

COST CUTTERS

The Best Dog Biscuit Recipe Ever

You do not have to be Julia Child to whip up something that your dog will sit, roll over, and beg for. And at less than a dollar a dozen, it's hard to beat the price. But the greatest thing about these biscuits, besides their taste and their price tag, is that you know precisely what's in them. Allow about an hour to make and bake these treats. The recipe yields approximately two dozen two- by two-inch biscuits.

- 3 cups minced parsley
- ¼ cup finely shredded carrot
- ¼ cup grated Parmesan or shredded sharp cheddar cheese
- ¼ cup olive or canola oil
- 2½ cups whole wheat flour
- ½ cup unbleached bread flour
- 1 teaspoon mild paprika
- 2 tablespoons crushed whole bran cereal
- 2 teaspoons baking powder
- ½ to 1 cup chicken, beef, or vegetable broth (or water)

Preheat the oven to 350°F. In a large bowl, stir together the parsley, carrot, and cheese. Add the oil and mix. Measure the flours by spooning them into a measuring cup. In a small bowl, stir them together with the paprika, bran cereal, and baking powder. Add the dry ingredients to the cheese mixture, then add ½ cup broth or water, stirring to mix well. Add more broth if needed to form a moist dough. Turn the dough out onto a lightly floured surface and knead four or five times.

With a floured rolling pin on a floured surface, roll the dough to a ½-inch thickness. Using a dog bone–shaped cookie cutter, the rim of a juice glass, or a clean, empty single-serving tuna can, cut out shapes and transfer them to a lightly greased baking sheet. (Other simple shapes also work well, as long as all the biscuits to be baked in one batch are about the same size.) Gather the scraps of dough, roll them out, and cut out more biscuits.

Bake for 20 to 30 minutes, depending on the size biscuits you're making. The biscuits should be brown and somewhat hard. They'll get crunchier once they're out of the oven. Cool on a wire rack or waxed paper. Store in an airtight container.

warned: Cats have been known to turn up their noses at any treat, no matter how many other cats have eaten it and loved it, no matter how much it cost, and no matter how much they loved it last week. They can be nearly as difficult as humans!

LIVING WITH PETS

FOR DOGS AND CATS

Let's Not Create Animal Overeaters

Be judicious in choosing times to dole out treats. When your pet behaves well during a trying experience—say, a trip to the veterinarian—it's appropriate to reward the animal with a treat immediately afterward. But don't shut the animal up in the laundry room with a ham slice for consolation because no one's given him the time of day in a week. If you offer a pet a food treat in lieu of attention or affection, then presto, an overeater is born!

FOR CATS ONLY

Every Litter Bit Stinks!

If yours is a strictly indoor cat, avoid giving him pungent fish products—sardines, mackerel, kippers, canned salmon—as a treat. His litter box output will be unbearably smelly if you slip up on this.

On Saturday, Tabby Gets Tuna

Try to limit treat giving to once a week or so. Otherwise, stick to kitty's regular fare. Don't play to a pet's finicky nature by getting more and more inventive with the treats. Cats will take advantage if you let them and can get diarrhea from many foods, so be firm and don't allow them to demand pâté on a regular basis.

How Could Morris Turn These Down?

If you're willing to risk rejection, try offering any of these as an occasional treat: a dollop of canned tuna in oil; two tablespoons heavy cream or half-and-half; an ounce or so of meat loaf; two or three sautéed chicken livers; two or three shrimp,

COMMON MISTAKES

This Treat Is a Trick

Some companies market packages of horses' hoof trimmings as chewy snacks for dogs. But these "treats" are dangerous to your pet. They are easy to choke on and may perforate the intestine once they are swallowed. When you buy a chewy treat for your dog, read the label to be sure you're not buying hoof trimmings.

cooked or raw, with shells on; one-quarter cup boned boiled or baked chicken.

FOR BIRDS ONLY

A Honey of a Treat

Cockatiels simply adore honey sticks, which consist of the usual pellets and seeds held together by coagulated honey. They cost so much ($3 to $5 for one) that giving them out as treats seems like the way to go.

A (Fruit) Cocktail Would Be Nice

Give your parrot a honey stick, too. Or tempt him with more creative fruit treats, such as kiwifruit (washed twice to remove even the slightest traces of pesticides) and strawberries cut into small chunks.

Egg Him On

When fresh fruit isn't in season, hard-boil some eggs, mash them, and watch your parrot gobble them up.

COST CUTTERS

These Two Flakes Are Alike

If the flakes labeled for goldfish cost less in your pet supply store than those labeled for tropical fish, buy them. The two products are essentially the same, and flake-eating fish are perfectly happy with either.

FOR FISH ONLY

Care for a Shrimp Cocktail?

Tropical fish really need consistent food more than anything—and not too much of it. But you might offer them an occasional treat of dried brine shrimp (available at pet stores). The fish seem to like it.

FOR POCKET PETS

What Makes a Hamster Happy?

If you want to give your gerbil or hamster something special, try a small dried cob of corn (available at pet or farm supply stores) or a honey stick (from a pet supply or discount store). Rats, mice, gerbils, and hamsters may not like honey sticks (or anything else) better

Lawn and Garden: What's Edible, What's Deadly

Rabbits and guinea pigs love grass, greenery, and even some flowers harvested from the great outdoors. But beware—their tiny systems can't tolerate much poison, so even a taste of the wrong plants can kill them.

What They Can Eat

Wildflowers

- Chickweed *(Stellaria media)*
- Coltsfoot *(Tussilago farfara)*
- Dandelion *(Taraxacum officinale)*
- Goldenrod (*Solidago* species)
- Green clover (*Trifolium* species)
- Groundsel *(Senecio vulgaris)*
- Mallow *(Malva sylvestris)*
- Plantain (*Plantago* species)
- Yarrow *(Achillea millefolium)*

Garden Flowers

- Asters
- Marigolds
- Nasturtiums (especially leaves)
- Sunflowers (especially leaves)
- Sweet peas

What Can Kill Them

Weeds and Wildflowers

- Buttercups (*Ranunculus* species)
- Deadly nightshade *(Atropa belladonna)*
- Scarlet pimpernel *(Anagallis arvensis)*

Garden Flowers

- Flowers or leaves from bulbs, such as tulips
- Lily of the valley
- Rhododendrons

than their usual food, but it's fun to watch them eat these treats.

Have You Ever Met a Finicky Guinea Pig?

Guinea pigs live to eat, so any offering is a treat. Still, if you want something truly special, give your pet one-half cup of one of those fancy prewashed salad green mixes. Look for one that's heavy on the darker greens and lighter on the lettuce (which has little nutritional value).

OTHER TREATS

Most pets thrive on routine, structure, and consistency. But they will get a lift from a little something special, and the owner offering the treat tends to get a good feeling, too. Here's how to perform random acts of kindness without going overboard.

FOR PETS IN GENERAL

Treat Your Pet Wisely

❑ Make each treat something unexpected, something a little extravagant. Treat giving should *not* be a three-times-a-day thing. When treats are offered too frequently, the unusual becomes the ordinary, and a pet can develop bad habits, such as demanding sugar at every meal or barking incessantly if she doesn't get to ride in the car when you go to work.

❑ Never handle a basic necessity as a treat. Daily walks for indoor dogs, for example, are not a treat. Nor is stroking cats every day or cleaning a dirty bird or hamster cage.

What Will Please Your Pet?

❑ Gear your pet's treats to the *pet's* needs, not yours. Pets are not humans. They don't need as much variety, as much spice, as we do. They do need plenty of attention. They don't need a different-flavored food for each meal, a pearl necklace, or a beer at the end of a hard day.

My, My, Don't I Look Lovely Today?

❑ Most birds, some toy breed dogs, and even goldfish enjoy a turn in front of the mirror. Just make sure the mirror is secure on the wall (or wherever it's propped) so that it doesn't crash if the animal makes a sudden movement.

Special Strokes for Special Folks

❑ Most folks know that their dogs and cats enjoy an extra brushing to

COST CUTTERS

If Mister Ed Shops Here, It's Good Enough for Me

You can often obtain rabbit pellets, guinea pig pellets, and cracked corn for ducks from a farm store or feed store. They're usually sold by the scoop for less than you'd pay at a pet store and for a fraction of what they cost at the grocery store. One warning, though: Ask up front whether the store gets plenty of pet customers, to ensure that your low-cost food also is fresh. And don't buy those 20-pound bags of rabbit pellets. They're intended for people who raise multitudes of rabbits for food. At the rate Mopsy eats, 90 percent of the bag will be stale before she gets around to it, and the pellets will lose the mineral composition that your tiny pet needs to thrive. About a month's supply is the most you should buy at once, whether you're shopping for rabbits, rodents, or birds.

A WORD FROM DR. DEVINNE

Something's Rotten in Your Living Room

DR. CHARLES DEVINNE *of Peterborough, New Hampshire, who has more than 15 years of veterinary experience and whose private practice currently concentrates on dogs and cats*

For dogs that need to chew and want to chew, I recommend rawhide—look for pieces that are shaped like big tortilla chips. They're something your dog can chew up, grind up, and swallow safely within an hour or two. And that's an important point.

You don't want your dog chewing on things that last day after day after day, because those things really start to stink. Those huge, length-of-your-arm rawhide bones that people get their dogs for Christmas aren't a very good idea. After about five days—ugh! If you smelled the end of one, believe me, it would just gag you.

remove annoying loose hairs. But other pets like this treatment, too. Try it on ferrets, rabbits, guinea pigs, and even potbellied pigs.

FOR DOGS AND CATS

Make Mine on the Rocks

In summer, place a couple of ice cubes in your cat's or dog's drinking water.

FOR DOGS ONLY

Time Is the Best Treat of All

Dogs live for their owners, and so the best treat for a canine will always be more time or more attention. A walk in the park before you go to work, for example,

will delight your canine friend. Or take your pet for an unexpected ride in the car, bring her along for a quick dip in a nearby pond, or include her on a family picnic.

There's No Pool Like an Old Pool

Fill an outdoor kiddie pool for your dog to dabble in. (This is particularly good for retrievers and shepherds.) The hard plastic kind is best, since dog toenails can puncture all but the best quality (and most expensive) inflatable versions. If you're treating a toy breed or small dog to a dip, make sure the water is either shallow enough so the pet can stand up or deep enough to swim in. The in-between height can cause a tiny pup to drown. Of course, don't leave a small dog unsupervised around a filled wading pool.

FOR CATS ONLY

The Picture of Comfort

Cats like a screened window left partially open in pleasant weather so that they can settle onto the sill and enjoy the breeze.

To give your kitty extra pleasure, let him rest in any warm, cat-size spot that's off the floor. He'll probably love relaxing on a towel placed on top of a clothes dryer, for example. Or leave the shades open so that direct sunlight will fall on an upholstered chair, a couch, or a cushion that you don't mind him sleeping on.

But I Want Your *Pillow*

Every large, soft object appeals to the lazy feline, but you'll make your pet especially happy if you place on a piece of furniture something slightly larger than your cat and with enough yield for the cat's body to create an indentation.

COMMON MISTAKES

For Cats, These Aren't Treats

Some substances that are treats for people are actually poisonous to cats. Certain foods may make your pet mildly ill or cause choking. Others can kill them. To avoid any of these possibilities, never feed your feline any of the following:

- Chocolate (can be fatal)
- Milk (upsets digestion)
- Pure tuna fish (upsets digestion)
- Chicken, meat, or fish with bones (can cause choking)

LIVING WITH PETS

Cats aren't trying to be perverse when they favor your pillow over the brand-new one you just set out. They love the smell of humans—especially *their* humans. So sleep with the new pillow yourself for a night, or "condition" it for a few days on the family room couch. You shouldn't be able to smell your scent after the conditioning, but your kitty's sensitive nose will know.

Let Kitty Look Down on You

Cats deeply desire to be above us all, so create a high perch by clearing an ample space on a dresser or a shoulder-high shelf on a stable, wide bookcase. Make sure there's some acceptable way for the cat to leap to her lookout point.

Just My Size

Any cat likes the security of a container he can just fit in. Leave out a hatbox, pail, or basket—preferably on a table, chair, or other waist-high surface. Or put a large, slope-sided ceramic fruit bowl on your coffee table (not too close to the edge). Leave it empty, and tabby will be happy to pose languidly in it to complete the decor.

COMMON MISTAKES

Chemical-Free or It's Not for Me

Many a bird or small pet has gotten a bellyache or even died from traces of pesticides in its food. Always wash twice any produce from the grocery store or farm stand (even produce labeled as organic) and scrub root vegetables with warm water and a brush. Beware of lawn grass unless you tend and mow it yourself. Fertilizers and pesticides are much more prevalent than you might think, and guinea pigs and rabbits can't stomach them. Never harvest from the side of the road, since exhaust fumes can stick to plants and grass.

FOR BIRDS ONLY

Spray It Again, Sam

Parrots enjoy a warm-water spritz. Buy a water bottle from a discount store for this purpose. Reusing chemical containers is too risky.

FOR FERRETS ONLY

Bring Them Outdoors—Carefully

Your pet ferret will have a great time if you bring her outdoors. But make sure you restrain her on a harness first, and keep a careful eye on her while outside to be sure she doesn't escape into the wild. Domestic ferrets have no hunting instincts, and they're very dependent on people for their survival—even more than dogs and cats. If your ferret picks up an interesting scent, her curious and fearless nature will cause her to wander off, and the prognosis for ferrets on their own is not good.

PETS AND CHILDREN

The bond between pet and child can be breathtaking to behold—unconditional love and tender care at their finest. But there's more to the kid-pet relationship than sentimental moments. Children can tend pets, but they need guidance to do the job right. Here's how to bring out the best and work with the worst when kids and pets live side by side—or just visit back and forth.

FOR PETS IN GENERAL

Age Is *an Object*

❑ The age at which a child can assume the basic responsibility for a pet depends on the animal and the child's maturity level. If a youngster really loves the animal, is willing to care for him, and enjoys him, somewhere around age nine is a good time to start. Some children are ready a year or two earlier, and some are never ready.

The Buck Stops with Mom

❑ Although it boosts a child's self-esteem to call a pet her own and she can certainly take on quite a bit of pet care, a pet is a living thing and a member of the family. Don't leave its well-being up to the kids. Be prepared to nurture the pet—newt or Newfoundland—with the best the

There's a Reason for That Gleam in Kitty's Eye

No, cats can't see in the dark; they need *some* light to activate the sensor cells of their retinas. But cats can see well in one-sixth the light needed by humans. One reason is the *tapetum lucidum*—Latin for "bright carpet"—a layer of glittering cells behind the cat's retina. When light comes into the cat's eye, it passes the light-sensing cells in the retina, is reflected by the mirror cells behind, and hits the retina a second time, enhancing the effectiveness of the light. Coincidentally, the reflection from this "carpet" of cells produces tabby's gleaming eyes.

household has to offer, independent of what the child is able or willing to do.

Let the Kids Choose Their Own Friends

❏ Accept that some children just aren't "animal people." Don't force them to feel guilty that they really don't want to be around the household parakeet or spend hours tending the dog, especially if it's a pet that was adopted when the children were babies or that they never asked for.

Skip the Empty Threats

❏ If you adopted a pet at one child's urging and whining and that child has lost interest, threaten to give the animal away only if you really mean it. Otherwise, you will just provoke guilt and bad feelings and will still end up caring for the animal yourself. Don't be a martyr!

Here's the Goal

❏ Forget lines such as "This is your pet. Don't expect me to feed it (or walk it, or change its litter box)." If you adopted the pet because you thought you'd never need to tend it, you must rearrange your thinking. Adults always have bottom-line responsibility for every member of the family. Better to say "If you aren't going to be able to take care of the cat this week because of football practice, you need to help me work out a schedule of who's going to fill in and how you'll make it up to them." That's a feasible project.

Let Me *Walk the Dog!*

❏ Establish pet care duties as a privilege, not a grudging chore. "Let" a child walk the dog only after she has proved that she can master the concept by, for example, "walking" a pull toy on a leash regularly for a week or two. Take away a pet care privilege as a consequence of other infractions: "You won't be able to brush Fifi tonight because you haven't finished your homework." Of course, to make the tasks seem alluring, you'll have to do them yourself with a cheery grin.

ONE PERSON'S SOLUTION

Different Strokes for Different Cats

Over the years, we've accumulated a number of cats—some of them lovingly chosen, some of them kittens or strays that someone has asked us to take in. Right now, we have ten cats. Every time we bring a new cat in, we have the challenge of determining what that cat needs for a good quality of life. We've learned that we can't go by what the other cats like and need because each animal is different. It takes weeks and sometimes months of experimenting to gauge what the new cat needs.

We've made an effort to give each cat the same *amount* of attention, but with time we've learned that it shouldn't necessarily be the same *type* of attention. Some of our cats want to be held and stroked, some want me to throw a ball or pull a string, and one just really likes being the curmudgeonly old uncle who rarely lets anyone touch him but gets caught being kind every now and then.

Another cat we rescued with his brother seemed as if he didn't want anything from us at all, except to be fed and hang around in the vicinity of the action. Then we boarded all ten cats when we went to Vegas on vacation. Ever since we brought him home, he's wanted a whole lot of loving. You have to stay flexible with cats.

—LIZ SCHIFFLETT
Columbia, South Carolina

Duties for Pet Deputies

❑ Although very young children shouldn't be expected to take full responsibility for a pet's care, even the youngest can *help* to tend pets. For a toddler, helping fill the dog's water bowl or clean the bird's cage is diverting and sets up an attitude of "It's my job to see that the pets are taken care of" that will last a lifetime. If you don't have children in your household, invite a neighbor's child to help out, or a grandchild or other relative.

❑ Give a child who's five to eight years old a regular duty, such as feeding the fish or brushing the cat. Once you've shown the youngster how and supervised him for five to ten days, set up a checklist or calendar so that you can note "job well done" each day. Work toward a small reward for consistent performance.

The Odds Are Good

❑ Surprisingly, the "prize" can work just as well if it's more for the pet than the child. For example, offer to let the child help you pick out a new water bowl for the dog after the youngster has done water detail for 21 days. (Odd numbers of days tickle children, as do unusual dollar amounts. For example, tell your young ones, "We'll spend $1.79 just on treats for Bandit after we've changed his cage three times.")

FOR DOGS AND CATS

Look Out—It's Walking on Two Legs

🐾 Keep the dog's or cat's food dish where a child younger than three years old can't sample the wares. Believe it or not, the concern here is not that the baby might eat something harmful—pet chow is fairly nutritious and digestible—but that the child could choke.

Mommy, Look What I Found!

🐾 Keep all pet medicines in a child-proof cabinet, particularly the heartworm medicine, which looks like brown bread pellets or gum balls.

If you have a small child, or if a toddler spends a lot of time at your house, don't buy those round kitty treats that look like gum balls and are the perfect shape for a toddler to choke on.

These Snacks Weren't Meant to Be Shared

To discourage your young child from habitually munching on dog biscuits, keep pet treats on a high shelf. But don't panic if a baby or child picks up a dog biscuit and gnaws on it—as long as the treat isn't broken into pieces so small that the youngster could choke. The ingredients won't harm the little one.

Polite Answers to Preposterous Remarks Parents Make

Whether at the park, on your porch, or in the veterinarian's office, some parents are bound and determined to let their boisterous tykes interact with your animal. Others are just as insistent about yelling "Bad dog" and scaring their children about calm, well-behaved pets. Here are some tactful ways to assert yourself.

Remark: "Isn't that cute? That puppy's letting her pull his fur!"

Response: "Shall I pull her off, or will you? I don't want my pup thinking I would let someone hurt him without helping him out."

Remark: "She's not scared of dogs!"

Response: "But my dog is scared of people, and sometimes he shows that by biting. He's kind of like a skunk—no trouble at all if we give him some space."

Remark: "It's okay if she gets scratched. She doesn't mind."

Response: "But I mind. You see, if my cat gets aggressive with your child, it could set up a bad habit, and who knows where it would all end. And the next person she scratches might mind." Or "I'm sorry, I just can't afford the doctor bill."

Remark: "Bad dog! He'll hurt you, Sugar Plum."

Response: "I understand that you might know some bad dogs, but Marmaduke here is really friendly. If you want to hold your little girl up, I'll hold him so she can pat him on the head, and then she'll know there are nice dogs, too." Or "I understand that my dog is making you nervous, but you're scaring him with your yelling. I'll move over here if you'll agree to give us some space."

LIVING WITH PETS

See, Dad? Bowser Really Likes *These Treats!*

Babies have a charming habit of giving people food to a dog or cat in undreamed-of quantities or of handing out every treat in the box. Monitor the children and pets when they're together. It doesn't take a supersmart cat or dog long to figure out how to take advantage of a youngster.

So Nice to Come Home To

Children who come home from school to an empty house feel much more secure and loved if a pet is waiting for them. If you don't have children, consider loaning your pet, especially a well-trained dog or playful cat, to such a household for the after-school hours.

COMMON MISTAKES

Toddlers and Tiny Pets: Curiosity Can Kill the Cat

Never leave a child under age four—yours or anyone else's—unsupervised with a puppy or kitten. The well-meaning child could hug the pet to death (particularly a kitten) or squeeze just hard enough to get nipped or scratched, which could create a lifelong terror of animals. Even a tot who has done fine before bears watching, since babies behave differently as they become more mobile and curious.

Bowser Will Be Expecting You

If you work outside the home during business hours, or if the child's home is strictly "no pets," consider loaning the youngster a key to your house. You'll be training a potential pet-sitter at the same time. Of course, you'll need to check with the child's parents first. You'll also need to lay down (and write down) ground rules about which areas of the house he may use and how long he should stay (probably 30 minutes or so). And make sure the youngster knows emergency phone numbers and how to lock the doors behind him.

FOR DOGS ONLY

Grumpy Old Dogs

Remember that an aging dog might not be able to handle the same boisterous treatment he could even a couple of years ago. When a child starts walking and

can pursue the dog, establish a "dogs only" area where your dog can keep away from sharp pokes and too-hearty thumps without resorting to nips and growls of his own.

FOR OTHER PETS

Incredibly Inedible

❍ Keep gerbils, hamsters, fish, water turtles, and frogs out of baby's reach. A baby might squeeze the tiny animals and hurt them. But it's even more likely that the tyke will pop a tiny creature into her mouth. If this happens, call the pediatrician for advice on whether the baby bears watching.

Screen All Visitors

❍ Install on top of the fish tank a tight-fitting screen that clicks into place. Available from fish stores, these screens keep toddlers from dipping in to terrify the fish or pull out seaweed, snails, or gravel for consumption.

But Mom! You Said We Should Share Toys!

❍ Other pet accoutrements are small enough for babies to choke on and fascinating enough to lure little folks. Keep small cat toys, seed sticks for birds, hamster pellets, charcoal for the fish tank, and similar objects out of children's reach.

TOYS

The best pet toys will keep life from being boring for your animals. They're good to have on hand for owner-pet play and even more important for animal entertainment when the owner's not around. But keep two things in mind: Most animals don't need many toys, and the perfect plaything is largely a matter of personal—um, animal—preference. Some pets want the latest gadgets and plastic toys; some play only with the traditional standbys. Some turn up their noses at whatever you spend good money on, and some prefer nothing at all.

Teach Your Dog to Play Frisbee

Quick. You have only about 15 minutes to spend with your dog, but you want to give him (and yourself) some vigorous exercise. The answer? Frisbee. Don't worry if you've never done it. If you have the right canine, Frisbee is pretty easy to teach.

What's the right kind of dog? Retrievers, sporting dogs, and herding dogs are likely candidates, as are any breeds (or individual dogs) that like to chase objects or play fetch. By contrast, dogs that like to lounge—mastiffs, for instance—are probably more interested in napping than Frisbee.

First, you need to get the right toy. The hard, commercial Frisbees are fine for dogs that are experienced players, but if your pooch is just starting out, it's better to opt for one of the small, fabric-covered models. They're sold in catalogs that sell pet toys and also in some backpacking stores. After your dog catches on to the game, you can graduate to the harder Frisbee.

Start with a basic game of fetch. Toss the disk into the air (if he follows it with his eyes, you're off to a good start). If the dog chases after the disk and fetches it, call him back and repeat the drill. Once you're sure he has the hang of it, begin gently tossing the disk to or at him. (Now you know why you start with the soft disk.) With some practice, you'll be on the pro circuit in no time.

FOR DOGS ONLY

Very Nice, but Can She Chew It without Choking?

Whenever you purchase a ball or toy for a dog, make sure it's large enough that if the pet tries to swallow it, the toy won't lodge in the animal's throat. A canine's primary designs on a toy are carrying it in his mouth, chewing it, tossing it, and catching it, so it's important that the toy is too big to swallow.

When you buy your pet a ball to chew on, pick one made of hard rubber or nylon so that the dog gets chewing satisfaction without ingesting bits of plastic. Soft foam balls, such as Nerf Balls, are really not a good buy because tearing them up is no more than an afternoon's work for the average dog. Besides, they make a neon-colored foam-drool mess that can be swallowed and cause blockages.

LIVING WITH PETS

Have a Ball!

If you plan to play fetch (outdoors, that is), make sure any ball you give your pooch will bounce.

Good Picks for Solitary Dogs

If your pet spends a lot of time unattended, look for balls and plastic toys with hard rubbery segments, nubs, depressions, and indentations. These allow a pup to latch onto one end and then flip the toy in the air or across the room—a one-dog version of catch that's great for stay-at-home animals.

Knot(s) for Dogs Only

Give your pet a rope with a knot in the end. This is a great chew toy, as long as it's made of nylon or cotton and as long as the manufacturer took care of the tying (you really want a commercial product here).

FOR CATS ONLY

Batter Up!

When choosing toys for your favorite feline, consider that kittens and cats like to bat small rolling objects, particularly on wood or tile floors. Pencils work, and so do Ping-Pong balls, which are inexpensive (available at sporting goods or discount stores). If you're willing to spend a bit more money, you can buy toys made specifically for this purpose, including light plastic balls with bells in the middle. Get them at pet stores, discount stores, and even full-service grocery stores.

COST CUTTERS

Give That Cat a Noisemaker

Looking for an inexpensive toy for a kitten? A wadded-up piece of paper will catch your kitty's attention—and paws. Make it craft paper or something thicker so that the animal can get it to make a noise. (Tissue paper won't do the trick.) Or delight your cat with a brown paper grocery bag turned on its side. All the pet has to do is creep inside and then punch, rattle, and roll to her heart's content.

LIVING WITH PETS

Let Her Play Cat and Mouse

Cats like to play with mice—or anything that's similar in size or shape. See if Fluffy will go for one of those stuffed mice with spring-wound wheels; you rev them up by scraping them on the floor. These are popular with many cats, and they don't have batteries to run down. If you can't find one at your local pet store or discount pet supply outlet, ask the store to order one for you.

COST CUTTERS

Grow Your Own Catnip

Some cats are fools for catnip. It's actually a *drug* for cats, and just a whiff of this mysterious mint turns many of them into zany, weaving, silly clowns. (*Caution:* It may even be addictive, so it's best offered only on an occasional basis.) If your cat's a catnip fan, you've probably already learned that a single catnip mouse can cost $3 to $4—if you can even find one. A cheaper alternative? For just a few bucks, you can grow enough catnip to supply the whole neighborhood. Here's how.

Start with seeds. You can usually get a packet for a couple of dollars from a local nursery or home supply store or from a mail-order seed company such as Park Seed Company. Call toll-free directory assistance (1-800-555-1212) to get the telephone number for Park, then call the company to place an order.

Plant outside. Sow the seeds in rows 18 inches apart in a garden or in one row down the middle of a flower box at least 16 inches wide and 10 inches deep. Plant in well-worked soil and in an area that receives moderate to strong sun. The seeds are fine, like basil seeds, so you might want to mix them with sand for easy sowing.

Mulch. The plants prefer rich soil but will settle for almost any soil as long as it's mulched with hay, dried lawn clippings, straw, or cocoa hulls.

Harvest. Catnip grows quickly and can reach a few feet high in a few months. When the plant reaches at least 18 inches high and has thumb-size leaves, but before it turns yellow, strip the leaves or cut the entire stalks.

Dry. Tie the stalks together and hang them upside down in the shade for a couple of days. Or lay the leaves on old newspaper in the shade.

Play. Bring a stalk out for the cats to rub against or roll on. Or crumble dried leaves and/or stems

Order Her a Toy to Go

Give your kitten one of the small toys from a McDonald's Happy Meal. Most of these are about the right size and shape (and have the right mechanics) to intrigue playful kitties.

Are You Through with That Box?

To create a Magic Kingdom for a kitty, set a small, empty, open cardboard box (about the size of a bread

and tie them into four-inch squares of material using cotton string or thread. The cats will bat them, bite them, and possibly eat the contents. If you want to get really fancy, try stitching up a homemade cat toy (see illustration). Use a laundry marker to add eyes and whiskers if you like. Stuff the toy with crumbled dried catnip (mixed with dried lentils if you don't have enough) before stitching the thing closed. Use a glue gun to attach some felt ears. Voilà! A catnip mouse.

Start a toy mouse with a felt circle (A). Fold it in half and stitch the edges (B) almost all the way around. Turn the fabric inside out (C) and decorate (D).

Peekaboo! Kitty will love a homemade hiding place.

box) on the floor—preferably a hard floor so that when the cat jumps in, she'll get some skidding action. For lots of fun, drum your fingers on the outside.

Set the same box on its side for a kitty "room with a view." Or close it up and cut a hole just larger than the cat's tummy in the side to give your cat an instant hidey-hole/crawl space.

IT'S PLAYTIME!

Pets aren't just comforting, companionable, and a fine measure of an owner's ability to take on responsibility—they're also fun. And this is never so true as when we get to play with them, whether it's a formal game of catch or an impromptu round of "what's behind this newspaper?" As long as you keep basic safety precautions in mind, this is your chance to innovate, experiment, and truly enjoy your pet.

FOR DOGS ONLY

The Paw Is Quicker Than the Eye

Hold a treat or a small rubber ball in one closed fist, with nothing in the other. Ask your dog "Which hand?" When he noses one, open your hand to show him whether he's right. If he's not, put your hands behind your back, then go again. (You can keep the treat or ball in the same hand or the opposite one. It makes no difference.) If you really want to impress friends and family, rub a beloved scent—say tuna fish or bologna—on a rubber ball, and your dog should "guess" correctly every time.

FOR CATS ONLY

And Now for the Late-Breaking News . . .

Looking for an easy way to entertain your kitty? Tap your finger on your side of an open newspaper page and watch the cat pounce.

Try Fishin' for Kitty Fun

At a pet supply store, purchase a stick that has a fishing line with feathers attached to the end. Then devise your own ways to tantalize your cat—for example, hold the stick as high as your pet can comfortably jump, then bring it down. Or crouch behind the couch and dangle the feathers on the cushions.

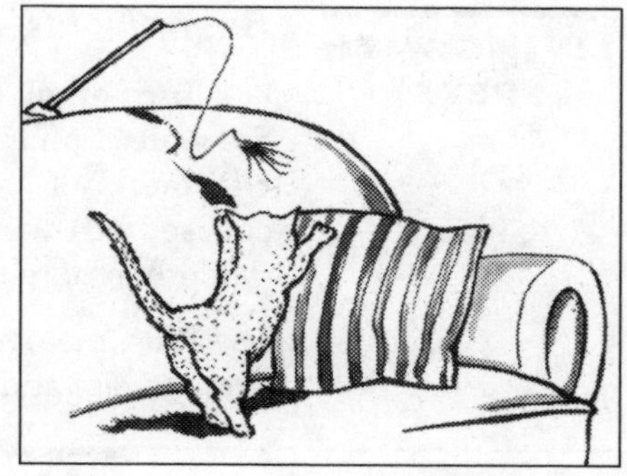

Gotcha! Watch your pet go for a good line.

Up the Down Staircase

Roll a tennis ball or a bouncy rubber ball down the stairs, or send a child's Slinky end over end down the same route. Then stand back and watch your cat charge. (Most canines aren't agile enough for stair play, so don't try this with a pup.)

Under the Covers

Run your fingers under the comforter on the bed and watch kitty pounce (but firmly say "No claws" if she unsheathes). If she gets bored with the game, use your fingernail to make a scratching sound on the fabric (polyester blends are the best), then stop. That will attract her attention. Start and stop the scratching noise at unpredictable intervals and keep insisting "I think I hear a mouse." She'll go along with the game for years after she knows it's just your fingers.

Me and My Shadow

Turn off the overhead light and turn on a low-light lamp. Then make shadows on an undecorated wall in an area your kitty can reach. Some cats will jump and pounce on the shadows as readily as they go after three-dimensional prey. For variety, make shadows with a reed, a feather, or another wispy object.

COST CUTTERS

Frugal Fun for Felines

Here's a cheap, homemade toy to add to your collection. Buy a little catnip at any pet store, then pour it into an old sock and knot the sock. Your cat will love it, it won't matter if he tears it apart, and most of us have an endless supply of mateless socks.

LIVING WITH PETS

Bright Lights, Big Kitty

Turn off all the lights and run a flashlight around the walls. Some cats will attack the light, while others will merely follow it with their eyes. Still others, of course, will wonder why you're acting so silly and patently ignore you.

With the overhead lights out, take a compact disc from its case and run it under a desk lamp that's turned

COST CUTTERS

One Man's Junk Is a Rodent's Treasure

Mice, hamsters, gerbils, and particularly guinea pigs are the ultimate recyclers. They'll be delighted if you take some of the household refuse you'd normally discard and instead turn it into great playhouses and climbing/hiding/jumping toys for them. Just make sure there's no chance that the cardboard has any sort of pesticide on it (avoid produce boxes, for example). And don't use plastic—it can break off and cut nibbling mouths or be ingested and cause gastrointestinal bleeding. The best part about all of these materials is that when they get gnawed, urinated on, or worn-out, you can just throw them away. For example, you could try:

Empty toilet paper rolls. These are great for mouse-size rodents to tunnel through or to hide in if you fasten a paper napkin over one end with a rubber band. Put the roll on the bottom of the cage or "play box," or add a little height by resting it or taping it on an empty cardboard pudding box (the large size). You can create a similar effect with empty paper towel rolls, but be sure to cut them to half their original length. Otherwise, a tiny pet can get stuck in the middle.

A napkin, a toilet paper roll, and a pudding box: heaven for a hamster.

Empty cardboard boxes. The big ones (such as moving boxes) make great playhouses for guinea pigs. Slightly smaller ones (such as book boxes) make good playhouses

on, tilting the disc from side to side. This will create a fascinating reflection on the wall—one that will move as you tilt the CD. Clear a path so that kitty can pounce at will.

Watch Out for Hairy Situations

When a kitten's lying on her back, never put your head on her belly and let her use you as a punching

for hamsters. To spruce things up a bit, let kids or creative friends draw some designs on the outside with nontoxic crayons or markers.

Old newspapers. Use several small-town newspapers or several sections of a metropolitan newspaper to line the bottom of a guinea pig's or mouse's cardboard playhouse. They will keep urine from reaching and ruining the cardboard, and they can be replaced when too many droppings pile up. Also use newspapers to make your own burrowing material by grasping a section at the fold, and shredding one-inch strips all the way down. Pile the papers as high as the top of the playhouse. The tiny guys can breathe through them just fine and will have them tamped down in no time.

Hold a section of newspaper at the fold and tear off strips (A) to create ideal burrowing material (B).

A broken clipboard or similar-size piece of plywood. Remove the metal from the clipboard and prop the end of the board or the plywood on a wooden block or a one-pound rectangular butter or margarine box. Place it in your guinea pig's play box or regular cage. Guinea pigs like to run up ramps and even jump off—if you start them on the habit before they're full-grown.

bag. It's fun the first few times, but an adult cat will eventually start using his claws, and it's hard to disentangle when your cat's got your head.

The same goes for letting cats play with long hair. Don't do it, because they'll come to think that all hair is fair game, even that on children and visitors who do not want a feline missile pouncing on their carefully coifed heads.

COST CUTTERS

5 Instant Toys for Kittens

Kittens are easy to please. If you can swish it and they can gallop toward it and pounce on it, they'll like it. Here are five possibilities to get you started.

1. A feather from a crafts store (Don't substitute a stray feather from the yard. It may not be sanitary.)
2. A long piece of grass gone to seed (Be careful not to let kitty swallow the awn, which can get stuck in a feline throat.)
3. A finger-width stick from the yard with a piece of string tied on the end
4. A dried sea oat
5. A drinking straw

Avoid anything with a wire attached or with a string that the kitten could detach and eat (and choke on). Most young cats will continue to enjoy any of these simple toys for at least a year.

FOR BIRDS ONLY

If She Ever Starts Teething, She'll Be All Set

Buy toys for parrots in the baby section of a discount or department store. Rattles and teething rings are particularly appealing to them.

Keep an eye on your parrot when she's out of the cage, or she'll find her own playthings, including bookbindings, telephones, and stereo and radio knobs.

FOR POCKET PETS

What Do You Have up Your Sleeve?

Never allow or encourage rodents to run inside your clothing while you're wearing it. It's just too tough to get them out without mashing them or getting bitten (those tiny buckteeth can draw blood).

Cut a sleeve from an old long-sleeved shirt—child size for hamsters and gerbils, adult size for guinea pigs. Thread three inches of the sleeve through a round cookie cutter or a clean, empty snack-size tuna can with both top and bottom removed, then fold the

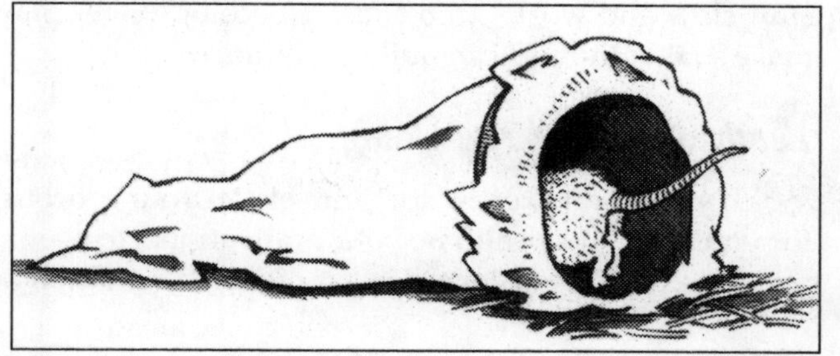

Grab a long-sleeved shirt from the rag bag and a tuna can (with top and bottom removed) from the recycling bin. Thread the shirt through the can, turn the fabric ends back, and let your pocket pet explore the new playhouse.

cloth back to make an opening. Let a small rodent run through this entrance and snuggle in the cloth.

PAIRING UP FOR EXERCISE

Here's yet another health benefit of pet ownership—physical fitness! Actually, unless you count waving your arms and running full tilt to chase the cat from the bird feeder, dogs are the only ones that can engage in fitness routines with their owners, and the right canine can keep any owner on the go. Read on to find out how to get moving with your dog, no matter which one of you would rather slouch on the couch.

FOR DOGS ONLY

Right Size for Exercise

If you want to move fast—say, you want to take up brisk walking, jogging, or in-line skating—don't plan to include a small dog or toy breed because she won't be able to keep up. But you can count on little pups for short walks or swims in the lake. You might even consider carrying a toy breed on a walk with you, leashed. That way, she gets an outing, you get some exercise, and you both get to bond.

Born to Run

Some breeds are more disposed to be active—for example, retrievers and German shepherds—than others. But any medium to large breed can be conditioned for walking, and most can swim. Just get in the habit as early in the pet's life as you can. And always

start slow and work up to a faster pace or longer distance so that the dog can build endurance.

Let the Guilt Get You Going

If you won't exercise for yourself, let your concern for your animal's health be your motivation. He needs regular exercise to prevent heart disease and obesity.

Before You Climb Every Mountain . . .

Always consult your doctor before starting an exercise plan of any sort. If your dog is more than six years old, is obese, or has a history of heart trouble, consult your veterinarian as well.

Walk the Walk

If you don't regularly exercise with your pet already, start with a walk of a couple blocks (or the approximate length of two football fields, or one-quarter mile around a track) and work up from there. Your goal should be at least 20 minutes of continuous walking three times a week for low-impact, inexpensive, heart-healthy, stress-relieving aerobic exercise. Cross-training, by adding a session or two a week of free weights and another of a sport such as tennis or volleyball—without your pet—will improve your overall fitness.

If you work your way up to five 20-minute walks per week, you can expect to lose a bit of weight and definitely some inches. And the pet you exercise with will certainly be healthier than in his couch potato days.

Gee, That Felt *Like Ten Miles*

Go for a drive and measure the distance you have walked or plan to walk. Or use a pedometer to track how far you've gone. It's just human nature to think you've covered more territory than you really have.

Downtime Doesn't Count

If your dog needs to do her "business" on the walk, work in some extra time and distance. Fits and starts don't count toward the continuous pace you'll need to increase your heart rate.

LIVING WITH PETS

No Need for Doggy Antiperspirant

Keep in mind that dogs can't cool off by sweating—they don't have the glands. That's why you'll need to watch the temperature and make sure to offer your pup at least 12 ounces of water before and after a workout. If the temperature is topping 70°F and you're out for more than 30 minutes, be sure to give your pet a drink *during* the outing as well.

Keep Fido Away from the Fountain

If you're driving the car to an off-site walk or run, always carry water with you in the car, in a plastic bottle such as a two-liter soda bottle. Also bring a plastic water dish. If the park has a water fountain, you may forgo the water, but not the dish. Dogs should not

COMMON MISTAKES

3 Warnings for Days When It's Too Hot to Trot

In hot weather, your dog or cat has fewer natural ways to cool off than you do, because pets perspire very little. Therefore, it's important that you follow these guidelines.

1. Plan your exercise for early morning or evening rather than taking your dog for a jog at noon on a hot day. Try to plan your route to go by a water source such as a stream so that your pet can splash right in to cool off. As you run, monitor how heavily your dog is breathing. If she seems to be panting hard or struggling, stop. Remember, your loyal pet will follow you anywhere, so it's up to you not to push too hard.

2. Make sure your pet has access to plenty of shade and water if you need to leave her in a pen. Never leave your dog outside in a sunny place from which she can't escape. Even if the animal's pen is nice and shady in the morning, consider whether it's in a position to get the hot sun later on.

3. Always keep careful track of your cat's whereabouts on sunny days. Make sure she hasn't sneaked up to the sweltering attic or gotten stuck somewhere hot by accident.

A WORD FROM DR. DeVINNE

Hike!

DR. CHARLES DeVINNE
of Peterborough, New Hampshire, who has more than 15 years of veterinary experience and whose private practice currently concentrates on dogs and cats

I live in an area where people go for hikes a lot, and many of those folks like to take their dogs with them.

It sounds obvious, but before you take your dog out for a three-hour hike, you should make sure that the animal is fit enough to exercise without tiring out. I wouldn't suddenly decide, "Gee, my 15-year-old dog's overweight, so let's go for a ten-mile hike today." It'd be like taking your 85-year-old grandmother out for a ten-mile hike! She'd probably drop!

A dog that's at least a year and a half old and is in pretty good shape should be fine. On the upper end of the age scale, it's harder to generalize because some dogs are "old" at six. If you're unsure, call your vet and ask, "Is my dog fit enough for a hike?" He'll look at the chart and give you an answer.

Once you've decided the dog can handle the exertion, be sure you keep the pet's needs in mind when you're planning your hike. A dog needs a tremendous amount of water, and dogs generally like to play for 10 to 15 minutes and then quit so that they can cool off. (Sure, you hear about sled dogs running for hours on end, but it takes a lot of physical training for them to get to that point.) So if you're going hiking for two to three hours, take a lot of rest stops and take plenty of water—or hike by a stream. The average dog needs at least 12 ounces of water both before and after the hike and the same amount every 30 minutes along the way. Don't bring your pet along if it's a terrifically hot day. Temperatures over 85°F will be too much for the average dog.

drink out of water fountains, even when no one is looking. Allowing them to do so risks spreading roundworms to humans who drink from the same fountain. This is also a sensitivity issue. The humans who are next in line may be uncomfortable drinking from a fountain after a dog has used it, and it's common courtesy to consider their feelings.

The Grass Is Always Softer . . .

The ideal route to seek is one where *you* can walk on a path or sidewalk and the dog can walk on grass.

City Sidewalks, Brutal Sidewalks

If city or sidewalk trotting will be the norm, build up distance slowly to let your dog's foot pads get conditioned.

Don't worry if your dog's paws get a little scraped or bloody from an outing. Just take a break for a couple of days. The scrapes will heal quickly, and your pet will eventually get the necessary calluses.

I See a Pattern Developing

If you're trying to make walking a weekday or daily habit, consider planning your walks for the same time each day. That conditions your dog to expect an outing, and his enthusiastic reminder at that time of day may overcome your inertia.

Choose a time when a walk really appeals to you. If you're a night person, don't think you have to walk in the morning.

Try the Buddy System

For a little extra motivation, buddy up with another dog walker. If you don't have a dog-owning friend or neighbor, talk with someone who frequently walks a pet about the same time and in the same place you do and see if that person wants to make it more official. So no one thinks you're making an inappropriate overture, simply say, "I noticed you walk your dog here about the same time I do every day. It might make me more motivated if I knew you were expecting me to show up. Could we meet here at 8:00 A.M. and walk together?" The worst that can happen is that the other person will say no.

COMMON MISTAKES

One More Reason Not to Leave a Dog Alone in a Car

You leave your energetic pet in the family station wagon while you make a quick stop. (It's a mild day, or you wouldn't *think* of leaving the animal alone in the car.) You figure the dog will guard the vehicle, so you don't even bother to take the keys. But pets left cooped up have a tendency to bounce off the walls—or, at the very least, to lean on doors so they can look out the windows. And if your car has the kind of door locks that activate when pressed down, guess what happens next? A locksmith we know reports being called on more than one occasion to get folks out of just such jams.

So far we haven't heard of any dogs that have learned to *un*lock the doors.

Take Some Baby Steps

Invite a friend who walks a baby—or might want to—to get in the walking habit with you. But keep in mind that the stroller, even an all-terrain stroller, will require a smooth walkway. And never try to hold the stroller and your dog's leash at the same time unless you're walking far from both automotive traffic and foot traffic. If anything startles the dog, you'll have a hard time keeping both her and the baby vehicle under control.

How Come Bowser Gets to Stay Up Late?

Respect your neighbors and never take a walk after a reasonable bedtime hour (say, about 10:00 P.M.). Even if you live in the safest of neighborhoods and are escorted by a Doberman pinscher, your trek will remind the neighborhood dogs that Bowser is out, and they'll alert their sleeping owners.

Run Away from It All

Just as it does for humans, running instead of walking places more stress on a dog's joints, muscles, and heart. But it *is* good exercise, so if it appeals to you—and if your doctor and vet give their blessings—start out with short distances (say, one-quarter to one-

half mile) and monitor your dog's paws for wear and tear. If you overdo it at the outset, you're much less likely to go again.

Tennis, Anyone?

Going out to hit a few tennis balls by yourself? If the park or tennis court allows dogs, take along a pup that likes to fetch and serve to him. Pack a few more aged balls than you might otherwise bring and count on losing some to slobber.

Get Things Rolling

If you plan to make in-line skating a habit, it's worth the trouble to train an active dog to be your companion. You need to learn the ropes of the sport first.

Saved by the Barryhund

Few dogs are as storied in history as the Saint Bernard. These dogs, credited with saving more than 2,000 lives over the centuries, are likely descended from Asian hounds brought to the future Switzerland by Roman armies during the first two centuries A.D. The dogs were adopted as pets by residents of the Hospice of the Great St. Bernard Pass, between Italy and Switzerland, beginning in the 17th century. The monks of the hospice soon discovered that their dogs were adept at finding and saving lost travelers. The burly animals would lie down and warm victims with their bulky bodies, and they seemed to have an innate ability to detect avalanches, perhaps by hearing the snow crack and settle when humans could not.

The king of the legendary Saint Bernards was Barry, credited with saving 41 lives from 1800 to 1810. For years after Barry's death, dogs of this breed were named Barry in his honor, and the name was passed on to the best male of each generation at the hospice. Barry's body was mounted and can be seen today at the natural history museum in Bern, Switzerland.

Barry also may be indirectly responsible for a persistent Saint Bernard myth. A contemporary artist painted the great dog's portrait and added a small cask of brandy hanging from his collar—a case of artistic license, not actual mountain dog equipment.

Then once you're riding smoothly, practice with the dog on a six-foot leash, in the driveway or during a very slow time at the park.

The Fallout Could Be Dangerous

If you're just going out for an occasional frolic on your in-line skates, leave Rover at home. A dog, even a calm one, tends to get tangled among skaters and can cause falls. If you're not worried about yourself or fellow skaters, worry about a skater falling on the pooch. Such an incident can result in serious injuries.

COMMON MISTAKES

Winter Bathing: Give Your Dog a Break

If a dog has encountered an irresistible pile of manure in December, a bath is in order. And it's okay to toss Fido in the tub once every six weeks or so during the cold months. But bathing any more than once a month depletes oil in the skin. This takes the gloss out of your dog's coat and makes skin already dried by cold air even drier, which can lead to a range of dermatologic ailments.

Let's Take a Dip

If a dog wants to swim in your household pool, take care to brush loose hairs off her first (assuming she asks permission before she takes the plunge). Also, be sure to clean the drains often so that they don't get clogged with pet hair.

Having a dog accompany you while you swim laps at a home pool or in calm water at a lake is great fun, but swim at least a body length away from a large dog. Paddling hind paws can really whack you.

You're on Lifeguard Duty

Always monitor dogs that brave the waves at the beach, and don't let your animal swim unless you can swim also. Dogs are just as susceptible to undertows, cold water, and rough waves as humans are.

BATHING AND CLEANUP

Humans are probably the only species that thinks of bath time as fun time. With pets, it's sometimes necessity time. Here are some tips on how to turn smelly old beasts into neat and tidy pets—and when you shouldn't bother to make the effort.

A Fairly Bearable Bath

Dogs usually aren't delighted about baths, but they'll generally tolerate them after they've been acclimated once or twice. Plan to clean your canine once a month when the weather is mild, unless you live in a particularly muddy area or have a toy breed, in which case you'll want to figure on more frequent dips in the water.

Showers Predicted; Dress Accordingly

When you bathe your dog, dress to get wet. A bathing suit is not carrying things too far if the dog being bathed is an unknown quantity.

Rub-a-Dub-Dub, Will He Fit in the Tub?

If the pup you're bathing is a small one, and if your furnishings can withstand the consequences should a sudsy mutt bolt and run, you can probably bathe the animal in the family tub. (To guard against a soap trail from a fleeing pet, always shut the bathroom door.)

Big dogs also may do okay in the tub, but in moderate or warm weather, move the bathing chores outside. Larger pooches fare best outside with the hose and a bucket of soapy water—and a place to shake off.

To hold a large dog still for bathing, straddle the animal's back.

Exercise Proper Restraint

The best way to restrain a medium to large dog that you're good friends with is to approach the animal properly before trying to bathe him. Straddle his back around his front legs and talk soothingly to him, explaining what you're going to do.

To keep a small dog from bolting in the middle of a bath, place one arm under the animal's stomach and the other across the back. Then alternate using your left and right hands to lather her up.

Use the Hands-On Approach

If you're dealing with a small dog, get the animal in a sitting position, then restrain her with one arm across her back and one under her belly. Keep the shampoo uncapped and nearby, and use alternating hands to lather her up, so that you always have at least one hand and both elbows on the dog. Use a leash as backup, in case you lose your grip in the suds or she gets any ideas about bolting.

Basic Washing Instructions

Make sure to brush off all loose hair before bathing your pet in the bathtub so that you don't clog the drain.

Unless your dog has particularly dry skin or you are treating her dermatology problems with a veterinarian-recommended product, use any standard pet store shampoo or Johnson's Baby Shampoo. Don't use conditioner designed for human hair, though. Some types just make dogs greasy, and other types don't agree with their skin.

The washing process is simple. Wet the animal with warm water, lather with shampoo as recommended on the bottle (or use about as much baby shampoo as you would if you had as much hair as your dog), rinse with warm water, and continue rinsing until the water runs clear.

Now We'll Put You under the Dryer

Once the dog is good and clean, let him shake off the water if you're outdoors. If you're indoors, swathe him in two old towels before he shakes. Once those towels are saturated with the bulk of the water, close the shower curtain and let him shake off the light droplets. Then towel him off lightly with a dry towel and put him outside to dry in the sun (preferably not near any dirt that he can roll in). Or keep him inside to dry by any heat source.

You can blow-dry a dog's hair, but it's a tedious process for all but the smallest breeds. If you decide to try it, use a low setting, and don't get the dryer so close that it can burn the dog's hair or skin. (Ears are particularly susceptible.)

No Need to Quarrel over a Few Suds

Some dogs do not like to bathe, and they will let you know that with a nip or an agonized howl or by not meeting your gaze for the three days following bath time. If your dog is in this category, consider delegating the task to a groomer. Most groomers will slosh some suds around a large dog just as enthusiastically as they'll paint a toy poodle's claws, and you can usually buy just the services you want—shampoo only, for example, no clipping or styling. You may pay anywhere from $12 to $45 for a sweet-smelling pooch. Ask your veterinarian for a local recommendation (he may offer such services right in his office) or look under Pet Grooming in the Yellow Pages. Some warehouse-type pet supply stores also offer these services, often at low prices.

FOR FISH ONLY

The Gleaming Goldfish Bowl

Clean your basic, no-pump, clear-glass, globe-shaped fishbowl once a week. The process is simple. Just dip out a cup of water from your pet's bowl (a large plastic stadium cup is the perfect size). Fish out the fish with a small net and place them in the cup for safekeeping. Dump the rest of the water from the bowl, then scrub the sides with an algae brush (available at fish or pet supply stores). Refill the bowl with clean

COMMON MISTAKES

One Fish, Two Fish, Red Fish—Dead Fish!

Many a fish fan has awakened to a newly scrubbed tank with all its occupants floating on top of the water. The culprit: soap in the water—a residue from washing the tank with shampoo, dishwashing liquid, or anything else that contains soap. Fish can't hack it. The safe alternative, even for the most disgusting gunk, is heavy-duty scrubbing with an algae sponge (available at most pet and all fish stores).

Cats and Baths, Oil and Water

Except for show breeds, which are bred to be fussed over, most cats feel that they do a fine job bathing themselves, thank you. And they really do stay clean without any human help. If a medical condition is serious enough to warrant bathing a cat (a deep wound perhaps), it's often wise to let your vet handle the process.

If you absolutely must bathe a cat—let's say someone dumped washable tempera paint on her coat—prepare to get scratched. Try the tub—the deeper the better for potential escapees—and make it quick.

water and then dechlorinate it. The last generation of fish owners had to leave water out for 24 hours or more to dechlorinate it, but we have dechlorinating tablets (available at pet supply or fish stores) to do the trick. Let the water in the bowl come to room temperature, then reintroduce Bubbles.

Tidying Up a Bigger Tank

If you have a tropical fish tank with a pump, give it a partial change of water (20 percent) once a month. Bail the old water with a large stadium cup, then pour it down the sink. Let the proper portion of dechlorinated water come to room temperature in one or more bowls or pitchers, then gently pour it into the tank.

It's also a good idea to pick up a tank vacuum at a pet store and use it to suction out yucky floating stuff and slime from the sides of the tank as needed. (Do not attempt this with an ordinary vacuum cleaner!)

Your Fish Has a Green Thumb

When you siphon off some of your fish's water every month, use it to water your plants. The water has been conditioned and softened, and the fish's waste will fertilize the soil.

SHEDDING

Shedding is like the weather—you can talk and talk about it, but no one can really *do* anything about it. Particularly if your decor favors plush carpets and upholstered furniture, pet hair tops the list of cleaning dilemmas—as well as most people's lists of "What I

Would Change about My Animals If I Could." Here's how to cope with what can't be changed.

FOR DOGS AND CATS

Bring Me That Brush!

If everything in your house has a fine layer of dog or cat hair that seems to reappear as soon as you vacuum, you need to go straight to the source. Establish a once-a-day brushing routine, always in the same place and at the same time. Furry pets will shed less hair if you brush them regularly, and a consistent pattern will get animals in the habit of reminding you that it's time for a currycomb.

Defeat Floating Fur

After brushing, pry the matted hairs from the tines of the comb or the base of the brush bristles and dispose of them. Do this each and every time you brush. Otherwise, you're just leaving the hairs to waft back into the air, scoot back under the bed, and form more dust bunnies—or creep back onto your clothing.

Throw a Damper on It

If, no matter how often you vacuum, it seems as though your upholstered furniture is still covered with fur, try this easy solution. Dampen a piece of fabric—chamois works best, but any cotton rag will do—with some water and rub it over the fabric. The pet hair will come right off.

> **COMMON MISTAKES**
>
> **Vacuuming: How to Terrorize a Cat**
>
> Why wait to vacuum until cat hair has collected on the carpet or furniture, when you can go straight to the source? Unfortunately, the vacuum cleaner's noise and the invasion of the cat's space will terrorize most felines. You could be left with scratches on your hands and face, and your pet could be left with a lifelong loathing of the machine. Even if you have the rare feline that will sit still for such treatment, the vacuum is more than likely to suck up more hairs than are ready to come out. And you run the risk of catching the cat's tail or whiskers in the attachment.

Guard against Static

No matter what method of fur removal you choose, you can make it even more effective by first

LIVING WITH PETS

spraying the affected area with some antistatic spray, such as Static Guard (which you can find at discount and grocery stores).

Don't Shed on Me

To keep hairs off wool and fuzzy clothing—their favorite clinging places—try to pet animals and say good-bye before you put on your coat to leave.

Keep a large shirt around to drape over "dry clean only" suits and sweaters when you're around the pets or sitting in their favorite chairs.

COST CUTTERS

Shed Hair with Masking Tape

No need to fork over hard-earned cash for a sticky lint roller, only to exhaust its meager layers on a few sweaters' and coats' worth of cat or dog hair. A roll of heavy-duty masking tape or duct tape does the same thing. Just rip off about a foot of it, wad it up with the sticky part on the outside, dab it on the garment (use a scattershot approach), and pull it away with the unwanted hairs attached. One roll of tape—depending on its thickness, of course—may handle as much hair as four or five lint rollers.

Neatness Counts

Always hang up coats and any other dry-cleaned clothing, preferably in a closed closet, and place sweaters in closed drawers. Dogs and particularly cats find these items irresistible when they are left lying around or are hung over the backs of chairs. And if your animal indulges, you may not appreciate the resulting dry-cleaning bill—let alone the fact that your clothing might still have hairs on it when it comes back.

FOR DOGS ONLY

The Pup's All Set—Now How about His Brush?

Keep your dog's brush clean the same way you clean your own. First, clean out all the dry hair with an old comb. Next, fill a basin or a bucket with some hot water and add a capful (a tablespoon or two) of your favorite shampoo. Rub it into the bristles, then let the brush soak for about five minutes. Rinse the brush clean with hot water and then a little white vinegar, which will remove any soap residue.

Bring in the Heavy (Cleaning) Artillery

If you've neglected your dog's brush for so long that shampoo doesn't do a good enough job of cleaning it, try this method. Pour some hot water into a bucket or basin and add a little ammonia. Soak the brush for about half an hour, then rinse well with hot water.

FOR CATS ONLY

Make Kitty Part of Your Decorating Scheme

If your decor is not terribly formal, consider working in a cat-size flat pillow on a couch or a soft, washable throw on a particularly appealing chair (at least for the spring, which is prime shedding season).

OTHER HOUSEKEEPING CONCERNS

One of the harsh truths about having animals as roommates is that they rarely clean up after themselves. Oh, sure, cats will swab themselves with their tongues, but they're the same beasts who think nothing of spraying, that malodorous challenge to housecleaners everywhere. The spectrum of animal "accidents"—in sickness and in health—provides unlimited chances to scrub, repair, and deodorize. Here's some down and dirty advice on how to clean up when animals mess up.

FOR DOGS ONLY

Wipe Out!

When a dog urinates on tiles, use paper towels to mop up the mess. And do it right away—otherwise, you'll get germs and a smell. Dispose of the towels in an outdoor trash can. Or use a cloth towel or rag and immediately toss it into a hot wash (cool rinse) with some household bleach or borax (available at hardware stores), then dry it on high heat.

Number Two's a Bit Harder for You

When a dog defecates on a bathroom or kitchen floor, the first priority is to get the mess off the

premises. If you're not too squeamish (and it's not really runny), just pick it up in a paper towel, put it in a plastic bag such as a small grocery bag, and plunk the whole thing in the outdoor trash can. If you are squeamish, use a broom along with a dustpan on the end of a long handle (available at home supply and discount stores) to perform the same operation. If the mess is rather runny, don rubber gloves before approaching the task. Amass a wad of paper towels big enough to cover the droppings, lay the towels on top, and then gently scoot the towels from the edges to the center, picking up the poop as you go. Without turning the bundle over, put it in a plastic bag and dispose of the whole thing. Then clean any streaks with bathroom cleaner or toilet bowl cleaner and more of those indispensable paper towels.

COMMON MISTAKES

Wash Your Hands of Salmonella

No matter how convenient it may seem, never wash your pet snake's cage in the kitchen or dispose of the animal's waste in the kitchen garbage can. And always be careful to wash your hands after handling your lizard or snake. The single greatest danger that any reptile poses to humans is the threat of salmonella poisoning. You can minimize the risk by keeping things clean and by keeping anything associated with your reptile away from your own food supply.

Be a Carpet Bagger

When a dog urinates, defecates, or vomits on the carpet, mop up the mess or pick it up with paper towels, then use a carpet-cleaning product such as Woolite Carpet Cleaner to remove what the carpet has absorbed. These products work remarkably well even on stains you don't discover for days.

Now Begin a Rapid De-Scent

As soon as you've cleaned up the tile or carpet that your pet soiled, treat the area thoroughly with a urine neutralizer such as Nature's Miracle (available at pet stores and from some vets). Or apply a mixture of equal parts baking soda and vinegar, then rinse well. (If it's carpet you're dealing with, first test a small, inconspicuous spot for colorfastness) Otherwise, no matter how clean you think you've gotten the area, your pet will pick up the scent and return there to do the same thing again.

Don't Make Him Lift His Leg

When a dog marks his territory on wooden furniture, wipe it off thoroughly and quickly with paper towels. Make sure you get it all, or the finish on your favorite heirloom can get trashed. Follow up with a urine neutralizer such as Nature's Miracle (available at pet stores), so that your pet won't be drawn to the same spot to repeat his performance.

For Pungent Poodles

Phew! If your pooch is rather ripe, here's a way to get him smelling sweet again. Sprinkle some baking soda on the animal's coat and work it into his fur with your hands. Then brush him well. The baking soda will absorb the odor and will brush out readily, along with

YOU'VE GOTTA LOVE 'EM

Puss in (Tissue) Box

My mother told me a story once about a very small cat that my dad had given my aunt. One day, my aunt came home from the store where she worked and couldn't find the cat anywhere. She started to panic and searched all over the house, but it was no use. Finally, everyone gave up. Later, when she was ready to turn in for the night, my aunt went to her room, got into bed, and turned off the light. She reached for a tissue, but it seemed to be stuck on something. She gave it a tug, but it still wouldn't come. Finally, she flipped on the light and saw her cat cuddled up inside the tissue box, where it had been all along.

That was one small cat.

—**CANDI ISHERWOOD**
Mesa, Arizona

any dirt in your dog's coat. Repeat the procedure if necessary.

Eau de Wet Pooch

Wet dog has to be one of the worst odors going, but it's not insurmountable. To rid a room of the odor, pulverize (in a coffee grinder or mortar and pestle) a tablespoon or so of ground coffee. Place the coffee in a frying pan over low heat. Roast the grounds until the odor is pronounced, then place the pan in the odorous room until the coffee cools down.

COMMON MISTAKES

Color Me Embarrassed

If you give a bird oddly colored food, he's going to have oddly colored stools from the same palette. Don't jump to the conclusion that the bird is passing blood before you check whether he's recently eaten strawberries.

FOR CATS ONLY

The Mess Is Gone, but the Smell Lingers On

Cats' urine is very concentrated, so odor—funky, lingering odor—is an issue when a cat sprays in the house or misses the litter box. You can pick up with a paper towel any urine or droppings that don't penetrate a surface, but you'll also need to follow up with a special cleaning product such as Nature's Miracle (available at pet stores and from some veterinarians). It's somewhat pricey but contains enzymes that will take care of stains and smells.

Let Dad Do It

Avoid dealing with any cat "output" if you're pregnant. It can cause toxoplasmosis, which will seriously threaten the health of mom and baby.

No More Encores!

Don't even think about cleaning cat spray with a product that contains ammonia. Cats can smell the ammonia long after humans, and it will attract them back to the area to spray again and again.

Something Just Didn't Sit Right

Cats are famous for vomiting guts—a small prey's, not their own—or leaving dead bird or chipmunk offerings to their beloved owners. Pick these up using a paper towel, drop the whole shebang in a plastic bag, and place it in an outdoor trash can with a tight-fitting lid (to avoid further kitty recycling). Carpets where the cat has dropped the treasure can be cleaned, if needed, with carpet cleaner. Spiff up slick surfaces with a nonammonia household cleaning product. Or use concentrated distilled cider vinegar (sold in a spray bottle) or regular white or cider vinegar in your own clean spray bottle.

LIVING WITH PETS

Right off the Bat

If your cat's dead prey happens to be a bat, put a bucket over the top of the dead animal, weight it with a brick, and call your local animal control agency. Don't touch the bat, as it could be carrying rabies, and you could be contaminated by handling it.

FOR OTHER PETS

Sometimes It's Easy

❍ Rabbits, mice, gerbils, guinea pigs, and hamsters all have vegetarian, alfalfa-based droppings, which don't really smell bad and are quite easy to pick up. Just make sure to ease them into a napkin or brown paper bag. If you squash them, they'll stick, much like Play-Doh pellets.

❍ You might want to consider tossing accumulated rabbit or rodent droppings into the compost pile. Un-

The Nose Knows

Dogs are justifiably famous for their sense of smell. With 220 million receptor cells in a dog's nose, versus 5 million in the human schnozzle, dogs are used to sniff out contraband such as drugs, bombs, and guns, as well as to locate people dead or alive. Trained dogs can determine whether twins are identical or fraternal because genetically identical twins share a characteristic odor. Bloodhounds have tracked human trails four days old and dozens of miles long, even when the fugitive used a vehicle or waded through large crowds or moving water.

Strangely, dogs are not sensitive to every odor. Although they are at least a million times more sensitive than we are to the butyric acid of human sweat, they appear almost completely indifferent to the lovely scent of a rose.

like dog and cat droppings, rabbit and rodent feces are actually a beneficial addition.

❍ Don't try to vacuum rabbit or rodent droppings unless they are very dry. Droppings up to three days old are still gummy enough to collect at the end of the vacuum hose and clog it up.

WHEN COMPANY'S COMING

If Ann Landers and Dear Abby are any indication, polite visitors constantly suffer at the paws of ill-mannered beasts and insensitive owners—and pet owners are besieged just as often by loutish guests who torment the

Mighty Dogs

If you notice a dog frantically barking and running in circles, don't assume that the pooch has seen too many *Lassie* reruns. There are countless cases of genuine canine heroism on record, and many times these dogs saved their masters or total strangers by causing just such a racket.

For more than 40 years, the makers of Ken-L Ration dog food have recognized untrained dogs that performed amazing rescues of all kinds with the Dog Hero of the Year award. Among their stories are the following:

• Willy, a nine-year-old weimaraner, pawed and barked at his owner to wake her up when a broken furnace leaked deadly carbon monoxide into the home.

• After his 227-pound owner suffered a heart attack, Sparky, a 130-pound yellow Lab, dragged the collapsed man nearly 200 yards to his home. The subsequent call to the ambulance, rush to the hospital, and stabilizing of the owner's condition would have been impossible if Sparky hadn't taken the first steps.

• Woodie, a mixed breed, followed his owner's fiancé off an 80-foot cliff when the man accidentally plunged into a shallow creek. Despite a broken hip from his leap off the crag, Woodie was able to keep the man's face above water until help arrived.

Not surprisingly, perhaps, collies, German shepherds, and Saint Bernards, along with mixed breeds, top the list of heroic dog breeds. But two poodles also have made the honor roll, including Mimi, a miniature poodle who ran through a burning house to wake a family, enabling eight people to escape the fire.

household pets. Here's how to encourage calm, sensible, even enjoyable interactions between your pets and people who visit your home—and how to know when the best interaction is no interaction at all.

FOR PETS IN GENERAL

Forget "Love Me, Love My Pet"

❑ As much as your pets might be members of the family, where visitors are concerned, it's smart to consider them more as "preferences"—like "smoking" or "nonsmoking," or country music versus jazz. Some people simply do not like cats, dogs, or little things that resemble rats (even though they're hamsters, for heaven's sake). It has nothing to do with the person's feelings for you, so don't take it personally if someone doesn't want anything to do with your beloved friend.

Fluffy Shouldn't Fight Your Battles

❑ Never use your pet to get back at another person. Say you still resent Aunt Margaret for calling you fat as a child, and you know that she hates having cats jump in her lap. Don't get even when she visits by letting Fluffy hop up to say hello.

But My Owner Thought That Was So Cute

❑ Never knowingly place pets in situations in which they are likely to annoy human visitors. Pets don't need enemies any more than you do, and they'll get confused when a behavior that always charms you—such as touching noses—draws a startled yelp from a new human acquaintance.

How Long Should You Keep Your Pet Cloistered?

❑ When you're expecting visitors for only an hour or an evening, go out of your way to accommodate those with allergies or those who don't appreciate pets as much as you do. Stash the cat in the laundry room for the duration, for example, or allow the dog only a brief

introduction before a neighborhood child whisks him out to the backyard for an afternoon of play.

❑ If your friend is planning an overnight visit or a stay of a couple weeks, you can't be as easygoing, or the entire household will be miserable. Either board your animal with a fun-loving friend or reputable kennel, ask a non-pet-owning relative to put the human visitor up, or offer to split the cost of a hotel room.

Everybody Comfy?

❑ Be firm about your feeling that you must try to make both your pet and your guest happy. Don't let anyone minimize your feelings for your pet with remarks such as "Couldn't you get rid of all your cats for the one week your mother is in town?" Simply reply, "You are a dear friend (or relative), and I simply couldn't bear it if your feelings about my animal got in the way of our having a wonderful visit. It would just be a waste of all the time and effort we've put into planning this."

This Is a Safe House

❑ Demand that your pet be treated with respect in your home. It's completely within bounds for you to insist that visitors refrain from squeezing, teasing, or thumping your pet—no matter whether the visitor is your three-year-old neighbor or an overzealous business associate. Simply say "That really bothers Marmaduke, so he'll be going to his space over here now, and you need to leave him alone."

When the Guest Is a Youngster

❑ When a child under the age of 12 comes to your home, take the lead in acquainting her with the resident pets. Introduce them and spell out any restrictions to the child, within the parent's hearing: "This is where my newts live, and I'm the only one allowed to touch the glass."

❑ You may give fanciful explanations for why a pet requires certain treatment, but for the under-eight crowd,

keep it to a few words: "Binky is shy. We can't chase him."

The Pet Pajama Party

❏ Warn overnight guests of any animal idiosyncrasies and how to deal with them: "The cat will come sleep on your bed if you don't keep the guest room door shut." "The hamster loves to run on his wheel at night. I've put him in the kitchen so he won't disturb you, but if you hear a noise, that's probably it." Or "Billy usually sleeps in here, so the dog might scratch on the door in the morning. Just say 'Go away, Bowser.'"

Do You Think We Should Get Out the Good China?

❏ Take pains not to repulse dinner or overnight guests by letting your pets eat off the dishes after a meal. If you're not worried about your company's sensitivity, consider that roundworms can be passed from the pet's mouth to humans via the dishwasher (although you can easily determine whether your pet has roundworms with a trip to the vet).

FOR DOGS AND CATS

Forewarned about Four Paws

When you invite someone to your home, make certain that person knows that your pet will be on the premises. Even people you've known for a long time through work, activities, or church may not remember that you have a dog or cat. So be explicit: "We're glad to have the bridal shower here, but you should know that we have three poodles and two cats that are definitely indoor animals."

COMMON MISTAKES

Too Many Pets

Your savings may dwindle, your carpet may suffer, or your neighbors may complain. But as long as you provide the basic necessities, you don't really have too many pets until you don't have the time or energy to give each one the attention the animal requires. At that point, you *do* have a problem. Many people who take on too many pets do so in an attempt to "rescue" unwanted animals. Ironically, if you rescue too many pets, you risk the emotional health and standard of living of the ones you already have. And it's rarely the animal you bring in that's unable to adapt to the situation. Consider the pets you already have before you agree to adopt another. Remember, charity begins at home.

YOU'VE GOTTA LOVE 'EM

The Squirrel That Fell from Heaven

A fellow named Tony Macula once owned a Siamese cat named Cecil, whose chief ambition in life was to catch a squirrel. Cecil was a devoted killer and spent all his time on terrorist attacks. Tony and Cecil lived in Middletown, Connecticut, in a Victorian house where the pigeons made themselves at home on the eaves. Cecil took care of crowd control. He did not discriminate against robins or rodents, either—all carcasses were laid on the living room rug for Tony's inspection. The only conquest missing was a squirrel.

Then one day the unthinkable happened. While Cecil was crouched in the driveway waiting to pounce on a pigeon, a squirrel missed a branch and dropped from the sky, landing six inches from Cecil's nose. It hit the ground square on four feet but was too dazed to run. A cat's dream come true. Cecil hadn't expected it to be so easy. Caught off guard, he stood frozen face-to-face with his prey in a cartoon moment. When he finally recovered and leaped to the attack, the squirrel had regained its senses as well and sprinted off. The chase was on.

Cecil would hate to admit it, but the squirrel got away. And Cecil, humiliated, got canned food for dinner.

It Can't Hurt to Ask

Ask point-blank, ahead of time, "Are you a cat (dog) lover?" and "Do you have any allergies to animals?" That way, you'll know what you're dealing with and can choose to relocate your meeting or social event to a local park, restaurant, or the visitor's home if the negative reaction is significant.

Dress Accordingly

Remind potential guests that your pets—and your furniture—are riddled with dog or cat hair, if that is the case. If they don't have the same problem at home, caution them to avoid wearing dark colors or wool.

FOR DOGS ONLY

Your Dog and Scaredy-Cats

Most adults won't come right out and say that they're scared of dogs, so be on the lookout for signs that a visitor is wary, jumpy, or nervous around your animal. This will be particularly obvious as a phobia, not just a well-warranted skepticism, if you have a cuddly breed such as a beagle. Be careful to keep your dog away from the tension before he picks up on it and gets defensive or protective—or confused.

You *Know He's Innocent—Avoid the Trial*

A guest who is afraid of dogs is more likely to imagine that your dog acted aggressively or even bit or lunged at her. Put your dog outside (assuming you have a fenced yard) or shut her in the laundry room, and you won't have to defend her against imaginary infractions or argue with a friend.

Be a Friend to the Fearful

Never confront a scared adult with your dog, however sweet and lovable the animal is. An adult can get over a dog phobia, but it's a slow process—first seeing pictures of a dog, then holding a collar, then looking at dogs through the pet store window, and so

forth. You cannot overcome a person's phobia simply by proving what a great guy Fritz is—and you don't want your dog to be offended or confused by someone yelling "Bad dog" or "Get away" when the animal is just doing his regular sniffing routine.

FOR CATS ONLY

Put the Squeeze on the Sneezes

To help a much-loved visitor who's allergic to cats, you can diminish, but not eliminate, the cat-caused allergens in the air with a plug-in air filter, available at home supply and discount stores. It also helps a little if you always restrict the cat to certain areas of the house where guests would never go. This won't make a five-day visit possible, but the person should be able to come over for an evening of card playing or to attend a birthday party.

FOR FISH ONLY

If I Eat Any More, I'll Pop

Even adults will compulsively feed fish at someone else's home. With children, it's almost a given. Plan a feeding for all to witness during the visit, and explain that the fish will meet an untimely death if they get a single additional food flake. (For kids, try the allure of the unmentionable: "If anyone else feeds this fish, he'll puke his guts out and die.")

If a public feeding won't fit into the schedule, hide the food wherever you keep your medicines and put a sign on the tank that says "Absolutely No Feeding." Or be creative. For example, the sign could read "Little-known species of piranha swimming here. If you feed them, they'll jump out of the water and continue to feed on you."

FOR POCKET PETS

No One Will Ever Know We're Here

When you're expecting visitors under age four, all gerbils, hamsters, and mice should be kept hidden from

view. Put their cage under a loose-weave towel, for example, and/or out of harm's way on a bookshelf or the bathroom counter. That's the safest way to avoid overhandling, squashing, and suffocating. Just make sure that the hiding place is warm enough and out of drafts and that you haven't created an escape opening while moving the cage.

Hold On!

If the child has come expressly to see the tiny rodent, make sure you know where both child and beast are at all times. If you feel that you must get the little fellow out of his cage, make sure to hold him in your hand and show the child how to stroke him lightly with one finger.

9 *Songs Birds Can Whistle Along With*

Birds are audio-oriented, so a good way to gain (or regain) a bond with them is to listen to new music together. The theme song from *Mayberry, R.F.D.* is a great choice to get birds twittering, but many other songs also are good possibilities. Here are a few.

1. "Whistle While You Work" from the *Snow White and the Seven Dwarfs* sound track
2. "Some Day My Prince Will Come" from the same sound track
3. "Give a Little Whistle" from *Pinocchio* (you know, Jiminy Cricket's theme)
4. "(Sittin' on) the Dock of the Bay" as recorded by Otis Redding
5. "Do Re Mi" from *The Sound of Music* sound track
6. The introduction to *Jungle Love* by the Steve Miller Band
7. The "Who Wears Short Shorts" jingle from the Nair commercials (You'll actually go out of your way to tape a commercial for once.)
8. The theme song from *Petticoat Junction*

If your tastes are more sophisticated, experiment, within the bird's earshot, with any type of music you like, particularly anything with some woodwinds. Accompany the recording with your own whistling. (You *do* know how to whistle, don't you?)

End of Discussion

If there are any arguments about getting a small rodent out of petting range, solve the issue with two words (which, for all you know, may be true): "He bites."

PETS AT CHRISTMAS, HANUKKAH, AND KWANZA

'Tis the season to be jolly—and careful. The holiday season is fun to share with pets, but it's also fraught with stress, temptation, and even danger. Here are some ways to protect your pet and still be full of good cheer.

FOR PETS IN GENERAL

Bows Are for Presents, Not Pets

❑ A holiday bow around a pet's neck can at worst strangle an animal that catches it on a paw and at best embarrass her in front of her friends. Much preferred are snap-away collars, which detach under pressure greater than that exerted by a straining dog on a leash and are available in holiday colors at upscale pet stores.

❑ If you can't resist the idea of putting antlers on your Great Dane or a Santa hat on your guinea pig, do it quickly, take a snapshot for the holiday card, and take off the topper right away. Most such items aren't made for wear and tear, safety, or comfort.

FOR DOGS ONLY

Out of Tails' Reach

Watch where you put treasures that enthusiastic tails could clear off with a single sweep. Place fragile or chewable decorations well out of reach. Avoid arranging Nativity or winter scenes on coffee tables, for example, or Christmas cards on the hearth.

FOR CATS ONLY

Cat-Friendly Trimmings

Some cats will ignore the holiday tree; some will consider it Santa's gift to the indoor kitty. To find out

YOU'VE GOTTA LOVE 'EM

The Disappearing Cat Trick

Two carpenters, Jeff and Larry, were hired to build an addition onto a friend's house in Dublin, New Hampshire. The owner, Mary, left them alone with her reclusive cat. The cat was so reclusive, in fact, that Jeff didn't even know there was a cat in the house.

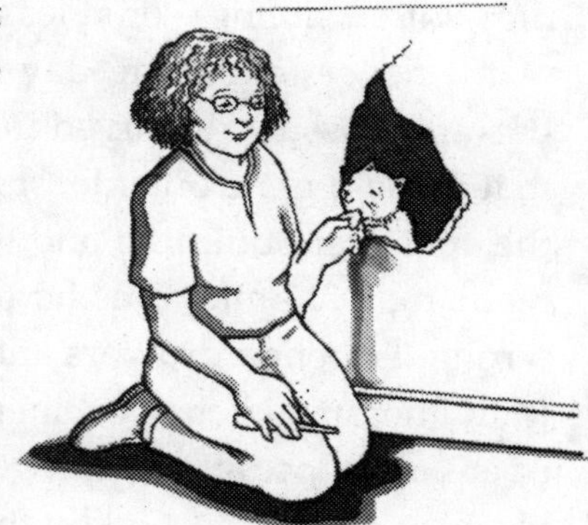

After completing the addition, the two men broke through to the old part of the house and framed and drywalled the transition area. Finally, they framed up the crawl space behind the knee wall on the second floor and went home.

Larry had his feet up when the phone rang. It was Mary, the homeowner. She hadn't been able to find her cat anywhere but had heard him meowing. By trial-and-error echolocation, she'd determined that her cat was trapped behind the carefully hung knee wall. Larry was ready to rush to the cat's rescue, but there was no need. Mary had taken a screwdriver to the wall, released the cat, and redone the drywall herself. Everything would have been fine except that word travels fast in small towns, and for months afterward people clutched their cats to their chests when they saw Larry and Jeff coming.

which variety you have, bring in the tree a day before you decorate it. Should a feline approach it with malice aforethought, zap her lightly with a water gun or slip four or five pennies inside an empty soft drink can and throw the can close by—very close by. The noise is likely to startle the cat, and she should get the message: Paws off.

YOU'VE GOTTA LOVE 'EM

Circus Act

My cat Barnum is a round, sweet ball of fluff, but she is not very bright. She spends almost all of her time staring off into space. Her sister, Bailey, is slim and sly, and protective of her dim-witted sibling—or at least I'd always assumed so.

I'll never forget the day I came home from work to find Barnum missing. We lived in the city at that point, and I knew that if she'd gone outside, she didn't have a chance. I searched the apartment building and the neighborhood for hours before realizing that Bailey was far too serene for anything to be really wrong. I opened drawers and closets, calling out to Barnum. I found her in a kitchen cabinet—one with an overhead door that opens and closes like a garage door. She meowed when she saw me and seemed startled by the sudden light. I had no idea how long she'd been in there but decided that Bailey had been responsible.

A few weeks later, I saw the two of them in the kitchen, near the open cabinet door. Suddenly Bailey started and studied the cabinet as if something was moving inside. Barnum was completely fooled. She walked inside to see what might be in there. As soon as she did so, Bailey reached up with one paw and slammed the door shut. Then she strutted out of the kitchen, right past me, with her tail twitching. She was pleased as could be.

—**ANN-MARIE CUNNIFF**
Medford, Massachusetts

It's the Leaning Tower of Temptation

A leaning tree is a vulnerable tree. To make yours less tempting for pouncing cats, tether it to a nearby window with clear fishing line. Hang the most valuable and/or breakable items near the top, securely fastened with hooks and further anchored with bread bag twists or florist's wire if necessary. That leaves the wooden and felt ornaments, and the candy canes, to hang where a cat can have some fun.

Tinsel and Tabby Don't Mix

Skip the tinsel. Instead, use any of the vinyl garlands and specialty lights now on the market. They'll brighten the tree, and you won't have to worry about their being eaten by your cat and causing digestive problems or choking.

Hey! Who Set the Curtains on Fire?

If candles are part of your holiday celebration, consider using some of the new holders that have glass domes, cups, or cylinders that cover the candle or flame. In households with cats, these are far preferable to traditional tapers because they're harder to tip over and less likely to singe fur. And no matter what kind of display you choose, don't burn candles unless an adult is there to monitor the paws of curious cats.

With menorahs, of course, tapers are the only option, so put them where your cat can't easily get a foothold—on a high mantel, for example, or a specially built shelf.

FOR FISH ONLY

Be Festive, Not Flashy

Holiday lights on the outside of the aquarium are a nice, reasonable touch. But make sure they're all the way on the outside. Even small fish can splash water on the bulbs. This can cause bristling electricity and

'Tis the season for decorations! Get in the spirit with holiday lights on the aquarium —but keep them out of splashing range.

maybe give humans or fish an electric shock (which can kill the fish). And by no means use blinking lights, which will stress the fish and possibly give them ich (a condition that causes slimy spots on fish and can be fatal if untreated).

FOR OTHER PETS

Let the Parakeet Join the Party

❍ Any cage can sustain a bow—on the outside, where little rodent teeth won't nibble away at it. You also might try a festive pattern for your bird's nighttime cage cover-up, something in red and green for Christmas or in an African weave to commemorate Kwanza.

CAR TRAVEL WITH PETS

Sometimes it seems that if God had meant for pets to ride in cars, he would have given them laps so that they could fasten their seat belts. Whether you're taking a

4 *Prerequisites for Travels with Charlie*

Here are the essentials to pack when you take a road trip with a dog.

1. A gallon jug of water, which you can replenish as needed, and a heavy water bowl (the one from home is fine).

2. A leash, which should be attached to the animal's collar and your arm whenever he's out of the car. Unaccustomed traffic noises and new friends and enemies in parking lots and rest areas could encourage him to depart hastily.

3. Enough food for the trip—both ways—and for a few extra meals should you end up stranded at an auto repair shop ("How about some vending machine crackers, boy?"), on the road, or in an area that's inconvenient for purchasing your usual brand ("No sir, most of the dogs in these parts just eat possums . . .").

4. A pooper-scooper and some plastic bags for disposal. Even if you needn't do these duties at home, consider that ordinances will probably vary in places where you stop or are forced to stop.

pet across town to the veterinarian or across the country to a new home, keep in mind that a car is not an animal's natural habitat. Here are ways to make the ride safe and enjoyable—or, in the case of cats, birds, and rodents, bearable.

COMMON MISTAKES

Don't Keep On Truckin'

Never let your dogs ride in the back of a pickup truck, no matter how long they've been doing it, how much they like it, or how hardy they are. Most areas have ordinances against this practice, and if that's not enough to deter you, envision the one time that your dog loses his footing and goes sailing into traffic—or through some innocent party's windshield.

FOR DOGS ONLY

You're in Back, Buster

Make sure all dogs, even toy breeds, ride in the backseat. That keeps them out of the driver's face, off the gear shift, off the brake, and out of range of the windshield if you stop suddenly.

If your dog is used to riding up front, put a long-lasting treat—a pig's ear or a nylon ring—in the back on your next couple of trips. This should encourage the animal to develop a new habit.

You Could Be Asking for a Real Mesh

Considering buying one of those plastic mesh-type barriers that you erect between front seat and backseat to keep eager animals in the back (particularly when you stop suddenly)? It could be a good move—*if* your car and your pet both meet certain requirements. Before

Before you invest in a plastic mesh barrier, make sure it will block your pet and not your view.

LIVING WITH PETS

you purchase one, ask the pet store or pet supply store whether you can install it in your car in the parking lot to check out how it affects visibility. And if you have a dog that's very aggressive about getting up front, forget it. A barrier like this won't deter him much.

Boy, Driving Makes Me Thirsty

Always give your dog extra water before and after drives if you're running the car's heater or air conditioner. Either will dehydrate the dog and dry up her mucous membranes, which can make her catch a cold easily.

A WORD FROM DR. DEVINNE

Too Hot?

DR. CHARLES DEVINNE
of Peterborough, New Hampshire, who has more than 15 years of veterinary experience and whose private practice currently concentrates on dogs and cats

One summer afternoon, as I was pulling out of my office parking lot, I passed by a car, owned by one of my clients, that was parked at the auto repair shop next door. In the front seat, I saw his dog, a Pomeranian, and I also saw that all the windows were up. The owner was nowhere to be seen, and the doors were all locked. I asked the attendant where the guy was.

"Oh, he left the car for service. Somebody was supposed to come pick him up, but he decided to walk downtown and catch his ride there." I asked the attendant whether he had the car keys, but he said the owner had walked off with them.

All I was thinking was "We've gotta get this dog out of the car." So finally we got one

Extra Driving Time with a Canine

When a dog is in the car for a long trip, be sure to stop every two to three hours and offer him a stretch, some water, food if it's dinnertime, and a visit to the facilities.

If you plan to take a lot of day trips and weekend trips with your dog, consider joining the American Automobile Association (AAA). On request, they'll map out a route to your destination, making sure to include properly spaced rest areas with dog facilities (gas stations tend to frown on dogs racing around or using the building or grounds as a bathroom). To get in touch

of those strips that the police use, and we jimmied the guy's door open and got the dog out.

I put the dog in my truck, and we drove downtown, looking for the owner. We drove around for a while, and I finally found him in a local convenience store.

"Hey! How's it going?" he said when I walked in. And I said to him, "I've got your dog in my truck."

I explained how we'd opened the door and how the dog had really been in a lot of danger—a dog left in a car, even with the windows open, can overheat in 20 minutes.

"My wife was supposed to pick me up," he said, "but she was late, so I thought I'd just start walking."

His wife never did show up. That dog could have been in that truck overnight—or certainly for hours—and might very well have died. And you know, the owner never gave it a second thought; he had no idea of the danger. He actually felt it was better to walk without the dog because he thought she'd get too hot and tired walking.

Don't make the same mistake. Don't *ever* leave a dog unattended in a car—especially in the summer.

4 *Vacations to Take with Your Dog . . .*

Traveling is quite stressful for a dog, but if you don't want to leave home without him, try one of these vacations.

1. State parks. These offer lots of walking and hiking, as well as many other activities in areas that are pet-friendly. Just don't plan long hikes if your dog isn't conditioned for it.

2. National parks. Attractions from Yellowstone to the Mall in Washington, D.C., allow leashed dogs. For more information about specific parks, search the Internet for the National Park Service.

3. Beaches. Hours of walking on the beach, Frisbee fun, and barking at waves are yours (and your pet's) for the asking.

4. Historical tours. Some landmarks, such as Colonial Williamsburg in Virginia, have "dogs welcome" walking tours and pet-friendly facilities to go with them. Although a leashed walk may not be the high point of your dog's life, if you're not outdoorsy, you might enjoy this type of "take-the-dog" vacation.

Your travel agent, the American Automobile Association (AAA; get the number by calling toll-free directory assistance at 1-800-555-1212), or the State Department of Tourism (call directory assistance for the capital city in the applicable state) can help you find an appropriate dog-friendly vacation spot.

with AAA, call toll-free directory assistance (1-800-555-1212) and ask for the number.

FOR CATS ONLY

Try to Change Her Point of View

To improve the car ride for a cat that hates to travel, try using a cat carrier with a front view. Tabby may be happier if she's able to see out.

Level the Playing Field

If your car's backseat folds down to a level surface, try placing the cat carrier there. It will feel more stable than if it's placed directly on the seat.

If you don't have the fold-down option, place the carrier directly on the backseat. Don't put it on the car floor. The floor is too close to weird road noises and will make the cat feel even more claustrophobic. Besides, it's usually more difficult to wedge the carrier into that narrow spot.

Talk Is Cheap

Cats keep calmer in the car if you talk to them soothingly. If they're not able to hear you well in the back, turn on the stereo speakers in the backseat and tune in talk radio. *All Things Considered* on National Public Radio is a great choice. Avoid sports call-in shows, which often have too many raucous voices and noises.

FOR BIRDS ONLY

When Polly Travels, It's Always Night

Always put a nighttime cover on your bird's cage before taking the pet in the car. It serves as a drug-free tranquilizer.

Carry a bird's water bottle and food separately from the cage. They tend to drain and spill in transit.

FOR POCKET PETS

Fur Balls Ride under Wraps

When traveling with gerbils, mice, hamsters, or guinea pigs, first prepare a basic traveling case. An old shoe box will serve the purpose. Just line it with newspaper and some soft rags, then use a vegetable peeler to poke about 30 quarter-inch holes in the top. Take the pets out of their cages and place them in the shoe box for the journey. That way, they can burrow in darkness on the drive, and while they're out of their cages, they won't startle and knock over food or water.

Pack the cages separately—in the trunk, inside a cardboard box or

. . . And 3 *Times the Pooch Should Stay Home*

It's not a good idea to bring a pet along on any of these kinds of vacations.

1. Expensive prepaid vacation packages. If having the dog along doesn't work out, you're all out of a vacation.

2. Ski trips. They're just too darn cold for most dogs.

3. Group tours. Even if the hotel and sites allow pets, you may have comrades who are scared of dogs or allergic to them.

Maybe We Should Try a Pup Tent

Whenever your dog comes along on a trip, make certain ahead of time that the place you'll be staying accepts—in fact, welcomes—pets. A night in the car is simply not an acceptable backup for a pup. There's no air circulation, temperatures vary, and she may get confused or lonely so far from home. In addition, most hotels that don't take dogs are equally unaccepting of barking dogs in their parking lots at 5:00 A.M. If you belong to the American Automobile Association (AAA), contact that organization for a list of accommodations that take pets. (Get the phone number for AAA by calling toll-free directory assistance at 1-800-555-1212.) Or ask any reputable travel agent to tell you about pet-friendly accommodations (or lack thereof) at your destination.

on a tray in case the cages leak stray seeds or bedding material. Bring food and water separately, too, if the animals will be gone most of the day (say, for a school visit) and will need sustenance. Otherwise, leave the vittles at home or get new food or water at your destination.

This Is No Time to Set the AC on "Icy"

Be careful to maintain a moderate interior car temperature during transit, and don't put your furry pet's box in a draft or on the floor. It's really easy for a tiny animal to fry or freeze.

PLANE TRAVEL WITH PETS

You may think that you want to take a cat or dog along on a plane trip, but you really, really don't. In the best circumstances, they'll be treated like third-class passengers; in the worst, like luggage. So reserve airplane rides only for those "must" excursions—you'll be gone for more than a month, you're moving, or you're sending a pet to a new home too far away for the reasonable person to drive. And if your four-legged friend must fly the friendly skies, an owner familiar with the drill can make a dismal experience bearable. Here's how.

FOR DOGS AND CATS

Drop Me Off on Your Way to Key West

If the long trip's a must and you're definitely flying, see if you can't buy a car ride for your dog or cat. Col-

lege ride boards, where student drivers post destinations and ads to share carfare, are a place to start. They're usually located in a college's student center.

If you're moving but someone else is driving your vehicle to your new home, find out whether that person is willing to bring your pet along for the ride.

But I Wanted to Show Fifi the Eiffel Tower

Don't plan to take an animal abroad unless this is a serious family pet and you're planning to relocate permanently. Most foreign countries will require that your dog or cat be quarantined for up to six months (at your expense) upon arrival.

First Stop, the Veterinarian

Before you leave on your trip, you'll need to get a certificate of health from your veterinarian for any animal that will fly with you. The airlines require it, and your pet will have to be up-to-date on all shots to pass muster. Check with the airline you're flying to find out how far ahead of time you can take care of this (the certificates are good for only a limited period).

Beethoven Won't Quite Fit

Before boarding a plane, find out whether an airline will allow you to take a small pet carry-on. Your pet usually must fit in an airline-supplied or airline-approved carrier that's small enough to go under the seat in front of you. Otherwise, your animal will travel in a cage with the luggage or in the cargo hold (on small planes, that may be the same place), where it's sometimes dark and cold.

COST CUTTERS

Cat Carriers: The Wonder of Plastic

Cats tend to tolerate the front-opening cat carriers better than the top-loading cardboard ones. But you don't have to invest in the most expensive kind, which have metal grate doors. Most cats do just fine with the plastic grate versions, which cost more than the cardboard carriers but less than their metal counterparts.

Let Fluffy see what's going on.

Best Bet: Same Flight

Ask your travel agent to find the least expensive way you can fly with your pet. Since travel agents work on commission and have loyalty to certain airlines, you need to make the request specific: "I want you to find the best rate for me and my cat to be on the same flight." Some airlines will give you an inexpensive rate for your pet or charge nothing extra if you and your pet take the same flight.

Even if you must pay extra, take the same flight so that you and your pet will share all the same delays and rerouting.

Plan On Separate Rooms

If you are traveling with two pets, no matter how well they get along, the airline will insist that they travel in separate containers. Plan accordingly.

Fido Can't Take This Flight

If you're a veteran commuter flyer, be forewarned that your pet won't be able to take certain commuter flights. Some of the turboprop aircraft don't have pressurized storage areas, and that's where Fido would ride.

Barking Baggage

When you simply must send an animal via air freight, ask for priority parcel service. That way, you can choose a flight, and the airline will guarantee when the animal will arrive at her destination (sort of like Federal Express, only the package is alive). You can plan when to drop the pet off at the airport, and the person at the other end of the line has a reasonable assurance of when to pick her up.

Limited finances should be the only reason that you opt for regular cargo, and you should understand that your pet might end up on any flight. Cargo is "standby," loaded on the plane after baggage *if* the weight limit hasn't been met. Your animal could wait for quite a long time before catching a flight, and you'll be expected to provide 24 hours' worth of food.

LEAVING HOME WITHOUT THEM

Whether you're a frequent business traveler or an "I would never leave Princess to fend for herself, but my daughter's getting married" type, every now and then

8 *Items for the Pet-Motel Checklist*

Having your veterinarian or a kennel board your cat or dog while you're out of town is never ideal, but you can choose the best possible arrangement by keeping these criteria in mind.

1. The welcome mat. Are you encouraged to come by and check out the facility at your convenience? True, kennel workers, particularly those whose homes are next door, value their privacy, but you should opt only for a facility where pet owners are welcome to observe and evaluate care ahead of time.

2. Space. Although your veterinarian's office is often the most convenient place to board animals, a more rural kennel may offer larger cages for cats and bigger runs or even an outdoor fenced-in area for dogs.

3. Shelter. Are your animals covered? Are there indoor/outdoor runs for large dogs?

4. Comfort. Is there heat in the winter and air-conditioning in the summer?

5. Price. Make some phone calls because prices can vary by as much as $10 to $20 a night.

6. Cleanliness. Even the cleanest accommodations will probably have a slight odor, but you shouldn't gag as you come in the door. Nor should there be piles of feces or pools of urine in the runs or cages.

7. Communication. Is the owner or manager available to answer your questions? Ask what schedule the animals are on and how the staff handles a barking dog, a pining pet, or a fight between two boarders.

8. Instincts. Trust your judgment. The most highly recommended facility isn't for you or your pet if you don't get a good feeling about it or the people operating it. No one knows where your animal will be happy better than you.

YOU'VE GOTTA LOVE 'EM

The Dog Who Would Be King

In a small town in southern New Hampshire, the dachshund Kaiser Wilhelm III was left to the care of pet-sitter Jim Collins with specific instructions. Willy (yes, Jim could call him that) must breakfast on Shredded Wheat 'N Bran cereal with milk, vitamins, scrambled eggs (but only three times a week because of cholesterol), and buttered toast cut into strips (he wouldn't eat it any other way). Dinner must include hamburger and cottage cheese or vegetables (the crunchy part of lettuce being a particular favorite). And at bedtime, the pet-sitter was to remove Willy's collar, help the dog into his turned-down twin bed, and then wait patiently while the dog scurried to the bottom of the covers and returned to have the sheet folded neatly back from his chin.

When Jim had done what was expected of him the first night, he climbed tiredly into the adjacent twin bed. A short time later, Jim heard a creature scurry across the room. It jumped onto his bed and ran over his back. Jim lay awake all night. Willy did not stir.

In the morning, Jim saw that the creature trapped in the room with them was a flying squirrel. The well-rested Willy, on the other hand, saw nothing. He whimpered impatiently, requesting that his eggs and buttered toast be served.

your pets must do without you, their routines, and maybe even their houses. Here's how to leave your pet behind without taking worries with you.

FOR PETS IN GENERAL

Home Is Best

❑ If your need for privacy can coexist with someone coming to your home to care for your pets, choose that option when you're going out of town. Your animals will be on familiar turf, you'll save a car ride or two, dogs won't be in danger of contracting kennel cough or worse, and cats won't have to spend days in small cages.

Visitors Should Come Early and Often

❑ You'll make your animal most comfortable by engaging a sleep-in caretaker so that he can stick to your everyday routine. But if the thought of someone sleeping in your home and eating your food makes you leery, try to find someone who can stop over frequently enough to approximate the same care you give your pet (walking the dog before work, after work, and in the early evening, for instance).

No One Can Replace My Owner

❑ Warn the sitter that a particularly attached animal may not eat as much as usual without his loving owner in the house. The sitter should comfort the pining pet and tell the animal you'll be home in a few days, but there's not much else that can be done. If you'll be gone for more than a week or so and the animal is still refusing food after three days, the sitter should call your veterinarian for advice. (The sitter should *not* call you unless you have the option of coming home to correct the situation.)

The Mary Poppins of Pet-Sitters

❑ Look for a pet-sitter who really loves animals in general and yours in particular. One good way to find out is to mention that you're looking for someone respon-

sible to help take care of your animals and wait to see whether you get a nibble *before* you mention that you're willing to pay.

❑ Don't take age as the best indicator of a good pet-sitter. A responsible 8-year-old with a mother who will back him up is preferable to an uninterested 20-year-old looking for a place to bring dates.

Fair Play in Paying

❑ If you're engaging a preteen or teenager, ask neighbors what the going rate for baby-sitting is, then offer to pay a daily rate equal to about two hours of baby-sitting time. If you expect a lot of extras—cleaning the fish tank or giving the dog a bath—you may need to pay by the hour.

❑ Remember to mention all the duties you'll expect the sitter to perform, including grooming, walking, treats to get the pet's mind off an absent owner, and nonpet duties such as taking in the mail and the paper or turning on the lights. These duties should be fully explained before you and the sitter agree on a price.

If Your Twin's Not Available

❑ Don't expect a sitter to do all that you do unless you're willing to pay for all the time and effort. For example, if you and the dog take a two-mile run each day, you may have to settle for someone who will take her to the park every couple of days.

So You Talk to the Animals?

You know the old joke that you don't have to worry about talking to yourself unless you start hearing answers? That's how it is with talking to pets. It's fine to converse with your pets constantly—telling them your woes, sharing your day, discussing what color you might paint the bedroom—as long as you don't hear them answering back. In fact, having an unconditionally supportive listener, even if she *is* just a goldfish, is one of the most meaningful aspects of the human-animal bond.

How to Keep the Sitter Happy

❑ Do you have a lure you're not aware of? You may be able to provide a responsible young adult from your neighborhood, church, or local community college with

12 Things Every Pet-Sitter Needs

Once you've found a sitter who's worth hiring, increase her chances of success with thorough preparation and foresight. Here are a dozen things your pet's keeper will require.

1. A key to your house

2. An extra key to your house, left with a neighbor, and an introduction to that neighbor

3. Enough of your pet's usual food to cover all meals during your absence

4. Some extra cash in case the food runs out (or is devoured by a lonesome pet)

5. A can opener (if you have canned food) and instructions on how to use it

6. A leash (if the pet-sitter will be walking the dog) and instructions on putting it on securely, particularly if your dog has escapist tendencies

7. Directions to setting the thermostat in case weather conditions change drastically while you're gone

8. The veterinarian's phone number and instructions on when to summon him

9. Potential transportation to the veterinarian's office, from either the pet-sitter's parent or a helpful friend

10. Written reinforcement of verbal instructions regarding food, medicine, and exercise

11. A list of tips on potential pitfalls around the house (for example, "Fluffy will zoom right into the living room if you don't remember to close the door tightly")

12. Your phone number and instructions on how often you'd like a call. Or, for absences of more than ten days, two or three preaddressed, postage-paid postcards to your destination that say "Fluffy is fine," to be signed and mailed by the pet-sitter

a reward in lieu of or in addition to cash. Think of free rein with the CD player, cable TV, a quiet place to study for exams, or a freezer full of home-cooked meals she can eat after she feeds the animals.

Blame It on the Authorities

❑ Tell teenage or young adult pet-sitters that your insurance company will simply not stand for smoking in the house, for more than two people visiting, or for minors drinking alcohol on your premises. You'd probably find that this was true if you actually consulted the

authorities you name, and it establishes ground rules without casting you as a nag.

She'll Watch Out, So You Should, Too

❑ Let any pet-sitter know that a trusted neighbor will be watching out for him, to make sure he's not having any trouble. This is a subtle way of saying "Other people will know you're here."

Runaways Need Not Apply

❑ If you engage a pet-sitter who's under 18, always make sure her parents know about your arrangement. You don't want to contribute to the delinquency of a minor.

Practice Makes Perfect

❑ Have your pet-sitter come over a few times before you leave to practice feeding the pets in your presence. This gives you a chance to gauge the person's interest level (is she asking questions about which pets want what and how much?) and competency, and it also gives the sitter your endorsement in your pets' eyes.

FOR CATS ONLY

Plan Visiting Hours Carefully

Indoor cats can usually thrive with a little less attention than you would normally give them, as long as they have fresh food and water and easy access to the litter box. For them, you can probably get by with a once-a-day visit.

Indoor/outdoor cats need someone who can come by to let them out as frequently as they're used to.

AS THE FAMILY EXPANDS

If you believe those "stress tests" we're all so fond of, it appears that happy events, such as marriages and new babies, are every bit as stressful as natural disasters. From a pet's perspective, that's certainly true: Marriage and babies throw an entire household off kilter, demanding new roles, new schedules, and compromises. Here's how to withstand the stress and win over your pet and your new partner. And remember, with a bigger family, there's more love to go around.

FOR PETS IN GENERAL

Can Man's Best Friend Be Best Man?

❑ Make certain that your intended knows just how attached you are to your animals. "Binky is like a

12 Questions for a Potential Spouse or Roommate

You never really know how someone feels about pets until you live with that person . . . and with a pet. Still, a lot of issues can be avoided down the road if you talk about division of labor and pets' rights before you move in together or get married. Sit down with this checklist and make sure you both agree on the answers before calling the movers. You might even want to write down your conclusions for easy reference after the honeymoon is over.

1. Will we consider certain animals "yours" and certain animals "mine," or will they both be "ours" (and we'll be equally responsible for them)?

2. If "my" animal and "your" animal are incompatible, would we consider finding one of them a different home? If so, which one?

3. Will dogs or cats live outside or inside?

4. Does "outside" include the garage, shed, or screened porch?

5. If they live outside, when can they come inside (for a visit, when it's cold, when it's hot)?

6. Who will wake up with early risers? (This can be tricky if one partner is a light sleeper and one is a heavy sleeper who can tolerate more pet pleading without waking up.)

7. Who will pay for pet food? Kitty litter? Equipment? Treats? Veterinary visits? Or will these things come from the household budget?

8. Who will feed the animals?

9. Who will purchase food, what will the quality be, and how much of the household budget will go toward this expense?

10. Do we agree that our animal should be spayed or neutered or that we'll eventually breed her?

11. Who cleans up "accidents"?

12. Who will walk the dogs and how often?

member of the family, and he goes where I go" is a good way to put it. Or "I've always believed in treating cats like cats, not humans, so she stays outside, and I feed her on the back porch."

FOR DOGS AND CATS

Sparky Could Be a Mother's Helper

Never make a decision to give up a well-loved pet before a baby is born. Hormones during pregnancy can really make a mom-to-be protective, so you need to wait until they've settled down a bit to decide whether your pet would genuinely pose a threat to the child. You'll be surprised at how quickly a dog or cat and a baby bond. Babies love to watch cats move around, and even the most cynical dog will get worried and summon you if the baby is crying. A baby's first word is often the pet's name.

12 More *Questions for a Potential Spouse or Roommate*

You made it over the first dozen pet hurdles, and you're still speaking. Can you agree on these as well?

1. Who will clean the fish tank and how often?

2. Who will clean the bird, gerbil, hamster, or guinea pig cage and how often?

3. Who will clean the litter box and how often?

4. Who will make sure the child who's responsible cleans any of the above?

5. May dogs or cats go for rides in the car?

6. Will our dogs go on vacation with us?

7. Will birds be allowed to fly freely inside the house at any time? Only in certain rooms of the house? If so, who will clean up the bird mess?

8. Will cats and dogs be permitted in the kitchen?

9. May they beg at the dinner table?

10. Is the dog or cat allowed in the bedroom? What if we're in there sleeping? What if we're in there being intimate?

11. Can a dog or cat sleep in the bed with us? On the floor next to the bed?

12. What is the household's absolute maximum number of pets?

FOR DOGS ONLY

How Can I Ever Make It Up to You?

Expect some one-sided sibling rivalry between your indoor dog and the newborn. Bowser won't appreciate the baby's demands for extra time and attention. See that he gets some extra attention, too, even if you can't give it yourself. Ask a persistent baby visitor to give Bowser some encouragement, a walk, or a treat, for example.

Solve Two (Potential) Problems at Once

Ask a two-legged sibling to keep Spot company more often, and sweeten the pot with a bit of extra allowance for "helping Spot adjust."

Two for the Two O'Clock Feeding

If you have a quiet, well-behaved adult dog, allow her to attend nighttime feedings, particularly if you ordinarily banish her to the garage or the backyard for the evening.

Hey, This Kid Came with Benefits!

Build a combined baby/dog walk into your routine as soon as your doctor gives the okay. That way, your dog will see that there are actually pluses to having a child in the house.

Rock-a-Bye, Binky, in the Treetop

Let the dog know that he's still important by working his name into the little nursery rhymes and songs you sing and the patty-cake games you play with the child. The pup will know you're talking about him and be pleased.

WHEN DIVORCE DIVIDES A HOUSEHOLD

Breaking up is so hard to do that sometimes a pet gets ignored in the process. But your pet is more than just another hassle that needs to be dealt with in this trying

time. She can be a source of comfort, a neutral topic for you and your mate to talk about to ease tension, a link to a happier time, or a focus to help you get out of bed in the morning. Here are some ways to provide for your pet during a divorce and to help make her a part of the healing process.

FOR PETS IN GENERAL

You Get the Car; I Get the Cat

❑ Always spell out in the divorce agreement who will get the pet, or who will be responsible for finding the pet a new home if neither party can keep her.

❑ Only contest "pet custody" if you can prove that you were the one who took care of the animal during the marriage or if you can unarguably offer the pet a better home (with a yard, for example). The judge will not care who originally brought the pet into the home or paid for her. Only the recent year or so counts.

❑ Never allow bitterness to get in the way of seeing that a pet goes to the best-suited owner.

Don't Take Buffie, Too!

❑ If the divorce involves children, make every attempt to allow the child to keep the pet. Losing an animal on top of all the other losses is just too much for a child to bear. Besides, a child also needs someone to listen and be there in this trying time, and who better than her loving dog (or iguana, or guinea pig)?

Consider Temporary Custody

❑ When finances prevent either parent from moving to a place that takes pets, find a family friend or relative to care for your child's pet until the animal can live with the youngster once again. Make sure everyone realizes that the arrangement is temporary, and schedule a regular once-a-week visit to the animal. In the meantime, have the child devote some allowance to the an-

ONE PERSON'S SOLUTION

Scent of a Friend

When my brother, Greg, left for his freshman year in college, our dog had as hard a time seeing him go as the rest of the family did. Greg's bedroom is in our refinished basement, and Sedeka, a black Lab–spaniel mix, was used to sleeping there with him every night. After he left, she would stand at the top of the basement stairs and just cry and cry. After several days of this same routine, we started letting her go down to his room so that she could see that nobody was there. She would run down the stairs and look all around, hoping to see Greg. But of course she never did.

Finally, after this had been going on for a couple of weeks, my mother went to Greg's room and got a blanket of his that was also a favorite of Sedeka's. She put the blanket in the dog crate where Sedeka now sleeps. Sedeka immediately went over to the blanket and snuggled right in. We don't know whether Greg's scent calmed her down or she just liked the blanket, but she has been content ever since.

—**ALISON MacEWAN**
Duxbury, Massachusetts

imal's regular upkeep. That helps the child realize that the pet is still his.

Give Your Child a Pen-Pet

❑ If the pet lives with the noncustodial parent or the noncustodial parent gets a new pet, use Sparky to open the lines of communication with your child. Sparky can

send postcards, E-mail, small gifts, audiotapes, or videotapes. More important, a child writing back to Sparky may open up more than she would writing back to the mom or dad who moved out.

CAN THIS OWNER-PET PARTNERSHIP BE SAVED?

No animal is perfect, but some animals have more problems than you care to deal with. Maybe the fault is strictly the owner's—you simply don't have time for that rowdy dog after a long day at work, or you shouldn't have adopted a sixth cat when you live in a small apartment. Maybe it feels like the animal's fault—she's untrainable, too aggressive, too dumb, too mean. But before you reach the decision to disown an animal, examine all the alternatives for improving the relationship. In your exhaustion, you may have forgotten that there are resources to call on. Don't give up until you've tried them!

FOR PETS IN GENERAL

This Could Be the Start of a Wonderful Partnership

❑ You want your pet but can't deal with all the responsibility. Someone else wants a pet but has restrictions of his own. Why not team up with that neighborhood kid whose dad is allergic to cat hair or with your sister who works out of town and is home only on weekends? Share the cost of the pet, the chores, or the activities—halve whatever concern keeps you from feeling good about your ability to keep the pet. Draw up a certificate of co-ownership for your partner or seal the bargain with a glass of wine or a birthday party for your "new" pet.

Suggestions from the Court of Last Resort

❑ Your local animal shelter may be able to advise you on handling your pet's specific situation, for free. Just call and explain what's troubling you. Tell them you're having doubts about your ability to keep this animal and are wondering what to do. The shelter is more interested than anyone else in seeing that your animal doesn't end up back there—they've seen how many animals never find homes. Look under Animal Shelters or Veterinarians in the Yellow Pages, or call your city or county animal control department (in the government listings of the phone book) and ask for a referral.

FOR DOGS ONLY

We Can Retrain You

Dogs of any age can benefit from obedience training. Don't delay—find a trainer through the

4 *Quick Pet-Bonding Pick-Me-Ups*

These are designed to give you warm fuzzy thoughts about pets in general, which might just inspire you to see your pet in a new light. And when you remember how neat and sweet pets are, don't forget to let your four-legged friends know. Have you hugged your pet today?

1. Rent a video. Try a tear-jerking classic such as *Old Yeller* or a light comedy such as *That Darn Cat!* (the classic with Hayley Mills is especially good), *Beethoven,* or *Benji.*

2. Read a story. Check out *The Incredible Journey* from the library and ask yourself, "Would my pets seek me out over thousands of miles?" Or get mysterious with Lillian Braun's "The Cat Who . . ." series. Koko—a mind-reading, mystery-solving Siamese—is a key character, and you can't find a better description of the confounding nature and mystique of the feline.

3. Take some photos and carry them around. Catch your pet's everyday life on film, then put the photos on your desk at work. When other pet lovers find out that you have pets, you'll hear stories about theirs, which can inspire you one of two ways: "Wow, pets can be really cool (or funny)" or "Am I ever happy I have my loyal, house-trained Fido instead of *her* dog."

4. Create a brag board. At the office or community center, set up a bulletin board where folks can post pet snapshots with scribbled captions. Bragging about your pet, even in a backhanded way, can renew your pride in the animal.

Yellow Pages under Pet & Dog Training or ask your veterinarian or pet supply store for a recommendation. If you weren't counting on the expense of training, ask for extended payments or seek a trainer who bases her rates on the client's ability to pay.

Pet psychologists can help you solve the specific behavior problems (jumping, spraying, fighting, and so on) that are marring your relationship. They're not as widely available as obedience trainers, but look in the Yellow Pages under Pet & Dog Training or ask your breeder, local animal shelter, or veterinarian for recommendations. Pet psychologists usually charge per session. You're likely to spend about the same as you would for a visit to a local veterinarian.

Biting Doesn't (Always) Have to Mean Good-bye . . .

Some breeds bite for specific reasons. (Sheepdogs, for example, keep the sheep in a circle and keep potential attackers out by nipping. They may transfer that biting instinct when they're playfully "herding" the family in the yard or when they're barring a stranger from entering the "circle.") Turn to an obedience trainer or a pet psychologist for help with such a pet—but don't delay. It's important to pursue retraining aggressively and to confine your biter until the behavior is corrected.

Famous Pets for Famous People

Albert Schweitzer, the Nobel Peace Prize–winning physician, theologian, and philosopher, had a pet pelican. Ah, the eccentricity of genius.

. . . But Sometimes It Does

Biting is the one area in which you really need to consider drastic action if a trainer can't quickly set bad habits right. If a dog, particularly one with a history of abuse, has snapped at a child or broken loose and bitten a passerby, it may be better to have the animal euthanized than to risk injuring or terrifying someone else.

FOR CATS ONLY

So She's Not a Lap Cat

You may need only to revamp your expectations to be able to see your way clear to keeping a cat you don't think you want anymore. Did you expect a fluff ball that wants constant affection and end up with a spitfire

Bedtime for Bowser?

A person who lives alone can make an independent decision about whether it's okay for a cat or dog to sleep on the bed at night. But when the issue affects another interested party, prejudice and emotion enter the picture. Here are six suggestions to help you (and your pets) make the right moves.

1. If one partner strenuously objects, don't even think about it. Sleeping with animals can be a deep-rooted aversion, and if the human loses this battle, she may resent the pet. Although it's not easy to boot a pet from the bedroom, an animal can adjust more easily than an adult human.

2. Come up with a compromise. Let the cat sleep on the bed in the afternoon when no one is home, or let the dog sleep in his own bed at the foot of yours. If your pet is a cat, don't expect the animal to sleep *near* the bed but not *in* the bed. Cats are biologically incapable of doing that!

3. Don't start early. Puppies can wet the bed just as readily as they do the carpet.

4. Don't start at all if you don't plan to make it a habit. Never let an animal sleep on the bed during an illness or when your mate's out of town, then expect her to give up the cushy mattress later without being unhappy. Instead, you and the dog or cat could both sleep temporarily in a spot—perhaps the couch or a futon mattress on the floor—that you're willing to let her return to later on.

5. Have the animal checked for worms and treated for fleas. Roundworms or hookworms can be passed to humans through the bedclothes. And fleas won't hesitate to jump off Fido and bite his owner.

6. Take sleep habits into consideration. If even one partner is a thrasher or roller, it may be best to keep kittens and cats out of the firing line. Otherwise, they could be flattened. Although it's not likely to be fatal, Fluffy may scratch or yowl in an attempt to survive—or just because he's surprised.

"Don't touch me" beast? Remind yourself that life is full of compromises and let Mr. Alley Cat be himself. Stop trying to hug him, and he'll likely stop scratching you. Stop expecting purr-and-cuddle sessions, and you may realize that his sparring with the neighborhood dog is

Adopted! How to Write a Classified Ad That Works

A "pet needs good home" classified ad should be no more than 25 to 30 words, but it must cover the details most important to prospective owners. Here are key descriptions and phrases to help you find the right prospective owner for your pet.

1. Type of animal—including gender, breed, and approximate age.

2. "Needs good home."

3. "Has shots" or "Has first shots."

4. "Spayed" or "Neutered." This is a real selling point, so you might offer to pay for sterilizing your animal ("Will fund spaying") if this hasn't been done yet.

5. "Good with children" or "Needs adult attention"—the great divide for most prospective owners.

6. "Declawed." This is not a recommended procedure for cats, but if the damage is already done, you may as well publicize it, since it eliminates those who want an outdoor cat and encourages others who don't want a furniture-destructive pet.

7. "Needs room," "Active," or "Great pal for walkers." Put a positive spin on the animal's need for space and exercise and eliminate those in the market for a docile lapdog.

8. "Good watchdog"—a potential drawing card for some, but only if it's true.

9. "Lover, not fighter." This draws in those looking for affectionate cats and animals that won't create conflict with other pets. It's also a polite way to say that Fido will probably lick intruders' hands.

10. "Needs one-pet household." This is for the pet that simply can't share an owner.

11. Phone number and "only" times to call. To protect your privacy, never include your name or address. You can decide whether to give that information when people call.

There's no need to go into great detail about why you can't keep the animal. You'll have plenty of time to discuss that when a prospective owner asks.

something you can admire on another level. It won't be as much fun as you envisioned, but it's not exactly fun knowing you sent a cat to meet his maker either.

WHEN YOU MUST PART WAYS

It's a wrenching decision, but sometimes you simply must admit that an animal has not worked out at your house and will have to go elsewhere. Or maybe your situation is changing, and you can no longer give a pet the standard of living the animal so richly deserves. There's a real temptation to cut ties quickly and completely, sending the pet to the animal shelter. But try to exhaust your other options first. In a different situation, your ugly duckling may turn into the swan prince of pets.

FOR PETS IN GENERAL

Back to the Breeder?

❑ If you have a ferret or a purebred dog or cat, seek out the appropriate breed rescue group. They'll help place the animal in another home or possibly retrain her so that she can stay in yours. Your veterinarian may know of such a group, or you can look for a breeder's card posted at a pet supply store or veterinarian's office and call for information. If you have a dog, check the Internet for the current phone number of the American Kennel Club. (Search on the organization's name.) Then call the club and ask them to direct you to a breed rescue group.

Finders' Fees

❑ Establish a network of friends and family interested in helping you place your pet elsewhere. Let them all know that you have an animal that needs to move on and why: "My house is too small." "No one here has time to walk him." "It's irrational, but I'm scared she'll scratch the baby."

❑ Offer a financial incentive—say, $10 for a lead that results in an interview or concert tickets for whoever finds a new owner.

LIVING WITH PETS

Better the Pet You Know Than the Pet You Don't Know

❑ Your neighbors are probably in the best position to know your pet, and they may already have a family member who's attached to the animal. So ask around—you may find new owners in your own backyard.

Would You Turn Your Back on This Pet?

❑ Don't try using guilt to convince friends or fellow animal lovers to take your pet. That just burdens another household with an unwanted animal, and after a

4 *Questions to Ask before They Adopt*

If you've decided that you must pass your pet along to some other responsible owners, you want to make certain of two things: (1) that they can give your pet a better life than you can and (2) that they are not merely a stop on your animal's way to a research lab. Start your fact-finding when the prospective owners first answer your ad, then double-check during the interview or visit. Here are four questions to ask anyone you don't know well already.

1. Where do you live? Establish what type of house these folks have and what facilities they can provide for the animal. Ask for an address so that you can drive by to check out the setup.

2. Do you object to my seeing your driver's license? Explain that although you hate to act paranoid, there's been a rash of less-than-honest folks obtaining animals under false pretenses lately and then selling them to research laboratories.

3. Have you owned a pet before? If so, ask for some details about the experience—what they liked best about the pet, for example, or what happened to the animal.

4. Who is your preferred veterinarian? The answer to this question lets you know whether they're likely to provide the animal with proper preventive and medical care, and it also gives you an honesty check. Track down the veterinarian and ask her whether these people would make good owners for the pet you're putting up for adoption. If the veterinarian turns out to be fictional, you have your answer.

few such shifts, the pet really *will* be impossible to live with.

Take a Flyer (or Two . . . or Three . . .)

❑ Another way to find a new home for a pet is to place flyers where your name will be recognized and where you know people—your child's school or day care center, your fitness center or church, the veterinarian's office, a nearby restaurant or convenience store. The flyers should state your case in a friendly but brief fashion—"I have this great cat, but I also have seven other great cats"—on a brightly colored 8½- by 11-inch sheet of paper.

❑ For a boost in responses, take a few extra dollars and make prints of a flattering picture of your pet. Then attach a print to each flyer.

Tall, Dark, Loves Long Walks

❑ If—and only if—you're unable to find your pet a new home with people you know, place a classified ad in the local newspaper.

Separate the Committed from the Dabblers

❑ Always ask for some sort of financial commitment, however small, from prospective owners. For example, offer to take care of getting your dog's upcoming booster shots if they'll pay for the flea dip. Or say you'll have the animal registered if they'll repay $10 of the cost of the tags. If they have to commit something, they'll consider the decision more carefully, and you'll eliminate anyone interested in the dog or cat for resale to a laboratory.

RECONNECTING WITH AN OLDER PET

The honeymoon is over. That cute little ball of fur whose feet rarely touched the floor is now that huge furry floor mat you have to step over to do laundry. The kitten you watched chase her tail is now the cat

you see only at meals. The gerbil hasn't been out of the cage in who knows how long. (Do you still *have* a gerbil?) Your relationship with your pet can really lose its shine over time. But that's a situation you can change by becoming aware of what's turning you away from your pet and taking steps to correct it. Here's how to start enjoying your friend again.

FOR PETS IN GENERAL

When the Disenchanted Owner Is a Kid

❑ If little Jimmy is not living up to his end of the pet care bargain, try to reestablish a routine. Call a meeting with the child and ask him what needs to be done with the pet and how best to get that accomplished. Mark those tasks on a calendar and ask your child to suggest consequences if he fails to follow through.

❑ Establish a tracking process for kids ages five through eight, using fun stickers (maybe a paw print stamp from a stationery store) and a chart noting that the pet has been fed, walked, and brushed today.

Is This Pet Too Much for a Youngster?

❑ The child may have lost interest in the animal because the pet is simply too high maintenance. Perhaps you have a big, smelly dog that drags the child when they walk and requires huge bowls of food from a too-heavy bag. If your expectations are out of whack, consider giving the child some of your manageable adult chores (such as dusting). In exchange, you could agree to take over some of the pet care duties.

That's Groosss!

❑ It may sneak up on you overnight. A child who quite happily changed the papers in the birdcage or dished out fishy cat food for years now thinks everything is, like, yuck! The best way to handle this is to say "Yes, it's gross, and yes, we still love Fluffy anyway, and yes, you'll still have to help us deal with the gross part of owning a pet." But pledge not to bring up the topic or make her do the chore in front of friends who might

YOU'VE GOTTA LOVE 'EM

Now That's *Hard to Swallow*

It was not unusual for Irv Liss to let his pet boa constrictor roam his Natick, Massachusetts, living room, but it *was* unusual for him to leave the outside door open. Nevertheless, that was what he'd mistakenly done one day when he was out back. The neighbor was asking Irv whether he had seen his pet poodle (whom we'll call Fifi). No, Irv said, he hadn't seen Fifi.

What Irv *did* see, upon returning to his house, was that his boa constrictor had a poodle-size lump bulging just behind his head. The fact that Fifi was no longer lost did nothing to help neighborly relations.

But what worried Irv the most was the health of his snake. The animal had never eaten anything larger than a rat, and certainly nothing wearing a rhinestone collar. Over the next few days, Irv fretted, keeping everyone apprised of the lump's move through the snake's body. Then one day the snake passed a rhinestone—proof in the pudding of the poodle's fate. Several more rhinestones followed. So far, so good. But how would the snake pass a dog tag? Worried, Irv enlisted the aid of a veterinarian. Using tweezers, the doctor performed the delicate operation, and Irv was happy to report that everything came out okay in the end (except for the poodle).

just be appalled that your child has to flush a goldfish or that her dear old beagle is flatulent.

First They Giggle, Then They Get It

❑ With kids younger than fourth grade, you can use humor to relay the message that the animals can't care for themselves, that they are totally at the owner's mercy. For example: "Imagine Buffie getting the car keys and putting on her sunglasses to go to the store to get food." Or "Buffie had to get up, walk to the phone, and call me at work to tell me that she needed to go outside to use the bathroom."

Don't Bother Nagging

❑ Look for ways to establish open communication and to encourage suggestions for improving the situation.

5 *Ways to Help an Aging Dog*

Surely it was only yesterday that your puppy literally ran circles around you when you took her for a walk or climbed a mountain with energy to spare. Now she has a tough time making it up the stairs. Her vision and hearing aren't as strong as they once were either. And she sometimes gets confused. Yet the vet says there's nothing seriously wrong with her; she's just getting older. Dogs age, just as humans do (only faster). If your pet seems to be slowing down, here are some things you can do to help.

1. Watch the animal carefully, keeping track of where she is in the house. She may need assistance finding her way around.

2. Watch with particular care as she ascends or descends stairs, and help your pet if need be. If she is small and you are strong enough, you may need to carry her up and down stairs.

3. If you also have younger dogs, walk the older animal separately from the puppies so that the older dog can go at a slower pace instead of struggling to keep up with the others.

4. Make sure your pet is eating properly. Don't give her hard bones to gnaw on; she may not be able to handle them.

5. Never let her loose outdoors. She may get lost easily or become the target of more aggressive animals.

Forget "You promised," "I'm disappointed in you," or "Once again, I fed your cat." Kids will block out nagging.

A Cut above Bribery

❑ Try to reinforce the positive rather than punishing the negative as you and your child rebuild the owner-pet bond. Say "Fido can watch *Scooby-Doo* with you after your walk," not "No TV unless you walk the dog." This makes it seem as if the child and the pet are working together for good things—not that the pet is keeping the child from doing what she wants to do.

❑ Every now and then, tape a dollar bill to the bottom of the dog's food bowl or the package of litter box liners. Do it unpredictably—that way the child will do his best every time, never knowing whether today is dollar day.

FOR DOGS ONLY

Outta Here with Those Muddy Paws

If you have a backyard dog and you live where it rains, the thought of slogging out in the mud to play with your pup might be subconsciously wearing you down. Make a stone or brick path so that you can walk to his area mud-free.

Sittin' in the Sun

In the warm months, it's easy to banish an outdoor dog to her post. Place a sun umbrella and a lounge chair or hammock in a strategic location near the dog's outdoor stomping ground. This will lure adults and children to hang out with the pooch.

When Did We Lose the Leash?

If no one is walking the dog regularly, you may need to purchase a leash. Keep it on the front doorknob so that no one can leave the house without remembering there is a dog in the house that needs to be walked.

LIVING WITH PETS

If you can't seem to find time to walk the dog during the day, force yourself to wake up a half hour earlier in the morning. If you truly love to sleep in, set up a "consequences" system: Anytime you forget to walk the dog at another time of day results in a week of waking up early.

Rex Is Not the Only One Who Needs Training

If you associate care and feeding of your canine with things you like, you'll be more likely to establish regular habits. So let Rex into the kitchen when—and only when—you're having your morning coffee and a leisurely look at the newspaper. Brush him whenever your favorite television program is on. Take it one step further—don't allow yourself to watch the program without Rex in attendance. Get these routines going, and soon they'll be second nature.

Will Rogers (Almost) Barks for His Supper

President Calvin Coolidge loved pets. He had raccoons, lion cubs, a goose, a donkey, and a mynah (bird) that flew around on the second floor of the White House. It landed on people's shoulders and pecked at their ears. Coolidge sometimes startled guests by pouring milk out of his own glass and into a saucer, then placing the saucer under the table for the cats waiting there. He often fed the dogs from his own plate. One startled guest, humorist Will Rogers, said later that he was sure the dogs ate better than he did. Rogers observed, "The butler was so slow in bringing one course that I come pretty near getting down on all fours and barking to see if business wouldn't pick up with me."

Dress the Part

Buy yourself some comfortable new walking shoes, some jazzy shorts, or a portable radio with headphones to encourage your regular walking. It's up to you whether these items are rewards or motivators—and your pooch never needs to know that you're not walking just because you love to be with her.

Teach an Old Dog a New Trick

Most older dogs can still learn, so renew your interest in your pet by training him to fetch your slippers, shake "hands," or catch a Frisbee. All it takes is some training treats and some patience. (If your dog has really turned into an old lazybones,

Falling in Love Again

An older dog may not fetch as many balls or rush to greet you after work quite as quickly, but she's likely to develop plenty of new habits that can be just as endearing and just as much fun to observe. Be sure to look for the special things old dogs do to make you fall in love all over again. For example:

1. Seeking sun or the hearth to warm her old bones

2. Flailing her legs while dozing, in remembrance of rabbits (or mail carriers) chased

3. Growling low and patronizingly when a young pup plays too rough

4. Going on "last hurrahs"—chasing the neighbor's cat, grabbing a roast off the counter—long after you thought she was past it

5. Barking at things she *thinks* she heard

6. Barking at someone she can't see too clearly and then looking sheepish when she realizes it's you

7. Dozing companionably at your feet while you read the paper instead of whining to go for a walk

8. Huffing and puffing for ten minutes after insisting on going for a walk uninvited

9. Performing her old tricks—more slowly, but recognizably—to show off

10. Sitting still for long sessions of patting and petting so that you have plenty of time to let her know how much you still love her

it may be trick enough if he learns to get up off the back porch without anyone calling "Suppertime!")

Double Your Treasure: Share with a Friend

Do you have a dog-adoring friend at work who lives in an apartment where she can't keep pets? Does one of the children in your neighborhood dearly long for a dog? Loan your pet to them for outings, or at least encourage visitors. There's no law that says an owner has to provide 100 percent of the attention a dog needs.

It's also acceptable to pay someone else to make your dog's life more enjoyable. Perhaps a schoolchild who comes home to an empty house wouldn't mind coming over to exercise your dog in the afternoons. Or a college student might agree to take her to a park or beach for a few bucks.

YOU'VE GOTTA LOVE 'EM

Rufus Was the Sensitive Sort

Winston Churchill had a brown poodle named Rufus, whom he adored. At dinnertime, the dog wore a bib and sat on a special cloth next to Churchill while waiting to be served. In fact, the butler always served the dog first, while everyone else waited. When they went to the movies, Rufus sat on Churchill's lap and watched with him. Once they went to see *Oliver Twist*. The movie got to the point where a main character decides to drown his dog to keep the police from discovering him, and Churchill quickly covered Rufus's eyes. "Don't look now, dear," he said. "I'll tell you about it afterward."

FOR CATS ONLY

Just a Few Magic Moments Will Do

- Cats need just a small portion of your day. Set them on your lap as you surf the Internet or hold them as you talk on the phone. They'll think you're talking to them!
- Let a cat share a ritual with you—for example, clear a space on the bathroom counter so that she can lounge while you brush your teeth. Or let her lie on a nearby stool while you iron clothes.

Meow! It's Mealtime!

- If your inattention to the cat includes forgetting to feed her, resolve the situation by feeding her at the very same time every day for a week. This will get her body clock on a routine, and soon she'll be reminding you that it's time to be fed with some meows and *"purrup"* noises.

WHEN THE OWNER DIES FIRST

It's a sad reality: Some pets outlive the only loving owner they've ever known. Some animals never seem to get over the loss; others pine for a bit and then are ready to move on to fill a space in someone else's heart. Whether your thoughts are with an elderly or ill friend or relative or with your own distant future, here are some ways to ensure that an animal left behind still has something to live for.

FOR PETS IN GENERAL

Where There's a Will, There's a Home for Felix

❑ For peace of mind, think about including in your will some instructions as to who should take your pet in the event of your untimely death—*after* discussing the provision with the potential caregiver. Consider bequeathing to that same person some funds for the animal's care.

❑ Since you'll probably have many pets over the years, you may want to make pet specifications very general—"I ask my daughter Marge to care for any dog I own and my daughter Julie to take the cats"—so that you don't have to update the will each time you adopt.

Holy Cat!

Buddhists believe that when a person dies after reaching a high level of spiritual achievement, he enters the body of a cat, where he stays until the cat dies. He then enters paradise.

Good Intentions Are Not Good Enough

❑ If a much-loved relative leaves an animal behind, don't take the pet simply out of sentimentality. Think about whether you can truly provide a good home. If not, put your goodwill to good use by helping find the pet a place where she can be happy.

The Injustice of It All

In 1968, a woman named Ella Wendel of New York passed away. Nothing unusual about that. What *was* unusual was Wendel's will: She bequeathed $30 million to her dog, Toby. Not surprisingly, Wendel's relatives contested the will, and the executors put the dog to sleep before the case was settled.

Comfort Is His Middle Name

❑ Pets used to living with people in poor health can actually be a godsend to another ailing or elderly person. When you're looking for a new adoptive home for a deceased friend's or relative's pet, seek out such folks. Call your local Humane Society first to see whether there are any programs emphasizing animals for shut-ins in your area. Also consult the local chapter of the American Association of Retired Persons (AARP), the Department of Human Services, and any local senior centers or AIDS or Alzheimer's support groups. You should be able to find any of these groups in the phone book (in the white pages, Yellow Pages, or blue government listings) or by checking with the reference desk at your local library. Or ask your veterinarian for leads.

AS PETS AGE

The gray in the muzzle, the ever-slower stretch in the morning, the longer naps—these things creep up on us, until one morning we realize that our pets are getting, well, old. While aging pets are certainly sad reminders of our own mortality, there is also a certain pleasure in watching pets evolve—in being the one to see them through, from paper-training to their last precious days of tottering around. Here are some ideas on learning to appreciate the final stages of life and keeping up with the issues that come with age.

FOR PETS IN GENERAL

Just How Old Is Old?

❑ As your animal gets on in years and starts seriously slowing down, make sure to ask your veterinarian how much longer you can expect to have your beloved pet around. Veterinarians are only human, and yours might feel uncomfortable broaching this painful topic.

A WORD FROM DR. DEVINNE

Don't Agree to Disagree

DR. CHARLES DEVINNE *of Peterborough, New Hampshire, who has more than 15 years of veterinary experience and whose private practice currently concentrates on dogs and cats*

It's hard enough for any pet owner to decide, as an animal's condition goes downhill, whether to have that animal put to sleep. It's even worse when there's more than one owner involved and they disagree. One thinks it's time, and the other doesn't. If there's one thing I've learned over the years, it's that if one person thinks it's not time, it's not time. It's *definitely* not time.

When that happens, I try to outline clearly where we're going. Of course, I do whatever I can to make the situation better in terms of medication. And then I make absolutely sure—it's cast in stone—that the owners bring the animal in for a follow-up visit in a short amount of time. I might have them come in again in, say, five days. And again in another five days. Each time, the goal is to make an assessment. Usually within ten days, the person who started out thinking it wasn't time has accepted that the situation isn't going to get any better. But those ten days give the person enough time to come to grips with the decision, which is really important.

When one party hasn't fully accepted the decision but agrees to go along with it anyway on the theory that it's the right thing to do, that person is going to have some bad feelings toward the spouse or partner. Each person really has to come to the decision in his own way.

Believe it or not, knowing is better than wondering because you can plan your pet's life accordingly and take pains to let her know she's loved before it's too late.

❑ Small animals can slip away quickly. The three or four years they have on this earth can pass in no time. Make a special effort to know their expected life spans, especially if your small child is the primary owner. Young children need time to prepare for a pet's passing.

FOR DOGS AND CATS

There's a Place in the Sun

🐾 Remember that older dogs and cats suffer from extremes of heat and cold more severely than young ones. Make certain to bring them inside on nights when the temperature goes below freezing.

A WORD FROM DR. DEVINNE

The Hardest Decision

DR. CHARLES DEVINNE
of Peterborough, New Hampshire, who has more than 15 years of veterinary experience and whose private practice currently concentrates on dogs and cats

Anytime you have to make the decision to have a pet put to sleep, it's a tremendously difficult thing. Usually you have a dog that's very ill—say, with cancer—and he can't breathe well. The owners are in the office, Fido's on the table, and the owners say, "We think it's about time." Tears are running down their faces. And then they ask, "What do you think?"

Of course, that's a hard one. As a professional, I can't make that decision. My job is to lay out all the information, then leave it up to the client. But I do tell people that it sometimes helps to look for three things to judge the quality of life the animal is experiencing.

Look for opportunities to create warm spots for sunning. Leave a curtain open near a window that gets direct sunlight, or, in spring and fall, leave just a transparent storm door between your pet and the morning sun.

Try a Warm-Up Routine

On cold mornings, give your pet a special warming treat. Throw a clean pet blanket in the dryer for ten minutes on medium heat, then let your pet snuggle in it.

FOR DOGS ONLY

Games for the Geriatric Set

For an older dog, develop a few games that are fun but not strenuous. Play "keep away" on the floor, for

The first is locomotion. Can the pet get up and walk someplace on his own if he wants to, or go down stairs? If he can, fine. But if the animal is in substantial pain or is frustrated by orthopedic problems that make moving around difficult, his quality of life is definitely lessened.

The second thing to consider is whether the animal is interested in food, on some level, on a routine basis. Unless an animal (like a snake) is in hibernation, not eating for extended periods of time is obviously not compatible with a good quality of life.

Finally, I think the animal should be able to recognize the owner. There should be some communication going on. When you walk into a room, if Fido lifts his head, looks at you, and gives a couple of tail wags, great. But if you're in a situation where he's unwilling or unable to recognize you—if he's off in his own little world, just trying to hang in there and survive the day—his quality of life is really pretty rough.

Making this decision is never easy, but in my experience it can be a little more manageable if you approach it in this way.

example. With the dog on his tummy, roll a ball to one paw. Then as he tries to paw it or get it with his mouth, roll it quickly to the other paw. Let him have it after a few rolls. If he drops it, get ready to roll it again.

Even an older pet that's no longer terribly active will enjoy it if, while she's lying on her back, you gently roll her from side to side (assuming she doesn't have painful arthritis).

Once a day, get your dog's attention and throw his Nylaring or chew toy down a long corridor or across the kitchen floor. It's up to him whether to run to retrieve it or to saunter over to get it at his leisure.

ONE PERSON'S SOLUTION

Knowing When to Let Go

I had a 15-year-old Yorkshire terrier. She'd been quite sick, and I knew that she was approaching her time to die, but I was worried about how I'd know when it was time to let her go. Then over the Fourth of July weekend, she jumped or fell off the bed, or had a seizure, and I found her in the bedroom flailing around. The next day and through the night, she couldn't stand up to pee and couldn't hold her head up. Then my other dog, Bailey, a golden retriever, started going berserk, and he wouldn't go near the room where she was. When I took the terrier outside on a blanket, Bailey was crying and whimpering at her and looking at me. He let me know it was time. There was no question in my mind, and I took her to the veterinarian's to be put down.

—**BARB DAUGHERTY**
Walland, Tennessee

The Mind Is Willing . . .

It's natural to allow a dog to set the pace for a walk, run, or play session. But when a dog reaches old age, she may not know when to stop, and she will be sore if you play too long or too strenuously. Make sure you halt the game of catch while your pet is still feeling frisky.

FUNERAL ARRANGEMENTS

It's the last labor of love you'll perform for a pet: making arrangements for burial or cremation. Those final decisions are probably something you'd rather not think about, but somebody has to make sure your pet rests in peace—and within legal limits.

FOR PETS IN GENERAL

The Vet as Undertaker

❑ You can count on your veterinarian to dispose of the body if you have your animal euthanized or if the pet dies at the veterinarian's office.

❑ If you'd like to have your animal cremated, with ashes to spread in a beloved area, ask your veterinarian for a referral.

❑ If you'd prefer to bury your animal in your yard, let the veterinarian know as you check in for your last visit.

When a Pet Dies at Home

❑ What do you do if your pet dies at home or is killed by a car and you don't want to deal with the remains? In a city or large town, call your local Dead Animal Disposal Unit, usually listed in the city or county government portion of the phone book. (If you can't find such a listing, try the Department of Sanitation or look under Animal Control in the Yellow Pages.) Such officials will usually come and take the body for disposal. Who pays depends on city or county policy, but don't be shy about asking whether you'll incur any charges.

❑ In a small town or rural area, find out whether similar services are available by calling the local Humane Society, sheriff's office, or police department. Folks there should know or should be able to put you in touch with someone who does.

❑ If you're more comfortable bringing your dead animal to the vet's office than having strangers cart off your pet, call and see whether your vet is willing to take care of the body. Most will be. Do this within a few hours of death, as decomposition begins quickly and is smelly.

Call Before You Dig

❑ If you're burying anything larger than a guinea pig, find out legal restrictions on burying animals in your yard by calling the county or city Dead Animal Disposal Unit, or look under Animal Control in the Yellow Pages. Most large towns and cities ban the practice because they're worried about runoff water pollution, but you can sometimes plead for an exception to be made.

❑ Animal burial is usually permitted in rural areas and small towns, but double-check with authorities. If you can't find a number for the Dead Animal Disposal Unit in the town or county listings in the local phone directory, call the local sheriff's office or police department, the county health department, or the town hall to find out whom to ask.

Burial Details

❑ When you prepare to bury your pet, dig a hole deep enough to have at least one to three feet of dirt on top of the body. (Use the higher measure if you live in a wet climate or have light or sandy soil that washes away easily in rain.) That keeps marauding animals from disturbing the body, discourages curious kids from digging up the remains, and keeps the body from washing away in heavy storms.

❑ It's a good idea to keep all animal graves at least 250 feet from natural water sources such as springs and wells.

Let There Be Life

LIVING WITH PETS

❑ Since you have the ground tilled anyway, consider planting some daffodil bulbs, a flowering bush, rosemary (to symbolize remembrance), or anything else that will commemorate your pet and give you a reason to come outside and think about the animal every now and then.

When the Cold, Cold Ground Is Too Cold

❑ Sometimes the ground is too firmly frozen to allow burial of even the tiniest gerbil. In this case, you have two options: (1) Ask your veterinarian, the city, or the county to dispose of the body, or (2) put the body "on ice" until the ground thaws. If you choose the latter, "bury" a tiny animal in a clay or peat pot (do not use plastic) of indoor potting soil, wrap the pot in a plastic bag, and store the whole thing in a shed, unheated garage, crawl space, or unused tree house until you can "transplant" the body. After the soil thaws, take off the bag and bury the animal, pot and all. The whole thing will eventually become part of the soil. Don't forget to take care of this as soon as the weather warms up. (Mark a reminder on your calendar!)

For a Bigger Animal, It's a Bigger Deal

❑ When the animal is larger than a toy breed or cat, it's best to let the authorities take care of disposal, if that's an option. But if you're attached to the idea of burying your pet under his favorite tree out back

COMMON MISTAKES

I Wish I'd Never Said That . . .

Grief can compel people to make really harsh remarks. One particularly hurtful statement is: "My pet's death hurt me the same way a child's death hurts a parent." Although you may mean every word of it, don't use this phrase in front of parents, especially those who have lost children. And even if you make the statement exclusively in pet lovers' company, word has a way of getting around. Not only does the sentiment cut deeply, but it also serves no purpose. You don't know how a parent who's lost a child feels, you're not in a competition over who hurts more, and those who don't understand the depth of your feelings aren't going to gain that understanding if you liken it to a human relationship. It *is* okay to say "Binky was a member of the family" or "Binky was the best family I had." That way you're not comparing relationships—you're just stating facts.

and he dies in the middle of January, you can wrap the body in four layers of plastic leaf bags and place it in one of those giant handle-lock plastic garbage cans (available at home supply and discount stores). Transplant the body the second the ground can be worked, engaging a backhoe operator (look in the classified ads of your local newspaper under a heading such as "Livestock and Farm") to dig up the area if necessary. Never proceed without first getting the approval of your city's or county's Dead Animal Disposal Unit or, in a small town, the local sheriff's office or county health department.

❏ Alternatively, check to see whether your vet might have a freezer storage area that you could use or rent until the ground thaws.

THE LAST GOOD-BYE

A wide range of emotions can attend the death of a pet. There's sadness that a loved companion and friend is no longer with us; contemplation of the "end of an era" that the animal signified in your life; and guilt, whether you're wishing that you had been a better owner or feeling bad that you weren't able to prevent an accidental death. But all these feelings are wrapped around a bigger emotion: love for your pet and the part he played in your life. Here's how to work through these feelings and learn to live with the sweet memory of your pet.

FOR PETS IN GENERAL

Plan to Fall Apart

❏ When your animal is in the final stages of life and you know it, create a plan for having things covered at work and at home if you fall to pieces once the animal dies. Explain to your boss, "This cat is a very big part of my life, and she always has been. I'm just not sure how I'll react when she dies. I may need Louise to pick up my projects for a day or two if I'm having difficulty coping." Many people find that they actually welcome

hard work and staying busy when an animal dies, but make sure you're covered if you just want to spend some time alone.

❑ Always offer to take vacation days or unpaid leave time. Despite the depth of your feelings, it's a considerable stretch to expect your company to pay for pet bereavement.

How to Deal with Rejection

❑ If your boss rejects your plan, accept it philosophically. At least you'll know what to expect when the sad event transpires. Don't sulk or make remarks such as "Fine, but I'm sure I won't be any help to you when I'm feeling so awful." You'll just harm your professional reputation, and it's doubtful that you'll change anyone's opinion about your heartfelt grief.

I'm Okay, You're Okay

❑ Tell yourself that your emotions are perfectly normal and acceptable, no matter how deeply you're grieving or how lightly you're taking the death. It's okay to grieve more for your pet than you would for a human. It's okay to cry for days or not at all. It's okay to feel very sad or to be anxious to get on with your life. Trust your instincts and do what feels right.

No Time Limits

❑ Don't expect to grieve and "get over it" on any set schedule. In fact, don't expect to get over it at all. Grieving for some pets is similar to saying good-bye to someone you love and will always love. You'll never forget them or stop thinking about them, but you must move on in your life and take their memory with you.

Reaching Out On-Line

Grieving pet owners can give and receive support on-line by searching on the keywords "Rainbow" and "Bridge." The Rainbow Bridge Web site offers owner-written inspirational poetry (it's not Walt Whitman, but it soothes the heart) and opportunities to chat with others experiencing the same grief. If you don't have Internet access at home, you may be able to go on-line through your public library, and at least print out the letters.

3 Ways to Commemorate a Dead Pet

There are many creative ways to keep your deceased pet's memory alive—and maybe to benefit living animals and their owners in the bargain. Here are a few.

1. Commission an oil painting. Some artists paint animal portraits as a specialty, and they will usually work from a photograph. To find a reputable artist in your area, ask your veterinarian or a local frame shop for a recommendation, then evaluate some work samples. Expect to pay at least $100 for a basic, one-animal, notebook paper–size work and more for more subjects or a larger work.

2. Create a shadow box. Shaped like a cereal box (but more nearly square), a shadow box is generally made of wood, vinyl, or metal and has a transparent front "door." It allows you to display a collection of photos and three-dimensional memorabilia—such as a favorite toy or a collar. You can prop the closed box on a tabletop or mount it on a wall. With some research, you can find a shadow box in any color or texture to match your decor. Prices vary widely, so it pays to do some comparison shopping in home supply stores, frame shops, boutiques, and mail-order catalogs.

Working on a shadow box can be good therapy for bereaved pet owners.

3. Donate a book in your pet's memory to the local library. Who said you have to be human to be a philanthropist? Most libraries allow donors to include a bookplate that says "In Memory of . . ." Choose a pet care book like this one or a book dedicated entirely to your animal or breed. This is a particularly thoughtful gesture if it's a book the library wouldn't normally have—one on ferrets, for example, or tarantulas. Children's fiction is another nice way for your pet to be remembered, as are picture books about animals from parrots (*Town Parrot* by Penelope Bennett) to guinea pigs (*I Love Guinea Pigs* by Dick King-Smith) to plain old cats and dogs. If you're not sure what's appropriate, ask the librarian what's on her wish list.

Take the High Road on Low Comments

❑ Some people cannot resist making remarks such as "Why are you still crying about that? That was last week!" Don't get into an argument with them, but simply respond, "You never really get over a loss. But I will accept it, learn from it, and move on with my life."

Keep the Memory Alive

❑ Talk about your animal whenever the opportunity arises. ("Remember how Binky loved to dig under that rosebush?") When you talk about your dead animal, you reinforce what she meant to you—and still does.

❑ Create a scrapbook of your pet and ask anyone who figured in your pet's life to contribute a memory on paper. Don't hesitate to call on relatives, ex-husbands, the postman, children who have grown up and moved away. You may be surprised at what an impact your pet had on other people—or just get a good laugh and something to show your grandchildren.

It's Okay to Speak Ill of the Dead

❑ Ask people to share their bad memories, too—the stinky breath, the favorite dress ruined, the scratch that got infected. It helps you to keep from feeling guilty about mixed feelings about a pet, keeps the memory from being impossible for another pet to live up to, and might just add some much-needed comic relief.

Help Your Child to Cope

❑ Never skirt the issue with a child of any age. Clarify that the animal is dead and not coming back and explain why he died (feline leukemia, his body wore out, or he ate poison in the woods). Children can sense sadness and deserve to know the uncomplicated truth. Otherwise, they might think they've somehow caused the sadness or their pet's disappearance.

❑ Explain to a toddler that the animal's heart and body have stopped working and that they'll never work

again. Repeat that as many times as is necessary. Young children have a hard time understanding the finality of death.

Let Her Picture This

❑ If it fits in with your religious beliefs, tell the child that the animal is safe in heaven now or say that although she's dead, we'll always carry her with us in our hearts. Drawing a picture together of the animal going to heaven is therapeutic and provides a visual image for the child to focus on.

No-Fault Reassurance

❑ Children in the six- to ten-year-old group are particularly prone to "magical" thinking. They're in a developmental stage in which they think they can create

Telling a Child about a Pet's Terminal Illness

Children should be able to share fully in a pet's final days, experiencing both the awe of a life well lived and the sadness of knowing that the pet will die and be missed. Here are some ways to draw youngsters in.

• Be honest. Tell the child that the pet is going to die and (in general terms) when you expect it. Say "The veterinarian has tried, and he just can't make Binky better. So we're going to love Binky and take care of him the best way we can until he dies."

• Help the child to feel blessed. Say "Aren't we lucky that we've had the pleasure of knowing Binky all this time? We'll miss him when he dies, but he's had a good life, and he's made our lives better, too."

• Let the youngster help. Be sure your child knows what an honor it is to sit up with the dog, hand-feed him soft food, or hold him in the car on the way to the vet's. Say "This is all we can do for Binky now, and I want you to help, just like you helped when he was brand-new."

• Celebrate a reprieve. If you get a few extra weeks or days, say "Aren't we lucky to have Binky even longer than the doctor thought we would? That gives us a little more time to get ready to say good-bye."

circumstances and cause disasters. Particularly if the pet died in an accident or the child might have wished him dead, you need to clarify that the child played no part in the pet's death. Here's a good way to put it: "You know how many times we wish for things, such as 'I wish I wouldn't have that test tomorrow'? Wishing doesn't really make things happen, does it? I hope you know that nothing you did or said or wished for made Simba get hit by that car."

When You Are *at Fault*

❑ Sometimes a child's or adult's actions *did* contribute to the pet's death—maybe an unleashed dog got hit by a car or an unattended gerbil was eaten by the cat. Then it's important to tell the child, "We made a mistake, but I'm the adult, so it was my responsibility that this happened. I couldn't be sorrier."

Let's Do Better This Time

❑ Publicly acknowledge how you contributed to your pet's death. It's a powerful tool for keeping other people from making the same mistake. And although you'll never feel good about failing to protect your pet, you will get comfort from warning others. Write a letter to Ann Landers or the local newspaper urging other animal owners to obey leash laws or get their pets vaccinated, so that they won't lose an animal, too. Or volunteer to speak on behalf of the Humane Society at local schools or day care centers. Your child can do the same, or he might write a report or give a talk at school about the importance of responsible pet care.

Release the Relief

❑ Sometimes there's no denying that your animal was a scratching, biting, or bird-killing bully; a slobbering, smelly embarrassment; or just really aloof and unlikable. If you're relieved that the animal is dead, go with the good feeling. Tell yourself or a child who's feeling guilty, "Marmaduke was part of our family, and we ful-

filled our responsibility to him, even when that cost us dearly. Now he's dead, and we know he's safe. Most important, we can feel good because we know he won't be bothering anyone anymore."

Tell Me a Story

❑ To help a child deal with the death of a pet, read with the youngster a picture book that has death as a theme and listen for questions about the story line. This is particularly helpful for parents and grandparents who are uncomfortable talking about emotions. You can facilitate the discussion by talking about the book, then relate it to your own situation and feelings. Two great titles for pre–second-graders are *The Tenth Good Thing about Barney* by Judith Viorst and *Nana Upstairs & Nana Downstairs* by Tomie dePaola. *Marvin Redpost: Alone in His Teacher's House* by Louis Sachar is good for preadolescents.

❑ Never hand a child a nonfiction work about death and dying to read on his own. It's your job—not the child's—to put it in the right context.

IS IT TIME FOR ANOTHER PET?

You can never really "replace" a pet that has died. That's what's so tough about the decision to adopt another animal. It seems so risky and sort of . . . disloyal. Here are some ways you can tell whether you're ready for take two in the wild world of reward and responsibility known as pet ownership.

FOR PETS IN GENERAL

Are You Ready to Love Again?

❑ Many a person quickly buys another pet because she misses the animal that died. But that can be a big mistake because you'll never have that animal again, and the new pet will suffer if you expect him to fill the old pet's role in the family. You're ready for a new pet when you can honestly say "I want to have a relationship with a dog (or parrot, or ferret, or hamster)," not "I want another Fluffy."

YOU'VE GOTTA LOVE 'EM

Friends for Life

Floyd is a two-year-old, fun-loving shih tzu. This little guy loves everyone and everything. If he sees a person, he runs over to say hello. If he sees another dog, he thinks it's his long-lost friend. It doesn't matter whether they're big or small, he runs right up to them with his tail wagging a mile a minute. Life is a big game to Floyd. I wish I had his temperament.

Floyd and I have enjoyed everything together. He comes along to the office, to the supermarket, to the bank, and anywhere else they allow me to bring him. I think he's more popular than me.

If you can't tell, I love this little dog. Unfortunately, some months ago he got very sick. He was diagnosed with kidney disease and has had several transfusions. I told my veterinarian that I wanted to keep up treatments only as long as it made sense and Floyd was still enjoying life. Now my vet has told me that we need to think about stopping the treatments.

Through all of this, Floyd has remained the happy-go-lucky dog he's always been. He even gets excited when we go to the vet's office, and you'd think he would hate that place. He's been a great dog and companion, and I dread the day when I will have to say good-bye.

Most people could learn a lot from Floyd. I have learned a lot, and when he goes, I will miss him dearly. He is my best friend.

— **ANDREW VEGA**
Biloxi, Mississippi

LIVING WITH PETS

Are You Too Old for This?

❑ Remember that you've gotten used to your pet at whatever age she—and you—were when she died. When you're evaluating whether to take on a new pet, consider whether you're ready for a puppy or kitten after losing your well-trained adult dog or lazy, easy-going adult cat. After all, you're not as young—and may not be as carefree—as you were last time you selected a pet. Start from ground zero as you evaluate your need for a pet and your ability to fulfill your responsibilities. If a frisky baby animal seems like too much to handle, think about adopting a slightly older pet.

COMMON MISTAKES

Getting a New Pet on the Rebound . . .

Not wanting a void in their lives for even a second, lots of pet lovers rush right out and buy another guinea pig or kitten or adopt another shelter dog within days of a pet's death. This is not a good idea. You need time to absorb the emotions associated with an animal's death, to deal with the grief and maybe the guilt, before making the major decision to include another animal in your life. How much time depends on the person and the relationship with the pet, but the bare minimum is a month. Take part of that time to evaluate your last owner-pet relationship and decide whether there are areas you might want to improve on. If it's been five or ten years since you were in the pet market, you may find that things have changed—-and your needs and wants probably have, too.

Will Things Be Different This Time?

❑ Take a long, hard look at the reason your last animal died, and don't repeat any mistakes. If your dog got hit by a car, for example, don't get another pup unless you're willing to fence in the yard. If your cat ate the fish or a gerbil, it's pointless to bring in another victim for her.

❑ If a young child owned the pet or had access to it, take particular care to investigate "mysterious" deaths, particularly with mice, gerbils, hamsters, or kittens. Did the pet get squeezed to death or smothered, or did she die of neglect? There's no point replacing an animal unless you can correct the situation.

You're Not Benedict Arnold

❑ Don't feel that you're betraying your deceased pet by replacing him. Tell yourself that no pet could ever

replace Old Yeller but that you still have love to give and receive.

❏ Count on still being sad about the pet that died, even though you have someone new to cuddle with, take on walks, or watch in the fishbowl. Each pet is an individual, so expect to have individual memories of each.

I'm Not Fifi; My Name Is Fluffy

❏ Always allow the new pet to develop her own identity—warts and all. If you ceaselessly compare the new animal to your former pet, you're not going to get maximum enjoyment from your new family member. You'll all too likely overlook some good traits, while resenting that the new pet doesn't resemble your other pet in certain ways. Constant comparisons can be miserable for the animal, too—especially for dogs, which live to please.

❏ If your deceased pet was a once-in-a-lifetime standout, you may need to take special precautions so that you don't expect a new pet to live up to his predecessor's reputation. Try a new breed of the same animal—an Abyssinian instead of a Siamese, for example. A pet of a different gender might take the pressure off, too, since (sexist or not) you'd rarely expect an animal of another sex to have exactly the same personality. Or you may be able to get that distance simply by selecting a pet of a different color.

COMMON MISTAKES

. . . Or Waiting Way Too Long

A pet's death can be such a painful loss that you want to take your time getting into another emotionally challenging relationship. But don't wait so long that you get out of the "animal habit"—changing litter boxes, waking up early, unwinding with your pet each afternoon. If you go more than three or four months without a pet, not only are you losing the stress release and bonding benefits, but you also may have to learn some hard-to-establish habits all over again.

REDUCING ANIMAL ABUSE

Once you have your own pet, it seems natural to take an interest in other people's animals. This heightened awareness makes it impossible to overlook the mistreated animals

you see in all walks of life. But you need not stand idly by. Without taking on the world's troubles, you can encourage more responsible pet ownership in your circle of friends and acquaintances and report to the proper authorities any incidents that are too hot for a single concerned citizen to handle.

FOR PETS IN GENERAL

Is It Abuse or a Difference of Opinion?

❑ Before you rush in where angels fear to tread, consider whether an animal that you feel is being mistreated is actually being abused. Some pet owners may not share your high standards for pet care—buying store-brand dog food, for example, is not abusive, nor is leaving a dog in a fenced-in area outside (except in extreme weather). It's okay to share your opinion with

A WORD FROM DR. DEVINNE

You Can *Remain Anonymous*

DR. CHARLES DEVINNE
of Peterborough, New Hampshire, who has more than 15 years of veterinary experience and whose private practice currently concentrates on dogs and cats

About once a week, I get a call from somebody who wants me to look into a case of possible animal abuse. One woman came to my office, and she was shaking like a leaf. She wouldn't give me her name, but she was so upset, she looked as if she was ready to have a nervous breakdown. She'd seen her neighbor from a couple doors down beating his dog, really laying into him. She said that it was a real thrashing that went on for a long time. Then later, she could hear—from two houses away—the man swearing at the dog. It sounded to her as if he was throwing the dog down some stairs.

Anyway, she was convinced there was a

a fellow pet owner ("You know, I could never bring myself to leave our puppy alone at home during the day"), but save your heartfelt arguments and energy for obvious incidents of abuse and neglect. They include beating, tormenting, and failing to provide food, water, and shelter.

Know the Animal's Rights

❑ If you feel that an animal is being abused and you're not confident that you can correct the situation with a few words to the owner, find out the laws in your area. You need to know what type of abuse local authorities will act on and how to report it. Start your phoning with city or county government agencies responsible for animal control. (They're usually listed in the white pages of the phone book along with other city or

lot of physical abuse going on, and she was afraid for her own safety. If this man found out that she'd reported it, she was afraid he'd retaliate. In our town, our dog officers are police. So after I called the Humane Society, I called one of my friends in the police department, and he reassured the woman that yes, the situation would be taken care of, and yes, she could remain anonymous.

The Humane Society actually posted someone near the man's house to watch the situation for a while, and they found that this man did indeed have a problem with the dog. So they approached the man to remove the dog. But rather than coming in with guns drawn and sirens blazing, they were very diplomatic, telling him that they were there to take this "problem" dog off his hands.

Of course, that "problem" dog was a real sweetheart—but those folks knew what they were doing. If you suspect a case of serious animal abuse in your town, don't say anything to the possible abuser. You may simply make him defensive, which could in turn make the situation worse for the dog—or for you. Instead, call the local Humane Society and ask them to look into the situation.

county agencies. Alternatively, you can get the appropriate agency's number by calling directory assistance or your local library's reference desk.) When you contact the government animal control entities, ask about applicable leash laws in your area. Also find out which offenses are punishable by citation, which ones merit an animal's removal from its owner, and what a concerned citizen can do to get the ball rolling.

❑ Alternatively, call a local animal shelter for the same information.

Know Who Your Friends Are

❑ Even the smallest towns and rural areas have groups that promote animal welfare. Call them to get behind-

Tact and the Neglectful Neighbor

You notice that your neighbor's dog is tied to a tree and the rope is long enough that it could get wrapped around the tree and possibly strangle the dog. Or a friend's cat always seems to be strolling in the road. Whatever the situation, if you're sure a pet isn't getting the best treatment and you have a reasonable hope of encouraging the owner to do better, press on. But choose your words carefully so that you come across as a fellow pet lover who maybe has a bit more knowledge about caring for animals—not a zealot who might just turn things over to the police.

For a tactful approach, consider phrasing your comments along these lines.

1. I've noticed that your dog howls a lot toward the end of the day, and I wonder whether I could help you out by going to let him out to go to the bathroom on days when you work late.

2. I see that you have one of those great Doberman pinscher puppies. Did you know that I have a lot of animals, too? I've really learned a lot over the years—like I know it's too cold tonight for a puppy to stay outside—and I'd love to exchange tips with you. I've even got some really good books if you're interested.

3. I know you probably don't want me nagging you, but I just had to let you know that your cat's been getting in the road because I had a horrible experience with that myself. My cat was hit in that very spot, and I couldn't bear it if it happened to yours without my speaking up.

the-scenes information about animal abuse cases in your area: Are the authorities tough on abuse or too busy to do much? Most animal welfare groups will be listed in the Yellow Pages under Veterinarians or Animal Shelters.

Don't Think You're Marshal Dillon

❑ It may be tempting to go spring that puppy that's chained in the heat without water, but you should never take the law into your own hands. That's a good way to get shot, bitten, or charged with breaking and entering. If you must sneak around, sneak some water to the dog, provide some shade, or buy the owner a leash. But leave the removing to the proper authorities.

INDEX

<u>Underscored</u> page references indicate boxed text. **Boldface** references indicate illustrations. *Italic* references indicate tables.

Underscored page references indicate boxed text. **Boldface** references indicate illustrations. *Italic* references indicate tables.

Underscored page references indicate boxed text. **Boldface** references indicate illustrations. *Italic* references indicate tables.

<u>Underscored</u> page references indicate boxed text. **Boldface** references indicate illustrations. *Italic* references indicate tables.

<u>Underscored</u> page references indicate boxed text. **Boldface** references indicate illustrations. *Italic* references indicate tables.

Underscored page references indicate boxed text. **Boldface** references indicate illustrations. *Italic* references indicate tables.

Underscored page references indicate boxed text. **Boldface** references indicate illustrations. *Italic* references indicate tables.

Underscored page references indicate boxed text. **Boldface** references indicate illustrations. *Italic* references indicate tables.

Underscored page references indicate boxed text. **Boldface** references indicate illustrations. *Italic* references indicate tables.

Underscored page references indicate boxed text. **Boldface** references indicate illustrations. *Italic* references indicate tables.

Underscored page references indicate boxed text. **Boldface** references indicate illustrations. *Italic* references indicate tables.

<u>Underscored</u> page references indicate boxed text. **Boldface** references indicate illustrations. *Italic* references indicate tables.

Underscored page references indicate boxed text. **Boldface** references indicate illustrations. *Italic* references indicate tables.

H

<u>Underscored</u> page references indicate boxed text. **Boldface** references indicate illustrations. *Italic* references indicate tables.

<u>Underscored</u> page references indicate boxed text. **Boldface** references indicate illustrations. *Italic* references indicate tables.

Underscored page references indicate boxed text. **Boldface** references indicate illustrations. *Italic* references indicate tables.

I

J

K

Underscored page references indicate boxed text. **Boldface** references indicate illustrations. *Italic* references indicate tables.

<u>Underscored</u> page references indicate boxed text. **Boldface** references indicate illustrations. *Italic* references indicate tables.

Underscored page references indicate boxed text. **Boldface** references indicate illustrations. *Italic* references indicate tables.

Q

R

Underscored page references indicate boxed text. **Boldface** references indicate illustrations. *Italic* references indicate tables.

S

<u>Underscored</u> page references indicate boxed text. **Boldface** references indicate illustrations. *Italic* references indicate tables.

<u>Underscored</u> page references indicate boxed text. **Boldface** references indicate illustrations. *Italic* references indicate tables.

<u>Underscored</u> page references indicate boxed text. **Boldface** references indicate illustrations. *Italic* references indicate tables.

Underscored page references indicate boxed text. **Boldface** references indicate illustrations. *Italic* references indicate tables.

<u>Underscored</u> page references indicate boxed text. **Boldface** references indicate illustrations. *Italic* references indicate tables.